TO BE
DISPOSED
BY
AUTHORITY

EXPANDING THE HORIZONS

His Honour John Toulmin CMG QC FKC
on the award of the Fellowship of King's College London on 18 July 2006

EXPANDING THE HORIZONS

On Active Service in Law and Education

His Honour John Toulmin CMG QC FKC

Wildy, Simmonds & Hill Publishing

Expanding the Horizons: On Active Service in Law and Education

British Library Cataloguing in Publication Data
A catalogue record for this book is available from the British Library

ISBN 978-0-85-490108-1

Printed and bound by CPI Group (UK) Ltd, Croydon, CR0 4Y Y

First published in 2012 by
Wildy, Simmonds & Hill Publishing
58 Carey Street
London WC2A 2JF
England

For my wife, Carolyn, our children Geoffrey, Alison and Hilary and all the family with infinite love and gratitude

John Toulmin has acted as Consulting Editor on:

EC Legal Systems, Butterworths, 1993
EFTA Legal Systems, Butterworths, 1993

Acknowledgements

This book includes a number of articles and speeches which are closer in time to the events which I describe. I warmly acknowledge permission to quote the following: the Academy of European Law (ERA) for the passages starting at pp 21, 30, 274, 283, 285 and 358 and particular thanks to Dr Wolfgang Heusel and Sir Konrad Schiemann for permission to re-produce their articles at pp 21 and 358; Thomson Reuters, publishers of the Construction Law Journal, pp 9 and 30; the Society of Construction Law, page 66; the University of Michigan Law Quadrangle notes, p 142; the Council of the Bars and Law Societies of Europe (CCBE) p 167; Fordham International Law Journal, p 215; Kluwer, p 240; the Middle Temple, p 344 and the Temple Church and Hart Publishing, p 349. I have given the appropriate references in each article which I have included. I am also grateful to King's College London for the photograph which forms the frontpiece, and to ERA, Kristine McGlothlin and the Middle Temple, Chris Christodoulou and the Temple Church for providing other photographs.

The six institutions covered in the book have been a substantial and very fulfilling part of my life. I wish to thank the many people who have made it such a rich experience. Some but no means all are acknowledged in the text.

Writing and compiling the book has been a fascinating undertaking for a novice. The original idea was to do something much less ambitious, and I shall always be indebted to Dr Brian Hill for suggesting that what I had thought of as a possible private publication, largely for the family, should be available to a wider public. I am most grateful to Wildy, Simmons and Hill and the printers Antony Rowe Ltd. who have helped to bring this project to fruition and enabled us to meet a demanding deadline.

I thank all people who have read parts of the book in draft and have made helpful suggestions and comments. They include Paul Farmer, the Rev Robin Griffith-Jones, Sir Vivian Ramsey, Professor Graham Thornicroft, Sir Rick Trainor and Michael H Trotter. There are many others, too many to mention individually, who have given help and encouragement to whom I am most grateful. I should however mention Dr Maurice Slevin.

I am particularly grateful to the Lord Chancellor for agreeing to write the foreword. We have known each other since Cambridge University days. I did not realise when I asked him to undertake the task that it would coincide with the passage of a very complicated and somewhat contentious legal aid bill through both Houses of Parliament.

This brings me to the immediate family. I thank most warmly our children Geoffrey, Alison and Hilary for their great encouragement and support. Without my wife, Carolyn, this book could never have been undertaken. As a senior reporter for the official law reports she possesses not only computer skills but also invaluable editorial skills. In addition, apart from total commitment to the project, she has also provided excellent ideas.

Contents

An Overview of Legal Practice

European Court of Justice

Academy of European Law (ERA)

Institute of Psychiatry / King's College London

Middle Temple

Temple Church

Epilogue: The Vineyard

Foreword

John Toulmin and I first met when we were students together at Cambridge. We both studied law there and we were both very active in political student life. I firmly expected that he would strive with me and our other Cambridge friends to become a politician, which is where Leon Brittan, John Gummer, Michael Howard, Norman Lamont, Norman Fowler and others all eventually met up again. John Toulmin virtually abandoned politics from the moment he left Cambridge and went on to pursue a distinguished legal career.

Our friendship remained unbroken and now I derive particular pleasure from this book, which combines serious essays based on judicial and legal experience with shrewd personal insight and which shows how eclectic and wide his interests became. He has an analytical view of the nature and purpose of litigation and the role of legal training. He has an extremely international approach to things which gives him a deep understanding, in particular, of the European dimension, of professional standards training and litigation.

In my present role as Lord Chancellor, I find myself in total agreement with him about the law as a public service. He asks all the fundamental questions that need to be asked about civil proceedings and the civil law. The aim is to help citizens and businesses to resolve even their most complex disputes in a reasonable time and at a reasonable cost. The law should not be needlessly slow and complicated, nor impossibly expensive. It certainly should not be too deeply rooted in professional conservatism and the traditions of practices which have tended to develop for the benefit of the judiciary and the lawyers, rather than the parties to the dispute.

In a readable and accessible way, John sets out in persuasive detail the role of the modern Judge in active case management and the resolution of disputes, preferably wherever possible by negotiation that is guided by the Judge's evaluation of the issues and the risks to each party in the proceedings.

I will not slip into the danger of seeking to paraphrase John Toulmin's expert analysis of every aspect of this approach. It is exactly the kind of approach that one would expect from a man who has mastered the intricacies of business, technology and modern commercial disputes. He undoubtedly played a part in the move towards promoting London as the centre of legal services to the global economy in the fields of commerce, trade and innovation. He played a part in the move to the Rolls Building as a suitable centre for delivering these services to the world.

Because of my own current policy interests, I have concentrated in these comments on just one part of John Toulmin's approach. The book covers a wider fascinating range of subjects. He deals as forcefully with law in the European Union and the training of the legal profession in Europe and the wider world. For such an esoteric range of subjects, he writes very easily and readably. The book is as accessible as it is surprising and entertaining. Any reader with any interest in the law is almost certain to find that his attention is caught by each of the essays and some of the judgements, lectures and speeches which make up the varied pages of this remarkable production.

The Lord Chancellor,
The Rt Hon Kenneth Clarke QC MP

Expanding the Horizons.

February 11, 2011 was my last day in court as a Judge of the Technology and Construction Court of the High Court of Justice. I was delighted to be offered a Valedictory farewell sitting because there were some topics which I wanted to raise with my fellow judges and court users relating to the future of court-based litigation. I assumed that, according to custom, the sitting would be a modest but warm send-off in my courtroom in St Dunstan's House, then an annexe to the Royal Courts of Justice. I was overwhelmed that it took place in the Lord Chief Justice's Court before the Lord Chief Justice, the President of the Supreme Court, the Master of the Rolls and many distinguished judges. It was equally important to me that the well of the court was packed to overflowing with barristers, solicitors and others who had come to wish me well. The speeches, referring to aspects of my life and rather varied career, are published in (2011) 27 Construction Law Review 399.

On May 28, 2011, I was presented with a "Liber Amicorum" by my fellow trustees of the Academy of European Law (ERA) on my retirement from the chairmanship of the Board of Trustees after more than 13 years. This was a second astonishing and touching tribute. The book, published as an annexe to ERA's publication *ERA Forum* Vol 12 supplement 1 – May 2011, consists of 22 chapters on aspects of European law and legal professional practice by very distinguished European judges, practising lawyers and academics. One theme referred to by many is the tension between the need for security worldwide and the preservation of fundamental human rights.

The introductory chapter by the Director of ERA, Dr Wolfgang Heusel, is a wonderful tribute to me which sketches my involvement with ERA's Board of Trustees since its foundation in 1993. The "Valedictory Speeches" (p. 9) and Dr Heusel's chapter (p. 21) provide an agenda for what follows.

My thoughts turned to whether it would be interesting to offer a volume of reflections based on articles and speeches which might provide some basis for the tributes which have been so graciously and generously given. In the written part of his Valedictory address, not delivered orally because of understandable pressures of time, my former pupil and close friend, Nicholas Davidson QC, noted that, apart from my professional practice as barrister and judge, I have served as a member of a number of voluntary bodies. It is a privilege to have done so. They have played as important and fulfilling a part in my life and that of my wife, Carolyn, called to the Bar on the same night in 1965, as the practice itself. Voluntary work with six of these bodies is covered in this book.

In his address in 2008 at the consecration of the window in the Temple Church commemorating the 400th Anniversary of the granting of the Royal Charter by

King James I and VI to the two Inns of Court, the Inner and Middle Temples (being two of the four Inns of Court, the other two Inns being Lincoln's Inn and Gray's Inn), the Bishop of London made the distinction between what we can learn from the past, "History", and how we should be planning for the future, "Destiny". This book may have some value because it is concerned, particularly in the introduction to each section, as much with destiny as with history.

I should explain the sub-title "On Active Service in Law and Education". The law theme is obvious but education is also a theme. Continuing professional development (CPD) is now an integral part of legal practice throughout most of Europe. There is now a Judicial College in England and Wales and judicial training has been acknowledged widely as an integral part of the preparation for judging. Of the institutions with which I have been involved, the Academy of European Law (ERA) is a legal training institution. The Middle Temple provides advocacy training and lectures which qualify for CPD points and The Temple Church also arranges lectures which widen the horizons. The Institute of Psychiatry and King's College London are, of course, academic institutions.

In his chapter in the *Liber Amicorum*, Dr Heusel refers to the fact that in the early years of ERA we were all pioneers. I am sure that those who take part in any organisation should have the spirit of pioneers. The pioneering spirit must be tempered by another wise saying by a long-forgotten Conservative back-room politician who said "We must have balance". I am also conscious of the lawyers' tendency to jump in too early and to forget that others have equal or more important contributions to make. We must also appreciate that the contributions must be appropriate to the position we are in. For example, the role of the non-executive chairman may well at some times be more hands on than others although, of course, he or she must not usurp the functions of the Chief Executive. I have tried to keep these considerations in mind when acting essentially as a non-executive chairman or as a non-executive director in the institutions in which I have participated.

It is interesting to look at and compare the seven apparently disparate institutions, with which I have been involved, including the Official Referees' Court and the Technology and Construction Court (TCC), to see how they relate to each other and how together they expanded my horizons far beyond those of the conventional judge. They have more in common than might at first be apparent. I put them here in the overall context. I shall provide later more detailed introductions to the articles and speeches.

I start with my time as a judge of the Official Referees' Court to which I was appointed in 1997. The court was founded in the latter part of the 19th Century. It has acted as a specialist court, hearing, amongst other things, complex construction and technology litigation and complex assessments of damages. In recent times it was responsible for promoting many of the innovations in civil procedure which are now regarded as standard, and have been incorporated into the Civil Procedure Rules (CPR) introduced in 1999 – active case management being perhaps the most important.

I was the last Official Referee to be appointed. In 1998 the court was re-named the Technology and Construction Court of the High Court (TCC). It continued to have the same jurisdiction as the Official Referees' Court. High Court Judges were introduced as permanent members of the court, and there followed a fairly painful transition until Judge David Wilcox, the last active former Official Referee, retired in 2012.

A separate initiative, started in 2002 by Sir Gavyn Arthur as Lord Mayor of London and me, referred to in my Valedictory speech, resulted, after much work by others, in moving the court to modern premises in the Rolls Building in 2011, along with the Commercial Court, as I had advocated in 2002, and the Chancery Division. I envisaged then that the TCC and the Commercial Court would have a common set of rules which would enable the two courts to be marketed actively internationally as the civil courts of choice for international commercial and civil disputes. Of course, this policy of encouraging international civil litigation runs rather contrary to the stated policy of discouraging domestic civil litigation except as a last resort. The period of assimilation of the Chancery, Commercial and TCC courts in one building is just starting. Therefore the TCC is still in transition. Those in authority would derive benefit from looking at the experience of King's College London after 1997, which is set out in pages 323 to 329 of this book.

Rather than give a history of the Court between 1997 and 2011, the section on "Judging" addresses the issues which I raised in my Valedictory address. First, Civil Procedure in England and Wales must, since the Lisbon Treaties, be seen in the context of the increasing competence in civil justice of the EU Commission as well as the worldwide problem of providing civil justice for ordinary citizens within a reasonable time and at a reasonable cost. These are among the matters addressed in this section.

It is clear that, as a consequence of the new civil procedure rules introduced in 1999 and other measures taken in the previous few years, far from being encouraged, civil litigation through the courts is regarded by the State as a last resort and significant obstacles have been placed in the path of the ordinary citizen seeking to use the courts. The article on "Civil Justice" (p. 44) examines this philosophy critically. It also addresses other issues raised in my Valedictory address.

In my Valedictory address I stressed the importance of active case management and in "Active Case Management" (p. 54) I set out how, in practice, I managed cases. This process should not be a mystery to the ordinary litigant. It is, after all, the litigant's case not the lawyer's and the article will, I hope, be of interest to the general reader. I also include a short exposition on "Early Neutral Evaluation" (p. 66).

As a judge for over 13 years, I gave a significant number of judgments, some of which are referred to in the Valedictory addresses. The two judgments which I have included are interesting in their own right, raising important points of legal principle. The aftermath of each judgment illustrates the importance of active and effective case management. The first is the last substantive judgment in the famous "*Factortame*" litigation (p. 72). I also set out how that litigation ended. The second case, *CIB Properties v Birse Construction Ltd*, sets out the scope of the adjudication process which is carried out by the equivalent of an arbitrator who gives a provisional but enforceable judgment which stands until it is superceded by a judgment of the court, an arbitration award, or a settlement between the parties (p. 123).

The second institution, the Council of the Bars and Law Societies of Europe (CCBE) was founded in 1960. At the start it was a tiny organisation with little funds but, largely through the efforts of eminent Presidents, it had an influence substantially beyond its apparent capacity. Various Presidents before me understood that we had entered a vicious circle. In recent more complex times its constituent Bars wanted the CCBE to do more to represent their members, but would not pay more unless the CCBE demonstrated that it was a more effective organisation.

By 1993 there was a direct challenge to its position as representative of the European Bars before the EU institutions from the Grandes Barreaux, an organisation representing many of the large City Bars on the mainland of Europe. As President of the CCBE in 1993, with help from my two Vice Presidents, and very able delegates, my internal task was to put the CCBE on a sound organisational and financial footing and to visit as many individual national Bars as possible. My external task was to represent the European legal profession at the European institutions, the Court of Human Rights in Strasbourg and internationally (pages 152-168). In particular, I was involved in two negotiations crucial to the development of the legal profession worldwide and within the European Union- the Uruguay Round (the GATT) which was concluded with an agreement in principle in December 1993, and the Lawyers' Establishment Directive which was not enacted finally until 1998 (pages 169-212). The CCBE's difficult negotiating position was assisted materially by the CCBE Code of Professional Conduct adopted in 1988 (p. 215). In "Ethical Rules and Professional Ideologies" (p. 240) I look back from the perspective of 1999 on a period of extraordinary change for the legal profession worldwide since the 1960s.

I was also Chairman of the CCBE Standing Committee at the European Court of Justice from 1986 -1992. In this capacity I wrote a paper on Legal Aid before the Court, and chaired the Committee which was responsible for the first draft of Notes for Guidance on the Written and Oral Procedures. This interest in the development of the European Court of Justice continued and resulted in a speech in Brazil in 2008 in which I set out the history of the Court, and addressed some of the current criticisms and future problems of the Court (p. 257).

The third institution, the Academy of European Law (ERA) (pages 272-287), was a totally new institution launched in 1991 but which really began its activities in 1993 at a time when I became a founding member of the Board of Trustees. The core activity, then as now, is its training programmes. In the early years the Board of Trustees, and particularly the Chairman, played a very active role which included areas which the organisation in its greater maturity deals with through its Management Board. I was Chairman of the Board of Trustees from 1997-2010 and remain involved as Honorary Chairman for Life. In the years 1998-2000, I played a crucial role in the development of ERA. This is referred to by Dr Heusel in his chapter in the *Liber Amicorum*. I include at page 274 my article in the 2010 ERA Annual Report.

The fourth institution is in fact two separate institutions which must be taken together. Having specialised in medical work in my early years at the Bar, I was nominated as a member of the Management Board of the Maudsley and Bethlem Hospitals (and its successor institution) from 1979-87. I was a Trustee of the Institute of Psychiatry (IoP) from 1982-1997, a member of its Advisory Committee from 1997-2009 and Chairman from 1999-2002. I was also Chairman of the Joint Committee of the South London and Maudsley Hospital NHS Foundation Trust (SLAM) and the IoP from 1994-2002 (p. 290).

In the 1980s and 1990s the NHS Health Authority was in a constant state of re-organisation. The IoP, founded in 1948, was a pre-eminent Institute for research and treatment of mental illness at the time when, in 1982, I became a trustee and member of the Committee of Management. Like the NHS Trust, it went through a very difficult period in the 1980s and 1990s both financially and, in the 1990s, when the IoP was under some threat of extinction. The IoP tackled the financial threat by changing its focus so that it could raise most of its funding through special projects. From 1997 it was assimilated within King's College London. This had to be achieved without prejudicing its pre-eminent international status. This transition brought its own problems.

I joined the Council of King's College London, the fifth institution, in 1997 as the IoP's nominee. I retired from the Council in 2009. In 1998 King;s was joined by the United Medical and Dental Schools of Guy's, King's and St. Thomas' Hospitals. The medical schools are known collectively as GKT. For much of the time between 1997 and 2009 I was a member, and then Chair, of the Governance Committee. I saw at first hand the process of assimilation of the IoP and the medical schools, at times painful, which had to take place before King's was able to move forward, effectively as a new university. This process of assimilation is now complete and King's is moving forward as a leading and innovative university. I also focus on the spirit of collaboration between the schools of the University and, with the additional perspective of a visiting Professor at the Law School, having a taught a course on Dispute Resolution to LL.M students, possibilities of further collaboration between the IoP, the medical schools and the Law School (p. 323).

The sixth institution is the oldest. There were lawyers on the land upon which now stand the Inner and Middle Temples from about 1340. The Inner and Middle Temples appear to have existed as separate entities from the late 14th and early 15th centuries (see p. 330 and following). By the sixteenth century the two Inns of Court were well established.

I joined the Middle Temple as a student in 1960, was called to the Bar in 1965 and started pupillage in 1966. I became a Bencher (member of the governing body) of Middle Temple in 1986.This was a time of change. The Bar grew in size from the late 1960s so that residential chambers in the Middle Temple were converted to professional accommodation and there were very many fewer people living in the Inn. This has changed its character. More importantly, the politicians decided in recent times that the legal professions could no longer be permitted to regulate themselves. Although the Inns of Court would retain the roles of formally admitting and dis-barring students, the Inns needed to find a new role. Part of this is being achieved by providing improved training for students, and in particular specialist advocacy training, but this is not enough. The changes provide new opportunities for the Inns to find a new and distinctive role as a market place of ideas and new thinking.

I had been a member of many committees of the Middle Temple, including the Executive Committee, before I became Reader in 2008. The Reader, whose primary responsibility is to work with and encourage students, gives a formal "Reading" on a subject of his choosing during his time in office. I chose as my subject "The Middle Temple and the Future" and in the Reading I suggested how the Middle Temple could expand its horizons with particular reference to its international connections (pages 332 to 343).

The seventh institution is the Choir Committee of the Temple Church, relatively recently re-named the Church Committee. It was formed in 1842, at a time when a regular choir was installed in the Church. It is a joint committee of the Inner Temple and Middle Temple whose responsibility it is to administer the Church.(This is not the responsibility of the full time clergyman appointed by the Crown who has the title of Master of the Temple.) I was a member of the Committee from 1990-2010 and Chairman in 2003 although, as a member of the congregation since we were married in the Church in 1967, I have an even longer perspective. "The Temple Church" (p. 349) is part of a chapter which I wrote in the "History of the Middle Temple". By the 1990s the Church had seen its regular congregation dwindle and needed a new infusion of enthusiasm and a new direction. In 1997, the Church Committee appointed a new Organist and in 1999 was instrumental in the appointment of a new Master, both of whom have been more actively supported by the Church Committee than were their predecessors. Both were outstanding appointments. As a member of the Temple Music Trust responsible for promoting music in the Temple Church since 1990, and as Chairman since 2002, I have been involved particularly in promoting the choir of the Church through new CDs. This has included funding three CDs in recent years from Signum Records, two by the choir, "The Majesty of Thy Glory" and "A Festival of Psalms", and an organ recital by James Vivian, the current Director of Music, "English Organ Music from the Temple Church", each of which has been highly acclaimed.

It can be seen that each of these institutions has been, during the time of my involvement, in an era of rapid change. Some have been under threat from outside – the CCBE and the IoP. My experience in one organisation has widened my horizons and informed my approach to the problems in the others.

What other experience have I brought to the task? At Cambridge University, at Trinity Hall, I was Chairman of the Cambridge University Conservative Association in Michaelmas 1962 and was a long-time member of the Cambridge Union Standing Committee. This was in the middle of a very active political period where, among other contemporaries, Leon Brittan, Norman Fowler, John Gummer, Kenneth Clarke, Michael Howard and Norman Lamont went on to be Cabinet Ministers. "The Cambridge Mafia" have remained good, and in many cases close, friends. Many thought that I too would go into party politics. As is becoming clear, much of what I have done, in particular my time as President of the CCBE, has been intensely political, although not party political.

After Cambridge, in the Autumn of 1963, I represented Cambridge University with Michael Howard in a two person debating tour of the United States – visiting 40 colleges and universities in 50 days west of the Mississippi. President Kennedy was assassinated when we were in Moscow, Idaho.

In 1964-65 I studied for a Master of Laws degree at the University of Michigan Law School. In 1993 I was honoured to be asked to return as the Professor WW Bishop Jnr Fellow. I spent a week on campus and gave a lecture entitled "Our Worldwide Legal Profession"(p. 142).

I then worked as a summer associate at the distinguished New York law firm of Winthrop, Stimson, Putnam and Roberts. A description of the firm, as it was when I was there, is included in "Ethical Rules and Professional Ideologies" written in 1999 (see post, p.242). My time spent in the United States, and the enduring friendships which I made, have left me with a great affection for that country, if not always for its politics.

In 1972 I was first elected to the Bar Council of which I was a member or an observer for 16 of the following 20 years. I was Chairman of its Young Barristers'

Committee in 1974/5. I was also a member of the Bar Council's International Committee for 20 years from 1972 and Chairman in 1988.

In my practice at the Bar as a junior barrister and as a QC from 1980, I specialised increasingly in international commercial work, often working with US lawyers, advising US and English firms on trends in international legal practice and on the advisability on setting up branch offices in London and on the continent of Europe, and in arbitration. My practice took place latterly from chambers at 3, Verulam Buildings, Gray's Inn and, after eight happy years there, and having acted as Chairman of the Committee responsible for organising the move from Gray's Inn Place to 3 Verulam Buildings, it was a very difficult decision whether to stay at the Bar or to go on the Bench. The decisive factor was that, as an Official Referee, I would in effect be acting as a specialist High Court Judge trying exclusively High Court cases, either in the Official Referees' Court or as a Deputy High Court Judge in the Chancery or Queen's Bench Divisions.

A further important influence since the 1990s has been Brazil. Dr Durval Noronha de Goyos Jnr has for more than 30 years built up one of the very few worldwide law firms which does not come from the United States of America or Europe. He invited me to Brazil in 1991, 1997 and 2008, and I have seen at first hand the rapid progress in one of the world's emerging economies and been able to study its legal system.

There is one other theme running through the Valedictory addresses and not only Dr Heusel's contribution in the Liber Amicorum, but also many of the other contributions – the 15th century house in Auxey-Duresses in the heart of Burgundy, 7 km from Beaune. It was a ruin when we bought it on January 31,1997. The vineyard surrounding it has a very modest appellation and is therefore uneconomic, but it produces between 1200 and 2000 bottles of our own good Pinot Noir, depending on the year. My wife Carolyn and I have restored the house and looked after the vineyard with considerable help from local experts. I say a little more about this in the introduction to The Vineyard on page 357. To our great joy, our children also enjoy the house. It is from Auxey-Duresses that much of this book has been written. It is to Carolyn, our children Geoffrey, Alison and Hilary and the rest of the family that this book is lovingly dedicated.

Valedictory Speeches on the Retirement of His Honour Judge Toulmin CMG QC

Royal Courts of Justice [1]

Lord Judge L.C.J., Lord Phillips of Worth Matravers J.S.C. (President), Lord Neuberger of Abbotsbury M.R., Rt Hon Sir Anthony May (President QBD) and Akenhead J. (Judge in charge of the Technology and Construction Court): February 11,2011

> The following valedictory speeches were delivered at the Royal Courts of Justice on February 11, 2011, on the occasion ofthe retirement of H.H. Judge John Toulmin CMG QC.

The Lord Chief Justice introduced the occasion as follows:

"Unrobed as we are, 'Is it a court that had to rise?' is a good question to ask with the Lord President of the Supreme Court here, but we are gathered, and it is a lovely turn-out, to pay a tribute to a wonderful Judge and actually a lovely man, who sits two away from me on my left.

This is the only court that would have been big enough to find a place for all the many people who want to join in the tribute that is going to be paid to John Toulmin, and when I was asked whether my court could be made available for the purpose I greeted it with alacrity.

It is not merely because it is John, but it is, in a strange way, symbolic of something that has been happening over the years which those of us who are older than some of you will remember as the old Official Referees' corridor tucked away in an out of the way bit of the building unknown, unheard of, where very strange people used to work! I did a couple of cases there myself, so I can speak with confidence. It shows a move from there by what is now the Technology and Construction Court right into the heart of the administration of civil justice. I think, therefore, it is salutary to just bear that in mind when we consider all the many wonderful things that can be said about John.

I am going to say no more. There are plenty of speeches to come. Some of us have work to do! All of you have work to do, and so I shall ask Mr. Justice Akenhead to go first."

---

[1]   This article was first published by Thomson Reuters in (2011) *Construction Law Journal* 399

Akenhead J.:

"Lord Chief Justice, this address will not be given in the form of a Scott Schedule. His Honour Judge Toulmin CMG QC is the last but one Judge still in the Technology and Construction Court who was, when appointed, an Official Referee. Unlike the first Official Referee, Sir Henry Verey, whose 44 years in office will never be exceeded, you have the fortune, John, to retire at a somewhat earlier stage.

When I came as something of an arriviste Judge to the TCC three years ago, you were extremely kind and welcoming, and that reflects not only your diplomacy but your essential decency which have been two of the hallmarks of your life.

After a stellar academic career you came to the Bar and practised in several sets of Chambers, represented here today, ending up as leading counsel in 3 Gray's Inn Place, as it was. I came across you several times in practice and you were always a fair and decent, but unfortunately always prepared opponent. Your substantial practice at the Bar included much international commercial work, and you appeared at all levels of the English court system as well as in arbitration. You had the real fortune to do some construction work, which also attracted commendation.

For many years you were a member of the Bar Council, including being on its International Relations Committee. Your services to European law were recognised by Her Majesty the Queen in making you a Companion of the Order of St Michael and St George in 1993. Those services included a close and long-standing connection to the European Bar Council in the 1980s culminating in your Presidency in 1993. Your crucial work there rightly attracted enthusiastic endorsement and praise.

For over 13 years now you have been an important member of what is now the TCC. You have performed your work as a Judge with assiduity, diligence and commitment. You have been the Judge in a significant number of important cases. I mention only four briefly. **In** *Smith v Bridgend,* the House of Lords restored your judgment, previously reversed by the Court of Appeal. Of course, the House of Lords, and now the Supreme Court, is always right. **In** the *Factortame* case, your judgment on the issue of whether a breach of European law can give rise to an action in tort is a masterpiece.

You materially contributed to the development of the law relating to adjudication. Two particular groundbreaking cases are worthy of mention. The first was *CIB Properties v Birse,* which addressed the then thorny issue of whether exceptionally complex disputes were referable to adjudication. The second was *Bloor v Bowmer & Kirkland,* which decided that an adjudicator can alter his decision to correct a clerical mistake or error arising from an accidental slip or omission.

You have helped to set up an innovative mediation process within the TCC, the Court Settlement Process, which has proved effective and successful. Others will speak perhaps in more detail about specific parts of your career and life.

I know that I will see a lot of you after today because, apart from anything else, we both have flats in the same block in Westminster.

Thank you very much on behalf of the TCC for your work in the court over those years and for your major contribution as a Judge of that court. I wish you and Carolyn a happy, fulfilled, healthy, vini-cultural, but busy retirement. The arbitration world awaits your visitation."

Lord Phillips of Worth Matravers J.S.C.:

"Lord Chief, I lead a team of six out of the eleven current Justices of the Supreme Court, and Lord Hope has asked me to say how much he regrets that his absence in Edinburgh prevents him being with us.

That is an indication of a man whose life in the law has taken him far beyond the confines of the court room. John, you and I go back a long way. We overlapped for a year at Cambridge, where you were a scholar at Trinity Hall, the college then pre-eminent in the law. After that, you looked outward going off with Michael Howard as a two-man Cambridge University debating team to tour the United States for 40 debates in 50 days. You formed strong links with the United States which you have maintained throughout your life. You went on to be a Fulbright Scholar of the University of Michigan, and later you had the distinction of serving for ten years on their Board of Visitors, and for five years you took week-long courses for the United States National Institute for Trial Advocacy. You are of course a long-standing member of the Pilgrims.

When you came back from the States we developed a very warm friendship as fellow members, and later Benchers, of the Middle Temple, and our practices at the Bar overlapped. It is as a friend rather than as a colleague that I am here this morning.

Not content with your American interests you turned your attention to Europe. Robert Akenhead has already described your quite extraordinary services to European law.

Coming closer to home, when I was Master of the Rolls I followed with admiration your initiatives at the TCC in setting up the court settlement process, under which Judges of the court, having trained as mediators, can mediate settlements in cases before them. I am sure they are very often tempted to do so. I know that you, yourself, have achieved a 100 per cent success rate in this form of alternative dispute resolution.

You have pursued a bewildering variety of interests outside the law, including serving on the Maudsley and Bethlem Hospital Management Committee, being a Trustee and for three years the Chair of the Institute of Psychiatry, serving on the Council of King's College, London, who made you a Fellow, serving on the Church Committee of the Temple Church, for a time as its Chair, and chairing the Temple Music Trust for the last eight years, and serving as a Trustee of the National Association of Young String Players. You are also a Member of MCC. So it is no surprise that you have earned the friendship of so many who are here to wish you well this morning.

I have saved the best for last: Chateau Toulmin, where I and my wife had the great good fortune to call when walking through Burgundy a few years ago. You regaled us well, and I would not dream of bringing coals to Newcastle. I did, however, take the liberty of selecting a decent bottle of Bordeaux from my cellars, and I hope that it will be one of the first of many pleasures that you and Carolyn will enjoy in your very well deserved retirement! *(Applause)"*

Mr Davidson:

"My Lords, looking at the vast volume of first instance submissions prepared by counsel, one of whom had the initials RA, a smiling member of the Court of Appeal asked me, with great sympathy to the Judges of the TCC and their families, 'Tell me, do the Judges of that Court ever get time to go home at week-ends?' That same Judge later produced a report, with an apology for writing a long one, explaining that he had not had time to write a short one. The attempt to distil intensively from information of the immense breadth of your life was bound to fail, as I have found.

I speak simply as one of your pupils, all of whom are grateful to you. Whether all from Paper Buildings have got here depends only on whether the most distinguished, Alastair MacGregor, now Vice-Chairman of the Criminal Cases Review Commission, has obtained early release from Birmingham. Each of us has great affection for you, not least because of your tolerance and your encouragement of our individualism as you led us across the 'Bridge of Surprise' , which is the crossing between learning the law and encountering facts.

For me, I take from enjoyment of your friendship for over half your life to date your humanity, courage and selfless service. I have said to you, entirely truthfully, that of all of the quarters I have had at the Bar-and I am about to make my 142nd VAT return-the one I most consistently enjoyed was that in the summer of 1974 as your pupil. **In** the mind's eye the sun streamed into your room every day as a wide variety of work, particularly medical and commercial, was tackled. I can still picture the pink flimsies and the notable grey pale type of the drafts of a long joint opinion you produced for the great

Robert MacCrindle, and the care which had gone into it produced the happy result that he changed hardly a word over about 30 pages.

There would be evenings when we worked late, and you were a generous host to me, sometimes at the Printer's Pie. **In** August there was an evening when you said, 'Let's hurry to Lord's', and for the first time in my life I watched a Test from the pavilion, and we happened to see one of the greatest catches which has ever been made on that ground. You loved your work but you maintained the right balance.

I want to mention one case, which is not in the Law Reports. To many it would have been just a so-called straightforward personal injury case, though it had two twists which meant it was not. One of the twists actually was that I gave good advice! I said, 'What we need is good advocacy, the Silk system is about good advocacy, send for JKT'. We did, and so it was. We had one of those days when the court was filled, not with the over-aggression one sometimes finds but with total charm as your opponent was also a Silk of charm and Technology in John Loyd. There was a dangerous point in cross-examination which was why I had asked for you. Our client was not going to work again. He did not mind that, and he did not mind about the ordinary financial side of the case. What mattered to him was that his case gave him the chance of realising his impossible dream. His recreation was shooting and he had heard of Purdey. The case was for him the chance of commissioning one. I was on the edge of my seat on the other side of this building as you cross-examined in that dangerous territory where one wrong answer meant no Purdey, and getting the right one got the Purdey. When you got it I thought to myself, and I remember the instant, 'John, you have just won a Purdey, you have given that man his life back'. That is the character of you.

At the Bar and on the Bench you have been always a bringer of civilisation. You used words with wisdom and pleasure. You would love Test cricketers to learn running between the wickets in the way that you did-from Shakespeare, 'Safe shalt thou go and safe return', you learned at Winchester, translating, 'Easy two!' (For your Lordship's last judicial note, the reference is *Cymbeline, Act III, Scene 5*).

You encourage and teach people gently, and will be so much valued in your Professorial role at King's. My daughters benefited from your then two-month-old Hilary, and you, explaining to me in your different ways that when cradling a baby it is desirable to keep the head above rather than below the rest of the body!

I wish to end with a word for your family. You and Carolyn are consistently charming and warm, and over more than 40 years together you have shown how drawing your talents together can lead to great achievement and happiness. Your children, Geoffrey, Alison and Hilary, do not need the

Fifth Commandment to remind them, Honour thy father and thy mother: they know very well that their father and mother are deserving of honour, which is why all of us are present in this court today."

Simon Tolson:

"My Lords, your Lordships, ladies and gentlemen, it is a great pleasure to have the honour to congratulate Judge Toulmin on his retirement as a distinguished Judge of the Technology and Construction Court. Coming on this line of such distinguished speakers, I represent TeCSA and the TCC solicitors who make up their membership, and also with a card on the TCC User Committee too.

TeCSA, its clients and the User Committee can be regarded, in the words of both Sir Michael Latham and Sir John Egan, as the *integrated* team and representing all points of view.

I am pleased that the law is one of the last bastions where valedictory speeches remain. How right Matthew Parris of *Radio* 4 fame was to mark the passing of the valedictory despatch, the traditional final telegram home in which British Ambassadors could let their hair down and settle a few scores at the same time-only marred most recently, I think, by the BBC choice of actors and perhaps marred slightly by Wikileaks too, but here everyone can speak for themselves in Court number 4.

We have a great deal to thank Judge Toulmin for. Professionally, he was called to the Bar in 1965, the first appointment of note was Chairman of the Young Barristers' Committee in 1973. You continued to impress as a barrister, becoming Queen's Counsel in 1980, appointed a Recorder in 1984, and then a Judge of the Official Referees, as it then was, in 1997, before making it to Technology and Construction Court a year later.

Judge Toulmin was quick, and this very important, to seize and hold on to the fact that it was becoming increasingly obvious to those in my industry, the construction industry, that they have a choice in the way disputes are resolved and managed. Judge Toulmin will be known to all of us for raising the spectre of Early Neutral Evaluation as an alternative to mainstream private sector alternatives.

I think many of us, and certainly a number of us in this room, will remember the turning point in relation to a paper he gave to the Society of Construction Law in 1999 entitled *Early Neutral Evaluation in the TCC* where he suggested that a judge could give the parties an indication as to what the outcome may be. I think that was a very important development in alternative dispute resolution available through the courts.

Then there is, of course, adjudication. There has been a little bit said about some of your cases. I just wanted to mention two. I think the first one is one that in my office is known as the *Yellow Banana"* case. That is the decision in *Bloor Construction v Bowmer & Kirkland,* which was mentioned a moment ago. I think it is important that the idea of a 'slip' being available as a matter of an implied term into the contract between the adjudicator and the parties was a very important clarification of the law, and of course Parliament has adopted it in Part 8 of the new 2009 Act when it comes into force.

The last case I wanted to mention was what I believe was actually your first case, I am reliably told by one of my partners, Vicky Russell, which was *City Access v Daniel Jackson.* I mention that case. As I understand it from Victoria, that case was down just to deal with some preliminary issues, but you managed to actually get through everything in two weeks for the entire disputes in the case. Thirteen years ahead of your time you actually brought the two quantity surveyor experts into caucus together as a 'hot tubbing' session. The abiding memory I am told in relation to that case was your ability with mathematics. You would sit there, I am told, quietly beaming as the quantity surveyors were thrashing away on their calculators, faffing around trying to sort things out, and then it was quite obvious to everyone in the court, except the quantity surveyors, that you were there in advance and had reached the answer. So if ever an expert's arithmetic did not tally with Toulmin's, they say, the Judge's arithmetic, unsurprisingly was always and without fail correct.

It is a great privilege on this splendid occasion and in this wonderful court-it really is lovely to be in here-as I am fortunate indeed to have become Chairman recently of TeCSA, to, on its behalf, on behalf of all the solicitors I represent and the Panel Adjudicators as well, have this opportunity to thank you most sincerely for your huge contribution that you have made as a Judge whilst you have been with the TCC. We wish you every success and much happiness wherever your energies may now be devoted."

Chantal-Aimee Doerries QC:

"My Lord, one of the pleasures and privileges of being Chairman of the Technology and Construction Bar Association is to be able to speak for the Bar on an occasion such as this, to celebrate your many and various achievements, and you will forgive me if I repeat some of them, speaking last, as I do today.

As a TCC Judge you tried a number of significant cases and Mr. Justice Akenhead has mentioned some. I wanted to mention but three very briefly-the famous case of *Secretary of State for Transport ex parte Factortame,* in which you found a breach of EU law constitutes an action in tort; *Smith v Bridgend County Borough Council,* which, as Mr. Justice Akenhead has mentioned, the House of Lords agreed with you, even if the Court of Appeal did not; and *CIB Properties v Birse Construction,* which considered whether an adjudication award could be upheld in a complex post-termination dispute.

It seems very appropriate that you, who had already achieved so much, on the international stage but in particular on the European law side should have been the judge in *Factortame*. The high esteem in which you are held by the Bar is demonstrated not just by the numbers here, but I understand that at the conclusion of *Factortame* you were entertained to dinner by counsel in the case-a real and indeed rare compliment for a Judge. I hope they served you a *'Clos Toulmin'*. A search on the internet has revealed that your Pinot Noir 2003 is described by someone in the know characteristically for this extraordinary vintage, 'This wine has unusually deep colour and a smell perhaps more reminiscent of a Rhone than of a Burgundy, this is nevertheless a delicious drink and recommended'.

There were, of course, many other cases, and I was lucky enough to appear in front of you in a number of them. No big case in the Technology and Construction Court is complete without a site view. Unfortunately, we never made it to Cyprus, but I well recall our visit to the supposedly cutting edge fire training facility in South London. We were walked through fire and flood. Of course, it was all simulated, and we were well togged up in a hard hat, gloves and boots.

As a Judge, you have left your mark on the court in a number of other· ways, some of which we have already heard about this morning. You were of course instrumental in devising and carrying through the rules for dispute settlement whereby a Judge of the court can now act as mediator between parties to the litigation and you were innovative in your promotion of this. I believe, as has already been mentioned, that your strike rate as a mediator is an enviable 100 per cent-perhaps not such a good thing for the Bar.

You continued to be active in European matters and have recently been honoured by being appointed as honorary President of the Board of Trustees of the *Europäische Rechtsakademie*, the Academy of European Law in Trier.

You have always been a strong advocate of the Bar. You were the Lent 2008 Middle Temple Reader and I know have offered much encouragement and support to a number of barristers applying for appointments. I very much hope that you will continue to play a role in the resolution of construction and technology disputes.

And I hope you will forgive me for disclosing that you are a Valentine's Day birthday boy, and on behalf of the Bar many happy returns! *(Laughter)"*

H.H. Judge Toulmin CMG QC responded as follows:

"I think 20 years ago I would have started off by saying Gosh! I think now I say Wow! What a wonderful send-off you have given me. Thank you very much to all those who have spoken and to all those who have come. Chantal Doerries mentioned the European Law Academy and the Director,

Dr. Wolfgang Heusel, got up at four o'clock this morning in Germany in order to be here today.

Thirteen years in one court is a long time. I thank all my Clerks, including Dawn and Val, my most recent Clerks, and especially Kim Andrews, my Clerk for five and a half years. I also thank Glenys MacDonald, who has looked after me as a supervisor to my Clerks. I thank all my fellow Judges, especially David Wilcox, who has made the judicial journey with me, and Peter Coulson, my next door neighbour. I thank the Court staff, and I thank all of you, barristers and solicitors, who have appeared in front of me over the years and, it has to be said, from time to time have had to put up with me.

I have in my hand my first brief. It was on April 6, 1966 and it was in the Supreme Court, except in those days it was called Middlesex Quarter Sessions! (*Laughter*) I arrived at court to watch David Webster who was, I think, all of 18 months senior to me, to see how one should do pleas in mitigation. Suddenly, a legal aider was put up. The difference between a legal aider in those days and a dock brief was that a legal aider was paid at £9.9 shillings and a dock brief was paid £2.4/6d. So I had to do my own back sheet and I received the antecedents, or the reason why the Petty Session Division of Edmonton had committed Kenneth Alfred Francis, *alias* Kenneth George Reynolds, for sentence, and I received two pages of antecedents, and that was that. I then had to go down to the cells and see my client. It was, as you can imagine, rather like the sort of advocacy exercise that students have these days. The Judge had heard that my client had a complete novice to look after him, and I must say Richard Vick was a sportsman and he gave him a sentence which was at least six months less than he would otherwise have got!

That was April 6, 1966. So the span from my first appearance in court to my last is nearly 45 years.

My wife Carolyn and I were called to the Bar on the same night by the Middle Temple in November 1965. We first started going out on October 2, 1966. She has made the journey with me, and I am very much blessed for that.

I have two claims to fame. First, I am proud to be the last Official Referee to have been appointed. Second, I must be the only Judge who started as the junior Judge of the court and, with the advent of High Court Judges, retires 13 years later as the junior Judge of the court! (*Laughter*) At this moment, I have to confess that I do not feel like the junior Judge of any court, but wonderfully among friends.

In 1998, as you have heard, the court was renamed the Technology and Construction Court and was opened with a fanfare by Derry Irvine as Lord Chancellor. There is still one tangible relic of this in the building-it was felt that the great man should at some point stand upon a red carpet. A square of red carpet was purchased, no doubt at great expense, and was installed on the floor of the Judges' lift, where it remains to this day! Rather an important relic and when the building is pulled down I hope that it will be preserved!

The Official Referees' Court has over the years produced some outstanding Judges. It was a unique court, which made a special contribution because, being outside the mainstream of courts, it was able to make innovations in the procedure in complicated litigation both in the period leading up to trial, and in the trial procedure itself. This was reflected in the Civil Procedure Rules, and I like to think that the Dispute Settlement Conference was the last initiative of the ORs. The fact that it came into being was largely the inspiration of Lord Phillips.

Secondly, the same judge case-managed the litigation from the first case management conference to the end of trial, as of course happens in arbitration. This enables case management to have the necessary continuity to further the twin objectives of preparation for a more just settlement through negotiation or mediation, and preparation for trial. This continuity is lost when all but the judge in charge go out on circuit. It cannot really be compensated for by double teaming a judge on circuit with one in London.

Thirdly, the Official Referees acted as a College. When I arrived we met not only among ourselves but also with Barbara Joy, the Court Manager. The court staff was part of the family. The court manager was not slow to talk to an individual Judge if there was a problem. This collegiate approach lasted through the time of John Dyson as Judge in Charge, but then sadly lapsed, although I am, happily, seeing signs of its revival.

The great advantage of the appointment of High Court Judges to the TCC has been that some outstanding practitioners have been prepared to put themselves forward as High Court Judges, but would not have applied to become Official Referees.

I have found the work here, together with my sittings as a Deputy Judge of the Chancery Division and occasionally the QBD, as most rewarding and challenging, and as is apparent from what has been said by those who have spoken to me today, I clearly have made many friends.

The case management work is as important a part of dispute resolution as the trials themselves. Unfortunately, it is little understood and on many occasions poorly done at all levels, as if by rote, by ticking boxes on a court form rather than tailored to the particular case. The Judicial Studies Board does not even cover it properly in seminars. Some of the most rewarding moments in my years on the Bench have been those where, with the active co-operation of the lawyers and their clients, we have achieved case management which was more appropriate and effective than anything that either the parties themselves or I, as the Judge, could have achieved on our own. I am, of course, acutely conscious that I have on some occasions fallen well below this high standard.

Three of the four cases I was going to mention have been mentioned already. *Factortame* has been covered by a number, and I think it was probably the most satisfying case which I was involved in, and one certainly where the lawyering on all sides by solicitors and barristers was of a quite extraordinary standard. At the end, I thought that we would achieve a settlement in advance of a six-month trial of the claims of over 100 fishermen who, as Mrs. Thatcher complained, were allowed to sue the British Government for stealing our fish, but only if I case managed correctly. Too much pressure from me and the parties would complain rightly that the work could not be done in time; too little and the essential work could not be completed before trial. As you have heard, the case was settled. We were given a sumptuous dinner by all counsel in the case, and David Friedman, leading for the Government-who I am delighted to see here today-remarked with a smile that we all seemed to be getting along so well that it was a pity we did not have the trial after all!

(Laughter)

I think I will simply mention one other case, and that is the *Mirant* litigation, which involved a power plant in the Philippines and was probably the most challenging case that I have had. There was a lengthy preliminary issue, a lengthy trial on liability involving the most complex technical issues, and an equally complicated trial on quantum centring on the issue of compensation for delays. On liability, which went to the Court of Appeal, I am happy to say that I was upheld, including by Lord Justice May, and on quantum my judgment was not appealed.

One last point: in November 2002, Gavyn Arthur became the first practising barrister to be Lord Mayor of London. He wanted to promote *Legal London* as an important part of his year of office. We talked about this, and I said that my vision of London as a worldwide centre included the promotion nationally and internationally of the specialist Commercial Court and the TCC as well as arbitration and mediation. If actively promoted jointly, these courts, with common or complementary Rules and Guides, would increase their international work and prestige, and their judgments would provide much needed guidance which would be followed worldwide. The increased work would provide much needed direct revenue through court fees and would also provide substantial invisible earnings. I said that the main problem was St Dunstan's House. I invited Gavyn Arthur to come and look at the facilities, or lack of them. He came and saw it for himself and was appalled. At the Mansion House Dinner for Judges in July 2003, he raised the topic directly on behalf of the City, saying that a specialist Court building, properly equipped and with proper facilities was badly needed. Lord Falconer, as Lord Chancellor, gave a reasonably encouraging response. I know that it took much work by Sir Gavyn Arthur's successor as Lord Mayor, Sir Robert Finch, COMBAR, in which my former pupil, Bill Blair, played an important part, as did Lord Mance and many others, to bring the Rolls Building project to fruition, but I hope that Judge Sir Gavyn Arthur will have an honoured place at the opening ceremony.

A common set of rules would, I hope, have the consequence that the TCC would jettison its pre-action Protocol, which has cost litigants unnecessary tens and even hundreds of thousands of pounds and, on occasion, has made settlements more difficult, if not impossible. I have never understood why procedures were devised to drive potential litigants from the courts, particularly since High Court civil litigation makes a profit for the Ministry of Justice.

Also in the Rolls Building is the Chancery Division. The Chancery Masters would, after appropriate mediation training, be excellent at conducting dispute settlement conferences. If successful, this could be extended to the QBD and further.

Well, my time is done. I am hoping to do mediation and arbitration. Carolyn and I will spend more time with the family and in our house in Burgundy. When a *vigneron* says of a bottle of wine, *'C'est interessant'*, he means, 'It tastes foul'. When he says, *'Ce n 'est pas mal'*, he means, 'It really isn't very good'. When he says, *'C'est tres bon'*, he means, 'It is good'. But when he tastes a bottle which he will always remember with the greatest pleasure and affection, he says, *'Merci! Merci!'* To you all, I say, simply, *Merci!, Merci! (Applause)"*

The Lord Chief Justice concluded the occasion as follows:

"Thank you all very much for coming. Thank you for the warmth of your reception of John Toulmin, and how wonderful that the efficiency of the Technology and Construction Court has meant that everyone who has spoken today has kept within the time limit!

Thank you."

There is a Tide in the Affairs of Men... A Tribute to John Toulmin

Wolfgang Hensel [1]

1 Leitmotiv

Be great in act, as you have been in thought.
Shakespeare, King John, Act 5, Scene 1

Judge John Toulmin QC CMG, Chairman of the Board of Trustees of the Academy of European Law (ERA) since 1997, retired as Chairman of the Board on 31 December 2010. On his 70th birthday, 14 February 2011, he also retired as a Senior Circuit Court Judge of the Technology and Construction Court of England and Wales. Following the suggestion by ERA's Management Board, the Governing Board presided by Jacques Santer appointed John Toulmin Honorary Chairman of the ERA Board of Trustees for life in October 2010.

This *Festschrift* or *Liber amicorum* is offered to John Toulmin by his fellow trustees and by the staff and friends of ERA. It is a tribute to an outstanding friend and supporter, a modest expression of our gratitude for ERA's untiring inspirer and an acknowledgement of his lasting contribution to European integration.

2 Pioneering

See first that the design is wise and just: that ascertained, Pursue it resolutely: do not for one repulse forego the purpose That you resolved to effect.
Attributed to Shakespeare

The first time I met John Toulmin was at the very first, the "constitutive" meeting of ERA's Board of Trustees on 5 July 1993. Following an initiative emanating from the European Parliament,[2] ERA had been set up as a public foundation in Trier in June 1992 by Luxembourg, Rhineland-Palatinate, the City of Trier and the "Association for the Promotion of the Academy of European Law", an association assembling very distinguished members of EU institutions (Parliament, Commission and Court of Justice) and eminent

---

[1] Dr. W. Heusel, Director (181) Academy of European Law, this article was published in Chapter 1 of *Liber Amicorum John Toulmin*, supplement to Vol 12 *ERA Forum*, p. 1, May 2011.
[2] Cf. EP Resolution of 10 September 1991 calling for the "immediate creation" of the Academy and requesting EC institutions to support ERA, OJ C267/33, 14.10.1991.

scholars of European law, which today is better known as the "Friends of
ERA" association.[3] ERA's Foundation Statute then provided for the institution
of three boards - the Governing Board as supreme organ representing the
patrons, the Management Board to run the Foundation, and the Board
of Trustees, or Advisory Board, to advise the other Boards on programme
planning, public relations and marketing, and to establish contacts with the
target groups and the Member States.

Those were exciting times: 1992 was the year of the "completion" of the
Single Market, 1993 marked the entry into force of the Maastricht Treaty
which for the first time introduced a "European Union" with its then three
pillars and new competences in Justice and Home Affairs yet to be discovered
and developed. The EU of the time had no more than twelve members, with
Austria, Finland and Sweden not joining until 1995. It was the time when
the practical relevance of Community law (as it then was) became gradually
apparent in the Member States, though many continued to ignore this,
particularly in the six founding Member States. The equally exciting mission
of ERA matched the challenge: to build up a consistent training offer in
European law for legal professionals of all kinds and from all Member States,
targeting also the former socialist countries of Central and Eastern Europe
which had yet to acquire official candidate status. It was a time for pioneers,
and as such we felt. No one could have told us how to succeed in setting up
a new European institute which was unique in concept and shape. There was
a model, certainly EIPA, the European Institute of Public Administration in
Maastricht, which had been created ten years earlier, also in the legal form
of a foundation. But EIPA was only targeting civil servants and did not have
an exclusive focus on European law; it was essentially funded by its Member
States and its internal governance reflected quite clearly its public-sector
orientation. ERA's mission was different and complementary; encompassing
all legal professions but exclusively dealing with European law made it wider
and narrower at the same time.

The founding years of ERA were a time for pioneers, and as such we were
in need of sound advice and of strong political and moral support. Many false
friends offered their suggestions -such as the invitation to be involved in well-
funded national initiatives aiming to export their legislative models to the
future candidate countries in the east. Many temptations marked our way
-such as the offers to participate in distinguished academic projects, which
essentially meant to sponsor them. There even came a time when we had to
fight for our autonomy. The best advice, the strongest moral support and the
soundest political guidance then came from our Board of Trustees.

---

[3]   Current Chairman is the former Spanish MEP Professor Manuel Medina Ortega, who in 2009
succeeded former Commissioner Peter Schmidhuber. For details see http://www.era.intl.

From the outset in 1993, the Board of Trustees was conceived as a genuinely European assembly of stakeholders. The original concept, still valid today, foresaw three core groups of members: representatives of the EU institutions; representatives of the target groups, judiciary, legal profession, in-house counsel, notaries etc ; and representatives of the member states. In 1993 John Toulmin was President of the CCBE, and the European Bar being a core target group made his nomination almost mandatory. To our great relief he not only accepted his nomination but also attended the Board's constitutive meeting which, when looking at its agenda and the list of participants, reveals the progress made. The agenda listed just five items (welcome; election of a chairman; report on ERA's activities; programme discussion; any other business). The meeting was scheduled to last only three hours and there were sixteen participants. Nowadays, despite breaking the 40 trustees present into working groups for part of the time, we have problems squeezing all topics into a full-day agenda.

3 ERA Years

'Tis not enough to help the feeble up, but to support him after.
Shakespeare, Timon of Athens, Act 1, Scene 1

In 1994, John Toulmin was elected Vice Chairman of the Board. In 1997, he succeeded Willi Rothley MEP as Chairman, a position to which he was re-elected in 2000, 2004 and 2008. He has not missed a single plenary meeting since 1993. He attended numerous other ERA meetings of subgroups of the Trustees, which on his initiative were first introduced in 2000, and of the Governing Board.

During an institutional history of nineteen years, the fourteen years of John Toulmin's chairmanship stretch from the very modest beginnings into the current phase of growth that has just been marked by the opening of a second conference building in Trier. One of his first requests as newly elected Chairman was a mid-term strategy for ERA's future role, which was discussed at the plenary meeting of the Board on the eve of the inauguration of ERA's new conference centre in 1998. It was a crucial moment, as local politics jealously defended their rather tight line of command and control over ERA's development just at the time when it was indispensable to open the Foundation to much broader European sponsorship and to allow it to pursue its way autonomously. It took us another year to get there, but it was above all thanks to John Toulmin's continuous support and political talent that eventually in March 2000 the Foundation Statute was substantially amended, separating management from political control and shifting strategic perspectives from external politics to the Foundation itself.

This change of perspective was a decisive factor in convincing other EU Member States of the added value of becoming institutionally involved. From

2000 to 2009, 20 further EU Member States became patrons of ERA, as well as Scotland and the present candidate country Croatia. Needless to say, John Toulmin was a key player in bringing the United Kingdom on board. The formal accession agreement was signed on 30 October 2002 at the chambers of the Lord Chancellor, Lord Irvine of Lairg, in the House of Lords.

John Toulmin never ceased to stimulate ERA's development and always considered consolidation as a step back. Besides his constant availability as adviser and admonisher, he was involved in numerous ERA events at a conceptual and implementation stage. To give a flavour: In 1998, he chaired the symposium inaugurating ERA's new conference centre on "The Euro -New Impulses for European Integration", with speakers including Pierre Werner, Lord Howe, Alain Lamassoure MEP and Piotr Nowina-Konopka. He was a member of various working parties preparing for example the 1998 annual congress on "Creating a European Judicial Space" or the congress on the occasion of ERA's Ten Years in 2002 (with sessions on "The European Constitution", "Judicial Architecture and Access to Justice in the EU" and "Judicial Cooperation -Preparing the National Judges for their European Role". In 1999, he inspired the English Bar European Group to hold their "Annual Overseas Conference" at the ERA premises; in 2007, he persuaded the "Chartered Institute of Arbitrators" to set up a joint conference with ERA in Trier. He spoke in numerous ERA conferences, in particular on mediation and arbitration and recently at a conference on legal aid in Brussels which ERA co-sponsored to mark the CCBE's 50th anniversary.

4 Profession

The first thing we do, let's kill all the lawyers.
Shakespeare, Henry the Sixth, Part 2 Act 4, Scene 2

John Toulmin studied law at Trinity Hall, Cambridge, and at the University of Michigan. He was called to the Bar at Middle Temple in 1965 and practiced as a barrister from 1965 to 1997. He took Silk in 1980, was called to the Bar of Northern Ireland in 1989 and to the Irish Bar in 1991. John Toulmin was a member of the Council of Legal Education of the Bar of England & Wales from 1981-83. In 1986 he was elected Bencher of Middle Temple and in 2008 he served as Reader and took advantage of his speech at his "Reader's Feast" to remind his fellow lawyers of the international and European challenges for the legal profession.

Between 1971 and 1993, John Toulmin served on various boards and committees of the English and European Bar. He led the UK delegation at the Council of the CCBE from 1982 until 1990, when he was elected Vice President (1991-92) and President in 1993. He was particularly involved in drafting what later became the "Lawyers' Establishment Directive,[4] and negotiated in the WTO Uruguay Round on behalf of the European legal profession. In 1994, he was made a Companion of the Order of St Michael and St George for his services to European law and in 1995 he was awarded the *Grosse Ehrenzeichen für Verdienste um die Republik Osterreich.*

In 1981, he started his judicial career as an Assistant Recorder and in 1984 became a part-time Recorder of the Crown Court. He was appointed Official Referee in 1997 and Judge of the Technology and Construction Court (TCC) of the High Court in 1998, where he dealt with domestic and international construction disputes. One of his most famous cases was *Factortame,* the case which in 1989 launched a cascade of decisions by the European Court of Justice and the English courts until it ended in John Toulmin's court on 27 November 2000. In its first judgment of 19 June 1990[5] the ECJ held that a national court has a duty to grant interim relief to safeguard alleged Community rights even if such relief is not foreseen under national law. In its second judgment of 25 July 1991[6] the ECJ made clear that national registration rules for vessels must not constitute obstacles for nationals of one Member State to establish themselves in the territory of another Member State and found the nationality requirements in the UK Merchant Shipping Act 1988 discriminatory and contrary to Article 43 EC as a restriction on the freedom of establishment. Finally, in its third judgment of 5 March 1996[7] the ECJ re-emphasised the principle of state liability in case of a breach of Community law, irrespective of which organ of the State was responsible for the breach, so even a breach of Community law by legislative acts (or omission) would trigger state liability if the breach was "manifest" and sufficiently "grave". The TCC, in the person of John Toulmin, was then called to decide on the substance of the tort liability claim brought forward by Factortame (which he found partly justified but, more essentially, managed to settle).

Furthermore, John Toulmin has remained engaged in academic activities, in particular at Michigan University Law School where he was a member of the Board of Visitors from 1996 to 2006, and at King's College, London, where he has served as Chairman of the Governance Committee since 1997 and which made him a Fellow in 2006. Arguably, his strongest professional and academic interests lie in alternative dispute resolution, where he was instrumental in setting up an innovative mediation process within the TCC, the Court Settlement Process.

---

[4] Directive 98/5IEC of 16.2.1998, OJ L77/36 of 14.3.98.
[5] C213/89, ECR 1990,1-2433.
[6] C221189, ECR 1991,1-3905.
[7] C46/93, ECR 1996,1-1029.

5 Leisure

Now go we in content
To liberty, and not to banishment.
Shakespeare, As You Like It, Act 1, Scene 3

Thankfully, John Toulmin's intellectual and cultural interests are not limited to law. He has always been a lover of ancient and modern classical music, from Georg Friedrich Handel to Sir John Taverner, and one of our favourite disputes has long been whether the former should be considered a German, an English, or an AngloGerman composer. (Funnily enough, we never had the same discussion about Hans Holbein *den Jungeren.* The obvious answer is that both were genuine Europeans ...) Among many other non-legal activities John Toulmin was also a Trustee of the National Association of Young String Players *Pro Corda* from 1992 to 1997 and since 1992 has been a Trustee and then Chairman of the Temple Music Trust. He is a fervent cricket enthusiast, a pastime to which I have not yet been admitted, a lover of good cuisine and an excellent connoisseur of wines and vineyards between Bordeaux and the Mosel.

While delicious cooking has always been provided by the *cuisine* of his wife Carolyn, who is also a Barrister and a Law Reporter, John had to wait until the late 90s to be able to produce his own quality wine. *Clos Toulmin* in Auxey-Duresses on the Côte de Beaune in Burgundy is an estate that is not only the source of an excellent pinot noir but also a wonderful residence, a resort to gather strength and ideas. We wish John Toulmin many years to come, to enjoy life, work and leisure, and we hope still to be able to count on his advice and support.

There is a tide in the affairs of men,
Which, taken at the flood, leads on to fortune.
Shakespeare, Julius Caesar, Act 4, Scene 3

Judging

The next section of the book is concerned with access to justice in the context of my time as a serving judge.

There are four articles. "Cross-Border Mediation" concentrates on the increasingly important European and international perspective. "Civil Justice" focuses on domestic litigation and amplifies many of the criticisms that I outlined in my Valedictory address. I observe that, as the legal world contracts, these observations relating to the English practice may well be helpful within civil law jurisdictions, just as the English courts must learn from the practices in civil jurisdictions and arbitration. In "Active Case Management" I set out a positive view of active case management and conclude that good case management can be taught as can the necessary grounding in Mediation and other forms of Alternative Dispute Resolution. Finally I include, a lecture on "Early Neutral Evaluation (ENE)", a form of alternative dispute resolution, which I gave to the Society of Construction Law in May 1999 and which Simon Tolson referred to in his Valedictory address.

"Cross-border Mediation and Civil Proceedings in National Courts" (p. 30), first published in *ERA Forum* (2009) 10 *ERA Forum* 551, and then in *Construction Law Review* (2010) 26 *Construction Law Journal* 516, was written after an important seminar at ERA in Trier in 2009. The article's focus is European. We need to be reminded that whatever the differences between and within the civil and common law systems, all countries have serious problems in providing civil justice at a reasonable cost and within a reasonable time.

The article starts by setting out a yard-stick against which the effectiveness of all dispute resolution procedures can be judged. In 1996 Lord Woolf published a devastating critique of the system of civil procedure then used in the courts of England and Wales which can be used to judge any system of civil justice, including that inaugurated by Lord Woolf's own reforms. This yardstick is used in the third of the four articles to test the usefulness of my case management practice.

The article goes on to consider what civil justice should achieve, and then considers the subject from the European point of view. As Professor Dame Hazel Genn suggests in her Hamlyn lectures, mediation has been embraced in the rest of Europe to cover for failings in those countries to provide any reliable means in their civil justice systems to enable parties to achieve a just resolution of their disputes within a reasonable time and for a reasonable cost. This represents a considerable change of attitude from the early1990s where civil law jurisdictions regarded mediation with suspicion. The article goes on to consider the development of mediation within the national court systems and to discuss the EU Mediation Directive (2008/52/EC of 21 May 2008) which came into force on 20 November 2010.

"Civil Justice: Competing Philosophies and Outcomes" (p.44) starts by turning the spotlight on competing philosophies in the delivery of civil justice in England and Wales, and concludes that access to court-based civil justice for the ordinary citizen has been reduced to the point where the European experience is highly relevant. The article traces the effect of the change in Treasury rules in 1993, the advent of adjudication which has none of the constraints imposed upon it by the CPR introduced as a result of the Woolf reforms, together with the punitive cost provisions to "encourage settlements" .

The article goes on to address the specific points raised by me in my Valedictory address – the disproportionate cost of pre-action protocols, judges' lack of understanding of, and training in, case management, and the lack of the continuous case management which was such an important feature of the Official Referees' court. It concludes with an outline of the Dispute Settlement Conference procedure referred to by Lord Phillips and others in the Valedictory addresses.

"Active Case Management in Civil Litigation" (p. 54) sets out in some detail my approach to active case management. It is, of course, not the only approach. I emphasise that poor case management can increase the cost of litigation substantially. I also conclude that case management can and should be taught as part of the training of civil judges. This view is supported by the Council of Europe in its report in 2007 on the efficiency of justice (see, Report of 7 December 2007, CEPEJ (2007)14, referred to below in "Cross-Border Mediation", p. 35). I note that the Judicial Studies Board, re-named the Judicial College, has a new and much more comprehensive course on case management for Judges in its 2012-13 programme but no comprehensive training such as I am advocating. I conclude by proposing what would be radical changes in the civil justice system to enable it to respond better to the needs of litigants.

"Early Neutral Evaluation" is an edited version of my paper to the Society of Construction Law on 4 May 1999. Early Neutral Evaluation remains very under-used. If judges were properly trained in case management and dispute resolution, parties might have more confidence in using it.

There is a new European significance to access to justice. Under Articles 81 and 82 of the Lisbon Treaties, the Commission has an enhanced competence in the field of civil and criminal justice. The Commissioner, Vice-President Vivien Reding, intends to table proposals on widening access to justice and on legal aid in 2012 and 2013 respectively. There needs to be a detailed survey of the effectiveness of civil justice in the Member States upon which informed decisions can be based. This requires much more than an analysis of the results of detailed questionnaires. It requires the work to be done by a team which includes trained lawyers who have a real understanding of the similarities and differences in the various legal systems.

The Commission will need the help of lawyers of high quality to evaluate the results and make positive and realistic proposals as to how access to justice can be improved at a time of acute financial restraints. It may be that some of the work will need to be carried out by an outside law institute, so that the EU Commission's proposals can be based on as reliable information as possible. Any proposals from the EU Commission will need to be taken into account in all Member States of the EU, including the United Kingdom.

The proposals need to be based on a full understanding of the similarities of the different legal systems in the Member States as well as their differences. It is important to recognise that it is not only the Common Law systems which are different to the civil law systems, but also that within the civil law systems there are many differences. Any proposals must also be realistic financially. Some of the proposals currently being made to the Commission to extend legal aid in civil cases and to provide legal aid for advice on contracts would be extremely costly for the Member States.

Cross-border Mediation and Civil Proceedings in National Courts

By HH John Toulmin CMG QC[1]

1. Introduction: the ERA seminar

On 14 and 15 May 2009 I co-chaired with Diana Wallis MEP[2], Vice-President of the European Parliament, a very important seminar at the Academy of European Law in Trier (ERA) entitled "Practical Issues of Cross-border mediation". It was co-financed by the European commission under its Civil Justice 2007-13 Programme and was supported by the Council of the Bars and Law Societies of the European Union (CCBE), the European Judicial Training Network (EJTN) and the Council of Notaries of the European Union (CNUE). Speakers came from ten different member states and the hundred or so participants came from 25 member states. The participants were legal practitioners, judges, government officials and academics and many ordinary participants were as distinguished as the speakers.

An important part of the work of ERA is to bring together those involved in different legal disciplines from different countries to study together legal questions which affect citizens within the European Union. The conference programme, expertly organised by Dr Angelika Fuchs, stimulated important discussions on mediation and civil justice which need to be carried forward at future conferences.

The participants were united in agreeing that it was important to develop effective systems of alternative dispute resolution for cross-border and domestic disputes within the European Union. Directive 208/52/EC of 21 May 2008 on certain aspects of mediation in civil and commercial disputes (the Mediation Directive) was welcomed although, as in the discussions leading to its adoption, those present were divided on whether it should have included domestic mediation as well as cross-border mediation. There was also a concern that the Directive was essentially an excellent first attempt, but would need to be revised well before the current review date of 2016. This Article represents my own thoughts but draws on and has been stimulated by the papers and the discussions at the seminar.

---

[1] MA (Cantab), LLM Michigan, President of CCBE 1993, Judge of the Technology & Construction Court of the High Court since 1997. Chairman of the Board of Trustees of ERA. Visiting Professor at the School of Law, King's College London University. This article was first published by Thomson Reuters in (2010) Construction Law Journal 516.
[2] Qualified Solicitor. MEP since 1999, Member of the Legal Affairs Committee of the European Parliament since 1999. Member of the Governing Board of ERA.

2. Mediation and National Courts

If it is successful, mediation (or negotiation) is a quicker and cheaper method of resolving disputes and will enable a solution to be achieved outside the strict confines of the dispute in a way which should benefit all the disputants. It enables matters which are not strictly the subject matter of the formal dispute, but are important to the parties, to be resolved in the mediation (or negotiation). It is worth noting that now, as well as before the advent of mediation, most disputes are solved by negotiation without the need for a mediator.

However in many cases parties need a mediator to guide the discussions and to assist the parties towards a fair solution. If a mediation is unsuccessful it carries its own cost which may be considerable. My definition of mediation would be different to that of the Mediation Directive in that I would define mediation as a structured process whereby two or more parties attempt by themselves on a voluntary basis *outside the court procedure administered by Judges* to reach agreement on the settlement of their dispute with the assistance of a mediator[3]. Much of the recent public impetus for referral to mediation as part of the civil legal disputes procedure, on either a voluntary or compulsory basis, has come from a failure of the domestic legal systems to provide adequate dispute resolution within the court system. More specifically, there has been an understanding within the Member States that the court procedures both at first instance and on appeal do not provide a reliable mechanism which enables parties to resolve their disputes within a reasonable time and at a reasonable cost within the court framework.

In addition, in the case of cross-border disputes there is the factor that one party may be perceived by the other to have obtained a procedural advantage in issuing legal proceeding in a jurisdiction with which it is familiar and the other party is unfamiliar.

2.1 The Woolf Test

In 1996 Lord Woolf, then Lord Chief Justice of England and Wales, published a devastating critique of his own legal system[4].

Lord Woolf found the system to be a) too unequal, giving an advantage to the well-resourced litigant b) too expensive c) too uncertain i.e. the parties could not forecast with sufficient accuracy how much the litigation would cost and how long it would take to be completed d) too slow e) too complicated in that the law and the procedure were incomprehensible to many litigants f) too fragmented in the way it was organised and g) too adversarial in that

---

[3] See Article 3(a) of the EU Mediation Directive. The words underlined are not included.
[4] See the Report of Lord Woolf entitled "Access to Justice" *Final Report* July 1996

cases were run by the parties and the Rules of Court were often ignored by the parties and not enforced by the courts.

These conclusions could be seen as answers to the following questions which would provide a checklist for the effectiveness of any system of civil justice a) Do the parties have, as far as possible, equality of arms before the court? Is the weaker party at as little disadvantage as possible, or ideally at no disadvantage? b) Is the cost of the litigation as reasonable as possible and proportionate to what is at stake? c) Can the parties make a reasonably accurate estimate in advance of how much each stage of the litigation will cost (including possible appeals) and how long it will take? d) Taking all the circumstances into account, will the preparatory stages, trial and (if necessary) appeal be completed within a time which is reasonable and consistent with doing justice between the parties? e) Is the court procedure capable of being explained to and understood by ordinary litigants? f) Is the court procedure organised so that it proceeds through logical and clearly defined stages from the start to the conclusion of the litigation? And g) Is the procedure too adversarial? Does the procedure itself foster confrontation, or does it, with the assistance of the judge managing the preparatory stages of the procedure, require the parties to cooperate in isolating for decision by the judge only those matters in genuine dispute? Does the procedure seek to resolve as early as possible those issues between the parties which can reasonably be agreed?

Put shortly, is the court procedure comprehensible to the ordinary litigant and does it enable the parties to obtain a final and just resolution of their dispute within a reasonable time and at proportionate cost?[5] In answering this overall question, it is necessary to take account of all possible delays including those which may take place to final appeal.

The Civil Procedure Rules 1998[6] which came into force in England and Wales on 26th April 1999 as a result of Lord Woolf's proposals, introduced significant reforms and remedied some of the defects of the old system. Court procedures have been speeded up. The power of the judges to control the procedure has been strengthened. The rules require the parties to cooperate in following the procedure. The procedures are explicit in encouraging mediation and other forms of amicable dispute resolution and have promoted earlier court settlements. However the procedure to trial is still far too expensive and is not readily understood even by sophisticated litigants. Parties still do not cooperate sufficiently in the procedure thus adding unnecessarily to the cost of the litigation. Judges are not trained in mediation and other forms of alternative dispute resolution or sufficiently in the overall case management

---

[5]   See also the overriding objective in the *Civil Procedure Rules* which implemented Lord Woolf's report and in particular the definition of the overriding objective CPR1.1(2)
[6]   These are amended from time to time by Statutory Instrument. *The Civil Procedure (Amendment Nº3) Rules 2008* (SI 2008/3327) commenced on 6 April 2009

of the litigation. Some of the reforms, far from reducing the cost, have added significantly to the cost of litigation without any compensatory benefit.

3. Mediation within the national court system

A threshold issue, which needs to be addressed clearly in all legal systems, is whether mediation should be delegated by the court system to outside providers or be integrated within the system. For example, should the parties be required to enter into a mediation first, and only if it is unsuccessful, should the parties be permitted to resolve their dispute through the court system.

There is an issue, much debated in the seminar and elsewhere, as to whether Article 6 of the Declaration of Human Rights permits compulsory mediation. In any event, there is an important underlying reason why mediation should be fully integrated into the civil justice system.

3.1 What Civil Justice ought to achieve

In her Hamlyn Lectures in 2008[7], Professor Dame Hazel Genn, set out what civil justice ought to achieve:

> The machinery of civil justice sustains social stability and economic growth by providing public processes for peacefully resolving civil disputes, for enforcing legal rights and for protecting private and personal rights. The civil justice system provides the legal architecture for the economy to operate effectively, for agreements to be honoured, and for the power of governments to be scrutinised and limited. The civil law (as opposed to criminal) maps out the boundaries of social and economic behaviour while the civil courts resolve disputes when they arise. In this way the civil courts publicly reaffirm norms and behavioural standards for private citizens, businesses and public bodies.

Put another way, if a party feels it is forced to mediate not out of choice but because of an inadequate system of civil justice which means that the party "cannot get justice" within the legal system that reduces respect for the legal system as a whole.

It is important therefore that mediation and other forms of alternative dispute resolution should be integrated into the court system. This requires first that all mediation agreements properly entered into should be speedily and inexpensively enforced within the court system. Secondly, where legal proceedings have been commenced in the courts, the procedure to trial should be administered by judges trained in mediation who are able to make orders within the overall case management of the litigation which will further both amicable settlement and the procedure to trial. I see no incompatibility in preparing a case for settlement and preparing a case for trial. It is properly

---

[7]   *Hamlyn Lectures 2008*, Lecture 2 deals with mediation.

part of the court procedure that the dispute should, if the parties wish it, be referred to mediation or other form of amicable settlement when it has the best chance of success. This will ensure the balanced relationship between mediation and judicial proceedings in Article 1 of the Mediation Directive.

In the Technology and Construction Court in England and Wales (TCC), which deals with complicated construction and information technology litigation, this stage frequently occurs only after the parties have been able to understand, and verify at least in outline, the other party's case. The judge trained in case management and mediation will know when this stage has been reached and can make orders designed to reach this stage in the most cost effective way[8].

3.2 The Slovenian experience

For me, one of the most important contributions at the ERA seminar came from Judge Jovin Hrastnik, a district judge in Lublijana, Slovenia. She explained how the district court, concerned at the backlog of cases, started a court-annexed mediation programme for civil disputes from 2001, family disputes from 2002 and commercial disputes from 2003[9].

In 2008 Slovenia enacted the Mediation in Civil and Commercial Matters Act. The Act transposes the EU Mediation Directive into Slovenian law. It sets out the basic principles of mediation procedure. The Act also provides that the mediators will be judges, lawyers and other accredited law specialists from whom the court will nominate a mediator in a particular case.

Judge Hrastnik explained that in the beginning there were no qualified mediators among the judges and no qualified teachers of mediation in Slovenia so that the first judges went to the United States to be trained and then returned to train their colleagues. In Slovenia the basic training takes 40 hours and there are about 60 accredited mediators.

As I explained at the seminar, a somewhat similar initiative was introduced in 2005 in the London Technology and Construction Court whereby the parties could ask for and, if appropriate, the case- managing judge could institute, a Court Settlement Process under which the case-managing judge or another judge of the court would assist the parties to achieve an amicable settlement of the dispute. If the attempt failed, the settlement judge would not be further involved in the court litigation. The judges, all of whom have had mediation training, have an over 80% settlement rate. These settlements have often been

---

[8]   In England and Wales it has only been in the TCC that the same Judge has always managed the case from the start of the procedure to trial. This is of great advantage to the parties.

[9]   In her synopsis included in the Seminar materials, Judge Hrastnik set out the mechanism of the Court-annexed mediation programme which in 2008 achieved settlement rates of 33.5% in civil cases, 66.5% in family cases and 49.6% in commercial cases.

achieved at a relative early stage in the procedure and have succeeded where previous attempts at settlement have failed.

3.3 Council of Europe – Awareness of the Judiciary

The need for judges to understand the process of conciliation and mediation as well as court-based adjudication was recognised and highlighted in the report of the Council of Europe, European Commission for the Efficiency of Justice 7th December 2007 CEPEJ (2007)14 on guidance for the better implementation of the existing recommendations concerning family mediation and mediation in civil matters.

Under the heading "Awareness of Judiciary" paragraph 3.3 said:

Fostering a culture of amicable dispute resolution it is essential that they [the judges] have a full knowledge and understanding of the process and benefits of mediation. This may be achieved through information sources as well as initiation in-service training programmes which include specific elements of mediation useful in day to day work of the courts in particular jurisdictions.

4. ADR an historical perspective[10]

Since the Middle Ages commercial men have often preferred to resolve their disputes in private outside the court system. Over one hundred years ago, in 1885, the predecessor of the London Court of Arbitration was founded to manage international disputes. The International Court of Arbitration (ICA) was founded in 1923. There was a similar development in the United States in 1925 when the Federal Arbitration Act recognised private domestic arbitration agreements.

In 1958 the United Nations (New York) Convention on the Recognition and Enforcement of Foreign Arbitral Awards was adopted. It is enforced in over 142 countries. It was described by Kofi Anan, a former Secretary General of the United Nations, as "one of the most successful treaties in the area of commercial law... [and] has served as a model for many subsequent legislative texts on arbitration." These principals have been followed in the rules of many arbitral bodies. The system of arbitration is now well established within the European Union and worldwide.

The development of mediation rules internationally and within the European Union is of more recent origin dating from the 1980s and 1990s and is still being developed. I remember drafting conciliation rules for the Hong Kong Transit Authority (with Arthur Marriott QC) in 1982[11].

---

[10]   For a distinguished US overview, see the article by Professor Menkel-Meadow, Professor at Georgetown University, one of the leading academic writers and mediators in the United States. In her contribution to *Melanges en l'honneur de Pierre Tercier* Schulthess.

[11]   The best general introductions in English are *Are Cross-Cultural Ethics Standards Possible or Desirable in International Arbitration?*, Brown and Marriott *ADR Principles and Practice* 3rd ed

As late as the early 1990s concern was being expressed by lawyers from civil law jurisdictions at this "tendance Anglo Saxon". There was still a strong feeling that legal disputes should be decided by judges not mediators.

5. Mediation Developments from 1998

Mediation within the European Union has had three separate strands: a) civil and commercial disputes, b) consumer rights i.e. resolution of disputes with the individual consumer often of small value, c) family disputes including in particular disputes involving children. The main discussion at the seminar was on a) but it was recognised that the discussion on cross-border and international civil and commercial mediation should be informed by b) and c). These topics were also included in the seminar.

The invaluable documentation of the Trier seminar would put the Europe-wide acceptance of the place of mediation in civil and commercial, consumer and matrimonial disputes at about 1998. On the 21 January 1998 the Committee of Ministers to Member States adopted Recommendation No R (98)1 on family mediation together with its explanatory memorandum[12]. The explanatory memorandum explained that the third European Conference on Family Law in Cadiz in 1995 had recommended that the Council of Europe give consideration to the question of family Mediation and examine the possible preparation of an international instrument setting out the principles of Family Mediation or other processes to resolve family disputes.

In December 2004 Evelyne Gebhardt MEP succeeded as the European parliament mediator for International Parental Child Abduction. She gave a progress report on 1 March 2007. Her report set out the progress that had been made within the European Union and at the Hague Convention conference.

In October 2006 the Hague Conference on Private International Law received a note on the development of Mediation, Conciliation and similar means to facilitate agreed solutions in trans-frontier family disputes concerning children especially in the context of the Hague Convention of 1980.

This was followed by a feasibility study on cross-border mediation in Family matters (in March 2007)[13] and a study on cross-border mediation in family matters analysing responses not only from the European Union but also from a range of States and non-governmental organisations world-wide. Finally the conference adopted conclusions and recommendations at its

---

2011, and Mackie Miles Marsh and Allen *ADR Practice Guide: Commercial Dispute Resolution* 3rd edn 2007, Butterworths, the authors of which are also well known through the Centre of Dispute Resolution.
[12]   Adopted by the Committee of Ministers on 21 January 1998
[13]   Prel. Doc. No20

Council on 31March/2 April 2009 and confirmed the continued relevance of the Strategic Directions set out in the Strategic Plan of 2002[14].

Over the last ten years the EU Commission has also been pressing ahead with initiatives on consumer mediation starting with the communication of 30 March 1998 (COM 1998 (198)) and ending with the green Paper on Consumer Collective redress of 27 November 2008 (COM (2008) 94 F) and the staff working document report on cross-border E-commerce of 5 March 2009. The explanatory memorandum attached to the communication of 30 March 1998 noted that Community action was highlighted in 1993 and in the action plan on "consumer action to justice and the settlement of consumer disputes in the single market" in 1996.

In civil and commercial mediation, earlier initiatives were followed internationally by the UNCITRAL Model Law on international commercial conciliation in 1992.

Within the wider Europe the Council of Europe recommendation 2002 (10) of the Committee of Ministers to Member States on Mediation in Civil Matters; the European Code of Conduct for Mediators ; the Council of Europe Guidelines implementing the 2002 recommendation concerning Family Mediation and Mediation in Civil matters of 7 December 2007 took matters forward.

6. The 2008 Mediation Directive

The most important initiative, and the one upon which the Seminar concentrated, is Directive 2008/52/EC of 21 May 2008 on Certain Aspects of Mediation in Civil and Commercial matters[15]. As is clear from the history of the development of civil and commercial mediation the Directive has come relatively early in the development of mediation within the European Union.

At the Seminar Diana Wallis MEP told us that there had been considerable discussion on whether the Directive should relate to domestic mediation as well as cross-border mediation and that the decision had been a narrow one. This was reflected in Recital 8 of the preamble to the Commission Draft COM (2004) 718 F which envisaged that the Directive should apply to cross-border and domestic disputes. The limitation to cross-border disputes is consistent with the approach taken to Family Mediation and E-Commerce (SEC (2009) 283) – Commission Staff Working Document, 5th March 2009. It avoids legislating on purely national disputes. This should be an encouragement to the Member States to continue to develop Mediation within their own legal systems and should assist in the development of common rules for mediation within the European Union and the wider International Community in the

---

[14]   See Prel. Doc. No5 of March 2009
[15]   The seminar also held workshops on consumer mediation and family mediation

coming years. The legal world is shrinking and the ultimate objective must be to establish codes of practice and conduct worldwide.

Article 1[16] sets out the purpose of the Directive namely "to facilitate access to alternative dispute resolution and to promote the amicable settlement of disputes by mediation and by ensuring a balanced relationship between mediation and judicial proceedings".

Article 2[17] of the Directive defines a cross-border dispute as a dispute in which at least one of the parties is domiciled or habitually resident in a Member State other than that of any other party on the date on which the parties agree to use mediation or it is ordered by the court or the obligation arises under national law or the parties are invited by the court to settle the dispute (see Article 5).

Article 3 defines mediation as "a structural process however named or referred to whereby two or more parties to a dispute attempt by themselves on a voluntary basis to reach an agreement on the settlement of their dispute with the assistance of a mediator".

Mediator is defined as "any third person who is asked to conduct a mediation in an effective, impartial and competent way regardless of the denomination or profession of that third party in that member state…"

Article 3 of the Directive attempts to provide clearly what is and what is not included within the Directive. Excluded are pre-contractual negotiations and arbitration. Also excluded are attempts made by the judge seized with the judicial proceedings to attempt to settle the dispute by conciliation in the course of those judicial proceedings. It is not entirely clear that other court resolution procedures, e.g. mini-trial, are excluded but they probably are excluded[18].

The Directive does include Mediation conducted by a judge who is not responsible for the judicial proceedings before the court and to whom the dispute has been referred for conciliation or mediation. As I made clear at the outset, in my view mediation by a judge as part of a recognised court procedure should have been excluded from the Directive. The distinction should have been made between procedures controlled by the judges of the national courts and those carried out separately. A mediation carried out by a judge as part of the court procedure is essentially part of the legal system of the member state and should not be included within the Directive.

---

[16]   Dr Felix Steffek LLM (Cambridge) of the Max Planck Institute for Comparative and International Private Law Hamburg gave an excellent analysis of the Directive at the Seminar. The Analysis in this paper takes account of his comments

[17]   Recital 8 of the Preamble encourages Member States to apply the Directive to domestic as well as cross border disputes.

[18]   See Recital 11 of the preamble.

There is an uneasy compromise within Article 3(a) in that a mediation within the Directive includes a mediation "ordered by the Court" or "prescribed by the law of a Member State"[19]. It is difficult to understand how such a mediation can be consistent with an attempt by the parties "on a voluntary basis" to reach agreement on the settlement of their dispute with a mediator. If a court orders the parties to attempt to reach an agreement it is difficult to see how a refusal by a party to undertake the mediation process in good faith (a voluntary act) can be regarded as compliance with an order for compulsory mediation.

Article 5 sets out minimum standards for courts. Article 5(1) is permissive. A court may invite parties to use mediation in order to settle the dispute or it may invite the parties to attend an information session on the use of Mediation.

However under Article 5(2) a Member State may make Mediation compulsory and impose sanctions on those who refuse to mediate. This provision is to apply within the context of Article 6 of the European Declaration of Human Rights which prescribes that a party must not be prevented from exercising the right of access to a judicial resolution of the dispute.

The uneasy compromise is continued within Article 5. If the parties are required compulsorily to have their dispute referred to mediation this conflicts with the idea that the parties attempt on a voluntary basis to resolve their dispute.

The qualification relating to the European Convention may also be important. In a number of cases the cost of mediation may be so significant that some parties may not be able to afford to pay for both mediation and litigation. If this is the case, the Convention requires that the parties are entitled to proceed to litigation without being required first to take part in mediation. If however the courts are able to develop procedures whereby orders are made for disclosure of documents as part of the preparation for trial, but which also further a successful mediation (or negotiation) between the parties, this problem may be avoided. Much of the duplication of cost can be avoided and the mediation will take place within the court procedure at a time when the judge can be confident that the mediation has a reasonable chance of success.

Article 6 of the Directive is concerned with enforceability of agreements resulting from mediation and provides that the content of such an agreement shall be made enforceable unless either the content of the agreement is contrary to the law of the Member State where the request is made, or the law of the Member State does not provide for its enforceability. In my view,

---

[19] See also Recital 13 of the Preamble.

it is essential that the Directive should require each Member State to provide for prompt enforceability of such agreements unless the content of any such agreement is contrary to the law of the member state where the mediation has taken place[20].

Article 7 concerning the confidentiality of mediation, seems to be straightforward enough. "Member States shall ensure that, unless the parties agree otherwise, neither the mediator nor those involved in the administration of the mediation, shall be compelled to give evidence in civil and commercial judicial proceedings or arbitration regarding information arising out of or in connection with a mediation process except in cases of:

a) overriding consideration of public policy, in particular in connection with protecting the best interests of the child or to prevent harm to the physical or psychological integrity of person or

b) where disclosure of the content of the agreement resulting from the mediation is necessary in order to implement or enforce that agreement".

Article 7(2) provides that nothing shall preclude Member States from enacting stricter measures to protect the confidentiality of mediation. As Michel Kallipetis QC, a leading international mediator, demonstrated very clearly to the Seminar, courts have had different approaches to the position of mediators. In England the courts have tended to regard mediation as "assisted without prejudice negotiation". In *Farm Assist Ltd (in liquidation) v SSEFRA* [2009] EWHC 1102 (TCC), decided a few days after the Seminar, on 19 May 2009, Ramsey J affirmed, in line with the Mediation Directive, the general rule of confidentiality between the parties and the mediator, and that the privilege lies with the parties and not with the mediator, and could be waived by the parties. He held, going beyond the Directive, that the mediator had a right of confidentiality but that this could be overridden "in the interests of justice" and that in the circumstances of that case, the mediator should be ordered to give evidence as a witness in subsequent proceedings.

In the end the case was compromised. The well-respected mediator was not in the event called to give evidence. The mediation agreement between the parties and the mediator had contained a confidentiality clause but Ramsey J held that it was not wide enough to encompass what went on at the mediation. Following the decision, a number of mediators have expressed concern at their position. An important topic to be considered in a review of the Directive is the extent to which, if at all, mediators should have a privilege separate from that of the parties not to give evidence or to provide documents in subsequent proceedings unless the mediator waives the privilege. The same

---

[20]   Dr Steffek pointed out at the Seminar that a mediation agreement is enforceable cross border under rules applying to judgments by consent see Art 32 et seq, 38 et seq Brussels 1.

public interest exceptions in Article 7(1)(a) would apply. There would be a further requirement that evidence otherwise admissible in court proceedings could not be rendered inadmissible because it was used in the mediation. Such a provision would remove the vague concept of "the interests of justice" and substitute a defined public interest exception. Account should also be taken of the reference to the confidentiality and compellability of mediators as witnesses in the Hague Conference report of 2007.

The position of mediation in the United Kingdom should no longer be developed by judges under the common law but should be set out in a short Act of Parliament, consistent with the Directive, which puts the position of mediators on a statutory basis. Both domestic and cross-border mediation have increased to the point where there is a need for such domestic legislation. In addition, it would clarify the law for those who wish to use England for cross-border mediation.

In relation to arbitration, Parliament has passed a series of Acts, most recently the 1996 Arbitration Act, which has put arbitration in England and Wales on a statutory basis. Mediation has developed to the point where it too should be put on a statutory basis. It should be noted that the 1996 Act does not deal with the issue of confidentiality of arbitrators. It would be entirely appropriate for this to be considered at the same time as the issue of confidentiality for mediators.

Article 8 provides that parties who choose Mediation in an attempt to settle their dispute are not subsequently prevented from initiating judicial proceedings or arbitration by reason of the expiry of the limitation period during the mediation process. On its face this appears to be a sensible provision but it has no time limit and could well be used by one party to delay the subsequent court proceedings and thus frustrate the overriding objective that a party should be able to resolve its dispute within a reasonable time and at a reasonable cost. The delay by a party in bringing proceedings until nearly the end of the limitation period may, itself, put the opposing party at a substantial and inappropriate disadvantage. In the United Kingdom the limitation period is 6 years for contractual disputes. The requirement that the proceedings be further delayed by mediation will delay the resolution of the dispute even further if the mediation is unsuccessful.

The alternative approach used in the Technology and Construction Court in England and Wales is that, if there is a risk that the limitation period may be relevant, a party must start legal proceedings and the court will then give Directions including, where appropriate, staying proceedings for a specified limited time to enable a mediation to be concluded within a reasonable time before or during the court procedure.

The Directive is due to come into force on 21 November 2010 at the latest (Article 12) and to be subject to a review by the Commission by 21 May 2016. In her address at the Seminar, Diana Wallis MEP said that this timetable was far too slow. There was general agreement with this opinion. I would hope that by 2016 there was not only a revised Directive but an International Agreement on cross-border mediation, and an agreed Code of Conduct for Mediators.

For completeness I should refer to the remaining Articles. Article 4 encourages Member States to provide mechanisms to ensure the quality of mediation. Article 9 requires member states to encourage the availability of mediation services and to publicise them. Article 10 requires the commission to make available information of competent courts provided by the Member States.

7. Conclusions

To summarise:

The ERA Seminar was extremely important. The Seminar with its wide membership both professionally and geographically was addressing Mediation in the context of access to civil justice for the ordinary citizen. This is a problem shared by all Member States and most, if not all, other jurisdictions worldwide.

There is a need for regular seminars at ERA on Mediation and Alternative Dispute Resolution in the context of access to civil justice for the ordinary citizen so that future initiatives can be discussed as they develop and ERA can act as a sounding-board on the progress of the Mediation Directive.

There is a need in the context of access to justice for the ordinary citizen to develop a common measure of the effectiveness of civil justice within the legal systems of the Member States and their ability to meet the increasing cross-border requirements of citizens within the European Union.

The machinery of justice sustains social stability within a State. It is desirable that effective provision for mediation shall be integrated within the legal system of each Member State rather than to operate as a referral activity outside the court procedure.

There is no incompatibility between preparing a court case for settlement through mediation (or negotiation) and preparing a court case for trial. Judges should be trained in mediation and other forms of alternative dispute resolution in order that in the course of the court procedure they are competent to make orders that will assist parties towards amicable resolution of the whole or part of their disputes (if necessary by mediation) as well as to trial. This will also assist judges in their attempts to achieve settlements in the course of legal proceedings.

The knowledge that a trial will inevitably follow within a reasonable time is, in itself, an important impetus to resolution of disputes by mediation.

Within the European Union there has developed within the last ten years an understanding of the importance of mediation in three separate areas: (i) civil and commercial disputes (ii) disputes affecting consumers and (iii) family disputes. A successful initiative in one area may point to a solution in another.

Within civil and commercial disputes, the cross-border Mediation Directive of 2008 represents considerable progress although there are a number of difficult issues which need to be resolved. It was right at this stage to confine the Directive to cross-border disputes.

The Directive provides that the current provisions will be reviewed by the Commission in 2016. It was the view of the Seminar that a substantial review will be required significantly before that date.

This article sets out various issues to be considered in the course of such a review. Mediation in England and Wales needs to be put on a statutory basis. The issue of confidentiality for mediators (and arbitrators) needs to be addressed at both international and domestic levels.

Mediation has important implications not only nationally for cross-border disputes within the European Union but also internationally. It is to be hoped that initiatives taken within the European Union will draw on experience obtained in the rest of the world and that at the time of the next review of the Directive attempts will be made for the amended Directive and Codes of Conduct for Mediators to be harmonised with rules to be applied internationally.

Civil Justice: Competing Philosophies and Outcomes

In my Valedictory address I was critical of a number of aspects of current civil procedure. These criticisms provoke a wider initial question, "What is the State's role in the provision of civil justice?" One view is that the State has no public interest in civil litigation. Its role is simply to provide a service which should be paid for in full by the litigant. If this goal cannot be achieved in full, potential litigants should be discouraged from using the courts except as a last resort, and be compelled or encouraged to use the private services of Adjudication and Mediation, thus reducing the cost to the Exchequer of providing for civil justice.

The alternative view is that the State has a public interest in providing a civil justice system which citizens can use readily and with confidence. The system should provide them, through the courts, with a process which enables the parties to resolve their civil disputes justly, either through a judgment of the court, or by earlier resolution using alternative forms of dispute resolution in order to achieve, as far as possible, a fair outcome between the parties in as reasonable a time and at as reasonable a cost as possible.

Successive governments have gone down the first route. For reasons which I shall set out later, and which have informed my practice as a Judge, I regard this approach as misconceived although I understand the financial pressures on the Departmental budget from legal aid for criminal and family cases which led to the Government's initial change in approach. In going down the alternative route, I am not suggesting any changes in the provision of legal aid or how litigation should otherwise be funded. I am suggesting that procedural reforms in the process of litigation at what should be a very modest cost would transform the administration of civil justice.

The Report on Costs by Lord Justice Jackson, published in 2010 (ISBM 9780117064041) is good on the subject of the funding of litigation; it is less convincing on the question of the process of litigation and its actual cost. I should add, purely for the record, that I was not invited to give evidence to Lord Justice Jackson, although the TCC High Court Judges did give evidence.

There is one other matter which I should clear away at the outset. Parties have, since the beginning of time, settled the vast majority of their disputes by negotiation. They do not need to be told that it is cheaper and quicker to settle their dispute, if they can, without going to law. They have also asked a third party neutral to help them to resolve their disputes. In relatively recent times an ever larger group of trained mediators has evolved to help parties more formally to resolve their disputes. Parties rightly often choose to use their services voluntarily. This article is not about that process. It is about the process which involves the recourse, or potential recourse, to law.

The route which successive governments have chosen, namely that access to civil justice should be a last resort, makes it difficult to argue that the Civil Justice system in the United Kingdom is any different to the civil jurisdictions in the rest of Europe. After an initial revulsion from the civil jurisdictions, on the grounds that it was importing an unhealthy common law solution, they have been forced to embrace Mediation and other forms of out of court dispute resolution, because of the failures in their own justice systems to provide reasonable access to civil justice for the ordinary citizen. The European experience, set out in the previous Chapter on Cross Border Mediation and Civil Proceedings in National Courts, is therefore highly relevant to the position in the United Kingdom.

The philosophy of successive governments and the Woolf Reforms is examined by Professor Dame Hazel Genn in her series of Hamlyn Lectures in 2008 entitled "Civil Justice, How Much is Enough?" In a section at p 45 entitled "The decline of the Civil Courts", she notes that historically the tax payer paid for the cost of civil judges and the court buildings, and the rest of the cost of civil justice was paid for by litigants through court fees.

The key change came not from a measured decision by the Lord Chancellor's Department or its successor the Department of Justice, but from a Treasury decision. In 1992, during a financial crisis, the Treasury decided that, like any government service supplied to paying customers, the civil justice service should pay for itself. As Professor Genn explains, they cut the financial provision in the Department's budget which paid for judges when carrying out their duties as civil judges, and also paid for the cost of providing court facilities for civil cases. These cuts took place at a time when the Departmental budget for crime and family litigation was expanding, but the cut in the civil justice budget also took place at a time when court litigation was very popular with litigants. The government's objective was achieved by discouraging potential litigants from using the courts and by promoting other forms of dispute resolution, particularly Mediation. By the year 2000 the use of the civil courts to resolve disputes had fallen dramatically.

This reduction had been achieved in the construction field through the enactment of the adjudication provisions of the Housing Grants Construction and Regeneration Act 1996 (the 1996 Act), through the Woolf Reforms and through (entirely legitimately) encouragement to parties to use voluntary conciliation and mediation. The latter was not a revolutionary step. As I have already indicated, this route had traditionally be used by parties. It had simply become more sophisticated.

The effect of the 1996 Act was, in effect, to privatise the resolution of construction disputes. The Act confers on parties a general right to refer a construction dispute or difference within the meaning of the Act to be adjudicated by a private individual acting as a neutral, provided it can be adjudicated in accordance with a procedure complying with section 108(2) of the Act. Some neutrals are legally qualified; others are often construction professionals – architects, surveyors, engineers etc. As I held in *CIB Properties Ltd v Birse Construction Ltd* [2005] 1 WLR 2252 (*CIB v Birse*)(see below), the 1996 Act can apply even to extremely complicated disputes. I have reached this conclusion with some misgiving. The original purpose of the Act was to provide a quick and simple method for insuring that sub-contractors would be paid promptly (see House of Lords Debate on the Bill).

Section 108(2) of the 1996 Act sets out the requirements, including time limits, within which the adjudication must be carried out.[The 1996 Act was revised in 2009 to widen the jurisdiction still further. The changes have not yet been brought into force.] The judgment of the lay neutral will be enforced by the courts. It will remain, in effect, a final judgment, or judgment nisi, unless it is superceded by a judgment of a court or arbitrator or by a settlement agreement between the parties.

It is to be emphasised that the procedure can easily be invoked to resolve a dispute or difference between the parties. Rather similar to the rules under the old Rules of the Supreme Court (RSC), this only requires a letter from the complainant setting out the nature of the dispute or difference, and a proper opportunity for a response by the other party before the procedure can be commenced. It does not require compliance with an elaborate and expensive pre-action protocol, such as that which was imposed on the Technology and Construction Court (TCC) by the new Civil Practice Rules (CPR).

The Woolf reforms came into effect in the CPR on 26 April 1999, but Woolf's final report pre-dated the 1996 Act. The civil procedure reforms were justified by a devastating critique of the previous RSC (see Cross Border Mediation and Civil Proceedings in National Courts, p.31). The critique provides a guide with which to judge the fairness and effectiveness of any civil procedure rules, including the new CPR.

There are nine pre-action protocols. The underlying purpose is set out in the Practice Direction – Pre-Action Conduct: "... Part 1.1(2). Support the efficient management by the Court and the parties of proceedings which cannot be avoided". (My emphasis).

In the Construction and Engineering Disputes Protocol efficient management is translated as "Proceedings will be conducted efficiently if litigation does become necessary".

In Chapter 10 of his final Report, Lord Woolf said that parties need to understand that litigation was to be viewed as a last resort and that before resorting to litigation the parties should understand the desirability of resolving disputes without litigation; they should be able to obtain the information they need in order to enter into an appropriate settlement, or make an appropriate settlement offer, or make an appropriate settlement offer, and if a settlement is not achievable, lay the ground for the expeditious conduct of proceedings. In order to achieve these objectives, the Protocol set out detailed requirements as to what must be done before the parties can start proceedings in the courts.

I have to comment, from over 11 years' experience as a Judge operating the CPR when case managing cases, that the pre-action protocol has been singularly unsuccessful in supporting the efficient management of cases which have come before me for case management. In all but a handful of cases it did not provide the necessary information to shorten the pre-trial court procedure. In effect, it added vastly to the cost of what is, in any event, a very expensive procedure for litigants.

TCC Judges managed to water down some of the prescriptive provisions to be found in other protocols, but I have had consistent complaints that, even in its present form, parties are required to spend tens, and even hundreds, of thousands of pounds in complying with the protocol before being permitted to start proceedings. Since I regularly asked the parties at the first case management conference how much money they had already spent on the litigation, I can support this contention from my own experience.

In smaller cases the Pre Action Protocol costs can easily exceed the amount claimed in the litigation. Also, in these smaller disputes, the lay clients will often feel that they know in general terms the nature of the claims for and against them. The elaborate procedure, which their legal advisers deem to be necessary, is really a waste of money and does not help either party to resolve its dispute early. On the contrary, the additional cost incurred may make the dispute unsettlable and it does not assist the pre-trial court procedure.

The legal advisers have a serious dilemma. The pre-action protocol is part of the adversarial procedure. It is not a question for the parties or their legal advisers of whether there have been potential breaches of the TCC Pre Action Protocol, the problem is that the legal advisers, doing their best, do not and by the nature of the process, cannot know in advance what the court will regard as proportionate. There is no provision in the rules for applying to the court in advance for directions as to how the Protocol stage should be carried out. There is only a Practice Direction which requires parties to make an application to the Court to commence proceedings after the Pre-Action Protocol has been complied with. Unless the parties comply fully with the Protocol, one party may block recourse to court proceedings by saying that the procedure has not been complied with, or may ask for costs sanctions under Pt 44(5)(a) because the opposing party has not followed sufficiently "the Practice Direction (Pre-Action Conduct) or any relevant pre-action protocol." In other cases, judges have criticised the parties' lawyers for taking too long over the protocol, or carrying it out in too detailed a manner, thus incurring unnecessary costs for the parties. Thus lawyers are entering into the realms of roulette, not justice. The absence of any proper provision of a right to apply to the court for directions as to how the pre-action protocol should be carried out, in circumstances where the steps to be taken are not and cannot be precise, seems to me to be contrary to a proper sense of justice.

I could also see circumstances, although the point has not been taken directly, where the procedure could offend against Article 6 of the European Convention for the Protection of Fundamental Rights and Freedoms (the European Convention). Article 6 provides that "In the determination of his civil rights and obligations ... everyone is entitled to a fair and public hearing within a reasonable time by an independent and impartial tribunal established by law". A party may be put in the position where, because of the costs which it has had to incur in the pre-action procedure, it does not have the finance to deploy its full case at trial and thus have a fair hearing. More particularly, where the parties are of unequal strength, the whole pre-action procedure is likely to exacerbate the position so that the weaker party is at an ever greater disadvantage when the case comes to court, making it more difficult for that party to have a fair hearing.

The extended time limits in the protocols are also objectionable in that they cause delay. This is inevitable in a procedure whose purpose is to divert litigation away from the court. Under the protocol (para 4), a defendant who wishes to take objection to the court's jurisdiction, or the named defendant, has 28 days in which to make the objection. Otherwise, within 28 days of the receipt of the claim, or a period of up to 3 months if the parties agree, the defendant must set out a detailed response to the claim. Thereafter, within 28 days, the parties normally should meet (para 5). There are detailed rules in relation to the meetings. Perhaps fortunately, and proportionately, I have never seen them carried out in full.

This procedure is to be contrasted with, for example, the most complicated trade disputes between nations in the World Trade Organisation (WTO). Article 4 of the conciliation procedure requires "adequate opportunity for consultation". Under Article 4(3) unless, mutually agreed, the Member State, to which the request was made, must reply within ten days and enter into consultations in good faith within a period of no more than 30 days. If a Member State fails to observe these time limits, the Member State requesting consultations may proceed directly to apply to set up a panel. If the parties fail to settle the dispute within 60 days after the request for consultations, or sooner if it appears to both parties that they have failed to settle the dispute, the complaining party may request the setting up of a panel (Article 4(7)). In case of urgency the parties are required to enter in to consultations within 10 days and conclude them within 20 days (Article 4(8)).

The second matter in the CPR which is objectionable jurisprudentially is the costs regime under Part 36.1. Under this Part, an opposing party can recover costs not only on an indemnity basis, but also interest on damages and costs at a rate not exceeding 10% above bank rate for the whole or part of the period after the time for accepting the opposing parties' offer has expired. This applies a) where a claimant fails to obtain a judgment more advantageous than a defendants' Part 36 offer (a formal written offer of settlement) or b) where a judgment against the defendant is at least as advantageous to the claimant as proposed in the claimant's Part 36 offer. If a private individual was to put such provisions into a contract, those provisions would be held by the courts to be a penalty and therefore unenforceable. I ask the question "Why should the State be able to do on behalf of an individual what would be unlawful for the individual to contract for him or herself?" I should add that an increase of 10% of the damages, with conventional orders for costs and interest, could well be regarded as a genuine pre-estimate of damage which would therefore not be regarded as a penalty.

The third matter about which I complained in my Valedictory address is a positive aspect of the Woolf reforms and the CPR which has not been followed up with appropriate training, namely the important shift in responsibility from the duty of the parties to manage civil litigation to that of the court. The duty of the parties under CPR Part 1.3 is to assist the court in carrying out this responsibility. This has had the positive effect of making the procedure much less confrontational. This change reflected the reforms in procedure of the Official Referees, the forerunner of the TCC, and the Commercial Court, and also incorporated some of the most positive aspects of international arbitration procedure. Previously lawyers often felt that to reach any agreement on procedural matters could be seen as a sign of weakness or of showing lack of faith in their client's case. The problem which I shall explore in the next chapter, is that insufficient resources are being devoted to training judges in case management, mediation and other forms of alternative dispute resolution to fit them to discharge the new responsibilities imposed upon them by the CPR, although the Judicial College's course for 2012-13 is a significant step forward.

The fourth matter which I raised in my Valedictory address is a problem which has been created by the arrival of High Court Judges to replace Official Referees. A crucial part of case management was that, as happens in arbitration, cases should be managed to trial by the same individual i.e. by the docket system practiced in the United States and elsewhere. High

Court Judges try cases out of London. They do not have control of their own itinerary which is organised by the administrators. The present system makes it extremely difficult for High Court Judges to undertake the continuous case management which is necessary in civil litigation. The lack of it makes court-based litigation even less attractive to potential litigants.

Lord Justice Jackson's approach to the docket system (broadly in favour) is far too tentative. Its introduction on a general basis would represent for many judges and administrators a very significant cultural change. As happened with the Official Referees, judges would need to take a much more substantial role in listing cases. On occasion, if they are away from London, they will have to insist that space is made in their lists for urgent hearings. This might well be very inconvenient for the administrators.

My approach is fundamentally different. I explored this topic at a lecture which I gave in Lisbon at the Autonomous University on 31 May 2001, relatively soon after the coming into force of the CPR. The lecture was published in Galileu, Revista de Economia Direito, Vol VII, No 1, 2002, p 7. My starting point was Article 6 of the European Convention. The right to a fair and public hearing within a reasonable time by an independent and impartial tribunal established by law identifies a public duty imposed on States. It is clear that the State has a public interest in providing a system for the fair and efficient disposal of disputes. The failure to provide such a system brings not just the civil justice system but the whole justice system into disrepute and lessens the respect in which it is held. After all, civil justice is the part of the legal system in which ordinary citizens, and certainly ordinary businessmen or women, are most likely to find themselves participating. The State also has a public interest in providing, through interpretation of legislation or through common law precedents, a guide to others as to how they should act in similar circumstances.

In her Hamlyn Lecture, at p 114, Professor Genn quotes with approval Sir Jack Jacob, former Senior Master of the Supreme Court, who, in an article in 1978, makes a wider point, namely that access to civil justice is a profound social need. He said as follows:

> We must enable legal disputes, conflicts and complaints, which inevitably arise in society, to be resolved in an orderly way according to the justice of the case so as to promote harmony and peace in society lest they fester and breed discontent and disturbance.

This objective could most easily be achieved by scrapping the Practice Direction "Pre-Action Conduct" and the Construction and Engineering Pre-Action Protocol. This would have the great advantage of bringing the TCC into line with the Commercial Court, which resisted the introduction of Pre-Action Protocols. A less attractive outcome would be to retain the Pre-Action

Protocol in a modified form as an exemplar of good practice. I can see no benefit in retaining the Protocols in a modified form as required procedures. If the Protocols were either scrapped or retained as exemplars of good practice, the criterion for starting litigation would be the same as for adjudication. The case would probably come before the judge for directions after a detailed claim had been made. The judge, who would have been trained in effective case management and the practice of mediation, would give directions for the future conduct of the litigation including any necessary stay in the procedure to ensure that the parties had the necessary information on the basis of which they could have further discussions and attempt to settle the case. The judge would also make appropriate disclosure orders to support the attempts to settle the dispute.

Importantly, the judge would impose a timetable within which this procedure should be carried out and fix a date for the first substantive case management conference if the dispute had not by then been resolved. At present some defendants use the time given for negotiation as an opportunity for delay.

I should observe that the taking of control by the case-managing judge would help to eliminate inequalities between the parties either of economic means or information. It would not supplant encouragement to the parties to mediate or otherwise to resolve their dispute justly. It should be noted that there is much in the mediation literature which emphasises that the purpose of mediation is to achieve an agreed settlement. It is no part of the mediator's duty to achieve a just settlement although the mediator may hope to do so. This system would frequently make the mediation a more just proceeding.

As far as costs are concerned, many cases now settle after the first case management conference. There is no reason to suppose that this might not happen under this new procedure. Appropriate fees could be charged for the additional service which is being provided. The procedure would also have the added advantage of enabling the parties to make a sensible choice between adjudication and court procedure. In some cases the parties would be able to achieve a final decision through the court in the same time that it would take for the adjudication and any subsequent enforcement proceedings to be completed. In such circumstances it is unjust that a party should be compelled to spend money on a provisional judgment when it could obtain a final judgment in the same length of time. It should also be noted that adjudication is not in itself necessarily a cheap procedure – for an extreme example, see *CIB v Birse*, p 124 below (costs of about £1m incurred by each party). I refer finally to two procedures which received favourable mentions from others at my Valedictory. The first is Early Neutral Evaluation (ENE), referred to by Simon Tolson. I include the paper at p 66 to which he refers.

I presented this paper to a meeting of the Society of Construction Lawyers in London on 4 May 1999. It sets out how the procedure can work in practice. Once the parties know that their cases will be heard by judges trained in case management and mediation, they will be much more prepared to trust them to assist in finding a quick and efficient way of resolving their disputes. This will include greater use of ENE.

With the encouragement of Lord Phillips of Worth Matravers and my fellow TCC judges, and in particular with the assistance of Sir Vivian Ramsey after he was appointed, I carried through a court settlement procedure which, although it has been used in relatively few cases, has achieved a high rate of settlement.

The idea originated because in a number of major and complex construction disputes which I was case managing, it became clear to me, as the procedure developed, that the parties wanted to find a way to resolve their differences without proceeding any further with the vastly expensive litigation, that I knew enough of the details of the case to be able to assist the parties to settlement and that I had the confidence of the parties to enable me to do so. There was no effective means to do this so I set about devising a procedure. The procedure came into effect on 31July 2006 initially for 1year but has since been made permanent.

The principles are that the procedure is voluntary, confidential and non-binding unless the parties themselves reach an agreement. Having considered other problems in other jurisdictions, it became clear that any proposal to invoke the procedure must be done jointly by the parties and not be the subject of an application by one party, or be imposed by the judge. In other jurisdictions there were complaints that one party had proposed to invoke a similar procedure knowing that it was going to be declined by the other party. The purpose of making the proposal appeared to the opposing party to be that the proposing party was attempting to ingratiate itself to the judge. There was a perception, on the part of the party declining to take part in such procedure, that the judge would be influenced at trial in favour of the party that had, unilaterally, proposed the settlement conference.

The principles are as follows:

1. It is voluntary, confidential and non-binding (unless an agreement is reached).

2. It must be requested by all parties in the litigation and then agreed to by the case managing judge.

3. The process normally, but not invariably, will be conducted by the case managing judge. If settlement is not reached, the judge will take no further part in the litigation. The case will be reassigned to another judge.

4. Unless the parties agree otherwise, the case managing judge may communicate with the parties together or separately, including private meetings with one party and the settlement judge may express opinions on the merits of the dispute.

5. No settlement shall have any effect unless it is set down in a settlement agreement, signed by the representatives of all the parties.

6. The court settlement process will come to an end on the signing of the agreement or when the judge directs. This is subject to the provision that any party can terminate the process at any time.

7. Nothing said or done during the procedure can be referred to or can have any effect on the rights and entitlement of the parties in the current or any subsequent proceedings.

8. The settlement judge has the same immunity from suit as he would have had if he had acted as the judge in the proceedings.

All the judges in the TCC had mediation training before the scheme started. The take up for the Dispute Settlement Conference has been relatively low but the success rate has been well over 85% and this includes a number of disputes where there had already been an unsuccessful mediation. I personally have undertaken five of these conferences and each has been successful although not always on the day of the conference. One of the advantages of the conference is that any settlement can take account not only of the precise issues in dispute, but also that other matters, which are of particular concern to the parties can be resolved at the same time.

The changes that I have outlined together with effective case management (see Chapter 6) would provide a much more effective system of civil justice, and one much better attuned to the needs of civil litigants. It would also fit in better with the Rules of the Commercial Court. This would enable the TCC and the Commercial Court to present themselves together as an attractive forum for the determination of international disputes. I have no doubt but that a fee structure for High Court civil litigation could be devised which at least cost neutral. Such a structure would no doubt take into account costs which the litigants would otherwise incur in arbitration or in adjudication.

Active Case Management

In my Valedictory address I was critical of the quality of case management by some judges.

Court litigation is extremely expensive and it is the responsibility of judges to manage cases justly in the most efficient and cost effective manner. At present the management of many cases is dealt with by parties' legal representatives by ticking a series of boxes, and by judges dealing with cases passively as though the Woolf reforms had not taken place and the pre-1999 Rules of Court applied.

The Civil Procedure Rules (CPR) require a complete change of approach by judges. It is now the responsibility of judges to manage cases, where previously the parties could dictate the pace of the litigation process. In any judicial training seminar the participants need to be reminded of this and of the detailed provisions of the CPR. This requires detailed training. There is a need for exercises which are designed to put the principles into practice and to give judges an opportunity to debate with each other the best way forward in the particular hypothetical case within the context of alternative dispute resolution (ADR).

What then is the purpose of case management? It is to provide a procedure, fair to the parties, which enables the parties to prepare for settlement or for trial, which leads the parties to agree issues which can reasonably be resolved at the earliest stage, and which provides for a fair resolution of the dispute at as reasonable a cost as possible and within as reasonable a time as possible. This, of course, also applies to arbitration. I set out the differences between court-based litigation and arbitration in "Arbitrators Taking Procedural Control: A Good Idea or Not?" 25 *Const Law Journal* 1 (2009) published by Thomson Reuters.

For this to be achieved, it is important, as I emphasised in the previous chapter, that the same judge should be responsible for case management to trial so that the judge can gain the confidence of the parties, follow through the procedure, and take responsibility for ensuring that the orders of the court are carried out.

The CPR provide the basis for effective case management. Their introduction signalled a radical change in case management in England and Wales in three major respects. First, as I have said, the judge is to take charge of the procedure leading to trial. Second, the parties are required to co-operate in the procedure. Third, great emphasis is placed on the use of mediation and the early resolution of disputes.

CPR Part 1 sets out the overriding objective, namely to deal with cases justly and goes on to set out important matters to be taken into account. Among these, in Part 1.3 it emphasises that the parties are required to help the court in achieving the overriding objective. Part1.4 stresses the requirement that the courts case manage actively, and sets out a "shopping list" of respects in which that should be done. It includes in Part 1.4(c) encouraging, and facilitating use of Alternative Dispute Resolution (ADR), and in Part 1.4(f) helping the parties to settle the whole or part of the case.

The provisions of the CPR are too detailed to be set out here, but there is much encouragement for ADR. As an example, CPR Part 26 requires the court to stay proceedings for one month for ADR if the parties request it. It also provides for a longer stay for ADR if the court considers it is appropriate to order it.

A key aspect of the CPR is the costs regime which provides an effective sanction for non-compliance with court orders or an unreasonable refusal to agree to mediate. The general rule is that costs follow the event, that is, that the unsuccessful party pays the costs of the successful party (CPR Part 44(3)(1)). However the court can make another order departing from the general rule (CPR Part 43.2)

Under CPR Part 44.4, among the matters the court must take into account when assessing costs are:

a)   the conduct of the parties;

b)   whether a party has succeeded on part of his case even if he has not been wholly successful; and

c)   any payment into court or admissible offer to settle made by a party which is drawn to the court's attentions, and which is not an offer to which costs consequences apply under Part 36.

CPR Part 44.5 explains that the conduct of the parties includes conduct before and during proceedings as well as the extent to which the parties followed the Practice Direction (Pre Action conduct) or any relevant pre-action protocol.

These rules form the context within which the case managing judge must take the necessary decisions. The criteria which I set out in Cross-Border Mediation and Civil Proceedings in National Courts (Chapter 4 above) can be used as a checklist against which individual case management decisions can be considered and judged. For example, does the order promote/maintain equality of arms within the procedure? Is the cost proportionate to what is sought to be achieved? Does the proposed order assist in the prompt resolution of the dispute, and so on.

Many of the cases in the TCC are complex but the court also deals with smaller cases which in other times would have been dealt with by County Court Judges or even in some cases, District Judges. It is clear that the procedure has to be tailored to the particular case, and what is appropriate in the very complex case may be disproportionate in the smaller case where the costs may well exceed the value of the claim after the pre-action protocol procedure.

My attitude to case management is as follows. The parties are entitled to have their dispute tried by the court within a reasonable time and at a cost which is proportionate. They are also entitled, as early as possible, to have the basic information which enables each party to evaluate the strengths and weaknesses of the case, the risks of litigation, and the chances of success.

I am aware that any risk assessment will include the costs of the litigation which one or more of the parties will have to pay in addition to the sums claimed. In addition, the parties must factor in the time spent by the litigants in instructing the lawyers and in the lawyers preparing the witness statements, and the time, the anxiety and the cost of giving oral evidence, being cross examined and sitting through a number of days of hearings. These are also part of the overall cost of the litigation. There will also be other matters which are confidential to the parties about which I have no knowledge, a fact which I must take fully into account.

The first case management conference is, or should be (as in arbitration) a most important occasion with lay representatives of the parties being present if at all possible. The lay clients need to understand at a very early stage what is involved in litigation and that they have an active role in the decisions to be taken. The judge has an important role in explaining the procedure to the parties and in particular in making it clear that the parties and their legal advisers are under a duty to co-operate in isolating those issues which are genuinely in dispute, and which therefore need to be vigorously contested and in agreeing other matters. It is also important for the judge to ensure that the lay parties understand the reason for the orders which the judge is making at the case management conference.

The first case management conference will take place in the TCC sometimes before and sometimes after the defence has been filed. There are a number of matters which must be decided at the first case management conference (which I will set out later) but a question at the forefront of my mind is always to try to ensure that each party has the essential information to enable it to evaluate its strengths and weaknesses in the litigation, and therefore to assess realistically its chances of success or failure at the earliest possible stage. You might have expected this information to have been provided in the course of the pre-action protocol procedure, but in my experience it rarely is. This is apparent from questions raised at the CMC in relation to the future conduct of the litigation.

In order to illustrate how the procedure works in practice at the first CMC and the PTR, it is helpful to have an example. A frequent dispute in the TCC is between a householder (owner) who has retained a builder to carry out extensive work in renovating the property. The owner has retained an architect to advise on the work and to prepare the plans. The architect has also been retained to oversee or project manage the project. The owner claims the renovation work does not accord with his expressed wishes; the work was poor and late. He sues the builder who in turn joins the architect in the proceedings saying that it was the architect's plans that were deficient and that the project was not properly project managed. The owner claims that much of the work had to be redone and he is claiming £300,000 for the work. He and his family had to rent accommodation for 8 months while the work was being undertaken. This cost £1200 a month or £9,600 a year. A schedule of defects has been prepared.

The claim is disputed by both the builder and the architect. Each party has expert quantity surveyors who have been round the property. If they meet at an early stage they can have confidential discussions and report back to the parties. As a result, early agreement can and frequently is reached on the sum required to do the necessary remedial work, subject to issues of overall liability. Equally the expert architects/building surveyors will consider whether the architect's performance was what could reasonably have been expected of a competent architect and project manager. Again, after the parties have heard from their own experts about the discussions between the experts, conversations which will remain confidential and cannot be referred to in court, they will be in a position to assess the chances of success and the risk of failure. I refer to these issues to underline the point that the parties may need to have at the earliest stage the information which enables them to have constructive settlement discussions with or without a mediator.

Before the first CMC, I send out my case management pro forma and I then require the parties to set out in a note their proposals for the procedure to trial and any particular contentious matters that they wish to raise. This directs me to the matters in the case management bundle which require my particular attention. I then make my own preliminary assessment and note the particular points which need to be raised at the hearing including those raised by the parties in their notes. This quite detailed preparation is essential if the CMC is to be successfully conducted and confined to relevant and important matters. I emphasise again that I have particular regard to the expressed wishes of the parties and to any agreements which they have reached. However I do not regard myself as bound to implement such agreements if I do not think it appropriate to do so.

Sometimes the agreements have been put together without much thought. One of the more frequent terms of such an agreement is that the experts do not even meet until very late in the procedure. This was proposed in a considerable number of cases where it was clear that, if the case was to be settled before unnecessary costs were incurred, it was essential that the experts should meet without prejudice at as early a stage as possible.

If this procedure is followed, a CMC in simpler cases, or in those where there is general agreement, will be completed within half an hour. Cases where there are more complex issues to be decided will take longer but rarely more than one hour, except in the most complex cases. Occasionally, like any other procedure, there will be complications or misunderstandings which will need to be resolved and will mean that the process takes longer.

At the case management conference I concern myself first with a number of matters which relate as much to preparation for settlement as for preparation for trial. Some may be the subject of appropriate agreement by the parties and can be disposed of quickly.

First, if it has not already been included in the case management information sheet, I ask the parties to say what the costs are which have been incurred to date, and the estimate of costs to the end of trial, the length of which has been estimated in the case management sheet. Clearly current and future costs in the litigation are an important factor, particularly in the smaller cases, and I check that the figures are realistic.

Second, I investigate the claim for damages. Parties may well be concentrating so much on liability issues that they fail to appreciate what in money terms is realistically at stake. In the hypothetical case, the damages have been specified. The owner is claiming £300,000 for work done and £1,200 per month for the cost of rented accommodation. It is to be assumed that documents supporting these costs can be readily produced and served on the other parties. This is important because whatever the merits of the claim, the fact that the work was carried out and the cost of rented accommodation for 8 months was incurred can be readily verified and agreed subject to liability. I may order those documents to be produced soon after the CMC. If the damage claim is insufficiently particularised, I may well order particulars – see below.

Third, it should be possible at this stage, if necessary, for the parties to produce a provisional agreed list of basic issues of expert evidence, fact and law, which they and the experts can use primarily as a working document for settlement discussions, but will also assist in the future conduct of the litigation. If it is helpful, I will order this to be produced. Unlike the Commercial Court, this document is at this stage "without prejudice" and therefore not available to the judge. A formal document at this stage is unnecessary if the formal pleadings have been done properly, and adds significantly to the cost of the litigation because every word has to be carefully considered. There is also a tendency, if this is a formal document, to include every conceivable issue because otherwise, at a later stage, advantage may be sought by the opposing party because some issue has not been included. In our hypothetical case, it should be relatively simple for the parties to set out clearly the issues in the case. This document can be amended as agreement is reached on some of the issues and, if necessary, be transformed into a formal document for the trial.

Fourth, the need for experts must be decided. If I grant permission for experts it will normally only be until the pre-trial review. At that stage, it is necessary to re-consider the need for the experts to give oral evidence, and to consider the scope of such evidence. It is at the first CMC that the court needs to consider with the parties whether or not a single or joint expert should give the expert evidence on a particular matter, rather than the parties appointing their own experts. There is a potential cost advantage in a single joint expert, but if each party has its own expert, they can reach agreements which will also save costs. Single joint experts have a rather more limited role than perhaps was envisaged by Woolf. In our hypothetical, it is clear that expert evidence will be needed from quantity surveyors to deal with the claim for additional work and to express views on the quality of the work. In addition there will need to be expert evidence from architects as to the standard of the architects' performance. The question however arises whether the defendants need separate experts or whether they need to have one expert nominated by the builder dealing with the quality of the work and the remedial works, and one by the architect dealing with the architect's standard of work and the standard of his project management.

Frequently it is the case that, before the parties are able to consider settlement, the experts need to meet without prejudice (i.e. the discussions cannot be disclosed to the court) to discuss the merits of a case as related to the expert's issues. I will frequently order the experts to meet at a very early stage without prejudice and report back to their respective clients. This is very important. The experts must meet in a spirit of co-operation in their primary role which is to assist the court. The meeting must take place before their views can become entrenched as protagonists for the party which is retaining them.

Fifth, the parties should now have the information on which it is possible to make a realistic estimate of their chances of success and of the risks in the litigation. So I will order that they meet without prejudice with or without a mediator, in order to seek to resolve the dispute or at least to narrow the issues. This will take place before the expensive processes of disclosure of documents and exchange of witness statements.

Sixth, I now turn to the pleadings. I consider whether the pleadings filed to that date set out in sufficient detail the claims of the parties. If they do not do so, I may raise with the parties the need for further clarification of the relevant pleading which can be achieved by amending the existing pleading. This preserves the necessary information in one document. After having heard the parties, I will also make orders for the service of any Reply and/or Defence to Counterclaim.

The seventh issue relates to the Schedule of defects. In the hypothetical example, a Schedule of defects has already been prepared and, provided it is in an intelligible form, it is only necessary to fix a date for the defendants to reply. If a Schedule has not been prepared, or it is not in a form useful for trial, I will make orders for the Schedule, known as a Scott Schedule, to be prepared by the claimants by a certain date specifying the information which is to be included in the Schedule, and for a Reply by the other parties a short time later to be incorporated in the same document. The Schedule of defects can be used by the experts for reaching agreement on many of the factual issues, subject to overall liability.

Eighth, I will order a timetable for disclosure of documents and the service of witness statements. I will also give directions for the experts' joint statement setting out matters which are agreed and not agreed, and if not agreed, with brief reasons for the disagreement. This will normally come after the service of witness statements. Finally, the experts should produce their reports for trial limited to matters not agreed.

Ninth, there may be other issues to be resolved e.g. a timetable for a summary judgment hearing, striking out part of the pleading etc. In a complicated case, a date for a further case management review conference may be fixed in case it should become necessary. It was at such a review conference in *CIB v Birse* (see Chapter 9 below) that I saw a problem which the experts were encountering and which enabled the case to be settled.

Finally, I will order a date for the pre-trial review, normally a month before trial and I will set the trial date after hearing representations of the parties to ensure that, as far as possible, it is convenient for all concerned including the experts, and counsel who is to present the case. I make it clear that once the trial date has been fixed, it will only be moved in exceptional circumstances. The parties know therefore that if the whole case is not resolved earlier, there will be a final determination on or soon after that date. This concentrates the minds of the litigants when having their settlement discussions. At the first CMC, I will also have raised with the parties, as a separate issue, the general question of mediation. As I have said in the previous Chapter, mediation in the United Kingdom should be put on a statutory basis after a process similar to that which took place before the Arbitration Act 1996.

I should emphasise that I conduct the first CMC by asking questions and by seeking to arrive at a consensus as to the best way forward. I avoid adversarial confrontation between the parties as far as possible. Frequently, after a preliminary discussion, I will ask the parties to agree a timetable to trial based upon what has been discussed.

Sometimes it is necessary to alter the dates fixed at the first case management conference. The process needs to be straightforward and inexpensive. A current practice in other courts is that the only immovable dates are the pre-trial review and the trial itself. All other dates can be changed by agreement between the parties. In my view this does not provide efficient case management. I found in my early days as a Judge that when an order had been made in those terms, parties arrived at the pre-trial review having failed to exchange witness statements or even complete the disclosure of relevant documents.

There are two alternatives. First, it is possible to order that the parties may agree a delay of up to one week without recourse to the court. I used a different order which worked extremely well and very largely eliminated unnecessary disruption to the timetable. The order was that no extensions of time were permitted without the permission of the court, such permission to be requested before the time and date for the step in the procedure. As a practical matter an extension of time was obtained by a party sending a fax to the court and to the opposing party with a specific request for an extension of time setting out briefly the reason for the request. If there was no objection and the overall time table was not adversely affected, I would fax back my agreement to the extension of time. Sometimes it became very clear that there were difficulties which needed to be resolved at an oral hearing and I would order such a hearing. It was this procedure which was used successfully in the Factortame litigation when the parties were working towards a settlement (see Chapter 8 below).

It is important for the legal representatives of the parties to set out in advance in a note to the court, copied to the other parties, the matters which the parties wish to raise at the Pre Trial Review(PTR). The note should also include specific proposals in relation to the matters set out below. There may be additional matters which a party wishes to raise, for example that another party has not fully complied with previous directions. The list of issues for trial may not have been entirely agreed.

The purpose of the PTR is to make orders which ensure that there is an orderly trial and to regulate the procedure leading up to the trial. Again, it is extremely desirable that lay representatives of the parties should be present at the hearing. In relation to the trial itself, the court will consider with the parties what witness evidence needs to be given and the form in which it needs to be given. Do all witnesses, whose witness statements have been filed, need to give oral evidence, or can their evidence be agreed because in essence it is not challenged, or be omitted because it is no longer relevant? Do the experts need to give oral evidence, and if so, on which issues is their evidence required?

Often at the PTR experts will also be ordered to continue their "without prejudice" meetings to see if further agreements can be reached. Often further agreements will be reached even as late as the end of the oral evidence at trial because, at that stage, the experts can consider the evidence as it has actually been given. I normally required the experts to be available for such meetings two court hours before the first expert in that discipline gave evidence.

There is often a question in construction cases as to how to deal with small value items of claim which it is not cost effective to deal with in the normal elaborate court procedure, unless they raise a particular point of principle. I may well suggest that I hear evidence on one or two sample items, or that the evidence relating to the small items is confined to written submissions. I have never had any difficulty in securing the agreement of the parties to sensible procedures designed to save costs.

The parties must also propose a detailed timetable for the trial assigning a particular length of time to each witness. Once this exercise has been undertaken, it gives a reasonable estimate of the actual length of the trial. It is not necessary to keep strictly to the timetable because inevitably some witnesses will take a longer and some a shorter time. However, unless there were unforeseen circumstances, I found that the overall estimate given was reasonably accurate.

The court will also give directions for the procedure leading to trial. This includes the nature and content of the trial bundles and the date on which they need to be exchanged. The normal procedure is that the claimant will serve a draft index on the other parties who will suggest amendments or additional documents which need to be included. In a complex trial I would normally require the parties to agree a core bundle of essential documents, often limited to two lever arch files. This would be supplemented by a bundle of documents in strict chronological order containing the documents which the parties regard as relevant. If documents in the large bundle are referred to, they can easily be interleaved in the core bundle.

Finally, a date will be fixed for the service of the trial bundle on the other parties to be followed by a date for the exchange of the detailed written opening statements of each of the parties. These must also be delivered to the court in time for the judge to have a reasonable opportunity to read them in advance of the oral openings.

The trial itself consists of detailed written openings delivered in the week before the trial starts, to be followed by short oral statements by each party. The witnesses of fact follow, starting with the claimant's witnesses followed by each defendant's witnesses. The experts then give relevant evidence on outstanding issues on which they have been unable to agree. There are then final written submissions followed by short oral submissions, often lasting in total half a day, or in more complex cases lasting a whole day. I have found it much better to have written final submissions in advance so that the opposing parties and I can read and understand them and then, in the course of the oral hearing the opposing parties can concentrate on commenting upon the written submissions, and I can ask the particular questions that are relevant to me. It is also of benefit to the parties, and particularly to the lay clients, who can review the written submissions before they are exchanged.

How does the procedure, which I have outlined, measure up to the criteria against which its effectiveness can be judged ?

a) The judge at the first CMC has done what he can to ensure equality of arms between the parties.

b) The procedure is tailored to keeping the cost of the resolution of the dispute at as reasonable a sum as possible.

c) The parties can at an early stage make a reasonably accurate estimate of the cost of the litigation

d) The parties can make a reasonable assessment of the risks involved in the litigation and the chances of success at the earliest possible moment.

e) In the TCC the time taken between referral of the dispute to the court and its resolution will be as little as 9 months in smaller cases and rather longer in more complex cases, and is reasonable and consistent with doing justice between the parties.

f) The procedure is capable of being explained and understood by the parties. The judge should explain the procedure to the parties at the first CMC and at the pre-trial review, at which the parties or their lay representatives should be present.

g) It follows through logical and clearly defined stages .

h) It does not foster confrontation, but rather requires the parties to co-operate in isolating for decision those matters in genuine dispute.

i) The procedure seeks to resolve the dispute or those parts which can be resolved at as early a stage as is possible in the procedure.

j) It focuses the parties' minds on mediation or other forms of early dispute resolution.

I return to the question whether or not case management can be taught. My clear answer is "Yes". As this chapter has demonstrated, there are many issues in case management which need to be thought through in advance and addressed at the case management hearing if the parties are to achieve the objective of having their dispute resolved at the most reasonable cost possible, and within a reasonable time. The Judicial College has a new and more comprehensive course for judges for the 2012-2013 programme.

However, the training needs to go further. The emphasis in the CPR is on promoting mediation and other forms of ADR. All civil judges, involved in case management, need, therefore, to be taught the basic principles and practice of mediation by an expert mediator. They also need to be taught the other options for alternative dispute resolution, including early neutral evaluation and, if it is to be extended, the TCC Dispute Settlement Conference procedure. All those who case manage regularly need to have more in depth training in mediation, similar to the excellent three session course arranged for the TCC judges. It may well be that further courses may need to be provided, tailored to the particular needs of groups of judges. The Judicial College could well learn from the Slovenian experience, see para 3.2 of Chapter 4 above.

These courses (one day) could be provided at an appropriate Court centre. This kind of training is particularly important when cases are normally managed by a judge who happens to be available and not as part of the docket system. The "new" judge, if he is to do his job properly, needs to have a basic understanding of these matters so that he can understand quickly the problems which he must resolve at his case management conference, or in applications associated with case management.

There are a number of ways in which case management can be and is being taught by the Judicial College. First, as is demonstrated in this chapter, there is ample material for a lecture on the principles and scope of case management and on the principles of mediation and other forms of dispute resolution. Second, the participants to the seminar can consider these issues in the context of a problem, or series of problems, to bring out the different approaches which may be required in different types of litigation. Specific topics which may be the subject of particular discussion include how to conduct the first CMC, and what orders should be made including consideration of mediation and other forms of alternative dispute resolution; problems that arise at the pre-trial review; the provisions of the CPR including topics like interim remedies (not discussed in this paper); when should costs be awarded for non-compliance with orders; the value of split trials; issues relating to expert evidence; and the differences in case managing complex and relatively simple litigation. There are no doubt many other important topics. It would also be possible to have a panel discussion involving judges who case manage different types of case to bring out the differences in approach which may be required.

I am conscious that I have set out what may seem to be a very elaborate procedure for case management. This procedure needs to be adapted to the particular case. A number of cases in my court have settled because the lay clients were present at the first case management conference and saw that the costs which they were incurring were disproportionate to the realistic value of the claim. Quite often intelligent case management at an early stage enables the parties to have the information on which they can reach a settlement based on fact rather than guesswork. A settlement based on disclosed facts, whether achieved by mediation or negotiation, is likely to be more just than a settlement which is arrived at by mediation before proceedings have started and before the necessary information is available to the parties, because it is based on evidence which enables each party properly to understand the strengths and weaknesses of its case and that of its opponent.

The proposals in these chapters, if implemented, would amount to a radical change in the current system of litigation. They place great emphasis on early dispute resolution as an integral part of the court service and not as a procedure separate from it. They emphasise continuing and active case management by the judge, acting sensitively with the co-operation of the parties. The general thrust of the proposals is in line with the overriding objective of the CPR, but with its emphasis in its process being carried out by a single judge, trained in case management and ADR, the proposals go further than the CPR. Crucially, far from doing everything to discourage the use of the civil courts, as at present, these proposals would encourage the use of the litigation process to assist citizens and companies in the efficient resolution of disputes. If one makes a comparison with the costs involved in arbitration, or in achieving a provisional result in adjudication, it should be possible to devise a costs regime for High Court civil litigation which means that the new process is at least costs neutral, and for higher value litigation is a source of income for the court service.

Early Neutral Evaluation in the Technology and Construction Court

His Honour Judge Toulmin CMG QC[1]

I must stress that the views which I am expressing are personal views. They are not necessarily the views which the Judges of the TCC will come to after discussion.

Some may find the idea of the Technology and Construction Court undertaking Early Neutral Evaluation to be a surprising one. They would no doubt be equally surprised to know that it is done as a matter of course in Israel and in New Zealand and in those two jurisdictions whose procedures are somewhat similar to our own, it operates very successfully.

I should put the initiative which Robert Stevenson [Solicitor acting for one of the parties] took to initiate Early Neutral Evaluation by me into context as far as I am concerned. Litigation is extremely expensive for ordinary litigants, only the very rich, and perhaps the very poor, are able to use our civil Courts. The Woolf Reforms address this problem. They set out the overriding objective that the Courts should deal justly and in a proportionate manner with the cases that come before them. One aspect of this is to link in Alternative Dispute Resolution to the procedures of the Courts. I believe that the Courts are in the age of Dispute Resolution, which is a twin track procedure. Dispute Resolution has a trial at the end of the procedure, but provides opportunities along the way to achieve a resolution of the disputes between the parties without requiring the trial. In fact, this is nothing new, in the TCC 90% of cases already settle before trial.

Early Neutral Evaluation

In the Early Neutral Evaluation case which I heard, the parties jointly put to me the suggestion that I should do an Early Neutral Evaluation. I was not, of course, told precisely the reason why this was thought to be the appropriate procedure at that stage, but I was assured that it was, in fact, regarded by all parties as the appropriate procedure. There are a number of forms of Early Neutral Evaluation ("ENE"). One form (which amounts virtually to a mini trial) is where the judge hears the core of the evidence from the parties or their legal representatives and then makes up his mind and gives an indication as

---

[1] Revised version of author's paper to Society of Construction Law, 4 May 1999.

to what the outcome would be. In my view, this can be too like a trial and is really a form of mini trial under another name. The procedure which was adopted in our case was rather different. On the 1st April 1998, we had what would now be called a further Case Management Conference and we worked out an order as to what should be disclosed before trial and how the ENE should proceed. The Order was that:

a) The hearing of the Neutral Evaluation would take place before me at 10.30 am on 8 June 1998.

b) The parties should, if possible, agree a Statement of Issues and a Chronology by 4 pm on 1st June 1998.

c) The agreed Statements of Issues and Chronologies were to be lodged at Court by 4 pm on 1 June 1998. In the absence of agreement, the parties were to lodge separate Statements of issues and Chronologies.

d) These should be lodged with the Court, by the Plaintiff, by 4 p.m. on 1 June 1998 together with a file containing the Pleadings, the consolidated Scott Schedule of Damages with the Defendant's response, the experts' report, the experts' joint statements of issues on insulation and drainage, and a core bundle of the most essential documents (if necessary).

e) Each party should lodge at Court and serve an outline of their case of not more than 10 pages by 4 p.m. on 1st June 1998.

f) Each party should have 30 minutes to open at the hearing and to respond to the other party's case.

g) There should he one hour during which 1 could put questions to the parties. The parties had leave to direct questions to other parties via myself.

h) There was to be a period of reflection before I made my assessment.

i) Nothing that was said at the hearing should be used in these proceedings or for any other purpose.

j) I was to be disqualified from further involvement in the proceedings unless the parties agreed otherwise. [This provides an exception to the normal rule that in making orders to assist the parties to achieve an early resolution of their disputes the Judge should not prejudice his ability to conduct the trial of the action]

k) Each party was to bear its own cost of the evaluation.

l) Representatives of all parties capable of making decisions to resolve the dispute between the parties were to be present at the hearing.

In fact, it took me a day to read all the documents that had been provided and to sketch out a draft Judgment, setting out the facts as they appeared from the statements and the reports and also to identify the precise issues which were in dispute between the experts.

The procedure followed the terms of the Order. Each party had 30 minutes to open the case and to respond to the other party's case. Following this, there was one hour during which I put questions to the parties and the parties directed questions to other parties through me. This procedure lasted from 10.30 until lunch time. Under the terms of the order, there was then "a period of reflection for the Judge to make his assessment". In fact, I took until about 3.15 pm to complete what was, in effect, an outline Judgment.

I considered what form of Judgment I should give. In the end I decided to give a Judgment which was in form similar to an ordinary Judgment of the Court. I analysed the facts as presented through the documents and Witness Statements and said on balance what evidence I was likely to accept and what evidence I was likely to reject and I produced an answer on the balance of probabilities.

An alternative approach would have been to have read the documents very quickly and to have said that, on the basis of what I had read, one party or another had a particular percentage chance of success. It seemed to me that this was not the most helpful way of proceeding, since it did not explain in relation to the issues, which were in contention between the parties, why I arrived at the conclusions which I did. It was also, of course, necessary to do the detailed work if l was to conduct a question and answer session lasting for an hour, which was, no doubt, as valuable as the judgment in bringing home to the parties what the issues were and what were the strengths and weaknesses of their respective cases.

The procedure seemed to me to be one which was reasonably satisfactory and economical, but at the meeting we held after the case had been settled to evaluate the procedure, one of the parties felt that 30 minutes was too short a time to open the case and effectively close it at the same time. That party felt that it was necessary to have longer to be able to go into detail in order to persuade the Judge against the initial impression which the Judge has formed.

[On reflection there is considerable force in this. It may be that each party should have had 15-20 minutes at the end to summarise its position and deal with matters raised in the question and answer session.]

We were told that there have only been four Early Neutral Evaluations in the Commercial Court and no one could think of another Early Neutral Evaluation that had taken place in the TCC. It occurs to me that one reason for this may have been that for many years until recently, the TCC calendar has been filled with valuation cases. The position has now been reached where parties can obtain a hearing date around the end of 1999 for a very short case, around March to May 2000 for a medium size case lasting more than five days and even a very long case will receive a trial date of either July 2000 or October 2000 (i.e. 18 months ahead). In short, there is substantially more flexibility in the system and cases will get on before the Court much more quickly than they would have done even a year or two ago. When I first arrived at the Court, 18 months ago, in November 1997, very long cases were receiving dates of more than two years ahead. This is no longer so.

Judgments

Two Cases form the section headed "Judging". I gave many judgments during my 13 plus years as a full-time Judge. Six of them were referred to by name in the Valedictory addresses. I have included two. Both are interesting in their own right. The aftermath of each is relevant to different aspects of positive case management.

R v Secretary of State for Transport, Ex p Factortame (the Factortame litigation) must be one of the best known European cases. It was referred to by two speakers at my Valedictory. I myself referred to it as the most satisfying case in which I was involved and one "where the lawyering on all sides by solicitors and barristers was of a quite extraordinary standard."

The case was concerned with giving private rights to individuals to recover damages against governments for breaches of European law. The case went twice to the European Court of Justice and twice to the House of Lords. I set out the previous history of the litigation at paragraph 8 and following of the judgment. The case was referred to me to deal with the issue of damages, but in fact it raised three important preliminary issues of principle: a) Was the action founded on tort? If it was, the English Limitation Act 1980 applied. If it was not, additional claims could be added. (My problem was that there was no definition in English law as to what constituted a tort.) b) Did the new claims arise out of the same facts? If they did, the Limitation Act might not apply and the new claims might be able to be added; c) Were the fishermen able to claim damages for distress and loss of personal esteem as a result of having to wait so long for the cases to be resolved? My judgment on these issues (*Factortame (No. 7)* was not appealed. The hearings took place over nine days from 24 October 2000 with judgment on 27 November 2000. The judgment was widely reported [2001] 1 CMLR 47; [2001] EuLR 207; [2001] 1 WLR 942.

Most law students know how the case started, but how did it end? The trial on the factual damages issues was due to start in January 2001 and was expected to finish in June or July 2001. Throughout the autumn of 2000 the experts worked on the 97 claims under the overall supervision of their legal teams. While the claims had much in common, they had to be worked through individually under my overall direction as case-managing judge. If I pressed too hard, the experts and the parties would say that the task of agreeing settlements was too difficult. If I was too generous in granting extensions of time, the work would not be completed before the trial was due to start. Final agreement was reached a few days before the trial date.

The parties told me afterwards that they did not think that a settlement before trial would be possible. I was reasonably confident that if I case-managed well a settlement could be achieved since the parties, including their experts, were co-operating constructively. This is an example of the importance of continuous case management by the same single judge operating the "docket system" - without such continuous case management a settlement certainly would not have been achieved and a very expensive trial would have gone ahead.

Predictably the settlement of £54.9m, of which £24.7 was interest (exclusive of the very considerable costs) provoked outrage in the Press. The Western Morning News of 10 February 2001 said that from the perspective of the West Country fishing industry, this was a huge compensation package to "flag of convenience vessels". The comment of Mr Portus, Chief Executive of the South West Fish Producers Organisation, which the Western Morning News quoted, was typical. He said that "While the government was writing out a compensation cheque to the Spanish and Dutch, calls for interim aid for their own beleaguered industry had fallen on deaf ears." The Cornish fishermen had asked for a £5m subsidy from the Ministry of Agriculture, Fisheries and Food (MAFF) which had been refused. In a written Parliamentary answer the Government said, claiming a degree of success, that the claim had originally been for £285m. Neither the Press nor the fishermen were impressed by this information.

**IN THE HIGH COURT OF JUSTICE QUEEN'S BENCH DIVISION
TECHNOLOGY AND CONSTRUCTION COURT**

Before:

HIS HONOUR JUDGE JOHN TOULMIN CMG QC

R E G I N A

-v-

THE SECRETARY OF STATE FOR TRANSPORT
(Now The Secretary of State for the Environment, Transport and the
Regions) (Respondents)

ex parte FACTORTAME LIMITED AND OTHERS (No. 7) (Applicants)

MR S MALES QC and MR C KIMMINS, instructed by Thomas Cooper
Stibbard, appeared on behalf of the "TCS" Applicants.

MR A GOURGEY and MR J MIDDLEBURGH, instructed by Edwin Coe,
appeared on behalf of the "EC" Applicants.

MR D FRIEDMAN QC, MRS M HALL and MS R ANSELL, instructed by
Treasury Solicitors, appeared on behalf of the Respondents.

MR D MARKS, instructed by Grant & Horton, appeared on behalf of the
O'Connors.

MR JAMES FLYNN, instructed by Brooks & Co, appeared on behalf of the
Haytons.

Judgment 27 November 2000

1. This is the judgment on preliminary issues in advance of the main damages
hearing of the remaining Factortame applicants due to take place in January
2001.

2. The parties have raised a number of preliminary issues of general
fundamental importance, on some of which there is no decided authority.

3. I am particularly grateful to counsel on all sides for their considerable
assistance.

4. The issues are in three broad categories. The first issue relates to applications to add additional parties to the proceedings. This raises the specific issues of whether or not the Limitation Act 1980 applies to individual claims against the Government for breaches of European law and, if it does apply, whether the period of limitation is 6 years or 12 years. It also raises the fundamental question of

"What is an action founded on tort?"

The parties are agreed that if the Limitation Act applies, time runs from either 1st April 1989, the date when the Merchant Shipping Act 1988 took effect, or 10th July 1990, when the offending part of the legislation was revoked. It makes no difference for the purpose of these applications which is the correct date and I am not asked to make a finding on this question. It is only if the six-year limitation period applies that the applications are outside the limitation period.

5. The second series of issues arise only if I find that a limitation period of six years applies. Even if the six-year period applies, a number of existing applicants contend that they are entitled to add claims for damages in respect of vessels for which they have previously made no claim and/or are entitled to make claims in a different capacity to their existing claims. This involves a consideration of section 35 of the Limitation Act 1980 and paragraph 17.4 of the Civil Procedure Rules.

6. The third broad category relates to claims brought by various TCS applicants for injury to feelings/distress and aggravated damages on the general ground that their claims under European law are broadly equivalent to domestic claims under the Race Relations Act 1976 for discrimination on the grounds of nationality, in respect of which they say that both damages for distress and aggravated damages would be recoverable. It is agreed that I should decide only whether in principle such a claim could be made, leaving detailed questions to the trial.

7. In the course of the oral hearings, I granted a number of applications from the applicants; some others were withdrawn by the applicants. There are a number of other issues which are of importance to the parties but not of general legal importance. I shall deal with those in a short further judgment.

Preliminary. The history of the Factortame legislation.

8. A number of fishermen from Spain have claimed against the United Kingdom Government for loss and damage as a result of the United Kingdom's breaches of European Community law in enacting the 1988

Merchant Shipping Act ("the 1988 Act") and the consequential Regulations on the ground that the Act and the Regulations discriminated against non-UK and particularly Spanish owners of fishing vessels which had licences to fish in United Kingdom waters. These claims have been made both through the fishermen's companies and also on their own behalf.

9. By a Notice of Motion dated 22nd December 1988 applications were made for judicial review of the Secretary of State for Transport's regulations which had the effect on 31st March 1989 of terminating the registration of fishing vessels owned, controlled and duly registered as British fishing vessels prior to 1st December 1988 unless certain conditions, later held to be discriminatory, were met.

10. A total of 69 applicants (including Factortame Limited) were identified in the annex. Although the annex showed all the applicants as being owners of the vessels, the applicants were described as including "the managers of the aforesaid vessels and the shareholders and directors of the said owners and managers".

11. The claim for interim relief was appealed through the English courts. On 18th May 1989, the House of Lords declined to grant interim relief but ordered a reference under Article 177 of the EC Treaty (now Article 234) to the European Court of Justice for a preliminary ruling on the question of whether Community law obliged or empowered a national court to grant interim relief in such circumstances -- see Factortame 1 [1990] 2 AC 85. On 10th October 1989, the President of the European Court of Justice made an order for interim measures, pending judgment in these proceedings, and suspended the application of the nationality requirements in the 1988 Act and the Regulations. Pursuant to that order, the United Kingdom adopted provisions amending the registration system from 2nd November 1989.

12. On 19th June 1990, the European Court of Justice, in what came to be known as Factortame 2 [1991] AC 603, answered the question referred to them: that the United Kingdom Government was required to grant interim measures in those circumstances.

13. On 9th July 1990, the House of Lords decided that the applicants should be granted interim relief and so informed them. They gave their reasons on 11th October 1990 -- see [1991] 1 AC 603 at 645. On 10th July 1990, the Government reversed the discriminatory legislation.

14. In Factortame 3 [1992] 1 QB 680 (judgment given on 25th July 1991), the European Court of Justice held that it was contrary to Community law and in particular to Article 52 of the EEC Treaty (now Article 43) for a Member

State to impose nationality requirements relating to registration of vessels which constituted obstacles to freedom of establishment within the EEC (now described as the "EU").

15. Article 52 applied because (page 735):

"22. Where the vessel constituted an instrument for pursuing an economic activity which involves a fixed establishment in the Member State concerned, the registration of that vessel cannot be dissociated from the exercise of freedom of establishment."

16. On 2nd October 1991, the Divisional Court ordered inter alia:

"(3) In respect of their claim for damages, the applicants are within eight weeks to give detailed particulars of their claim, setting out in a Statement of Claim or Points of Claim: (i) the cause of action or actions on which each of the applicants rely; (ii) the nature of each applicant's interest in each vessel; and (iii) the Heads of Damage under which the claims are made."

17. On 24th January 1992, pursuant to that order, a statement of applicants' claim for damages was served on behalf of 47 applicants. The applicants were companies and individual owners of the vessels. Some had been named in the original Notice of Application for Judicial Review, others had not been identified in the notice. The pleading did not include any claims for damages on behalf of shareholders or directors, although the pleadings referred to the allegation that shareholders and directors had been denied rights of establishment.

18. On 16th November 1992, the Divisional Court gave leave for new parties to be added as applicants. The order provided that:

"(i) Such of the companies and individuals referred to in the Amended Statement of Claim in the annex hereto, together with the shareholders and directors in such companies as are not already applicants and/or claimants be given leave to be joined as applicants and/or claimants for damages on condition that (ii) leave be given for the Statement of Claim herein to be amended as set out in the annex hereto."

19. The amended statement of applicant's claim for damages identified the claimants as:

"1(a) The vessel-owning and vessel-managing companies specified in schedule A, together with the shareholders and directors in such companies and (b) the shareholders in the vessel-owning companies listed in schedule B hereto."

20. Schedule A listed in its final form 84 companies. All but three of the companies were vessel-owners. Those three (Cmaine Shipping Limited, D-Tect Securities Limited and Portfish Limited) were managers. Schedule B identified Mr and Mrs O'Connor as applicants 85 to 97. The companies in which they held shares and the vessels owned by those companies were specifically identified.

21. Two days later, on 18th November 1992, there was a further hearing before the Divisional Court. In the course of this hearing applications by new parties to be added as applicants were dealt with. Leave was given to Pesca Fisheries to be joined as the 83rd applicant. Mr Barling, QC, referred to a possible 84th applicant.

22. Glidewell LJ said, addressing counsel for the respondents:

"Mr Richards, it is important that there should be finality. I would be minded to say that, unless you are informed of all details regarding that vessel by the end of normal working hours today, the Minute of Order will be drawn up in accordance with the intimation already given."

23. There were a few claims notified in 1995, but otherwise this completed the claims made before those which were made earlier this year, partly in response to advertisements, setting a deadline for new claims to be included in these proceedings.

24. The European Court of Justice, in Francovich [1991] ECR 5357, [1995] ICR 722, had decided in 1991 the important principles of Community law which were later developed in Factortame 4 [1996] QB 404:

"37. It is a principle of Community law that the Member States are obliged to make good loss and damage caused to individuals by breaches of Community law for which they can be held responsible."

25. Three conditions were required to be met:

"40. The first of those conditions is that the result prescribed by the Directive should entail the grant of rights to individuals. The second condition is that it should be possible to identify the content of those rights on the basis of the provisions of the directive. Finally, the third condition is the existence of a causal link between the breach of the State's obligation and the loss and damage suffered by the injured parties."

26. The court went on to emphasise that, in the absence of Community legislation, it is for each Member State to designate the appropriate courts and to ensure that there was an effective remedy which was not less favourable than those relating to existing domestic claims

27. In Factortame 4, decided on 5th March 1996, the European Court of Justice developed further the right of individuals to recover damages for a breach by the Government of European law.

28. At paragraph 51 of the judgment, the court held that three conditions must be met: (1) the rule of law infringed must be intended to confer rights on individuals; (2) the breach must be sufficiently serious; and, (3), there must be a causal link between the breach of the obligation resting on the State and the damage sustained by injured parties -- see *Brasserie du Pecheur v Federal Republic of Germany* [1996] QB 404 at 499.

29. On 31st July 1997, the Divisional Court found that the UK Government's breaches of Community law were sufficiently serious to give rise to a right by the applicants to damages, provided the first and last conditions were met. Those damages could not include exemplary damages. The finding in relation to exemplary damages was not appealed -- see Factortame 5 [1997] EuLR 475

30. This decision was upheld by the Court of Appeal in Factortame 5 [1998] EuLR 456. Judgment was given on 6th July 1998. The Court of Appeal remitted the case to this court for the assessment of damages.

31. On 28th October 1999, the House of Lords dismissed the Government's appeal -- see [1999] 3 WLR 1062. I heard the claims of the first 15 claimants, in what became known as the "fast-track", in a trial which started on 6th March 2000. The last of the claims was settled on 15th May 2000, just before the end of the trial. I am due to hear the rest of the claims in a trial starting on 15th January 2001.

The first issue.

The broad issue is: does the Limitation Act 1980 apply and, if so, what is the applicable period of limitation? The specific issues relating to the Limitation Act (if it applies at all) are agreed to be:

33. 1. Is the limitation period six years by virtue of section 2 of the Limitation Act 1980, ie is it an action founded on tort within the meaning of that section? This involves the following sub-issues: 1.1. What is meant by "an action founded on tort"? 1.2. What is the correct categorisation of the cause of action in this case? 1.3. What is the significance, if any, of the fact that the source

of the obligation is the European Treaty rather than domestic law? (I have deliberately rephrased this question.) 1.4. What is the significance, if any, of the fact that the 1980 Limitation Act was passed before the decision which established the State's liability in cases of this sort?

34. 2. If the period of limitation is not six years by virtue of section 2 of the Limitation Act, is the limitation period six years by virtue of section 9 of the 1980 Act?

35. 3. If the period of limitation is not six years by virtue of sections 2 or 9 of the 1980 Act, is it 12 years by virtue of section 8 of the 1980 Act or is there no period of limitation?

36. It is agreed, rightly, that if a limitation period of six years does apply, such a period of limitation would not offend against the Community law principles of equivalence and effectiveness.

37. It is necessary, first, to consider the nature of the right that is being claimed by analysing the right as formulated in the Factortame litigation in the ECJ, secondly, to consider other relevant cases before the ECJ and, thirdly, to consider the right as formulated by the English courts in Factortame and other relevant cases.

38. I shall then consider how Community law rights are incorporated into English law, the specific provisions of the 1980 Limitation Act and then I shall set out my conclusions. The Factortame litigation in the European Court of Justice (ECJ).

39. This section is also particularly relevant to the issue of damages for distress and aggravated damages, which I shall discuss later.

40. As has already appeared, the ECJ reached its conclusions in two stages. In Factortame 3 [1992] 1 QB 680, the ECJ concluded that the United Kingdom Government was in breach of Article 52 of the EEC Treaty in imposing nationality requirements relating to the registration of vessels which constituted unlawful obstacles to freedom of establishment within the EC.

41. In Factortame 4 [1996] QB 404, the court held that individuals were entitled to recover damages in respect of the breach, provided the three conditions were met.

42. In Factortame 3, [1992] 1 QB 680 at 751, the court held: 1. It was for the Member States to determine, in accordance with the general rules of international law, the conditions which must be fulfilled in order for a vessel

to be registered on their registers and granted the right to fly their flag. But, in exercising their power, the Member States must comply with the rules of Community law.

43. 2. It was contrary to the provisions of Community law, and in particular to Article 52 of the EEC Treaty, (Article 43) for a Member State to stipulate as conditions for the fishing vessel in its national register

44. (a) that the legal owners and beneficial owners and the charterers, managers and operators of the vessel must be nationals of that Member State or companies incorporated in that Member State and in the latter case that at least 75 per cent of the shares in the company must be owned by nationals of that Member State or by companies fulfilling the same requirements and 75 per cent of the directors of the company must be nationals of that Member State; and

45. (b) that the said legal owners, charterers and managers, operators, shareholders and directors, as the case may be, must be resident and domiciled in the Member State.

46. In *Brasserie du Pecheur v Federal Republic of Germany (Factortame 4)* [1996] 1 QB 404, the ECJ analysed the conditions under which an individual was entitled to obtain damages for a breach of Community law by a Member State.

47. The court said at paragraph 25 of the judgment (page 496) that the existence and extent of state liability for damage in suing as a result of a breach of obligations incumbent on the State by virtue of Community law were questions of Treaty interpretation which fell within the jurisdiction of the European Court.

48. It noted (paragraph 27, page 496) that it must make its ruling by reference to the fundamental principles of the Community legal system and, where necessary, by reference to general principles common to the legal systems of the Member States.

49. At page 496 of the judgment, the court explained how the liability for Member States arises:

50. "29. The principle of the noncontractual liability of the Community expressly laid down in Article 215 of the Treaty (now Article 288) is simply an expression of the general principle familiar to the legal systems of the Member States that an unlawful act or omission gives rise to an obligation to make good the damage caused. That provision also reflects the obligation on public authorities to make good damage caused in performance of their duties."

51. Article 215 of the Treaty says that in the case of noncontractual liability the Community shall, in accordance with the general principles common to the laws of the Member States, make good any damage caused by its institutions or its servants in the performance of their duties.

52. This principle is further explained in paragraph 42 of the judgment in Factortame 4:

"42. The conditions under which the State may incur liability for damage caused to individuals by a breach of Community law cannot, in the absence of particular justification, differ from those governing the liability of the Community in like circumstances. The protection of the rights which individuals derive from Community law cannot vary depending on whether a national authority or a Community authority is responsible for the damage."

53. The general principle of the liability of a Member State is therefore derived from general principles familiar to the legal systems of the Member States. The extent of the liability is the same as that for which a Community authority or its servants would be liable.

54. At paragraph 39 of the judgment (page 497), the court identified the following specific reasons for its decision:

"first, the full effectiveness of Community rules and the effective protection of the rights which they confer and, secondly, the obligation to cooperate imposed on Member States by Article 5 of the Treaty (now Article 10 -- obligation on all Member States to ensure the fulfillment of all obligations arising out of the Treaty".)

55. Paragraph 51 of the judgment (page 499) sets out the all-important three conditions to which I have already referred.

56. The court made it clear at paragraph 58 that the national courts have the sole jurisdiction to find the facts and to decide how to characterise the breaches of Community law. The court emphasised (paragraph 65) that it is for the national courts to determine whether there is a causal link between the breach of obligation borne by the State and the damage sustained by the injured parties.

57. At page 506, the court ruled as follows:

"(2) Where a breach of Community law by a Member State is attributable to the national legislature, acting in a field in which it has a wide discretion to make legislative choices, individuals suffering loss or injury are entitled to reparation where the rule or Community law breached is intended to confer rights on them, the breach is sufficiently serious and there is a direct causal link between the breach and the damage sustained by the individuals. Subject to that reservation, the State must make good the consequences of the loss and damage caused by the breach of Community law attributable to it in accordance with its national law on liability. However, the conditions laid down by the applicable national laws must not be less favourable than those relating to similar domestic claims or framed in such a way as in practice to make it impossible or excessively difficult to obtain reparation."

58. "(3) Pursuant to the national legislation which it applies, reparation of loss or damage cannot be made conditional on fault (intentional or negligent) on the part of the organ of the State responsible for the breach, going beyond that of a serious breach of Community law."

59. In (4) the court warned that:

"National legislation, which generally limits the damage for which reparation may be granted to damage done to certain specifically protected individual interests, not including loss of profit by individuals, is not compatible with Community law. Moreover, it must be possible to award specific damages, such as the exemplary damages provided for English law pursuant to claims or actions founded on Community law, if such damages may be awarded pursuant to similar claims or actions founded on domestic law."

60. The remedy against the State is framed on the basis of a remedy which is given to individuals in all Member States to obtain reparation for damages which the State has caused. Community law has laid down conditions, some of which are similar to those under the English law of tort, ie a requirement that the legislation is intended to confer rights on individuals, that the State is in breach of those obligations and that the individual suffered loss as a result of the State's breach.

61. The courts pointedly rejected common law requirements of fault (intentional or negligent) and substituted its own requirement that the breach should be sufficiently serious. The court made it clear that remedies were a matter for the national court but must comply with the principles of equivalence and effectiveness.

Other EC authorities.

62. It is clear that the right of an individual to claim damages against the State for breaches of Community law was not fully understood at the time when the Limitation Act 1980 was enacted.

63. In Rewe [1981] ECR 1805 at 1838 (judgment 7th July 1981), the court held at paragraph 44:

"Although the treaty has made it possible in a number of instances for private persons to bring direct actions, where appropriate, before the Court of Justice, it was not intended to create new remedies to ensure the observance of Community law other than those laid down by national law."

64. It was not until Francovich [1991] ECR 5357 (see above) that the European Court of Justice gave a right to individuals to recover damages against the State for the State's failure to implement a directive, provided the appropriate conditions were fulfilled.

65. The court said at paragraph 41:

"Those conditions are sufficient to give rise to a right on the part of individuals to obtain reparation, a right founded directly on Community law."

66. This finding must be read in the light of the explanation given in paragraph 42 of Factortame 4; that the individuals derive their rights from Community law, but the means of enforcing those rights are derived from the principle of the Member States, that an unlawful act or omission gives rise to an obligation to make good the damage caused.

67. I note in passing that in Palmisani [1997] ECR 4025 (following Rewe [1976] ECR 1989, which emphasised the need for legal certainty in tax legislation), the ECJ held that a Member State has the power to impose a time limit within which an individual may bring proceedings to recover damages against a Member State, provided the period of limitation does not offend against the principles of equivalence and effectiveness. The principle that there must be an end to litigation is one which is acknowledged in all Member States.

68. Finally, in Norbrook [1998] ECR 153, the ECJ reiterated the three conditions set out in Factortame 4. The court went on, at paragraph 111, to confirm:

69. "It has been settled case law since the judgment in Factortame and others cited above (paragraphs 41 to 43) that, subject to the existence of a right to obtain reparation, which is founded directly on Community law, where the three conditions mentioned above have been met, it is on the basis of the rules of national law on liability that the State must make reparation for the consequences of loss and damaged caused, with the proviso that the condition for reparation of loss and damage laid down in the national legislation must not be less favourable than those relating to similar domestic claims and must

not be so framed as to make it in practice impossible or excessively difficult to obtain reparation."

70. I conclude that, viewed from the standpoint of the ECJ, the remedy is framed as a remedy for breach of Community law which is available to individuals when the three conditions are met.

71. Two of those conditions, (a) that the rule of law infringed must be intended to confer rights on individuals and (b) there must be a direct causal link between the breach of the obligation resting on the State and the damage sustained by the injured parties, are ones which are familiar in the English law concept of tort.

72. The third condition, that the breach is sufficiently serious, was intended to replace common law tort notions of fault – see Factortame 4 [1996] 1 QB 506

The European Communities Act 1972.

73. In 1972, at the time of the United Kingdom's accession to the Treaty of Rome and in order to enact the Treaty into English law, Parliament passed the European Communities Act 1972.

74. Section 2 provided:

"2(1) All such rights, powers, liabilities, obligations and restrictions from time to time created or arising by or under the Treaties and all such remedies and procedures from time to time provided for by or under the Treaties as in accordance with the Treaties are without further enactment to be given legal effect or used in the United Kingdom, shall be recognised and available in law and be enforced, allowed and followed accordingly, and the expression 'enforceable Community right' and similar expressions shall be read as referring to one to which this subsection applies."

75. Section 2(4) makes it clear that the directly applicable Community provisions are to prevail over existing and future Acts of Parliament and reinforces the binding nature of legally enforceable rights and obligations imposed by Community law. The domestic statute in imposing such obligations acts as a bridge or conduit enabling obligations imposed by Community law to become part of United Kingdom domestic law. It is the means by which enforceable Community rights become requirements of domestic law.

76. As Neill LJ put it in *Biggs v Somerset County Council* [1996] ICR 364:

"Section 2 of the European Communities Act established the primacy of Community law in English law."

77. The English decisions to which I now refer must be considered with this in mind. Guidance from the English Courts' decisions in Factortame.

78. In Factortame 5 [1997] EuLR 475, the English courts address two questions: first, whether the Government's breaches of Community law were sufficiently serious to give rise to an entitlement by the applicants to damages and, secondly, whether the applicants are entitled to recover exemplary damages.

79. They answered the first question "yes" and the second question "no."

80. At page 530, the court analysed the claim as follows:

"In Community law, the liability of a State for a breach of Community law is described as non-contractual. In English law, there has been some debate as to the correct nature of the liability for a breach of Community law. In our judgment, it is best understood as a breach of statutory duty. The reasons which lead us to this conclusion are fully set out in the judgment of Mann J in *Bourgoin v The Ministry of Agriculture* [1986] QB 727-734.

81. That case was concerned with the revocation of a licence to import frozen turkeys from France, which the ECJ held to be a breach of Article 30 of the Treaty (now Article 28, prohibiting quantitative restrictions on imports). He reviewed the authorities and followed what had been said by Lord Diplock in *Garden Cottage Foods Limited v Milk Marketing Board* [1984] AC 130 at 141. A breach of the duty imposed by Article 86 (now Article 82) not to abuse a dominant position in the Common Market, or a substantial part of it, can thus be categorised in English law as a breach of statutory duty imposed for the benefit of private individuals to whom loss is caused by a breach of that duty."

82. At page 733 (in Bourgoin) Mann J said:

"Accordingly, I hold that a contravention of Article 30 which causes damages to a person gives to that person an action for damages for breach of statutory duty, the duty being one imposed by Article 30 (as interpreted by the European Court) and section 2(1) of the Act of 1972 when read in conjunction."

83. The court in Factortame 5 went on to emphasise that it was on the question of remedies that the decision of the Court of Appeal in Bourgoin had been overtaken by later decisions and in particular Francovich (see also *Kirklees*

Metropolitan Borough Council v Wickes Building Supplies Limited [1993] AC 227 at 281).

84. The Divisional Court went on:

"Thus, whilst it can be said that the cause of action is sui generis, it is of the character of a breach of statutory duty. The United Kingdom and its organs and agencies have not performed a duty which they were statutorily required to perform."

85. The judgment then goes on to deal with the issue of exemplary damages as if the cause of action were a breach of statutory duty.

86. This exposition, while extremely helpful, is not conclusive, since the judgment starts by saying that the cause of action is for a breach of Community law and ends by saying that it is sui generis, with a character of a breach of statutory duty.

87. The nature of the remedy was considered further by the House of Lords in *R v Secretary of State ex parte Factortame* [1999] 3 WLR 1062 (Factortame 5).

88. At page 1079 Lord Slynn of Hadley said:

"The deliberate adoption of legislation which was clearly discriminatory on the grounds of nationality and which inevitably violated Article 52 of the Treaty (since it prevented establishment in the United Kingdom) was a manifest breach of fundamental Treaty obligations. It was a grave breach of the Treaty, both intrinsically and as regards the consequences it was bound or at least was most likely to have on the respondents. It has not been shown to have been excusable."

89. He went on to conclude that the domicile and residence provisions in the 1988 Act also constituted serious breaches of the Treaty.

90. He concluded as follows:

"I therefore conclude that the United Kingdom's breach of its Community obligations by imposing or applying the conditions of nationality, domicile and residence in and pursuant to the Merchant Shipping Act 1988 was a sufficiently serious breach so as to entitle the respondents to compensation for damage directly caused by that breach. I consider also the United Kingdom was in breach of Community law by failing to give effect to the order of the President of the European Court of 10th October 1989 until 2nd November 1989 and that this also constituted a serious breach of Community obligations, which would, had they not succeeded on the first ground, have entitled Rawlings (Trawling) Limited to compensation directly caused by that breach."

91. In his speech at page 1083, Lord Hope of Craighead noted that paragraph 55 of the judgment of the ECJ in Factortame 3 attempted to set out factors which the domestic court might wish to take into account in reaching a conclusion as to whether the breach was sufficiently serious. He made it clear that such matters were for the national court and not for the European Court.

92. He went on at page 1083E:

"It is a novel task for the courts of this country to have to assess whether a breach is sufficiently serious to entitle a party who has suffered loss as a result of it to damages. The general rule is that where a breach of duty has been established and a causal link between the breach and the loss suffered has been proved, the injured party is entitled to damages. In the present context, however, the rules are different. The facts must be examined in order that the court may determine whether the breach of Community law was of such a kind that damages should be awarded as compensation for the loss."

93. From the passages in the two speeches, I derive the following conclusions. First, the breaches by the United Kingdom Government amount to breaches of Community obligations. Secondly, that although the nature of the breaches can be characterised as breaches of duty or obligations, the assessment of those breaches is undertaken in a way which is novel under English law.

Other English decisions.

94. Other English cases have analysed breaches of Community law in terms of breach of statutory duty, misfeasance in public office and actions sui generis.

95. I have already referred to the judgment of the Divisional Court in Factortame 5, where the court concluded that liability for breach of Community law was best understood as a breach of statutory duty and where the court referred to the speeches of the House of Lords in *Garden Cottage Foods Limited v Milk Marketing Board* [1984] 1 AC 130.

96. In *Garden Cottage Foods Limited v Milk Marketing Board* [1984] 1 AC 130, Lord Wilberforce, at page 151, dissented from the view of the other Law Lords, as expressed in the speech of Lord Diplock, that a breach of Community law was properly characterised as a breach of statutory duty.

97. He said that the point had not been argued fully and it was at least arguable that on a proper construction of section 2 of the European Communities

Act 1972, rights arising under the Treaty were to be available in the United Kingdom as "enforceable Community rights" and not rights arising under English law. In such a case, it was arguable that Community law, which the English court would be applying, is sui generis.

98. The applicants say that Lord Wilberforce's tentative formula is the correct one and that a new remedy was created sui generis outside the provisions of the Limitation Act 1980.

99. They say that I am entitled to take this view because Garden Cottage Foods was decided before Factortame and Francovich and Lord Wilberforce's formulation is consistent with the way in which the law has developed since Garden Cottage Foods.

100. Before considering other formulations of the categorisation of breaches of Community law as English law rights, it is convenient to consider breach of statutory duty under English law.

101. In *X (minors) v Bedfordshire County Council* [1995] 2 AC 633 at 730, Lord Browne-Wilkinson analysed breach of duty in English law as a public law right which by itself gives rise to no claim in damages. It is the common law which gives a private right to damages.

102. He went on:

"Private law claims for damages can be classified into four different categories: viz (A) actions for breach of statutory duty simpliciter (ie irrespective of carelessness); (B) actions based solely on the careless performance of a statutory duty in the absence of any other common law right of action; (C) actions based on a common law duty of care arising either from the imposition of the statutory duty or from the performance of it; (D) Misfeasance in public office ..."

103. Lord Browne-Wilkinson defined misfeasance in public office as the failure to exercise or the exercise of statutory powers either with the intention to injure the plaintiff or in the knowledge that the conduct is unlawful.

104. He went on:

"Breach of statutory duty simpliciter. This category comprises those cases where the Statement of Claim alleges simply (i) the statutory duty, (ii) a breach of that duty, causing (iii) damage to the plaintiff ..."

105. "The basic proposition is that in the ordinary case a breach of statutory duty does not, by itself, give rise to any private law cause of action. However, a private cause of action will arise if it can be shown, as a matter of construction of the statute, that the statutory duty was imposed for the protection of a limited class of the public and that Parliament intended to confer on members of that class a private right of action for breach of the duty."

106. At page 734 of the judgment, he emphasised that in order to found a cause of action flowing from the careless exercise of statutory powers or duties, the plaintiff has to show that the circumstances are such as to raise a duty of care at common law.

107. In *Banque de Bruxelles v Eagle Star* [1997] AC 191 at 211, Lord Hoffmann made a similar analysis. He emphasised that a duty of a care does not exist in the abstract:

108. "A plaintiff who sues for breach of duty imposed by law (whether in contract or in tort or under statute) must do more than prove that the defendant has failed to comply: he must show that duty is owed to him and that it was a duty in respect of the kind of loss which he suffered."

109. At page 213, Lord Hoffmann said:

"Rules which make the wrongdoer liable for all the consequences of his wrongful conduct are exceptional and need to be justified by some special policy. Normally the law limits liability to those consequences which are attributable to that which made the Act wrongful."

110. Both Lord Browne-Wilkinson and Lord Hoffmann analysed breach of statutory duty in English law in terms of duty, breach and damage which are recognisable to individual claimants for damage against the State for a breach of Community law, subject to the Community requirement that the breach should be sufficiently serious.

111. There is no general right to damages for breach, either under Community law, where serious breach is required, or under common law principles of negligence. Where there is a right to damages it is to be assessed under the common law rules. Lord Hoffmann classifies all breaches of duty imposed by law within the categories of contract, tort or under statute.

112. It is interesting to consider the following cases with this analysis in mind.

113. In *Three Rivers District Council v The Bank of England* (3) [1996] 3 All ER 558, Clarke J considered the question of whether an action for breach of

Community law could properly be characterised as an action founded on tort, but in the event he did not have to reach a conclusion on this question.

114. At page 624, he said that in order to recover damages for breaches of Community law, including the failure properly to transpose an EC directive, the claimant must establish a relevant right.

115. He went on:

"If he does so, the court has now laid down clear rules which must be met. These criteria are different from the criteria which must be established on any view of the tort of misfeasance in public office.

116. It will be a matter for future consideration whether in such a case the claimant's remedy is properly to be regarded as a remedy for that tort. It appears to me that, in such a case, the claim should not be regarded as a claim for the tort of misfeasance in public office but rather as a claim of a different type, not known to the common law; namely, a claim for damage for breach of duty imposed by Community law or for the infringement of a right conferred by Community law.

117. That view seems to me to be consistent with the dicta of Lord Goff in Kirklees [1992] 3 All ER 717 at 734 when discussing the decision of the majority of Court of Appeal in Bourgoin."

118. The passage of Lord Goff's speech to which Clarke J was referring was the passage quoting, with approval, paragraphs 33 to 37 of the judgment in Francovich in the European Court of Justice and in particular paragraphs 35 to 37:

119. "35. It follows that the principle of the liability of the State for damage to individuals caused by a breach of Community law for which it is responsible is inherent in the scheme of the Treaty.

120. 36. The obligation on Member States to make good the damage is also based on Article 5 of the Treaty under which the Member States are bound to take all appropriate measures, whether general or particular, to ensure fulfilment of the obligations arising under Community law.

121. 37. It follows from the foregoing that Community law lays down a principle according to which a Member State is obliged to make good the damage to individuals caused by a breach of Community law for which it is responsible."

122. Clarke J's analysis was supported by the House of Lords -- see [2000] 2 WLR 1220.

123. In the House of Lords, Lord Hope of Craighead said, at page 1242, that there were two approaches. First, that United Kingdom legislation properly construed implemented the directive; the other that it did not fully implement the directive, with the consequence that the United Kingdom courts must have direct recourse to it and that the rights of redress were wider under Community law than those dependent on bad faith or the common law action of misfeasance in public office.

124. Lord Steyn, at 1235, and Lord Millett, at 1273, agreed that the requirement of the mental element in misfeasance in public office meant that it was not an appropriate way of characterising State liability for breaches of Community law.

125. Lord Millett set out the elements of the tort of misfeasance in public office as follows:

"The tort is an intentional tort which can be committed only by a public official. From this, two things follow. First, the tort cannot be committed negligently or inadvertently. Secondly, the core concept is abuse of power. This involves other concepts such as dishonesty, bad faith and improper purpose ... they are all subjective states of mind ... It is important to bear in mind that excess of power is not the same as abuse of power, nor is breach of duty the same as abuse of power. The two must be kept separate from breach of statutory duty, which does not necessarily found a cause of action."

126. I conclude from this that whatever categorisation is appropriate in this case it is not that of misfeasance in public office

127. Finally, in *Arkin v Borchard Lines* [2000] UK CLR 504, Colman J accepted that a claim for damages for breach of Article 85 or 86 of the Treaty (now articles 81 or 82) was properly classified as a right of action analogous to a claim for breach of statutory duty which arises where the breach causes damage to the defendant.

An Irish case.

128. Although the classification of the remedy of individuals to recover damages against the State has not been decided in the courts in the United Kingdom, it has been decided in the Irish High Court in *Tate v Minister of Social Welfare* [1995] 1 ILRM 507. The case concerned the implementation of

Council Directive 79/7/EEC which requires the Member States to afford equal treatment to men and women in social security matters.

129. Carroll J found that the plaintiff had suffered discrimination by reason of the fact that the regulations enacted in Ireland did not implement fully the rights granted under the directive. The learned judge held that Community law had domestic effect by reason of Article 29.4 of the Irish Constitution and section 2 of the European Communities Act 1972 (which was the Irish counterpart of the United Kingdom legislation and in identical terms). The issue of damages for distress does not appear to have arisen.

130. At page 522 of the judgment Carroll J characterised the wrong committed by the State in failing fully to implement the directive as:

"... a wrong arising from Community law which has domestic effect. It is not a breach of Constitutional rights; it is not a breach of statutory duty and it is not a breach of the duty of care. It is a breach of a duty to implement the directive and approximates to a breach of Constitutional duty."

131. Carroll J then went on to address the question of whether the Statute of Limitations 1957 applied to this type of claim and in particular where the claims were barred by section 11(2)(g) of the statute, namely:

"Subject to paragraphs b) and c) of this subsection, an action founded on tort shall not be brought after the expiration of six years from the date on which the cause of action accrued."

132. This provision is in identical terms to section 2 of the 1980 Limitation Act.

133. Carroll J held at page 525:

"I do not accept that the breach of obligation by the State to implement the directive is a breach of statutory duty. It is, as I already said earlier, a wrong arising from Community law which has domestic effect and approximates to a breach of Constitutional duty ... Just as the word 'tort' in the Statute of Limitations is sufficiently wide to embrace breach of statutory duty even though not specifically mentioned, so also in my opinion the word 'tort' is sufficiently wide to cover breaches of obligations of the State under Community law. There is nothing strange in describing the State's duty do fulfil its obligations under the Treaty as a tort. Therefore I am satisfied that section 11(2) of the Statute of Limitations does apply to a breach of obligations to observe Community law."

134. This important decision suggests clearly that one possible answer to the first question is that the breach of duty of the Government falls within the definition of an action founded on tort and leads into consideration of the Limitation Act itself. The applicants say that the intervention of the Irish Constitution is decisive and that the Irish case is of no relevance to this case.

The Limitation Act 1980.

135. I shall consider first the general policy and scheme of the Act and then section 2 of the Limitation Act, which must be construed with the general purpose of the Statute in mind.

136. The long title of the Statute is "an Act to consolidate the Limitation Acts 1939 to 1980".

137. It is a consolidating Statute whose purpose is to bring together in one Act of Parliament the Limitation Acts of 1939, 1963, 1975 and the Limitation Amendment Act 1980. It is not therefore intended to change the existing law, and I am entitled to consider previous Limitation Acts and cases decided under them.

138. The Act is the successor to the Limitation Act of 1623. The general purpose of imposing a limit on the time within which proceedings may be brought before the court was described by Lord Atkinson in *Board of Trade v Cayzer Irvine & Co* [1927] AC 610 at 638 in these terms:

139. "The whole purpose of this Limitation Act is to apply to persons having good causes of action which they could, if so disposed, enforce and to deprive them of the power of enforcing them after they have lain by for the number of years respectively and omitted to enforce them. They are thus deprived of a remedy which they have omitted to use."

140. In the *Ampthill Peerage Case* [1977] AC 547 at 575, Lord Simon of Glaisdale explained the reasoning behind the Statute of Limitations 1939 as amended in these terms:

141. "There is a fundamental principle of English law generally expressed by a Latin maxim (going back to Coke's commentaries on Littleton p330) which can be translated; `It is in the interest of society that there should be some end to litigation.' This fundamental principle finds expression in many forms. Parliament has passed statutes (the last only last year) limiting the time within which actions at law must be brought. Truth may be thus shut out; but society considers that truth may be bought at too high a price; the truth bought at such expense is the negation of justice."

142. This policy is equally applicable to claims against public authorities for sums payable by them pursuant to statute -- see *CEGB v Halifax Corporation* [1963] AC 785.

143. The avowed purpose of the Limitation Amendment Act 1980 consolidated into the Limitation Act 1980 was as the Law Commission reaffirmed in 1977 (a) to protect defendants from stale claims; (b) to encourage claimants to institute proceedings without unreasonable delay and thus enable actions to be tried at a time when the recollections of the witnesses was still clear; and (c) to enable a person to feel confident after a lapse of a given time that an incident which may have led to a claim is finally closed.

144. This principle is well understood in both common law countries and civil law countries and, as we have seen, was upheld by the European Court of Justice in Palmisani [1977] ECR 4025.

145. That this general principle was intended to apply to all actions brought in the English courts is clear from section 1 and the scheme of the Limitation Act

146. Section 1 of the Limitation Act 1980 provides:

"1 -- (1) This Part of this Act gives the ordinary time limits for bringing actions of the various classes mentioned in the following provisions of this Part. 147. "

147. (2) The ordinary time limits given in this Part of this Act or subject to extension or exclusion in accordance with the provisions of Part II of this Act."

148. Part I sets out the time limits for actions founded on tort, section 2; conversion of chattels, section 3; theft, section 4; contract, section 5; loans, section 6; enforcement of arbitration awards, section 7; actions on a specialty, section 8; sums recoverable by statute, section 9; contribution, section 10; personal injuries or death, sections 11 to 14; and actions relating to land, sections 15 to 27. This includes actions relating to trust property and mortgages and time limits for enforcing a judgment.

149. Part II deals with the extension or exclusion of ordinary time limits dealing with disability; acknowledgment or part payment; fraud, concealment and mistake; discretionary exclusion of time limits for actions in respect of personal injury or death.

150. Part III is concerned with miscellaneous and general matters, including the application of the Act to arbitrators, section 34; new claims in pending actions, section 35; and equitable remedies, section 36.

151. This last provision provides that the time limits under the Act in sections 2, 5, 7, 8, 9 and 24 shall not apply to equitable remedies including specific performance and injunction and preserve the court's equitable jurisdiction to refuse equitable relief to an applicant on the grounds of acquiescence or otherwise.

152. Neither the 1980 Act nor the earlier 1939 Act defines tort or action founded on tort, although it does define personal injuries, settled land and trust.

153. I conclude therefore that the approach to considering section 2 of the Limitation Act 1980 must be to give the term "action founded on tort" a wide construction.

154. Section 2, headed "Time limit for actions founded on tort", says:

"2. An action founded on tort shall not be brought after the expiration of six years from the date on which the cause of action accrued."

155. The crucial question in this case is: what is "an action founded on tort?" It raises the fundamental question of: what is a tort?

156. It is surprising that, although this has been discussed by learned textbook writers, there is no settled authority on the point.

157. The 17th edition of Clerk & Lindsell on the law of torts (soon to be superceded by the 18th edition) concludes at paragraph 1-01 that "no entirely satisfactory definition can be offered."

158. It cites Professor Winfield's classic definition in 1931:

"Tortious liability arises from a breach of duty primarily fixed by the law; such duty is towards persons generally and its heads are redressable by an action for unliquidated damages."

159. The learned editors readily acknowledge that this was intended as a description and may not now be entirely accurate.

160. At paragraph 1.04 and 1.05 Clerk & Lindsell goes on to say that where an individual enjoys a remedy for damages for breach of Community law, such a remedy is often referred to as a "Eurotort".

161. There is no decided legal authority on the point, and the question remains: is it properly so classified and, if so, is a "Eurotort" a tort for the purposes of section 2 of the Limitation Act 1980?

162. The claimants say that whatever you call it the action is sui generis and outside section 2 of the Act.

163. The respondents say that it is properly so classified and within the terms of section 2.

Conclusion.

164. Two questions must be considered. Can the cause of action be classified as an action founded on tort because it is founded on a breach of statutory duty?

165. Secondly, can it be so classified because the cause of action itself comes within a proper definition of the word "tort"? The expression "cause of action" is extremely wide and encompasses all proceedings in a court of law, and certainly applies to these proceedings; see *Hillingdon Borough Council v ARC Ltd* [1997] 3 All ER 506 at 518.

166. An action for breach of English statutory duty is properly classified as an action founded on tort. It is argued that this can be properly extended to breaches of Community law by the Government in these circumstances. The breach relied on in relation to breaches of the Treaty is the Government's breach of its obligations under section 2(1) of the European Communities Act 1972 which requires domestic law to give effect to all rights, powers, liabilities, obligations and restrictions arising out of the Treaties and provides that where there is an enforceable Community right it should be enforceable as a matter of domestic law.

167. In this case so the argument runs there is an enforceable Community right which the Government is required to enforce, namely not to impede free movement of individuals who have rights under Article 52 of the Treaty. It is in breach of its obligations in failing to do so.

168. The European Communities Act 1972 was intended to and does provide a conduit or bridge by which Community obligations are translated into domestic law. It is conceded that it does not define the primary obligation in the way in which United Kingdom statutes said to come within the definition of tort do. Nevertheless it can be argued that it would be within the all inclusive nature of the Limitation Act and consistent with its purpose to hold that what was being alleged was indeed a breach of statutory duty and therefore within the classification of an action founded on tort.

169. This answer is somewhat unsatisfactory in that it does not address the fundamental problem of whether or not an action by an individual against

a government for breach of Community law can properly be described as an action founded on tort. Nevertheless, giving the statute the widest construction in accordance with its purpose, a combination of a breach of Article 52 of the Treaty and section 2(1) of the European Communities Act 1972 does amount to a breach of statutory duty which is within section 2 of the Limitation Act.

170. This does not absolve me from answering the fundamental question. I start from the fact that the term "action founded on tort" is not defined in section 2 of the Limitation Act and that it is within the purpose of the Act that the words should be given a wide construction.

171. Following the approach suggested by Lord Hoffmann in Banque de Bruxelles [1997] AC at 211, I define a tort as:

"A breach of non-contractual duty which gives a private law right to the party injured to recover compensatory damages at common law from the party causing the injury."

172. This covers not only the present case but those few torts in English law where violation of a plaintiff's interest without proof of actual damage is sufficient to found a claim in tort.

173. This definition is also consistent with the judgment of the ECJ in Factortame 4 [1996] 1 QB 404 cited above which sets out the general principles of non-contractual liability familiar to all Member States.

174. It is also consistent with Lord Browne-Wilkinson analysis in X *(Minors) v Bedfordshire County Council* [1995] 2 AC 633 at 730, which emphasises in particular that it is the common law which gives a private right to damages.

175. The ECJ has emphasised that, while it is Community law which establishes obligations under the Treaty, it is for the Member State to afford a remedy which is effective and equivalent to comparable domestic remedies. It is also for the Member State to decide whether the breach of Community law is sufficiently serious.

176. The definition which I formulated differentiates between a section 2 right, where damages are compensatory at common law, and a section 9 right, where quantum of damages is fixed by statute. It is consistent with the purpose of the Act and with the guidance which I have derived from the authorities. It may well be that the term "Eurotort" is apt to describe the particular characteristics in Factortame 4 [1996] 1 QB 404 at 506 to differentiate it from the somewhat different requirements under English domestic law.

177. The fact that the source of the obligations is European law makes no difference to the analysis. The conduit or bridge of section 2(1) of the European Communities Act translates the obligations into English law and renders it an English law obligation. The definition in section 2 of the 1980 Limitation Act properly construed is wide enough to encompass it.

178. Equally, the fact that the precise nature of the Government's obligation was not fully defined until 1996 makes no difference. The Limitation Act is drafted in wide terms consistent with its purpose. It would be well understood by the drafters of the Act that the classification of torts has always included new rights, e.g. the tort of conspiracy. It has never been suggested that the Limitation Act did not apply because the new cause of action arose out of a new type of obligation which had arisen since the last enactment or amendment of the Statute of Limitations and in respect of which the claimant was entitled to relief.

179. I conclude therefore that section 2 of the Limitation Act 1980 applies to all new claims since 10th July 1996.

Relationship between Sections 2, 8 and 9 of the Limitation Act 1980.

180. Section 8 of the Limitation Act 1980 provides as follows:

"8(1) An action upon a specialty shall not be brought after the expiration of twelve years from the date on which the action accrued. 181. "

181. (2) Subsection (1) above shall not affect any action for which a shorter period of limitation is prescribed by any other provision of this Act."

182. Section 9 of the Limitation Act provides as follows (insofar as it is relevant):

"9 -- (1) An action to recover any sum recoverable by virtue of any enactment shall not be brought after the expiration of six years from the date on which the cause of action accrued."

183. A specialty is a contract or other obligation contained in a document under seal. An action for money recoverable by statute is an action upon a specialty. But for the exemption in section 8(2) of the Limitation Act 1980, the limitation period would have been 12 years.

184. Since I have held that section 2 of the Limitation Act applies, and since the same period of limitation of six years applies under section 9(1), a discussion as to whether section 9 also applies in the present action is largely academic.

In my view the two sections were intended to be comprehensive but were not intended to overlap.

185. I therefore construe the words "any sums recoverable by virtue of any enactment" in section 9 as referring to cases where those sums which are recoverable by the claimant are specified in or directly ascertainable from the enactment. This is to be contrasted with damages recoverable under section 2 which are compensatory damages assessed under common law principles and which cannot therefore be directly ascertained from the statute.

186. Within the meaning of the word "enactment" I would include any provision of Community legislation by reference to which compensation could be directly calculated. Such legislation would be incorporated into English law by virtue of section 2(1) of the European Communities Act 1972 with which it would have to be read. In the present cases the sums are ascertainable by common law principles and fall within section 2 of the Limitation Act.

Issues of principle arising out of section 35 of the Limitation Act 1980.

187. The preliminary issues raise the two fundamental questions of whether applications can be made by existing applicants to add claims for additional vessels and whether existing applicants can make claims in a different capacity.

188. Section 35 of the Limitation Act 1980 provides as follows:

"35 -- (1) For the purposes of this Act any new claim made in the course of any action shall be deemed to be a separate action and to have been commenced -- "

(b) in the case of any other new claim, (ie not made in or by way of third party proceedings) on the same date as the original action."

189. Section 35(2) makes it clear that any new claim includes (a) the addition or substitution of a new cause of action; or (b) the addition or substitution of a new party.

190. Section 35(3) provides:

"(3) Except as provided by ... rules of court, neither the High Court nor any County Court shall allow a new claim within subsection 1(b) above, other than an original set-off or counterclaim to be made in the course of any action after the expiry of any time limit under this Act which would affect a new action to enforce that claim ..."

191. Rules of Court must satisfy the conditions set out in subsection (5):

"a) in the case of a claim involving a new cause of action if the new cause of action arises out of the same facts or substantially the same facts as are already in issue on any claim previously made in the original action.

192. "b) in the case of a claim involving a new party if the addition or substitution of the new party is necessary for the determination of the original action."

193. The relevant Rule of Court is CPR 17.4, which provides that where a period of limitation has expired under the Limitation Act 1980:

"(2) The Court may allow an amendment whose effect will be to add or substitute a new claim but only if the new claim arises out of the same facts or substantially the same facts as a claim in respect of which the party applying for permission has already claimed a remedy in the proceedings."

194. Mr Males on behalf of the TCS applicants makes a submission in which the Edwin Coe applicants join, that the amendments do not raise a new cause of action. He submits that the existing cause of action is for breach of European Community law caused by the Merchant Shipping Act 1988 or arising out of the Merchant Shipping Act 1988 and is a single cause of action and not multiple different causes of action. He says that the only new element in relation to the application is to add in new vessels.

195. He goes on to say that, if I am against him in that submission, the new claims (if I categorise them as such) arise out of substantially the same facts as are already in issue in the original action and that I should exercise my discretion in the claimant's favour to enable the court to do justice in accordance with the overall justice of the case.

196. Mr Friedman for the respondents submits that both the claims in respect of new vessels and the claims by applicants in a different capacity are new claims and do not arise out of the same or substantially the same facts. The respondent's fall-back position is that, if the matter depends on my discretion, I should not exercise it in favour of the applicants in view of the time that has elapsed since the limitation period expired. The law.

197. It is common ground that there is no change in the law from that which prevailed before the implementation of the CPR; see *International Distillers and Vintners v Hildebrand UK Ltd* The Times January 25 2000. Therefore the law as expressed before May 1999 is relevant.

198. The classic definition of "cause of action" is that set out by Brett J in *Cooke v Gill* [1873] LR 8 CP at 116:

"'Cause of action' has been held from the earliest time to mean every fact which is material to be proved to entitle the plaintiff to succeed -- every fact which the defendant would have a right to traverse."

199. In *Paragon Finance v Thackerar* [1999] 1 All ER 400 at 406 by way of illustration Millett LJ said after citing this definition:

"In my judgment, it is incontrovertible that an amendment to make a new allegation of intentional wrongdoing by pleading fraud, conspiracy to defraud, fraudulent breach of trust or intentional breach of fiduciary duty where previously no intentional wrong doing has been alleged, constitutes a new cause of action."

200. An alternative definition of a "cause of action" is that set out by May LJ in *Steamship Mutual v Trollope and Colls* [1986] 33 BLR 77 at 91 and since often cited:

"It is sufficient for the purpose of this judgment merely to quote a short dictum from the judgment of Diplock LJ (as he then was) in the case of *Letang v Cooper*. It is unnecessary to refer to the facts of that case. On the question 'what is a cause of action' the learned Lord Justice said this: "

'A cause of action is simply a factual situation, the existence of which entitled one person to obtain from the court a remedy against another person.'"

201. In *Steamship Mutual v Trollope and Colls* at page 93 May LJ approved the decision in *Brickfield Properties v Newton* [1971] 1 WLR 862 a case where the architects alleged negligence in design was held to constitute a different cause of action to his alleged negligence in supervising the construction of the building.

202. Lord Justice May held that a proposed amendment to a claim alleging defects in the central heating system in order to allege defects in the wall ties constituted a new cause of action.

203. At page 98 he explained his approach:

"I do not think one can look only at the duty on a party but one must look also to the nature and extent of the breach relied on as well as the nature and extent of the damage complained of in deciding whether as a matter of degree a new cause of action is sought to be relied on. The mere fact that one is considering what are, as it is said after all, only different defects to the same building does not necessarily mean that they are constituents of one and the same cause of action. Thus I conclude that whether there is a new cause of action is a mixed question of law and fact."

204. The Casper Trader [1991] 2 Lloyds Reports 237 arose out of a fire. A number of allegations were pleaded that the fire was caused by the builders. The plaintiffs sought to add a claim that the builders owed a duty of reasonable care and skill and that the work should be reasonably fit for the purpose. There was no amendment to the claim for damages.

205. Webster J had no difficulty in considering that there was sufficient overlap with the existing claim and allowed the amendment.

206. Staughton LJ in the Court of Appeal (page 246) said that sufficient overlap is little more than a paraphrase for the requirement that the facts must be substantially the same. He then went on to consider the phrase "if it is just to do so". He said that the court must take into account the fact that the defendant will be deprived of an accrued defence. He said:

"The court may grant leave if it thinks that it is just to do so after taking into account together with all other relevant factors."

207. The Court of Appeal upheld Webster J's decision. It rejected other amendments which sought to add an allegation of breach of duty in the design and the carrying out of the modifications framed in the alternative in contract and tort.

208. Finally in *Lloyds Bank v Rogers* [1999] 38 EG 187 where a pleading made no claim for a monetary judgment, although it set out the essential particulars which would have justified such a claim, the Court of Appeal held that it was not necessarily a new cause of action since it did not raise any new issues between the parties.

209. At page 85 Auld LJ in considering the distinction between a new claim and a new cause of action said:

"That the draftsmen of section 35 and order 20 rule 5 had the distinction in mind is underlined by their respective provisions for new claims by reference to substituted new causes of action as well as additional new causes of action. The remedy claimed -- any claim -- may or may not be the same. What makes the claim 'a new claim' is the newness of the substituted cause of action. Thus a claim for damages is a new claim even if in the same amount as originally claimed if the claimant seeks by amendment to justify it on a different factual basis from that originally pleaded. But it is not, even if made for the first time, if it does not involve the addition or substitution of an allegation of new facts constituting such a new cause of action."

210. Evans LJ disagreed with Auld LJ on this issue but agreed with the result. He said:

"I would hold that amending the particulars of claim to include a claim for sums due as principal and interest under the guarantee adds causes of action that are 'new claims' under section 35 and order 20 rule 5 respectively. They are different causes of action from the claim for possession of the appellant's property under the legal charge and guarantee which was the only claim first made ..."

Conclusions.

211. I conclude therefore that the following principles apply. First, the provisions must be construed in accordance with the words of the section of the Act and the provisions of the CPR, and in accordance with the overall purpose of the Act. This means the special provisions must be construed as exceptions to the general rule that no new claims must be introduced once the limitation period specified in the Act has expired.

212. Secondly, a cause of action means every fact which is material to be proved to entitle the plaintiff to succeed -- every fact which the defendant would have a right to traverse (challenge).

213. Thirdly, "any claim" includes the addition or substitution of a new cause of action or the addition or the substitution of a new party.

214. Fourthly, if the court is satisfied that the claim involves a new cause of action, the court must consider whether it arises out of the same or substantially the same facts as a claim in respect of which the party applying for permission has already claimed a remedy in the proceedings.

215. Applying these tests in the present case, it is clear that the claims by existing applicants for loss and damage in respect of additional vessels are new causes of action. The facts which the applicants need to prove are specific to those vessels and relate to complicated claims which need to be proved in order that the claims can succeed.

216. Permission to amend can only be given if I conclude that the applicants can bring themselves within CPR 17.4. The new claims do not arise out of the same facts or substantially the same facts as a claim in respect of which

the party applying for permission has claimed a remedy in the proceedings. They arise out of different facts and circumstances relating to those particular vessels.

217. It is of course correct to say that in terms of issues some of the underlying claims in respect of the new vessels have much in common with existing claims. But they inevitably do not arise out of the same or substantially the same facts because the facts are specific to each vessel and must be considered specifically in relation to each vessel.

218. In relation to the application to add claims for existing claimants in a different capacity, it is clear that these are also new claims which require the addition of new parties.

219. With reference to section 35(5)(b) of the 1980 Act the new parties are not necessary to determine the claims in the original actions. The new claims by the parties claiming in a different capacity inevitably involve new claims which will be proved on the basis of new facts. I therefore also refuse these applications.

220. In relation to both these heads of claim, if I had a discretion in the matter I should refuse to exercise it in the applicants' favour. The limitation period expired at the latest in 1996. These claims were made for the first time in about September 2000 and were heard promptly in October 2000 in respect of a trial starting in January 2001. They are simply too late.

Damages for distress/injury to feelings and aggravated damages.

221. Although other issues were originally included as preliminary issues, the parties are agreed that the only issue for determination at this stage is whether in principle claims can be made by shareholders and directors for damage for injury to feelings and aggravated damages.

222. The applicants contend that the courts have already held that they have suffered discrimination on the grounds of their nationality contrary to Article 52 (now Article 43) and Article 6 (now Article 12) of the Treaty. They say that this is comparable with the fundamental discrimination prohibited by the Race Relations Act 1976. They say that section 57(4) of the 1976 Act permits the court to award damages for distress and aggravated damages and that therefore these remedies should in principle be available to these applicants.

223. They go on to say the court should not need much persuasion in these circumstances to conclude that the anger, distress and anguish caused by the Merchant Shipping Act 1988, which discriminated against the applicants on

the grounds of their nationality, had injured their feelings -- see *Ministry of Defence v Cannock* [1995] 2 All ER 449.

224. They also say that, where damage for injury to feelings is recoverable, aggravated damages which are compensatory in nature are available where a defendant has acted in a high-handed, insulting and oppressive manner -- see *Alexander v Home Office* [1988] 1 WLR 968.

225. Finally they contend that aggravated damages are in principle available to them on the basis of the existing findings by the European Court of Justice and the English courts, and do not depend upon proof of malice.

226. The respondents say that damages for injury to feelings are not normally recoverable in English law. They argue that the remedy in damages is one for English law subject to the principles of effectiveness and equivalence. They contend that it is necessary to consider the nature of the breach of Article 52 of the Treaty, and that if one does so it is clear that it is concerned exclusively with the economic and not social activity and is not comparable with a breach under the Race Relations Act 1976 or the Sex Discrimination Act 1975. In summary, the respondents say that there is no statutory equivalent in English law to a breach of Article 52 of the Treaty and that neither damages for distress nor aggravated damages are payable in these cases but only damages for economic loss.

General principles of English domestic law.

227. The general rule is that damages for injury to feelings or mental distress -- grief, fear, anger and the like -- will not be awarded under English law unless the injury to feelings has resulted in physical or mental harm -- see Devlin J's judgment in *Behrens v Bertram Mills Circus* [1957] 2 QB 1 at page 28. In the case of mental harm, the mental harm complained of must amount to a recognisable psychiatric illness -- see Lord Lloyd in *Page v Smith* [1996] 1 AC 155 at 189.

228. The circumstances in which damages can be awarded as injury to feelings and as aggravated damages as exceptions to the general rule have been developed in a line of cases starting with *Rookes v Barnard* [1964] AC 1129 and *Broome v Cassell* [1972] AC 1027.

229. The starting point is the well-known passage in Lord Devlin's speech in *Rookes v Barnard* at page 1221:

"Moreover it is well established that in cases where damages are at large, the jury (or the judge if the award is left to him) can take into account the motive and conduct of the defendant when they aggravate the injury done to the Plaintiff. There may be malevolence or spite or the manner of committing the wrong may be such as to injure the Plaintiff's proper feelings of injury and pride. These are matters which the jury can take into account in assessing the appropriate compensation. Indeed, when one examines cases in which large damages have been awarded for conduct of this sort it is not at all easy to say whether the idea of compensation or punishment has prevailed."

230. In *McCarey v Associated Newspapers No. 2* [1964] 3 All ER 947 at 957 Pearson LJ said that:

"Damages may also include the natural grief and distress which he may feel at being spoken of in defamatory terms and if there has been any kind of high-handed, oppressive, insulting or contumelious behaviour by the defendant which increases the mental pain and suffering which is caused by the defamation and which may constitute injury to the plaintiff's self-confidence -- those are proper elements to be taken into account where damages are at large."

231. In *Broome v Cassell* [1972] AC 1027 at 1085 Lord Reid described aggravated damages in these terms:

"Damages for any tort are or ought to be fixed at a sum which will compensate the plaintiff, so far as money can do it, for all the injury he has suffered. When the injury is material and has been ascertained, it is generally possible to assess damages with some precision. But that is not so where he has been caused mental distress or where his reputation has been attacked -- where, to use the traditional phrase, he has been held up to hatred, ridicule and contempt. Not only is it impossible to ascertain how far other people's minds have been affected, it is almost impossible to equate the damage to a sum of money. Any one person trying to fix a sum as compensation will probably find in his mind a wide bracket within which any sum could be regarded by him as not unreasonable -- and different people will come to different conclusions. So in the end there will probably be a wide gap between the sum which on an objective view could be regarded as the most to which the plaintiff is entitled to compensation.

232. "It has long been recognised that in determining what sum within that bracket should be awarded, a jury, or other tribunal, is entitled to have regard to the conduct of the defendant. He may have behaved in a high-handed, malicious, insulting or oppressive manner in committing the tort or he or his counsel may have aggravated the injury by what they there said. That would justify going to the top of the bracket and awarding as damages the largest sum that could fairly be awarded as compensation."

233 In *Broome v Cassell* [1972] AC 1027 at 1124, Lord Diplock set out three categories for which damages are at large, the third of which relates to exemplary damages.

234. The second category is particularly relevant:

"(2) additional compensation for the injured feelings of the plaintiff where his sense of injury resulting from the wrongful physical act is justifiably heightened by the manner in which or motive for which the defendant did it."

235. It is important to place these observations in context. They relate to the tort of defamation where holding up the plaintiff to hatred, ridicule and contempt is an integral part of the tort and where it is foreseeable that such conduct will result in distress and injury to feelings as a direct result of the defendant's conduct. The observations are also made in the context of giving guidance to juries in defamation actions where the bracket of damages which they could legitimately award is extremely wide.

236. In *Alexander v Home Office* [1988] 1 WLR 968 at 975 May LJ, referring to Lord Diplock's second category in *Broome v Cassell*, said:

"Nevertheless damages for this relatively new tort of unlawful racial discrimination are at large, that is to say they are not limited to pecuniary loss that can be specifically proved. Further even when exemplary or punitive damages are not sought nevertheless compensatory damages may and in some instances should include an element of aggravated damages where, for example, the defendant may have behaved in a high-handed, malicious, insulting or oppressive manner in committing the act of discrimination."

237. He went on:

"Although damages for racial discrimination will in many cases be analogous to those for defamation they are not necessarily the same. In the latter case the principal injury to be compensated is that to the plaintiff's reputation; I doubt whether this will play a large part in the former. On the other hand, if the plaintiff knows of the racial discrimination and that he has thereby been held up to hatred, ridicule and contempt then the injury to his feelings will be an important part of his damages. That the injury to feelings must have resulted from the knowledge of discrimination is clear from the decision of this court in *Skyrail Oceanic Ltd v Colman* [1981] ICR 864."

238. Apart from the damages arising from the statutory tort, May LJ held that a number of factors could legitimately be taken into account by the judge in

aggravation of the compensatory damages to which the plaintiff was entitled. These included:

239. "f) The aggravation of these factors: ii) by a persistent abuse of power on the part of the State authority charged by law with the duty of seeking to reform and deal equitably with the plaintiff;

240. iii) by the high-handed conduct of a defendant in whose sole power the plaintiff was;

241. iv) by the attempt, persisted in to the end of the proceedings to justify the defendant's treatment of the plaintiff by injurious and untrue allegations against him and in favour of other white prisoners;

242. v) by the conspicuous want of any withdrawal or apology for the damaging and unjustifiable reports used by the defendant to the plaintiff's detriment."

243. While it is helpful to set out these considerations, it is essential to put them in the context of that particular case. It concerned prison officers and officials in the Home Office who discriminated against a prisoner in a way that was found to be racially motivated. The Home Office then sought to justify the unfounded allegations against him by injurious and untrue allegations and by continuing that conduct to the end of the proceedings. It is easy to see how such behaviour aggravated the initial injury.

244. In *AB v South West Water Services* [1993] QB 507 the Court of Appeal considered the nature and development of aggravated damages.

245. At page 527 Stuart-Smith LJ pointed out the distinction between ordinary compensatory damages and damages for distress in a case where the claimant claimed that the defendants had aggravated the feelings of the claimant by their conduct in continuing to permit the claimant to drink contaminated drinking water.

246. He said:

" Likewise if uncertainty as to the true position caused by the defendant's lack of frankness following the initial incident led to real anxiety and distress that is an element for which they are entitled to compensation under general damages for suffering. But anger and indignation is not a proper subject for compensation; it is neither pain nor suffering."

247. In his judgment at page 532 Sir Thomas Bingham MR considered the development of the concept of damages for distress and aggravated damages in these terms:

"The question is whether in addition to that full compensatory measure (of conventional damages) the plaintiffs have pleaded a sustainable claim for additional compensation by way of aggravated damages. This is claimed in paragraph 27 on the basis that the plaintiff's feelings of indignation were aroused by the defendant's high-handed way of dealing with the incident. I know of no precedent for awarding damages for indignation aroused by a defendant's conduct.

248. Defamation cases in which a plaintiff's damages are increased by the defendant's conduct of the litigation (as by aggressive cross-examination of the plaintiff or persistence in a groundless plea of justification) are not in my view a true exception since injury to the plaintiff's feelings and self esteem is an important part of the damage for which compensation is awarded.

249. In very many other tort actions (and for that matter in contract, boundary disputes, partnership actions and other disputes) the plaintiff is indignant at the conduct of the defendant (or his insurers). An award of damages does not follow nor in my judgment should it since this is not damage directly caused by the defendant's tortious conduct and this is not damage which the law has ever recognised."

250. This judgment reaffirms the general rule set out in *Behrens v Bertram Mills Circus* and identifies, as a separate category where damages for distress may be recoverable, torts where injury to the plaintiff's feelings and self-esteem is an integral part of the damage for which compensation is awarded. To this may be added aggravated damages where the defendant's conduct after the tortious act has aggravated the damage which the plaintiff has suffered.

251. In *Ministry of Defence v Cannock* [1995] 2 All ER 449 at 480 in the Employment Appeal Tribunal Morison J emphasised that tribunals were well used to making assessments of damages for distress in respect of sex discrimination by one person against another.

252. He emphasised that compensation for injury to feelings was not automatic but had to be proved:

"It will often be easy to prove in the sense that the tribunal will not take much persuasion that the anger, distress and affront caused by the act of discrimination has injured the applicant's feelings but it is not invariably so."

253. The nature of this discrimination is a claim brought by individual plaintiffs against individual defendants who are acting unlawfully in breach of legislation passed by Parliament.

254. In *Thompson v Commissioner of Police* [1997] 2 All ER 762 at 775 Lord Woolf MR, in the course of setting out the method of assessment of damages against police officers for unlawful conduct against members of the public, set out the guidelines which a judge should give when summing up the case to the jury in relation to aggravated damages:

255. "(8) If the case is one in which aggravated damages are claimed and could properly be awarded, the nature of aggravated damages should be explained to a jury. Such damages can be awarded where there are aggravating features about a case which would result in the plaintiff not receiving sufficient compensation for the injury suffered if the award were restricted to a basic award. Aggravating features can include humiliating circumstances at the time of the arrest or the prosecution which shows that they behaved in a high-handed, insulting, malicious or oppressive manner either in relation to the arrest or the imprisonment or in conducting the prosecution. Aggravating features can also include the way the litigation and the trial are conducted."

256. "Aggravating features listed take account of the passages in the speeches of Lord Reid in Broomes Case [1972] AC 1027 at 1085 and Pearson LJ in *McCarey v Associated Newspapers No. 2* [1964] 3 All ER 947 at 957, which I have already cited."

257. Lord Woolf MR went on:

"It should be strongly emphasised to the jury that the total figure for basic and aggravated damages should not exceed what they consider is compensation for the injury which the plaintiff has suffered. It should also be explained that if aggravated damages are awarded such damages though compensatory and not intended to be a punishment will in fact contain a penal element as far as the defendant is concerned."

258. In summary I conclude that the following general principles apply:

259. 1. The general rule remains that damages for injury to feelings or distress will not normally be awarded in English law unless the injury to feelings has resulted in physical or mental harm.

260. 2. Damages to compensate a claimant for distress caused as a direct consequence of the tort are confined to those torts where the claimant's loss of self-esteem is an important part of the damages for which compensation is

awarded. This is the case in defamation actions and actions brought under the Race Relations Act and the Sex Discrimination Act.

261. 3. In cases involving unlawful discrimination, damages must be proved but will in appropriate cases be readily inferred.

262. 4. In cases where damages for distress have been awarded, aggravated damages may also be awarded where the defendant has behaved in a high-handed, insulting, malicious or oppressive manner subsequent to the tortious act but only to compensate the claimant for the unnecessary additional distress which the claimant has been caused and not to punish the defendant.

Damages: European Law Principles

263. The general principles of European law can be put into a series of propositions: 1. An individual has a remedy under Community law when three conditions are met. a) the rule of law infringed must be intended to confer rights on individuals b) the breach must be sufficiently serious, and c) the injured party must establish a causal link between the breach of obligation by the State and the damage which the injured party has sustained -- see Brasserie du Pecheur (Factortame 4) [1996] QB 404 at 499.

264. 2. Where the State must make good the damage sustained by individuals the conditions for recovery must be no less favourable than those relating to similar domestic claims or be framed in such a way as in practice to make it impossible or excessively difficult to obtain reparation (principle of equivalence and effectiveness) -- see Factortame 4 at 502.

265. 3. At page 506 of the ECJ's judgment in Factortame 4 the court emphasised that the applicants would be entitled to specific damages such as exemplary damages (including presumably damages for distress and aggravated damages) if such damages could be awarded pursuant to similar actions or claims founded on English law.

266. 4. The Divisional Court held in Factortame 5 [1997] EuLR 475 at 530 that exemplary damages could only be awarded for torts in respect of which they would have been awarded before the decision in *Rookes v Barnard*. This head of damage was not available in these proceedings. That decision was not appealed.

267. 5. The Divisional Court in Factortame 5 left open the question of whether damages for distress and/or aggravated damages could be awarded to the claimants [1997] EuLR at 527.

268. 6. The House of Lords in Factortame 5 [1997] 3 WLR 1062 held that the adoption of legislation in breach of unambiguous and fundamental Articles of the Treaty was a sufficiently serious breach to satisfy the second requirement in Factortame 4 (that the breach was sufficiently serious) and therefore entitled the applicants to recover damages for losses directly covered by the breach. It was not asked to and did not express any opinion on the availability of damages for distress or aggravated damages.

Previous observations on the gravity of the Government's conduct.

269. The applicants say that the previous observations make it clear that the defendant's conduct is analogous to a breach of the Race Relations Act 1976 and that therefore they are entitled in principle to recover damages for distress. They say that the seriousness of the allegations is clear from the findings of the Divisional Court, the Court of Appeal and the House of Lords.

270. The Divisional Court referred to four factors which in particular constituted sufficiently serious breaches of the relevant Articles of the Treaty:

271. 1. Discrimination on the grounds of nationality was the intended effect of the domicile and residence conditions

272. 2. The Government was aware that the imposition of the conditions must necessarily injure the applicants because they were intended to ensure that the applicants would no longer fish against the British quota

273. 3. The United Kingdom decided to achieve its objective through primary legislation. This made challenge to the legislation difficult. Furthermore, hopes were expressed that no damages could be awarded against the Government for breaches of Community law if such were eventually established

274. 4. The United Kingdom Government went ahead with the legislation despite the fact that the Commission had expressed the view that it was unlawful under Community law. This was clear from the letter from Mr Fitchew of 28th March 1988. Mr Fitchew was at the time a very senior civil servant in the Commission. His letter went so far as to threaten that the Commission would bring infringement proceedings under Article 169 of the Treaty.

275. The Court of Appeal [1998] EuLR 456 at 473 said:

"The ECJ clearly regarded the condition relating to nationality as being a breach of Community law falling into a special class. This is readily understandable in view of the terms of Art 6 of the Treaty which specifically provide

276. 'Within the scope of application of the Treaty and without prejudice to any special provisions contained therein, any discrimination on the grounds of nationality is prohibited'."

277. The court endorsed the status of the requirements of Article 6 expressed by Advocate-General Jacobs in the Phil Collins Case [1993] ECR 1-5145 at 5162 where he said:

"9 The prohibition of discrimination on the grounds of nationality is the single most important principle of Community law. It is the leit motiv of the EC Treaty."

278. In the House of Lords Lord Slynn of Hadley said at page 1076:

"The nationality condition was obviously discriminatory and in breach of Article 52 ... as Factortame No. 2 [1992] QB 680 ... had found."

279. He went on at page 1076:

"It is to be noted that in Factortame 3 [1996] QB 4041 at 500, para 61 the European Court stated bluntly that the nationality condition constituted direct discrimination which was manifestly contrary to Community law."

280. Lord Slynn concluded at page 1079:

"Accordingly despite the arguments of the United Kingdom and the advice it received it seems to me clear that the deliberate adoption of legislation which was clearly discriminatory on the grounds of nationality and which inevitably violated Article 52 of the Treaty (since it prevented establishment in the United Kingdom) was a manifest breach of fundamental Treaty obligations. It was a grave breach of the Treaty, both intrinsically and as regards the consequences it was bound, or at the least was most likely to have an adverse effect on the respondents ... What was done therefore in regard to nationality plainly constituted a sufficiently serious breach for the purposes of the second condition of liability."

281. Lord Slynn went on to say that discrimination on the grounds of domicile and residence was also sufficiently serious. He concluded that it was somewhat artificial to separate out the various conditions which should be treated as cumulative.

282. Lord Hope of Craighead agreed. At page 1083 he affirmed that it was for the national courts to decide how to categorise the breaches of Community law which are in issue. But he had no doubt that the breaches were sufficiently

serious to entitle the claimants to damages. He came to this conclusion on three grounds:

283. 1. The three conditions of nationality, domicile and residence in section 14 of the Merchant Shipping Act 1988 constituted direct breaches of the fundamental principles of the Treaty

284. 2. The potential for causing obvious and immediate damage to those who are likely to suffer loss as a result of it was clear

285. 3. The methods which were used to achieve the result amounted to serious breaches of the Treaty.

286. Lord Hope concluded at page 1084:

"This then was more than a trivial or technical breach of the Community obligations. The words 'manifest' or 'grave' are not easy adjectives to apply in this context. But I have no difficulty at all in seeing what was done here as a breach which was sufficiently serious as to entitle the respondents to compensation by way of damages for such loss as they can show flowed directly from the breach. If damages were not held recoverable in this case, it would be hard to envisage any case short of one involving bad faith where damages would be recoverable."

287. At page 1084 Lord Hope found that "the government's good faith is not in question". At page 1089 Lord Clyde specifically agreed.

288. I adopt the above conclusions as encapsulating the conclusions of the judges of the House of Lords. Lord Nicholls of Birkenhead and Lord Slynn specifically endorsed the reasons given by Lord Hope. The speeches of Lords Hoffman and Clyde are consistent with it.

The issues to be decided.

289. a) Taking into account the specific purpose of Article 52, are the damages confined to economic damages? b) Is the Race Relations Act 1976 the appropriate equivalent under English law? c) If it is, can the applicants in principle recover damages for distress and/or aggravated damages? a)

a) The general purpose of the Treaty and the specific purpose of Article 52.

290. This issue does not involve a detailed examination of English law. It asks the question whether or not Article 52, taken with Article 7 and Article 221, on its true construction contemplates anything more than economic loss.

291. Article 52 (now Article 43) provided:

"Within the framework of the provisions set out below, restrictions on freedom of establishment of nationals of a member state in the territory of another Member State shall be [prohibited] abolished by progressive stages in the course of the transitional period. Such [prohibition] progressive abolition shall also apply to restrictions on the setting up of agencies, branches or subsidiaries by nationals of any Member State established in the territory of [any] another Member State.

292. "Freedom of establishment shall include the right to take up and pursue activities as self-employed persons and to set up and manage undertakings in particular companies or firms within the meaning of the second paragraph of Article 58 [Article 48] under the conditions laid down for its own nationals by the law of the country where such establishment is effected, subject to the provisions of the chapter relating to capital."

293. Article 7, which became Article 6 in the Maastricht Treaty signed on 7th February 1992, with minor amendments is now Article 12 in the Treaty of Amsterdam. It is in Part One of the Treaty headed "Principles".

It provides that:

"Within the scope of application of this Treaty and without prejudice to any special provision contained therein, any discrimination on the grounds of nationality shall be prohibited.

294. "The Council may, on a proposal from the Commission and in co-operation with the European Parliament, adopt by a qualified majority rules to prohibit such discrimination."

295. The second paragraph was added by Article 6(2) of the single European Act 1986. Article 221 (now Article 294) requires Member States to accord nationals of other Member States equal treatment as regards participation in the capital of companies or firms.

296. The relationship between Article 7 and Article 52 is that Article 7 is within the basic principles of the Treaty to be applied within the scope of application of the Treaty and therefore within the application of Article 52.

297. As was made clear in the decision of the *Commission v UK* C 246/89 dated 4th October 1991, at paragraph 17 of its ruling, Article 7 had been implemented in Article 52 of the Treaty in the specific domain governed by

that Article, and that consequently any rules incompatible with Article 52 were also incompatible with Article 7 of the Treaty.

298. The court concluded in paragraph 39 that the United Kingdom had failed to fulfil its obligations incumbent upon it by Articles 7, 52 and 221 of the Treaty. It was clear to the court that the breach was a breach of one of the basic principles of the Treaty.

299. In Factortame 4 [1996] 1 QB 404 at 506 the Court of Justice issued a warning to the United Kingdom court in a passage which I have already quoted:

"National legislation which generally limits the damage for which reparation may be granted to certain specifically protected individual interests not including loss of profit by individuals is not compatible with Community law. Moreover it must be possible to award specific damages such as the exemplary damages provided for by English law pursuant to claims or actions founded on Community law if such damages may be awarded pursuant to similar claims or actions founded on domestic law."

300. The Government's claim, not I think advanced in the last round of proceedings before the English courts, is that, on a proper analysis of Article 52, damages for injury to feelings and aggravated damages are not available because the Treaty as a whole and Article 52 in particular is concerned with economic matters. This is not to be confused with economic torts in English law, which is a totally different concept. Facilitating the right of freedom of establishment under Article 52 as an economic matter is to be equated with normal torts under English law which only allow compensatory damages.

301. It seems to me that this analysis which I have expressed in my own words has much merit. It is supported by specific finding in paragraph 22 of the ECJ's judgment in Factortame 3 (see paragraph 15 above). It involves an analysis of the purpose and effect of the Treaty at the relevant time, although it would not necessarily provide the same answer after the amendments in the Treaty of Amsterdam which import social provisions into the Treaty and in particular the new Article 13, which empowers the Council to take appropriate action to combat discrimination based on sex, racial or ethnic origin, religion or belief, disability, age or sexual orientation.

Is the Race Relations Act 1976 the appropriate equivalent under English law?

302. In my view, the starting point is the nature of the breach of Article 52. This provides for the right of nationals of one Member State to establish themselves in another Member State. This, as I have already said, is not couched in terms

which are comparable to the test of Sir Thomas Bingham MR in *AB v South West Water*. A breach of Article 52 cannot be said to be comparable to a tort under English law where the claimant's loss of self-esteem is an important part of the compensation for which damages are awarded.

303. Part of the answer to the question lies in the fact that "nationality" within Article 7 of the Treaty does not have the same connotation of hatred, ridicule and contempt as can be applied to the term within the Race Relations Act; see *Nabadda v Westminster City Council* [2000] ICR 957 per Buxton LJ. It has been used widely to enforce economic rights to free movement of persons to exercise their rights of establishment within the European Union in a whole variety of circumstances.

304. If one considers the precise nature of the breach of Community law by the Government using the same test, one reaches the same result. The nature of the breaches of Community law within the Merchant Shipping Act 1988 were held in Factortame 3 [1992] 1 QB 680 at 751 (quoted again for ease of reference) to be as follows:

305. "a) that the legal owners and beneficial owners and the charterers, managers and operators of the vessel must be nationals of that Member State or companies incorporated in that Member State and in the latter case that at least 75 per cent of the shares in the company must be owned by nationals of that Member State or by companies fulfilling the same requirements 75 per cent of the directors of the company must be nationals of that Member State; and

306. "b) that the said legal owners, charterers and managers, operators, shareholders and directors, as the case may be, must be resident and domiciled in the Member State."

307. The group of persons adversely affected was substantial in number, and no individual so affected can reasonably claim to have suffered personal loss of self-esteem by being included in the category. The terms of "hatred, ridicule and contempt" in the sense which they are used in relation to the English law of defamation or the Race Relations legislation are simply not applicable.

308. This is not to the say that the Government was not in serious breach of the Treaty; it was, but the English case law has made it clear repeatedly that the right to recover damages for distress is not available as a punishment on the defendant but to permit claimants to recover compensatory damages in particular and limited circumstances.

309. Since I have concluded that the claimants have no right in principle to recover damages for distress, I do not need to consider the question of aggravated damages which are ancillary to damages for distress. It is sufficient to say that in *Thompson v Commissioner of Police* [1997] 2 All ER 762 at 775 Lord Woolf in summarising the well established authorities emphasised that such damages can only be awarded if the plaintiff did not receive sufficient compensation from the injury if the award was restricted to a basic award. A party can only recover such additional damages for conduct which would not otherwise be compensated. The Race Relations Act 1976.

310. Even if the Race Relations Act 1976 had been the appropriate comparator, the claimants would still not have been entitled to recover damages for distress or aggravated damages.

311. The Race Relations Act 1976 provides that:

"1(1) A person discriminates against another in any circumstances relevant for the purposes of any provisions of this act if:

"(a) on racial grounds he treats that other less favourably than he treats or would treat other persons.

"(b) he applies to that other a request or condition which he applies or would apply equally to persons not of the same racial group as that other ..."

312. Section 3(1) defines a racial group as:

"A group of persons defined by reference to race, nationality or national origins."

313. There is considerable doubt as to whether the expression "nationality" under the Act means the same as it does under Community law.

314. In *Nabadda v Westminster City Council* [2000] ICR 951 at 957, at paragraph 12 of his judgment, Buxton LJ said:

"While it is correct that section 3(1) of the Act repeated the definition of racial grounds in section 1(1) of the Race Relations Act 1968 but with the addition of the word 'nationality', that was not done with Article 6 (of the Treaty) in mind. Rather it was generally understood at the time of the Act of 1976 that the addition was made to offset the effect of the House of Lords' decision in *Ealing London Borough Council v Race Relations Board* [1972] AC 342 that 'national' in the expression 'national origins' meant national in the sense of race and not of citizenship."

315. If this is correct, the Race Relations Act 1976 does not cover the type of discrimination which is inherent in the Merchant Shipping Act 1988 and the regulations. Such a view would be consistent with common sense. The term "nationality" in relation to free movement of persons, goods and services and to the right of establishment is much wider and does not have the same connotation as nationality as it is used in the Race Relations Act.

316. On the basis that the comparison does not fail at this stage, I go on to consider the scheme of the Act and the relevant provisions. The argument proceeds on the basis that the applicants are a group of persons defined by reference to nationality and therefore prima facie come within the scope of the Act.

317. The scheme of the Act is to set out in Part III the prohibited acts of discrimination -- section 20, to which I shall return, is particularly relevant. Section 57 of the Act provides that unlawful discrimination may be the subject of civil proceedings in like manner as any other claim in tort. It provides specifically that damages for an unlawful act of discrimination may include compensation for injury to feelings "whether or not they include compensation under any other head".

318. The Act specifies under section 75 that the Act of Parliament applies to an act done by a minister of the Crown or a government department as it applies to a private person and that acts done under statutory authority under section 41 are exempt from the provisions of the Act.

319. Under section 20 of the Act it is unlawful for any person concerned with the provision of goods, facilities or services to the public to discriminate against a person who seeks to obtain or use those goods, facilities and services by:

"a) refusing or deliberately omitting to provide him with any of them."

320. Section 20(2) provides that the following are examples of the facilities and services mentioned in subsection (1):

(g) the services of any profession or trade or any local or other public authority."

321. The wording of section 20 is identical to the wording of section 29 of the Sex Discrimination Act 1975. In Amin [1983] 2 AC 818 the House of Lords considered the section in the context of a United Kingdom passport holder resident in Bombay who applied to an entry clearance officer in Bombay for a

special entry voucher to enable her to settle in the United Kingdom. She was refused on the grounds that she was not the head of the household.

322. Lord Fraser of Tullybelton said at page 835:

"My Lords, I accept that the examples in section 29(2) are not exhaustive of section 1. Section 29, as a whole, seems to me to apply to the direct provision of facilities or services and not to the mere grant of permission to use facilities ...

323. "Example (g) seems to me to be contemplating things such as medical services, library facilities which can be directly provided by local or public authorities. So in Savjani Templeman J took the view that the Inland Revenue performed two separate functions -- first a duty of collecting revenue and secondly a service of providing taxpayers with information ..."

324. At page 835:

"In the present case the entry clearance officer in Bombay was in my opinion not providing a service for would-be immigrants; rather he was performing a duty of controlling them."

325. In *Farah v Commissioner of Police* [1997] 1 All ER 289 the Court of Appeal held that police officers came within the class of persons in section 20(2) (g) when they were providing services to the public. Section 57 of the Race Relations Act 1976 provides that:

326. "(1) A claim by any person (`the claimant') that another person (`the respondent') (a) has committed an act of discrimination which is unlawful by virtue of Part III ... may be the subject of civil proceedings in like manner as any other claim in tort ...

327. "(4) For the avoidance of doubt it is hereby declared that damages in respect of an unlawful act of discrimination may include injury to feelings, whether or not they include compensation under any other head."

328. Section 57(4) has prompted the submission that if damages for distress are available under the Race Relations Act they should be available in this case. Under this section awards of damages for distress have become commonplace in race relations cases; see e.g. *Ministry of Defence v Cannock* [1995] 2 All ER 449 at 480.

329. The main sections dealing with the relationship between the legislation and the Crown are set out in section 75 and 41 of the Race Relations Act 1976.

330. Section 75 provides:

"(1) This act applies -- "

a) to an act done by or for purposes of a Minister of the Crown or government department; or

"b) to an act done on behalf of the Crown by a statutory body, or a person holding a statutory office, as it applies to an act done by a private person."

331. In Amin Lord Fraser of Tullybelton explained the equivalent section 85 of the Sex Discrimination Act 1975 as follows:

"That section puts an act done on behalf of the Crown on a par with an act done by a private person and it does not in terms restrict the comparison to an act of the same kind done by a private person. But in my opinion it applies only to acts done on behalf of the Crown which are of a kind similar to acts that might be done by a private person. It does not mean that the Act is to apply to any act of any kind done on behalf of the Crown by a person holding statutory office.

332. "There must be acts (which include deliberate omissions -- see section 82(1) [section 78(1) in the Race Relations Act 1976] done in the formulating or carrying out of government policy which are quite different in kind from any act that would ever be done by a private person and to which the Act does not apply. I would respectfully agree with the observations made by Woolf J in *Home Office v Commission for Racial Equality* [1982] QB 385 at 395.

333. "Part V of the Act of 1975 [the Sex Discrimination Act; my explanation] makes exceptions for certain acts including acts done for the purpose of national security (section 52) and for acts which are 'necessary' in order to comply with statutory requirements (section 51). These exceptions will no doubt be effective to protect acts of a kind that would otherwise be unlawful under the Act but they do not in my view obviate the necessity for construing section 29 as applying only to acts that could be done by private persons."

334. In this case it is clear that in enacting the Merchant Shipping Act 1988 the Government was performing an act which was quite different in kind from any act which could be done by a private person. Indeed, in the case of primary legislation, while it is carried through the legislature by the Government, the Act of Parliament is enacted by the Queen in Parliament under the Royal Prerogative.

335. This requirement that a claim for compensation against the Crown can only be made in respect of acts that could be done by private persons is reinforced by and consistent with section 41 of the 1976 Race Relations Act:

336. "41(1) Nothing in Parts II to IV shall render unlawful any act of discrimination done --

"a) in pursuance of any enactment or Order in Council; or "

b) in pursuance of any instrument made under any enactment by a Minister of the Crown; or

"c) in order to comply with any condition or requirement imposed by a Minister of the Crown (whether before or after the passing of this Act) by virtue of any enactment."

337. In *Hampson v Department of Education and Science* [1990] 2 All ER 513 the House of Lords held that statutory protection under section 41 extended to acts done in the necessary performance of an express obligation contained in the instrument but not to acts done in the exercise for power or discretion conferred by instrument.

338. The Crown's immunity was reinforced by the enforcement provisions. Section 53 provides:

"(1) except as provided by this Act no proceedings, whether civil or criminal, shall lie against any person in respect of an act by reason that the act is unlawful by virtue of a provision of this Act.

"(2) subsection 1 does not preclude the making of an order of certiorari, mandamus or prohibition."

339. Section 53 was also explained in *Hampson v Department of Education and Science* [1990] 2 All ER 513.

340. At page 521, Lord Lowry said:

"The remedies of certiorari, mandamus and prohibition where expressly preserved by section 53(2) of the 1976 Act despite the general limitation imposed by section 53(1) and no doubt with a view to allaying any misgivings which might attend the prospect of such widespread immunity."

341. Section 53(2) enables any public misuse of power of the Government and its servants to be challenged by the public law prerogative writ. This is a

separate remedy to the private law remedy being claimed by these claimants in this action.

Conclusion.

342. I conclude that the Government is not liable in principle to pay damages to the claimants for injury to feelings and aggravated damages for the following reasons:

343. 1. Damages for distress are not normally awarded under English law.

344. 2. They can only be awarded in relation to those torts where the claimant's self-esteem is an important and integral part of the damage for which compensation is awarded.

345. 3. They can only be awarded in respect of torts committed by private persons or by Government officials acting in circumstances where the claimant could recover damage if the act was done by a private person.

346. 4. At the time of the breach Article 52 of the Treaty incorporating Article 7 granted rights to persons entitled to benefit from its provisions which were economic in nature. These Articles of the Treaty were not concerned with social rights which were matters exclusively within the competence of the Member States. Therefore only economic damages are recoverable in this case for a breach of Article 52.

347. 5. If contrary to the finding in 4 it is open to the claimant in principle to recover damages under the Treaty, it is not open to them in this case because the group which had in it 100 persons and probably more is distinguishable from the individual cases of discrimination where a loss of the claimant's self-esteem was a foreseeable part of the damage that the claimants would suffer.

348. 6. The Race Relations Act 1976 is not a comparator for a group such as were discriminated against in the Merchant Shipping Act for the reasons set out in 5 above.

349. 7. If the Race Relations Act 1976 is an apt comparator, it does not assist the claimants because it contains a specific exemption from claims for damages for acts done by or in pursuance of any enactment or Order in Council (section 41 and section 57). Liability under the Act is confined to acts by the Crown, Crown servants and statutory bodies which are comparable to acts done by private persons. The enactment of primary legislation is not comparable to an act done by a private person.

350. I conclude therefore that damages for distress/injury to feelings and aggravated damages are not available in principle to the claimants in this case.

CIB Properties Ltd v Birse Construction Ltd

CIB Properties Ltd v Birse Construction Ltd [2004]EWHC 2365(TCC); [2005] 1 WLR 2252 is mentioned a number of times in the Valedictory speeches as a landmark case. It is an extreme example of the use of adjudication. The costs of the adjudication alone amounted to around £1m for each party. My judgment, rejected the challenges to the validity of the award and upheld the decision of the very experienced adjudicator. In particular, I rejected the claim that the issues were too complex to be the subject of the adjudication process.

I reached this conclusion on the wording of the Statute, although it was clear from the Debate on the Bill in the House of Lords that this was not what the promoters of the legislation originally intended. The original purpose was to provide a quick and cheap means of obtaining redress, particularly for small sub-contractors, from whom payment was being withheld and who desperately needed to be paid promptly if they were to remain in business.

My judgment was not appealed. The adjudicator's award stood, therefore, as being enforceable until it was superceded by a judgment of a court or arbitrator(s) or, as in this case, by settlement. The result of the adjudication was not accepted by the parties and the parties failed to achieve a subsequent settlement on their own. The case came back to me as substantive litigation. It was settled in the course of case management before me. This was because, knowing the case well, I saw something in the position of the experts which had not been appreciated by the parties.

It is a further example of the value of positive and continuous case management by a single judge. Without a very detailed and instinctive grasp of the case, I would not have identified the circumstances which would have enabled it to settle. If the "docket system", continuous case management by one judge, a strength of the Official Referees, disappears, and case management is done by another judge, who just happens to be available, the attraction of the TCC to litigants will be substantially diminished. After all, case management in arbitration is not undertaken by a third party who just happens to be available. I have substantially abbreviated the judgment to focus on the issues relating to adjudication enforcement in complicated cases and the power of the adjudicator to amend an award, an issue also referred to in the Valedictory speeches (see *Bloor Construction(UK) Ltd v Bowmer & Kirkland* (London) Ltd [2000] BLR 314). The result of my judgment in Bloor, namely that in limited circumstances the adjudicator has power to amend his award, was incorporated in the recent amendments to the Housing Grants Construction and Regeneration Act 1996.

CIB Properties Ltd v Birse Construction Ltd (QBD)

Counsel: Vivian Ramsay QC and Jonathan Lee for the claimant.

Paul Darling QC and Sarah Hannaford for the defendant.

19 October 2004. JUDGE JOHN TOULMIN QC delivered the following judgment.

1 This is an application by CIB Properties Ltd ("CIB") to enforce the decision of the adjudicator, John Uff CBE QC, made on 24 February 2004 that Birse Construction Ltd ("Birse") should pay CIB £2,164,892.

2 Birse seeks to prevent the enforcement of the adjudicator's award by raising a number of defences including the plea that adjudication is inappropriate in a dispute of this complexity. This is a defence which goes to the root of the adjudication process. The point has not previously been decided.

3 I give this judgment after hearing oral evidence. The judgment is, therefore, a final judgment. The grounds on which CIB's application is contested are set out in para 18 of the defence and have been amplified in detailed and most helpful submissions. They are:

There was no dispute in being at the date of the notice of adjudication so that the adjudicator had no jurisdiction to hear and determine the matters before him. Birse says that any possible dispute had not crystallised because there were ongoing discussions to resolve CIB's claim and CIB had agreed to a further meeting due to take place after CIB served the notice of adjudication.

Birse claims that the adjudication could not be and was not conducted fairly and impartially because: (a) it was irredeemably prejudiced by CIB's tactics and conduct before the notice of adjudication was served which meant that Birse was put at a disadvantage before the adjudication started which could not be cured. The limited and piecemeal extensions of time given to Birse in the course of the adjudication could not eliminate the prejudice which had already taken place. (b) The pressure, which not only Birse but also the adjudicator was under, led the adjudicator to act unfairly and to the prejudice of Birse in relation to (i) the time for Birse's response; (ii) the timetable and timescales generally; (iii) the expert evidence; and (iv) the documentation generally. (c) It led the adjudicator, because of pressure, in to making a slip in his award which transformed what should have been an award in Birse's favour into the present award in favour of CIB.

The size and complexity of the dispute meant that it could not be resolved fairly by adjudication. Birse cites in support comments made by judges in other adjudication cases.

The adjudicator made a slip which the court has power either to correct itself or, in the circumstances of this case, the court has power to invite the adjudicator to correct. Birse contends that the adjudicator decided in section 9 of his decision that Birse had no liability for defects in the cladding but in section 14 of his decision he awarded CIB the costs of remedial works in relation to defects in the cladding for which, in section 9, he had said that Birse was not liable. Birse contends that the adjudicator's letter in response to their own constituted exceptionally an invitation to the court to make a finding on this issue which the court should accept.

4 At the start of the hearing, Birse relied on two other defences which are no longer being pursued: (a)that the allegation that the service of new documents with the referral notice created a new dispute ; and (b) that Birse was entitled to set off its own claim against CIB's enforcement claim.

The law

5 The starting point of any consideration of these issues is section 108 of the Housing Grants, Construction and Regeneration Act 1996. Section 108 provides:

"(1) A party to a construction contract has the right to refer a dispute arising under the contract for adjudication under a procedure complying with this section. For this purpose 'dispute' includes any difference.

"(2) The contract shall-(a) enable a party to give notice at any time of his intention to refer a dispute to adjudication; (b) provide a timetable with the object of securing the appointment of the adjudicator and referral of the dispute to him within seven days of such notice; (c) require the adjudicator to reach a decision within 28 days of referral or such longer period as is agreed by the parties after the dispute has been referred; (d) allow the adjudicator to extend the period of 28 days by up to 14 days, with the consent of the party by whom the dispute was referred; (e) impose a duty on the adjudicator to act impartially; and (f) enable the adjudicator to take the initiative in ascertaining the facts and the law."

6 In relation to the duty of impartiality, paragraph 12(a) of the Scheme for Construction Contracts (set out in Part I of the Schedule to the Scheme for Construction Contracts (England and Wales) Regulations 1998 (SI 1998/649)),

provides: "The adjudicator shall-(a) act impartially in carrying out his duties and shall do so in accordance with any relevant terms of the contract and shall reach his decision in accordance with the applicable law in relation to the contract."

7 The history of the events leading up to the passing of the Act was set out by May LJ in *Pegram Shopfitters Ltd v Tally Weijl* (UK) Ltd [2004] 1 WLR 2082. It is clear that Parliament has introduced an intervening stage in construction disputes which enables the parties to achieve a temporary solution in advance of the full process of litigation or arbitration.

8 The purpose of the litigation was described by Lord Ackner in the debate in the House of Lords (see Hansard (HL debates), vol 571, cols 989-990): "[adjudication] was a highly satisfactory process. It came under the rubric of 'pay now argue later', which was a sensible way of dealing expeditiously and relatively inexpensively with disputes which might hold up the completion of important contracts."

9 There is no doubt that the procedure is being used in disputes which are to be resolved long after the contract which is the subject matter of the dispute has come to an end. It has come to be used, as in this case, as a form of intense confrontational litigation which can be very costly. I was told that CIB's costs of the two adjudications amounted to £973,732.41 and Birse's costs to £1,161,341.70, in each case excluding VAT. To this must be added the adjudicator's costs in the two adjudications. The adjudicator's costs, including the costs of the expert assessor, in the second adjudication amounted to over £150,000. This could not be described as inexpensive.

10 The procedure, as in this case, can often encourage the parties to engage in tactical manoeuvring of a type that is these days deprecated in litigation before these courts.This manoeuvring continued up to and throughout the adjudication.

11 There is no doubt that a wrong or unenforceable decision of an adjudicator can lead to great unfairness to one side or the other. This is inherent in the legislation. On the other hand, the proponents of adjudication point to the very many cases where adjudication (or the threat of adjudication) leads to the early resolution of the dispute. They also perceive it to be an advantage that, unlike ordinary litigation, each party bears its own costs in any event and it is only the cost of the adjudicator that can be the subject of a conventional order.

12 The background policy which the courts must respect is well set out in two passages in the judgment of Dyson J (which was approved by the Court of

Appeal) in *Macob Civil Engineering Ltd v Morrison Construction Ltd* [1999] BLR 93, 97:

"The timetable for adjudications is very tight (see section 108 of the Act). Many would say unreasonably tight, and likely to result in injustice. Parliament must be taken to have been aware of this."

13 In his judgment in the Macob case Dyson J also said, at p 97: "... Parliament has not abolished arbitration and litigation of construction disputes. It has merely introduced an intervening provisional stage in the dispute resolution process."

14 The jurisdiction has been developed primarily by judges of this court in conformity with the legislation. The following steps are relevant in adjudication. (a) There must be a dispute arising under a construction contract which is capable of being referred to adjudication. (b) Notice must be given to the other party to refer that dispute to adjudication. (c) A timetable must be provided under which, if there is no designated adjudicator, the adjudicator must be appointed within seven days. (d) The adjudicator must reach a decision on the dispute which has been referred to him. (e) The adjudicator must (subject to (f) below) reach his decision within 28 days of the referral or such longer period as is agreed by the parties after the dispute has been referred. (f) The adjudicator is permitted to extend the 28-day time limit to up to 42 days with the agreement only of the referring party. (g) The adjudicator has an overriding duty to act fairly and impartially. This requires the adjudicator to direct the procedure so that each party has a proper and equal opportunity to present its case.

15 The question of what is a dispute was decided by the Court of Appeal in *Halki Shipping Corpn v Sopex Oils Ltd* [1998] 1 WLR 726, 761. Whether there is a dispute depends on the ordinary meaning of the word and the facts of the case. In the Halki case Swinton Thomas LJ, citing a passage of Templeman LJ in *Ellerine Bros (Pty) Ltd v Klinger* [1982] 1 WLR 1375, held that in appropriate cases, where there had been a demand, a dispute could be inferred to exist where a party had failed to respond to the demand.

16 I do not understand the word "difference" in the Act to add any additional concept. Rather it prevents barren arguments over whether a situation can properly be characterised as a dispute or a difference.

17 In *Sindall Ltd v Solland* (2001) 80 Con LR 152, a decision approved by Forbes J in *Beck Peppiatt Ltd v Norwest Holst Construction Ltd* [2003] BLR 316, 318, para 4, Judge Humphrey Lloyd QC carried the analysis of what is a dispute a stage further. He said 80 Con LR 152, para 15:

"For there to be a dispute for the purposes of exercising the statutory right to adjudication it must be clear that a point has emerged from the process of discussion or negotiation has ended and that there is something which needs to be decided."

18 I accept entirely the spirit of this analysis as an expression of a common sense approach. There is a danger that it can be taken too literally. It is clear that in this case each side was engaged in tactical manoeuvres in relation to its own claims. In relation to the threat of CIB starting an adjudication Birse was anxious to keep discussions going so that it could say that the process of negotiation had not ended.

19 In my view the test is whether, taking a common sense approach, the dispute has crystallised. Even after it has crystallised, parties may wish to have further discussions in order to resolve it. Whether or not it has, in fact, crystallised will depend on the facts in each case including whether or not the parties are in continuing and genuine discussions in order to try to resolve the dispute.

20 The court has, from the beginning, declined to enforce an adjudicator's award on the grounds of bias or procedural unfairness: see, e g, *Glencot Development and Design Co Ltd v Ben Barrett Son (Contractors) Ltd* [2001] BLR 207, *Discain Project Services Ltd v Opecprime Development Ltd* [2000] BLR 402 and *McAlpine PPS Pipeline Systems Joint Venture v Transco plc* [2004] BLR 352. There are a number of decisions where the court has refused to enforce a decision where the adjudicator has conducted the procedure in a manner which is unjust or to the unfair disadvantage of a party. In considering these questions courts must have in mind section 108(2)(f) of the Act which enables the adjudicator to take the initiative in ascertaining the facts and the law provided he acts in a way that is fair. This applies to orders relating to the disclosure of documents as much as to any other aspect of the procedure.

21 In this case, Birse challenges the adjudicator's decision not only on specific grounds but also on the general ground that the dispute was too complex to be decided by means of adjudication.

22 Although this point has not been decided directly, Birse cites in support comments of judges in previous cases. In particular, in London and *Amsterdam Properties Ltd v Waterman Partnership Ltd* [2004] BLR 179, 196, para 146, Judge Wilcox said:

"It must also be recognised that there may be some disputes particularly arising at the end of a project which are too complex to permit a fair adjudication process within the time limits of the scheme."

23 In *AWG Construction Services Ltd v Rockingham Motor Speedway Ltd* (2004) 20 Const LJ T107, para 123 I raised the possibility that there may be disputes which are so complex, and where the advantages of the procedure are weighted to such an extent against the defendant, that there is a conflict between the right to refer to adjudication and obtain a decision within the time limits laid down in section 108(2)(c)(d) and the adjudicator's duty to act impartially under section 108(f) of the Act. I went on to suggest (erroneously as I now think) that this was a conflict which it might be impossible to resolve.

24 The answer to the problem lies in construing the Act itself. The Act confers a general right to refer a dispute or difference to adjudication provided it can be adjudicated in accordance with a procedure complying with section 108(2). This general right exists irrespective of the apparent complexity of the dispute but it does not require an adjudicator to reach a decision if he is unable to do so within the time limits imposed by section 108(2) of the Act.

25 Section 108(2) sets out requirements (including time limits) within which the adjudication must be carried out. Section 108(2)(c) is permissive. A party is not bound to agree to an extension of time beyond the 28 days. If a defendant does not agree to further extensions of time after the dispute has been referred, the time limit for the adjudicator's decision is, therefore, 28 days or up to 42 days on the application of the adjudicator with the agreement of the referring party: see section108(2)(d).

26 It is argued by CIB that if a defendant agrees to one extension of time, it must be taken to have agreed to further necessary extensions of time. I do not agree that this is necessarily the case. It will depend in each case on the circumstances in which the initial extension of time is agreed. There will be cases where this is a proper inference. There will be other cases where no such inference can be drawn, for example, where a defendant has made it clear that the initial extension of time is agreed without prejudice to any further extensions. The test is not, therefore, whether the dispute is too complicated to refer to adjudication but whether the adjudicator was able to reach a fair decision within the time limits allowed by the parties.

27 In complex cases it is likely also that issues will be raised as to whether (1) the adjudicator acted fairly in the procedure and (2) whether his decision was properly responsive to the dispute that was referred to him or, as it was put in *Bouygues (UK) Ltd v Dahl-Jensen (UK) Ltd* [2001] 1 All ER (Comm) 1041, 1045, para 12, did he answer the right question or questions?

28 In addition to these arguments, Birse has an additional argument that there was a slip which the adjudicator should be ordered, or at least encouraged, to correct. Birse cites in support my decision in *Bloor Construction (UK) Ltd v*

Bowmer Kirkland (London) Ltd [2000] BLR 314. CIB argues that this decision was wrong but says that in any event it does not go far enough to assist Birse in the present circumstances.

29 In the Bloor case I said, at p 319:

"in the absence of any specific agreement to the contrary, a term can and should be implied into the contract referring the dispute to adjudication, that the adjudicator may, on his own initiative or on the application of a party, correct an error arising from an accidental error or omission. The purpose of the adjudication is to enable broad justice to be done between the parties. Parties acting in good faith would be bound to agree at the start of the adjudication that the adjudicator could correct an obvious mistake of the sort which he made in this case."

30 In reaching this conclusion I was careful to analyse what amounted in law to an accidental slip or omission. I referred to Sir John Donaldson MR's analysis of what amounted to a slip under the old procedural rules in *Mutual Shipping Corpn v Bayshore Shipping Co Ltd* [1985] 1 WLR 625, 633:

"It is the distinction between having second thoughts or intentions and correcting an award or judgment to give true effect to first thoughts or intentions, which creates the problem. Neither an arbitrator nor a judge can make any claim to infallibility. If he assesses the evidence wrongly or misconstrues or misappreciates the law the resulting award or judgment will be erroneous, but it cannot be corrected either under section 17 of the [Arbitration Act 1950] or under RSC Ord 20, r 11. It cannot normally even be corrected under section 22 of the 1950 Act. The remedy is to appeal, if a right of appeal exists. The skilled arbitrator or judge may be tempted to describe this as an accidental slip, but this is a natural form of self-exculpation."

31 The distinction under the Arbitration Act 1996, which received the Royal Assent a few weeks before the Housing Grants, Construction and Regeneration Act 1996, is summarised in Mustill Boyd, Commercial Arbitration, 2nd ed (1989), ch 27, p 406:

"They enable the arbitrator to make an award on a claim which he has inadvertently overlooked, such as an award of interest, or to correct errors of accounting and arithmetic, such as attributing a credit item to the wrong party. But the section does not give the arbitrator licence to give effect to second thoughts on matters on which he has made a conscious act of judgment."

32 This is only one of the two hurdles which Birse must overcome in relation its claim that the adjudicator made a slip which should be corrected. The

threshold question is whether the adjudicator is prepared to admit or correct the slip at a time when it does not prejudice the other party. If the adjudicator is not prepared to make a correction promptly that is an end of the matter. In the Bouygues case [2000] BLR 49, 55, paras 33, 34, there was an error by an adjudicator which Dyson J (at first instance) concluded was a mistake which fell into the category of a slip. The adjudicator refused to admit or correct the mistake. Dyson J held, at para 33, that the adjudicator's decision had to stand because the adjudicator was not exceeding his terms of reference: "he was doing precisely what he had been asked to do, and was answering the right question, but he was doing so in the wrong way." The appeal was dismissed [2001] 1 All ER (Comm) 1041. The Court of Appeal held that (subject to a separate point relating to bankruptcy law) Dyson J had stated correctly the relevant law and its application to that case.

33 I conclude, therefore, that the law before this case is that in relation to a slip or alleged slip there are two questions: (1) is the adjudicator prepared to acknowledge that he has made a mistake and correct it? (2) is the mistake a genuine slip which failed to give effect to his first thoughts? If the answer to both questions is "Yes" then, subject to the important question of the time within which the correction is made and questions of prejudice, the court can if the justice of the case so requires give effect to the amendment to rectify the slip.

34 Having considered the matter again, I adhere to my decision in the Bloor case [2000] BLR 314. It found some limited support from Dyson J in *Edmund McNuttall Ltd v Sevenoaks District Council* (unreported) 14 April 2000, decided a few days after the Bloor case, when he concluded in relation to the decision in the Bloor case: "In my view, putting the matter at its lowest, it is at least arguable that it is right."

35 The decision in the Bloor case is, however, of very limited and narrow application. In this case I am being asked by Birse to say that the court should review the adjudicator's decision, conclude that he has made a slip, and either invite or order him to amend his decision. This is a very difficult argument on which to succeed in the light of the existing law. Birse contends that while under existing law this may normally be the case, the position is different where the adjudicator has invited the court to rule on the matter. I shall consider this argument after I have considered the adjudicator's letter dated 19 March 2004 in response to Birse's request that he reconsider his decision.

The facts

36 CIB and Birse entered into a contract dated 8 August 2000 for the construction of a new building which was to be called the Riverdale Data

Centre, Molesworth Street, London E13. CIB was to be the owner of the property and Birse was the main contractor. Clause 16.14.3 of the contract provided:

"Owner or contractor may at any time give written notice of its intention to refer any dispute arising under the contract for construction to adjudication. The adjudication provisions of the Scheme for Construction Contracts shall apply."

[Paragraphs 37 – 160 contain facts only and have been cut] 161 On 24 February 2004 Mr Uff delivered his adjudication decision.]

162 On 5 March 2004 Hammonds wrote to the adjudicator. They referred to paras 9.6-9.15 of his decision and said that:

"You decided in para 9.15 that Birse did not have liability for patent or latent defects in the work of façade and that these costs should be excluded from the claims against Birse."

163 The letter went on:

"We are concerned that, when you later considered the amounts which should be deducted from the cladding claims at paras 14.20 and 14.21 of your decision you have made an accidental slip by not fully taking into account this finding when undertaking your valuation."

164 The letter went on to suggest how the decision should be amended. The long letter concluded by saying that one of the real risks of adjudicating a dispute of this kind meant that slips leading to injustice were almost inevitable:

"Hence our submissions as to the overall unfairness of this whole process. Since the ultimate effect on our clients of this accidental slip amounts to over £2m they are understandably extremely concerned about this huge discrepancy and would be grateful if it could be rectified as soon as possible."

165 Also on 5 March 2004 Knowles responded to Hammonds' letter by saying that it was not a correct characterisation to say that Birse was requesting the correction of an accidental slip or omission: "In fact, Birse's complaint is that you have misapplied the law to the facts of the case. This cannot be an accidental slip or omission."

166 On 19 March 2004 (the delay having been caused by his unavoidable absence from chambers) Mr Uff responded:

"The matter which has been raised by Hammonds, namely the way in which the decision at paras 9.6-9.15 of the decision have been applied in section 14, is an issue with which I am familiar. I am aware that it could have been argued on both sides that the figure to be deducted from the E3 account by reason of the decision at para 9.15 could have been materially different from those which I, in fact, accepted. In the circumstances of the adjudication, particularly the pressure of time, I consider the appropriate decision was to accept Mr Crowter's figure for categories Z2, Z3 and Z4 in full. I fully accept that had time been available Birse would have contended for much greater deductions and CIB for lesser deductions. Given the exchange between the parties I do not consider that it would be useful for me to express any view on whether my approach contains any error. If the parties or the court decide that there is any error I should be happy to review the decision and to receive further submissions from the parties ..."

The decision

167 The decision of the adjudicator runs to 139 pages. It is divided into sections. They consist of the preamble, CIB's claims, Birse's response, CIB's reply, CIB and Birse's evidence, final submissions, a discussion of the evidence, a discussion of whether Birse was entitled to an indemnity from CIB as claimed and the decision with reasons on each of the claims. It is clearly a conscientious and careful piece of work from a very experienced adjudicator.

168 At paras 7.09 and 7.10 he notes the guidance given by Judge Wilcox in *London and Amsterdam Properties Ltd v Waterman Partnership Ltd* [2004] BLR 179, 201, paras 184, 185, where Judge Wilcox noted:

"184. The scheme does not envisage that there should be a provisional resolution of a dispute by an adjudicator at all costs.

"185. That would be far greater an injustice than that which the Housing Grants, Construction and Regeneration Act 1996 was enacted to remedy."

169 The adjudicator said:

"In the light of such guidance it is appropriate to record that if I came to the conclusion that I had not sufficiently appreciated the nature of any issue referred to me, I would not give a decision on that issue."

170 He said that undoubtedly the availability of more time would have refined the process of investigation but he went on: "I am confident of having understood the case of each party in relation to the principal issues."

171 In relation to the determination of quantum, which he acknowledged proved exceedingly complex and difficult, he said that what was important was that the figures and sums of money to be allowed or awarded individually should be approximately correct and should reflect the merits of the case. He concluded: "I consider that I have been able to do substantial justice between the parties and to arrive at an overall figure which reflects the merits of the case as I find them."

172 The adjudicator's assertion is disputed by Birse who say that in the decision the adjudicator concedes: "I fully accept had time been available Birse would have contended for greater deductions and CIB for lesser deductions in relation to allocated costs within the E3 account."

173 In my view, the test which the adjudicator set himself, namely that he could only reach a decision if (a) he had sufficiently appreciated the nature of any issue referred to him before giving a decision on that issue, including the submissions of each party, and (b) if he was satisfied that he could do broad justice between the parties, was impeccable.

174 He was also correct to acknowledge that if he had had more time he could have refined his decision further. That is inherent in this adjudication procedure. I still have to consider whether, in fact, he achieved his own standard.

Birse's contentions

175 I should set out Birse's criticisms in more detail. Birse contends first that no dispute had crystallised in relation to the demand. The stage had not been reached when CIB gave notice of adjudication where a point needed to be decided by an adjudicator. Birse makes this point both as a general submission and specifically on the basis of the contention that on 5 November 2003 the parties agreed to have further discussions to settle the dispute, which rendered premature the referral on 14 November 2000.

176 In relation to its claim that Birse was irredeemably prejudiced by CIB's conduct before the notice of adjudication, it relies on: (1) the alleged secret preparation for adjudication; (2) the alleged failure to refer to the possibility of an adjudication in correspondence with Birse; (3) after they decided to go to adjudication CIB allegedly gave the false impression that they were prepared to enter into meaningful discussions; (4) refusal to answer and/or dilatory conduct in answering Birse's questions; (5) the dilatory conduct in copying the 52 files; (6) the statement that they would consider further Birse's points made at the meeting on 5 November 2003; (7) the statement on 5 November 2003

that CIB would be providing further information in relation to its corporate structure.

177 Birse contends that the adjudication did not cure the overwhelming disadvantage arising from CIB's conduct. The adjudicator granted piecemeal extensions of time which did not cure the mischief. Birse suggests that if the adjudication had been timetabled to last 100 days at the outset it might have cured the problem.

178 In relation to claims that the adjudicators acted unfairly in the conduct of the adjudication, Birse makes complaint of the amount of time the adjudicator allowed for submissions on jurisdiction; the preparation of the response which was not as good a document as Birse would have wished to put forward; the tight timetable for expert evidence which was, as they put it, shoehorned into January 2004. This, it is alleged, was particularly the case with E3 which involved consideration of how CIB managed to spend such considerable sums over such a short period.

179 In relation to that particular issue, Mr Crowter said in oral evidence:

"I was able merely to make inferences as to the magnitude of the cost relative to the work that was left and draw inferences about the time it took but I was not able to quantify or understand why these things happened or understand the processes that had gone on after Birse left the site. Birse did not have that information other than the 52 files which were merely an audit trail to the money. There was no explanation as to how the money had been spent."

180 In relation to the size and complexity of the claim Birse relied on: (1) the fact that over £12m plus VAT and interest was claimed; (2) 49 files were filed with the referral notice containing 24 experts› reports on defects, 18 lever arch files of reports on quantum, and 16 witness statements; (3) a further 52 files relating to CIB›s E3 claim; (4) a further 55 files served by the parties in the course of the adjudication. (5) There were very significant issues to be considered in the course of the adjudication.

181 Birse claims that CIB was determined to have an award by the end of January 2004 or shortly afterwards.

182 Birse›s contentions in relation to the slip have been already fully set out. It is right to add, in relation to the slip, that in her final submission Miss Hannaford said that in the adjudication: «It has taken account of some deduction but not the total figure for the cost of remedial works.» Miss Hannaford explained the slip by saying that in para 14.20 Birse was not responsible for costs in category Z2, Z3 and Z4. She says that it follows from the finding that not only

the costs in category Z but those in Mr Hart›s category B and Mr Crowter›s categories B, X and Z should be deducted. Put another way, Miss Hannaford sees procedural unfairness in the adjudicator declining to express a view on whether or not he had made a slip and for that reason she says that the decision should not be enforced.

CIB›s contentions

183 CIB›s contentions can be summarised by saying that by 14 November 2003 Birse had had a proper opportunity to respond positively to the 30-day demand received by Birse at the latest by 6 August 2003. In relation to the claim of unfairness in starting the adjudication, CIB says that this was not unfair. The 2002 adjudication which Birse had started did not resolve the dispute because Birse would not concede that CIB was entitled to terminate the contract under clause 14.2.4. It was clear that at that stage both parties were looking to see what sums should be paid. The parties were, in effect, in dispute at that stage and this was acknowledged by both parties who agreed to have a mediation in March 2003.

184 Birse was put on notice in late 2002 that CIB reserved the right to take any steps to resolve the dispute and it must have been clear to them that this included adjudication. CIB says that the reason why Birse asked the various questions and failed to consider expeditiously the documents disclosed by CIB was that Birse was anxious to be able to say that the dispute had not been crystallised and, therefore, any adjudication would be premature. CIB contends that the dispute had crystallised long before 14 November 2003.

185 With regard to the adjudication itself, CIB says that the adjudicator took the initiative in the procedure as he was entitled to do. The timetable which extended the period of 42 days was agreed as a result of the meeting on 22 December 2003 when the 12-month timetable was put forward. It might have been a different position if Birse had refused any extension to the 42 day period and said that the issues were too complicated to be adjudicated in the time, but this was not the case here.

186 In relation to the claim that the adjudicator did not require full disclosure of documents, CIB contends that it was for the adjudicator to decide what documents he needs in order fairly to determine the issues before them. This he did in this case.

187 In relation to the issue of a slip Mr Ramsey, on behalf of CIB, argues that: (1) in his letter dated 19 March 2004 the adjudicator indicated that the figures in his adjudication represented his considered view; (2) the decision is explicable by the fact that the adjudicator was unable to accept in full either

of the experts> figures and came to his own conclusion which was properly reflected in his award; (3) in saying that he was prepared to review his decision if the parties agreed that he had made an error or that he would review it if the decision of the court was that he was required to do so, he was not making any concession or admission that he had, in fact, made an error.

Conclusions

188 I have already made a number of findings in the course of this judgment but it is appropriate to draw the findings together in a series of conclusions. These are as follows:

189 (1) I am satisfied that the claim notified by CIB on 28 July 2003 was disputed by Birse and that the dispute had crystallised by the date of the referral to adjudication on 14 November 2003. In the 15 intervening weeks there had been a proper opportunity for Birse to consider the claim and provide a constructive response which may or may not have led to further discussions. Instead, Birse attempted to manoeuvre tactically so that it could make the claim that the dispute had not crystallised. Both sides had, for a long time before the start of the adjudication, been engaged in tactical manoeuvres. Looking at the history it is impossible to conclude that Birse was ambushed by CIB.

190 (2) At the meeting between the parties on 5 November 2003 CIB may have said in general terms that it was prepared to have a further meeting with Birse but this was not on the understanding that it would delay any steps to enforce its rights, including adjudication, until such a meeting had taken place. CIB was entitled to refer the dispute to the adjudicator on 14 November 2003.

191 (3) The conduct of CIB before the notice of adjudication did not render the whole process unfair or put Birse at an overwhelming disadvantage. It is clear that this was a very complex dispute and that Birse would require more than the 30 days originally stipulated in which to consider the claim. There was a 15-week period in which Birse could have made a constructive response. CIB at all stages carefully reserved its legal rights. Birse was aware, although CIB did not make it explicit, that this included the likelihood of a referral to adjudication of part or all of the claim. At an earlier stage Birse itself had sprung an adjudication on CIB.

192 (4) In relation to the specific claims of bad faith made by Birse I conclude that CIB did not act in bad faith before the referral in not explicitly referring to the possibility of adjudication, in having discussions and taking part in the mediation and in relation to the copying of the 52 files, and also in relation to providing further information on corporate structure. CIB did not prejudice

the adjudication by conduct which rendered the adjudication which followed an unfair proceeding. Birse›s problems were largely caused by its own tactical decision to play for time.

193 (5) I have considered the conduct of the adjudicator, John Uff QC. At all stages he was careful to consider how he could conduct the adjudication fairly and he succeeded in doing so. He was mindful of his duty to ensure that both parties had a fair opportunity to put their case. I accept without reservation his assurances in his decision that if he had not felt able to reach a decision which was fair to the parties he would not have done so. It is acknowledged that adjudication is not a final proceeding and I find that, within the limits of an adjudication proceeding, the adjudicator fully discharged the duty not only to act fairly but to reach a fair determination on the evidence. In relation to the experts› issues, the adjudicator gave the parties a fair opportunity to deploy their cases before him. The adjudicator felt he was able to deal with the experts› issues on the basis of the evidence he received. I see no reason to doubt his judgment.

194 In the light of the decision of the Court of Appeal in *AMEC Capital Projects Ltd v Whitefriars City Estates Ltd* [2005] 1 All ER 723, handed down while this judgment was being revised, I should note that the Court of Appeal held that a party has no absolute right to make submissions on the issue of jurisdiction even though, if the adjudicator considers that he has jurisdiction, the immediate consequences set out in paras 9 and 11 of this judgment will follow. Birse›s challenge must also fail on this ground.

195 (6) The adjudicator was not bound to agree to Birse›s proposal at the hearing on 22 December 2003 that a timetable should be agreed, that there should be an extended procedure lasting one year or that adjudication should be followed by a dispute resolution procedure which would be concluded similarly by December 2004. He was acting entirely within his jurisdiction to set a timetable which he felt would enable the adjudication to be fairly concluded in the early part of 2004.

196 (7) The adjudicator was not bound to accede to Birse›s request for extensive disclosure made in the course of the adjudication. These requests were inappropriate and may well have been made largely for tactical reasons.

197 (8) It is clear that the claim was complex. If the adjudicator was to reach a fair decision he clearly needed more than the 42 days to which he was statutorily entitled under the Act (provided that the referring party CIB agreed). He sought and obtained the agreement of Birse to extensions of time which enabled him to reach a fair conclusion having given both parties a proper opportunity to put their case. Birse is not to be criticised for agreeing

to extensions of time but, having agreed them, this enabled the adjudicator to reach a decision on the matters referred to him after making a due and impartial enquiry.

198 (9) I appreciate that Birse has taken the position that it objected to the adjudication on the grounds that it was irrevocably prejudiced by CIB›s conduct and the complexity of the dispute which it had to deal with in a relatively short time. I have concluded that it was not prejudiced because (a) it had 15 weeks from the demand in which to make a substantive response and (b) in the course of the extended adjudication it had a full opportunity to make further investigations and to put its substantive case to the adjudicator within the limits imposed by the adjudication process, and it did so.

199 (10) I have already considered the question of whether there are some disputes, including this one, which are so complex that they are not suitable for adjudication. I conclude that this issue is governed by the Act. There is a general right under section 108(1) for a party to a construction contract to refer a dispute or difference to adjudication. There is a duty on the adjudicator to reach a decision provided that the conditions in section 108(2) are met. This means that the adjudicator must be able to discharge his duty to reach a decision impartially and fairly within the time limit stipulated in section 108(2)(c)(d). A defendant is not bound to agree to extend time beyond the time limits laid down in the Act even if such a refusal renders the task of the adjudicator to be impossible.

200 (11) I am doubtful how far I should investigate the alleged slip. In the Bloor case [2001] BLR 314 I reached the very limited conclusion that in certain circumstances an adjudicator may, on his own initiative or at the request of a party, correct an accidental error or omission. In this case Birse asks me to extend the principle to circumstances where the adjudicator declines to take any such step. I do not understand the adjudicator›s letter dated 19 March 2004, properly read, to constitute an invitation to the court to reach a conclusion in relation to the alleged slip and to indicate whether or not the adjudicator should correct it. Even if he had gone this far I should have to consider the adjudicator›s invitation in the context of the decision of Dyson J in *Bouygues (UK) Ltd v Dahl-Jensen (UK) Ltd* [2000] BLR 49, upheld by the Court of Appeal [2001] 1 All ER (Comm) 1041. The conclusion in that case was that if the adjudicator was answering the right question, the decision ought not to be reviewed. It seems to me that Parliament intended the procedure to be an interim procedure which, if carried out fairly and in a manner which is procedurally correct, is not subject to review by the court. I conclude that even if the adjudicator had invited the court to carry out a review the court should decline to do so. However, I do not understand the adjudicator›s letter to be making such a request but rather to be saying politely that if the court

concludes that he has made a slip and orders him to correct it, of course, he will do so.

201 As far as the merits of Birse›s contention are concerned I will merely give the indication that I incline to the view expressed by CIB that this was not a slip at all and that the decision is explicable by the conclusion that the adjudicator was unable to accept in full the figures of either expert and, doing the best he could, he came to his own conclusion which was reflected in his final monetary decision which was a sum substantially less than the original referral to adjudication of £14,687,205.63.

202 I conclude that the adjudicator›s decision should be enforced and order Birse to pay CIB the sum of £2,164,892.

An Overview of Legal Practice Worldwide

As Lord Phillips notes in his most generous Valedictory address, in 1964/5 I went to the University of Michigan Law School on a Ford Foundation Fellowship and a Fulbright Scholarship to take a Master's degree in Law. This was a formative time. A flavour of my experience in 1964/5 is to be found at the end of my lecture. In 1993 I was invited back to give the annual lecture founded in honour of Professor W William Bishop Jnr, late Professor of International Law and author of the leading student text book . In view of my positive and formative experience, it was appropriate that I should set out my core views on the worldwide legal profession at the University of Michigan Law School.

The lecture crystallised the view, much expressed in this book, that all lawyers are part of a worldwide legal profession, are to a greater or lesser extent interdependent, and that we need to view our activities in that context. I note in the lecture that it is the clients who are driving change in the legal profession. This continues to be the case with less-promising financial consequences for the lawyers (see "Ethical Rules and Professional Ideologies" p. 240). The concept of a world-wide legal profession is one that I carried with me in the Council of the Bars and Law Societies of Europe (CCBE) and the Academy of European Law (ERA). Both are Europe-wide institutions which also need to take account of the world outside. Many of the University of Michigan students go on to major international law firms and were a very enthusiastic audience. The lecture expanded the horizons of many in the audience including some of the law Professors who were present. It was published the following year in the *University of Michigan Law Quadrangle Notes* (1994) Vol 47, No 7, p 46. At this time the countries were part of the European Community (EC). I have preserved this distinction rather than use the current designation of European Union (EU). I have abbreviated the section on the legal framework in Europe which is covered extensively in "Avocats sans Frontières", p 172 ff.

Our Worldwide Legal Profession

In 1965 it did not make sense to talk about a worldwide legal profession. There were many different legal professions which, in the spirit of those times, had little need to harmonise their rules or consider what effect changes in the rules would have on the pattern of practice in other countries. Indeed, until the last few years, there was, except for a few specialists, little practical need for ordinary lawyers to study either the law or law practice in other countries.

What was until recently an academic pursuit of the few is now recognised as being of great practical importance to all of us. It is clear that we now have a worldwide legal profession and that it is developing at a considerable pace. Lawyers provide services for clients; clients respond to and take advantage of changes in the political and economic situation and in technology, thus driving change in the profession. In order to understand what our worldwide profession requires, it is necessary to look at the extent of the changes that have taken place.

The political and economic map has changed. On this continent, you now have the North American Free Trade Area. Recently, the GATT agreement was signed. Legal services are included in GATT as part of business services. The European Community (re-named the European Union in 1993 by the Maastricht Treaty) of six member states has enlarged to twelve, and is still growing. On January 1 1994, a number of the European Free Trade Association countries entered into close association with the full members of the EU.[1] Central and Eastern Europe are now part of the free world. This region has cooperation agreements with the EC and strong links with the United States and other countries. The Mercosul countries in South America-Brazil, Argentina, Uruguay and Paraguay – have formed their own free trade area. There are trading agreements in the Pacific Rim. In each case, there is increasing co-operation between nations and lowering of regional trade barriers, which allow law firms to expand and become multi-national.

The development of technology, particular computers, facsimile and voice mail, has made worldwide communications easier, not only for businesses but also for law firms. The world also seems a smaller place when satellites beam news around the world. For instance, the Rodney King trial and the Senate hearings of Judge Clarence Thomas received a great deal of television coverage in many countries.

---

[1]   Most members of the EFTA-Austria, Finland, Iceland, Norway and Sweden- joined the European Economic Association (EEA) as part of an enlarged trading market on Jan 1, 1994. Switzerland and Liechstenstein did not join.

Within the United States, the change in the pattern of legal practice has been marked. In 1965, the largest American law firm had about 175 lawyers. Now there are more than 200 US firms with 250 lawyers or more. Then, there were no national law firms in the United States. Now it is wrong to think, for example, of Winthrop Stimson Putnam and Roberts solely as a New York firm, or of Morrison and Foerster as a San Francisco firm. They have offices in other parts of the United States and the rest of the world. At least 12 firms in Detroit have out-of-state offices. Meanwhile the profession has grown in size. In 1971 there were 350,000 lawyers in the United States. Now there are over 900,000.

In Europe, too, there have been great changes, particularly in the last few years. Until 1970, English solicitor firms had a statutory maximum of 19 partners. Now there are at least 10 firms with more than a 100 partners. As a result of changes in the rest of Europe, there are large law firms in Germany and France and especially in the Netherlands which has a number of firms with more than 200 lawyers.

Throughput Europe, the practice of law is increasingly transnational. In 1965, there were two US firms with offices in London. By 1992, more than 50 of the 100 largest US law firms had offices there. This expansion of practice is not confined to Europe and the United States. It has taken place in all the major commercial centres of the world, particularly in the Far East.

There have been other changes for lawyers. In the 1960s, and indeed after, lawyers' privileges and immunities were accepted by politicians and the general public. Now, throughout the world, they have to be justified at the bar of public opinion. Law firms, particularly in the United States, are regarded as commercial enterprises. There is talk of "one-stop shopping"; a proposal in the United Kingdom for reform of the legal profession questioned why all professional services – legal, accounting, architectural, surveying etc – could not be provided by one partnership.

I am told that in the United States, lawyers are poorly regarded by the public. Former Vice-President Dan Quayle's speech at the 1991 American Bar Association convention, which was deeply critical of lawyers, was the most sympathetically reported speech he ever made. Lawyers' mystique is disappearing in other countries as well.

Something positive must take the place of that mystique. If there is contempt for lawyers, contempt for the law is not far behind. What is needed worldwide is a vigorous assertion of those values which are important for the functioning of the legal system so that these values are preserved in this time of rapid change. To do this, lawyers must play a constructive role in bringing about necessary change. It is, for example, a blot on the legal system that in most of the free world, the majority of citizens cannot afford to use the civil courts.

Increasingly, we lawyers are interdependent in thought and deed. What happens in one country will affect directly not only the practice in another country, but even the way in which lawyers are regarded in that country.

The speed of these changes in the pattern of legal practice has largely taken unawares those who regulate our profession. Yesterday, the movement of lawyers affected only a few and could be dealt with by informal arrangements. Now it is necessary to make clear the regulatory process by which lawyers can qualify as members of the bars in other countries; the rules of conduct which will apply when they visit other countries; whether they can establish branch offices abroad and, if so, what scope of practice they should be permitted to undertake.

In dealing with these questions, there is a need to understand each other's legal systems. Such an understanding is particularly important in Europe, where we have many different legal systems. There may be a good reason why a particular proposal causes difficulty in a country. For example, Germany and France give lawyers a monopoly on providing paid legal advice. There is no such monopoly for lawyers in the United Kingdom, Ireland and Belgium.

It is also important to understand that we are at the start rather than at the end of a period of rapid change for the profession. For example, there are at present only three foreign legal consultants registered under the Michigan Law, but it is not hard to see that foreign lawyers may wish to establish offices in Detroit to serve clients connected to the automobile industry, or in Kalamazoo for the pharmaceutical industry, or that there may be a need for greater interchange of lawyers across the Canadian border.

Shaping cross-border practice – the profession's role.

As the EC has developed, the legal profession in Europe has been forced, often unwillingly, to face up to problems in the profession and consider not only in a theoretical but also in a practical way how solutions can be found. The Council of the Bars and Law Societies of Europe (CCBE) plays a major role in insuring that the views of the legal profession are understood and taken into account when changes affecting the profession are considered by the European institutions and national governments.

The CCBE consist of national delegations from the legal professions of all twelve EC states and the countries in the EEA as full members; five other nations are observers.[2] This umbrella organisation represents the legal professions of

---

[2] EEA countries were admitted to the CCBE as full members on Jan 1, 1994. Observer countries are Switzerland, the Czech and Slovak Republics, Hungary and Cyprus.

these nations before the institutions of the EC and other international bodies. The CCBE delegates also meet to discuss topics such as multinational and multidisciplinary partnerships, access to justice, a common code of conduct for lawyers, the GATT round and alternative dispute resolution.

Professor Bishop taught me a very valuable lesson – that if negotiations are to succeed, they must not only be based on principle, but must also be practical. In discharging the duties of president of the CCBE, I found it was important to keep in mind at all times what is practical and what is possible when trying to reach a common position between a large number of legal professions operating different legal systems in different languages. Before the legal professions can influence others, they must reach agreement amongst themselves, however difficult that may be.

The legal framework in Europe.

The Treaty of Rome, as U-M Professor Eric Stein taught me, provides in Article 3(c) for the abolition of obstacles to the freedom of movement of persons, services and capital within the member states and prohibits discrimination on the grounds of nationality.[3] Under Article 52 of the treaty, restrictions on freedom of establishment by nationals of one member state in the territory of another member state should be progressively abolished; this applies specifically to professional activities. Under Article 59 there is a right to provide cross-border services. Article 54 and 57 (2) require the Council of Ministers of the Governments of Member States to issue directives on the mutual recognition of diplomas, certificates and other qualifications for the exercise of professions.

The general programme for the professions was originally set out in 1961. Progress toward these objectives was very slow. It wasn't until 1977 that the EC adopted the Lawyers' Services Directive (77/2491 EEC)which permits lawyers who are nationals of and qualified in one member state to provide a wide range of cross-border services including, in particular, giving legal advice on host state law.

In 1989, the Council of Ministers adopted a Directive on the Recognition of Higher Education Diplomas, also known as the Diplomas Directive (89/48/EEC). This directive, which applies to all professionals, has special provisions for lawyers. It outlines how EC member states must recognise relevant professional qualifications acquired in another state. Under the directive, an EC national admitted to the bar in a member state may, without examination, become a full member of the bar in another member state where the legal

---

[3]   Article 8(a) added by Article 13 of the Single European Act of 1986 establishes the specific aim of establishing the internal market by Dec 31, 1992. "The internal market shall comprise an area without internal frontiers in which the free movement of goods, persons, services and capital is ensured in accordance with the provisions of this treaty".

systems are similar. They may join the bar in a member state where the legal systems are different after taking a shortened version of the bar examination which takes into account relevant knowledge acquired in the home state.

There is one other piece of EC-wide legislation that is important for lawyers. In 1988, the CCBE unanimously adopted a code of conduct that applies to all cross-border dealings between EC lawyers. The code has been adopted by all the legal professions represented in the CCBE.

The joint committee of the CCBE and the ABA has compared this code with disciplinary rules in the United States. There are some differences, notably on contingency fees, but if there was a desire to have a code of general principles that applied to cross-border activities between EC and US lawyers, this could be achieved. The Japanese disciplinary code is also consistent with the principles in the CCBE code. A worldwide code would help to build confidence not only between lawyers, but also for their clients. When delegations from the American, European and Japanese legal professions met together for the first time ever at Évian-les-Bains in October 1993, they agreed that this task should be undertaken.

A practical proposal within the European Union.

To complete the freedom of movement for lawyers within the European Union, the CCBE has drafted its own directive giving a lawyer the right to establish an office in another member state and act as a legal consultant, carrying on a limited range of activities under his or her own title of qualifications. Such consultants would be subject to the host's professional rules and discipline and have the right to participate in host bar committees.

The draft directive is intended to help lawyers in border areas who wish to establish offices in the neighbouring state, and those who wish to provide a service for their own nationals residing in another member state as well as those who wish to carry on international practice from foreign offices in major business centres. Like all other EC directives, it applies to EC nationals who are members of a recognised EC profession but not to non-nationals, even if they are members of a bar or law society in a member state. Currently the CCBE and members states are discussing what the rights of non-EC lawyers should be, but at present there is no consensus on this question and it is difficult to achieve any consensus until the internal question is settled.

Although the EU draft directive will take time to be adopted and take effect, it will have a more immediate influence. In the event of a challenge to existing bar rules, the Court of Justice will look to the CCBE and Commission drafts when deciding if the rules can be regarded as objectively justified.

The US system.

Regulation of foreign lawyers in the United States has taken a different route. Unlike the European process, it is the courts in individual states – not the profession itself – which decide the questions of admission to practice in that state. At present, the number of foreign legal consultants is small- about only 200 are practising in the United States, of which about 170 are in New York. This compares with more than 500 in London and Brussels and just under 200 in Japan. The right for foreign lawyers to practice as legal consultants exists only in about 14 states, including Michigan. In half of the states, there is no reciprocity allowing interstate practice; lawyers from other states must pass the state bar exam to be admitted to practice, so it is argued that it is difficult to permit foreign legal consultants from other jurisdictions to establish offices as legal consultants albeit to undertake limited areas of work.

All the states permitting foreign legal consultants have a rule requiring a period of practice in the law of the home state before admission to practice as a foreign legal consultant. Many states require the practice to be undertaken exclusively in the country where the lawyer qualified. Foreign legal consultants generally may not advise on US states and federal law. In some states, however, they may do so if it is based on the advice of a locally-qualified lawyer. Formal requirements include due diligence investigations by the state bar to verify the status and suitability of the applicant.

Some states, particularly California and Texas, have indemnity insurance requirements with which it is almost impossible for foreign legal consultants to comply. As a result, there are only six legal consultants registered in California and only one in Texas. Some in the ABA, including former International Section chairs, Steven Nelson of Dorsey Whitney and Joe Griffin of Morgan Lewis and Bockius expressed concern that the lack of a general right to establish as a foreign legal consultant in the United States was inhibiting discussion for liberalising rules in other countries. They drafted the Model Rules for Foreign Legal Consultants which the ABA adopted as official policy in August 1993, although the actual decision to adopt the rules is a matter for each state alone.

The model rules are carefully drafted to leave residual discretion on admitting legal consultants to the competent authority of the host state.[4] Under the rules, the foreign lawyer should have five years' experience in the laws of the home state, but it could be obtained in offices outside the home state. As a result of the strong position taken by the CCBE and others, this requirement is not mandatory. A shorter period may be substituted, or the qualifying period may be omitted entirely.

---

[4]   See eg Michigan Code Article 5E(a)(1).

Article 1(c) and Article 2 preserve the right to make due diligence searches into the character of the legal consultant, rather than the due verification procedure. Article 1(d) has an age limit of 26, although it is optional. (Michigan has an age limited of 18.) Article 3 has a clause giving the right, but not the obligation, to make reciprocal treatment for members of the bar of a US state a precondition in accepting foreign legal consultants.(Michigan Code Article 5E(b) requires that Michigan lawyers should have a reasonable opportunity to practice in the applicant's jurisdiction). In discussions within the CCBE, there has also been a strong feeling that there should be some broad element of reciprocity.

Article 4 of the model rules permits a much narrower scope of activity than under the EC draft directive. Court work is excluded; legal consultation is confined to advice on foreign law, although advice on local law can be given if based on the advice from a locally-qualified lawyer. However, the forms of practice allowed under Article 5(b) are wider than in the EC draft, in that a foreign lawyer is entitled to employ locally qualified lawyers and take them into partnership. The explanatory memorandum to this rule says that it thinks only a limited number of foreign legal consultants will register. I disagree. I expect the movement of lawyers which is taking place increasingly in the rest of the world will also take place in the United States.

The model rules also contain provisions on discipline, application and renewal fees, revocation of licence, and admission to the bar. They do not deal with the problems of compliance with insurance requirements, which in some states are a significant barrier for foreign lawyers wishing to become legal consultants. The ABA's adoption of model rules is a positive and welcome step forward, although, as can be seen, much remains to be discussed before these basic differences in approach can be reconciled.

Beyond the Atlantic Area – the GATT Round.

Our worldwide legal profession does not, of course, only include Europe and the United States but also the rest of the world. Both the CCBE and the ABA and their governments have been having separate discussions on foreign legal practice not only with each other but also, particularly with the Japanese. These discussions have often taken the form of demands that the Japanese liberalise their rules for foreign legal consultants. Japanese rules are indeed too restrictive, but it is right to point out that foreign legal consultants are permitted to establish offices in Japan whereas they are not permitted to practice as such in the majority of US states, or in a number of countries in Europe.

At the insistence of the US Trade Representative, with the support of the ABA, legal services were included in GATT as part of business services.[5] European lawyers raised objections to this. On one occasion, the head of the Belgian delegation asked a senior representative of the EC Commission why he thought lawyers should be treated as traders in the same way as sellers of tomatoes. However, the EC Commission itself was sympathetic to keeping legal services in the GATS.

The CCBE had a choice to object to the inclusion of legal services and do nothing constructive, or to try to play a constructive role. We chose the latter. In our view, business legal services are essentially advisory services. Court-related activities are essentially participation in the process of justice and cannot properly be characterised as business services. If legal services were to remain part of the GATS, we argued that inclusion should be confined to advisory services and should not deal with questions of access as full members of the local profession, employment and partnership, which should be left to individual countries.

The United States in its discussions with the Japanese, in its Annex on Legal Services of Oct 3, 1990, took the opposite view and demanded extensive rights for foreign attorneys, including the right to recruit local lawyers as employees and to take local lawyers into US partnerships. The EC Commission took the position that the GATT should not regulate the status of lawyers as partners or employees, but should concentrate on activities. These activities should include advice on the law in which a person is qualified and on international law , but not local law. For this purpose, EC law was to be treated as local law.

At a private sector meeting with EC senior officials in 1991, I suggested that the CCBE could aid negotiations by meeting its counterpart professions in other countries, in cooperation with EC officials. Officials welcomed the idea, and, since then, the CCBE has had many discussions on the GATT Round with representatives of the ABA, the EC Commission and the US Trade Representative. Similar meetings were held with the Japanese.

There are, of course, many other countries in the world for which additional freedom for lawyers to provide services to their clients in other countries is of the greatest importance. It is dangerous to single out any in particular, but among others, Hong Kong, China, Singapore, Malaysia, Australia, New Zealand, Canada, Brazil and Egypt spring readily to mind. All interested countries must have the opportunity to take part in the detailed discussions. The experience of past discussions shows that we must strike a balance between the progress urged by the exporters of legal services and

---

[5] These are covered under the General Agreement on Trade in Services, known as GATS. Specific provisions for lawyers are contained in the Annexes on Legal Services prepared by the participating countries.

the concerns of the importers. We must understand the concerns of smaller countries which fear domination by the larger ones. The arrival of one lawyer from a small country in the third world in the United States or the United Kingdom should not necessarily trigger a large exodus in the opposite direction on the basis of reciprocity.

In my mind, I can hear Professor Bishop asking what is the practical method for obtaining more liberal offers in the GATS framework to extend the very limited liberalisation so far achieved. The present offers from the European Union, the United States and Japan provide a confusing patchwork. If other countries follow suit, the objective of progressive liberalisation will not be met. It also will be difficult to put pressure on those countries that do not wish to open their borders to foreign lawyers.

Taking into account the different views expressed at the historic Evian les Bains meeting with representatives of the Japanese, American and European legal professions, and at other meetings that I attended during my year as president of the CCBE, I believe it may be possible to form a consensus around the following positive proposals, which countries would be encouraged to offer as a minimum:

The scope of activities for foreign lawyers in other jurisdictions would be home state law and international law. (This would not include EC law for lawyers from countries outside the European Union.) In addition, foreign lawyers would be permitted to advice on third-country and local law provided it was based on the advice of an appropriately qualified lawyer.

The foreign lawyer would be required to register with the host bar, but have a right to be registered after fulfilling formal requirements. He or she would be subject to host rules and discipline, provided that they conformed with accepted principles of conduct.[6]

Where the present rules in any state are more liberal for foreign lawyers than the GATS rules, existing rules apply. This provision would apply, for example, in the United Kingdom.

Foreign qualified lawyers should be entitled to conduct all arbitrations except for purely domestic ones.

Courts will decide whether to admit a foreign qualified lawyer to plead a particular case before a domestic court or tribunal (as in the present system in the United States).

The foreign qualified lawyer practising from a branch of a firm should be entitled to use the name by which the firm is habitually known.

---

[6] Perhaps these principles could be similar to the Common Code of Conduct set out in my article in the *Fordham International Law Journal*, Vol 15, No 5, p 673 (1991-92).

An agreement by all the states in the GATT along the lines of these proposals would substantially liberalise the provision of legal services that support business services. It would create its own momentum for change. The requirements of clients inevitably would provoke additional liberalisation in those countries which offered only the minimum. In this area, it is much more important to start the process than to wait for years in the hope of achieving the perfect agreement.

I wish to end with a tribute to the farsightedness of the Law School Faculty. My year at the Law School was one of the most rewarding and enjoyable of my life. Professor Bishop, a brilliant teacher, who combined rigorous scholarship with a sense of fun, gave us a lesson in practical skills at my first seminar in international law. He gave us a treaty of friendship, commerce and navigation to construe, then told us that one clause meant "absolutely nothing but we had to put it in because the point had to be covered". He taught us the importance of working out in advance the practical future consequences of action taken on behalf of your client. I know that he was loved and revered not only by his students and fellow teachers, but also by his colleagues in the State Department where he served as legal advisor from 1939 -1947.

Professor Bishop was among a number of other remarkable teachers: Professor Paul Kauper teaching American Constitutional Law; Professor Jerry Israel teaching a seminar on the American law of free speech; Professor S Chesterfield Oppenheim teaching American antitrust Law; Professor Jackson giving a seminar on international trade law; Professor Whitmore Gray teaching a comparative law course on contracts and Professor Eric Stein teaching the law and institutions of the Atlantic area.

I never thought when preparing for Professor Stein's class that I would ever need to know about the GATT round, or even be directly involved in the EEC, since the United Kingdom had just been rejected for membership. There was no course similar to Professor Stein's anywhere in Britain. When I attended a seminar of law Professors and members of the European Court of Justice in 1991, it was agreed that a course along the lines of his was essential background for all lawyers in the EC, so you can see how far-sighted it was in 1965. The Faculty today continues to reflect in its courses the changing times in which we live. The professions regulatory authorities, too, must keep up with the pace of change; otherwise they will lose the respect of both the legal profession and the public.

[Editorial note: John Toulmin, Queen's Counsel, was a student of Professor William Bishop when he attended the U-M Law School as a foreign Ford Foundation Fellow and Fulbright Scholar in 1964-5. As the President of the Council of the Bars and Law Societies of Europe (CCBE), he returned to Ann Arbor as the William W Bishop Jr Fellow to give the 1993 Bishop Memorial Lecture on the international practice of law. This article is based on his lecture.]

Council of the Bars and Law Societies of the European Union (CCBE)

The second institution with which I have been involved is the Council of the Bars and Law Societies of the European Union (CCBE). The CCBE consists of delegations representing the member states of the European Union and national observer delegations. The United Kingdom delegation consists of a representative of the Bar and Law Society each of England and Wales, Scotland and Northern Ireland. In 1983 I became the English Bar's representative. In 1987 I became leader of the UK delegation, and I was elected Vice-President of the CCBE for 1991 and 1992 and then President in 1993. The task of the President is a difficult one. The internal task is to secure the maximum agreement among the national delegations of the Bars and Law Societies, each of which has different, and very often divergent, interests. The external task is to represent the views of all European lawyers before the EU Commission, the Council of Ministers, the European Court of Justice (the Luxembourg court), and the European Court of Human Rights (the Strasbourg court).

I had had good practice in this difficult art because I was leader of the United Kingdom Delegation between 1987 and 1990. During that time the English Bar and Law Society were on opposite sides of the reforms of the legal profession carried through by the then Lord Chancellor, Lord Mackay of Clashfern. I was proud that in the United Kingdom delegation we never even needed to have a vote. Indeed we submitted the only evidence agreed by all the Bars and Law Societies of England and Wales, Scotland and Northern Ireland, being a detailed paper on the impact of the proposed reforms from the European perspective.

The section on the CCBE is divided into two parts. The first three articles (pages 154 to 169) deal generally with my time in the CCBE, and particularly as President. The final three articles (pages 172 to 212) deal with the detailed negotiations in the Uruguay (GATT) Round and for the EU Lawyers' Establishment Directive.

As I said in my introduction, at the time when I assumed the Presidency, the CCBE was the subject of criticism from its constituent national Bars and its position was threatened by the Grands Barreaux. I start by giving a picture of the activities of the CCBE by including my Report of the Presidency from October 1992 to June 1993 (p. 154). The Report gives details of the work of the CCBE and the visits which I had undertaken as President.

It emphasises the need for a common approach to be agreed between the European Bars which make up the CCBE so that it can be put forward positively to the Commission and the other Community Institutions. It also emphasises the need for the CCBE to forge good relations between itself and those Institutions. Although the CCBE has grown in size, as the number of Member States has grown, these should remain cardinal priorities of the CCBE. The report goes on to set out the detailed work of the CCBE in 1992-3, including that undertaken by the new working parties set up under my Presidency on Legal Aid, Access to Justice, the Single Practitioner, ECO/Legal Audit, the Young Lawyer, and Human Rights.

I also include the English version of a speech made to the Deutscher Anwaltstag in Stuttgart in May 1993 (p. 165) as an example of a speech given to a national Bar Association. It was a rather formidable experience since I spoke immediately after Manfred Rommel, the legendary Mayor of Stuttgart, son of the Field Marshal, and a wonderful speaker. My German was negligible. I was told that if I spoke in English everyone would leave for an early lunch. I was fortunate to have the help of a German colleague, fluent in English, who provided a German translation. The audience even laughed at the jokes!

Finally, I also include the brief summary of the work of my year as President which I wrote for the Commemorative Book on the History of the CCBE, prepared for the special 50th Anniversary meeting of the CCBE in Basle in September 2010 (p. 167).

As Head of the UK Delegation to the CCBE from 1987-1990 a major part of my task was representing the Law Society of England and Wales. My father was a practising solicitor and I was very honoured in 1994 to be elected an Honorary Member of the Law Society of England and Wales. I was also very honoured in 1995 to receive the Grosse Ehrenzeichen für Verdienst of the Austrian Republic and to be elected a Senator of the Annual Vienna Bar Presidents' Conference.

Report of the Presidency on CCBE Activities

October 1992 – June 1993

Introduction

At the Standing Committee Meeting on 4th June 1993, attended by Heads of Delegations representing the Bars and Law Societies of the Member States and the 10 Observer Countries, we agreed, at the suggestion of the Presidency, that I should report directly to Bar Leaders and their Members on behalf of the Presidency on the work of the CCBE during the last six months and that I should report again at the end of my Presidency. Here is my report on the period since the CCBE Plenary Session in Lisbon from 22-25 October 1992.

Links with Member Bars -The Need for a Common Approach

Earlier this month my wife Carolyn and I were the guests of the Danish Bar at their meeting in Elsinore. It was attended by over 20% of the whole Danish legal profession. We felt very much at home. Not only could we see Hamlet's Castle from the hotel but there was a statue of Hamlet outside. Before speaking to the 600 Danish lawyers I listened (with the assistance of a translation from the First Vice-President, Niels Fisch-Thomsen) to speeches from the Minister of Justice and Jan Erlund, the President of the Danish Bar. The speeches had a familiar ring. The Minister of Justice told us that the Danish government had no additional money for legal aid and that in three years' time they would be ending the prohibition on estate agents doing conveyancing. Jan Erlund talked about the abolition of fixed fees for certain types of work. He also talked about multidisciplinary partnerships and the attempt of Arthur Andersen, the accounting firm, to provide a full range of legal services in opposition to the Bar. He also stressed the importance of developing good relations with the government so that the Danish Bar's views would be fully understood.

I suspect that similar topics might be discussed at Bar meetings anywhere in Europe. I was again struck forcibly by how many problems we all have in common and how important it is that they should be discussed within the CCBE representing as it does the Bars and Law Societies of the 12 member states and the ten observer countries -Austria, Cyprus, the Czech and Slovak Republics, Finland, Iceland, Hungary, Norway, Sweden and Switzerland. Where possible we should try to formulate a common approach to problems and at least be aware that similar problems exist in other countries.

It is becoming particularly important to try to achieve a common approach not only because the provision of legal services is becoming increasingly international but also because changes made in one country can affect the practice of law in other countries. For example, if multidisciplinary partnerships are permitted in one country and lawyers from that country set up a branch office in another country through which work can be referred to the first country, then multidisciplinary practice can effectively be introduced into the country where it is not permitted. Airlines are well aware of the hub system. If the rules are changed in one country, that country can be used as a base or hub for providing legal services in other countries in the same region. The American Bar Association and the accountants, Arthur Andersen, are making separate efforts both at EC level and at national level to obtain agreements which would permit US lawyers and accountants to provide a wide range of legal services within Europe. Within the EC, representatives of Ministries of Justice now meet regularly to discuss policies for the legal profession. Frequently, too, the legal profession comes within the remit of the national Department of Trade.

This underlines the need for close co-operation between the Members of the CCBE and good relations between the CCBE and the EC Commission. We need not be too defensive in our attitudes. I have found that the view of officials in the 1980s, as Robert Boccart (then Head of the Belgian Delegation now Dean of the Belgian Bar) described it, that "lawyers should be treated like sellers of tomatoes", seems to have given way to a rather more balanced view of the legal profession by non-lawyers. Certainly when dealing with non-lawyers in the EC Commission I have found an impressive willingness to understand the particular position of the legal profession and to take it into account when formulating policy.

I started my speech in Elsinore by saying that the CCBE is increasingly discussing the subjects which affect lawyers generally. It is important that the Presidency of the CCBE should have an opportunity to visit Member Bars, to speak, and to listen, so that we have a feel for the problems which affect all practising lawyers and take these fully into account when discussing priorities within the CCBE, and, in particular in order to seek common approaches to problems which can be presented to the EC Institutions.

Fortunately there has been a general wish on the part of the Delegations to bring this about. Since I was elected President in Lisbon last October, I have spoken to a Conference of Italian and United Kingdom lawyers in Bologna, to Spanish lawyers in Barcelona, to Austrian lawyers and Bar Leaders at the Vienna Presidents Conference, to lawyers from all over Europe at the Europac Conference in Brussels, to French avocats in Paris, to lawyers from the North of England in Manchester, to Scots lawyers in Edinburgh, to German lawyers in Stuttgart and to Danish lawyers in Copenhagen. Before the end of the year I shall have spoken to Spanish lawyers in Madrid, Czech lawyers in Prague, English solicitors in Stratford-on-Avon and in Brighton as well as to American lawyers at the American Bar Convention. All three Members of the Presidency regard these visits as an essential as well as a rewarding part of our work. We are very happy to accept such invitations if our expenses are paid. The number of visits is such that clearly the cost can no longer come out of CCBE funds.

Before moving to specific topics I should add that as the provision of legal services becomes increasingly pan-European and international and as the importance of EC Regulations grows for all lawyers, the essential work of the CCBE is increasing and will do so even more after the Maastricht Treaty and the enlarged European Economic Area take effect. The first will add access to justice as an EC responsibility. The second will mean that the countries in the enlarged area must also be directly represented before the EC institutions.

The Working of the Presidency

In 1991 a new system was instituted under which the President had two years as Vice-President before taking office. My predecessor Jose Manuel Coelho Ribeiro started to develop what could be described as a "rolling Presidency" where the two VicePresidents were increasingly involved in the work of the Presidency. This has been taken further this year and Niels Fisch-Thomsen and Heinz Weil have been fully involved in all the work of the Presidency. It means that there is a proper identity of purpose in each Presidency and continuity of policy from year to year. The Presidency of the CCBE now involves 80% of the President's time and a very substantial amount of time for the two Vice-Presidents. I should like to pay tribute to them for their great help and support. It is also becoming extremely difficult for the very small secretariat to cope effectively with the range of work which the CCBE must undertake if it is fully to represent the European legal professions. The staff with Mrs Janice Webster as Director is small and dedicated but overstretched. I would like also to acknowledge the work of the Delegations and the Special Committees, in particular the Finance Committee, in what has been a demanding six months.

The Detailed Work of the CCBE

European Economic Area

At the Plenary Session in Manchester on 23 April 1993 the CCBE statutes were changed so that those countries which join the EEA will automatically become full members of the CCBE. For many years representatives of the Observer Countries have played an important part in our work. This change is in line with the Policy of the EC Commission as well as being the unanimous wish of the full Member Delegations.

Multidisciplinary Practice and Multinational Practice with non-EC lawyers

As became evident at the Danish Bar Meeting and also in discussions which I have had on my visits to other Bars and Law Societies, these are important topics for all lawyers since changes in the rules will affect the shape of legal practice for all lawyers. We had a lengthy debate at the Plenary Session in Manchester on both topics. There appears to be a clear consensus against cross-border multidisciplinary partnerships. All Delegations have been asked to send their views to the office in Brussels by 1st September so that a detailed policy paper can be prepared for debate at the Plenary Session in Brussels in November. There was a similar debate in Manchester (and a similar timetable for a policy paper) on forms of association with lawyers from outside the EC where there was no unanimity except that there was a general feeling that rights should only be given on a broadly reciprocal basis. There were those who feared the over-commercialisation and over-litigiousness of US firms. Others took a contrary view. We take these views fully into account when we represent the CCBE in discussions with outside bodies. We hope, however, that a clearer position can be achieved at the end of the Consultation period.

Draft Establishment Directive on Rights of Establishment for EC lawyers

The CCBE draft Directive on Rights of Establishment for lawyers was passed by 10 votes to two in Lisbon, Luxembourg voting against because the draft was too liberal; Spain voting against because it was not liberal enough. The Presidency formally presented the draft Directive to the Director of DGIII, M. Riccardo Perissich, on 9th December 1992. He told us that it was part of the work programme of the Commission for 1993. This was confirmed by Sir Leon Brittan in a letter to me dated 25th February 1993. The EC Commission has virtually completed its own draft and it should be published within the next two months. [It was not published until December 1994, see Chapter 14 below.] Thereafter it will go to the Council of Ministers and the European Parliament.

The attitude of the Member States is of crucial and continuing importance. We were fortunate that under the United Kingdom Presidency, on 1st October 1992 the Ministers of Justice agreed that the CCBE draft provided a constructive basis for discussions and that they would not make their own proposals for an Establishment Directive until they knew whether or not the CCBE draft would be passed. Before the detailed work of drafting the Directive was undertaken by the EC Commission, officials from the Ministries of Justice were again consulted about the draft Directive at a meeting with the Commission on 1st April 1993. They gave a positive response. Once the draft appears from the Commission, the speed of progress will depend on the Council of Ministers and, in particular, on the Government which holds the Chairmanship of the Council of Ministers. We have already had a meeting with the Belgian government which takes over the Presidency on 1st July 1993. Another meeting is planned for July.

The role of the Parliament and, in particular, the Legal Affairs committee is also of vital importance. On 25th March 1993 we had a meeting with M. Reinhold Bocklet and M. Ricardo Passos, respectively President and Secretary of the Legal Affairs Committee of the European Parliament, who told us that we should have an opportunity to give evidence to the Committee when they considered the Commission's draft later in the year. The Directive must be debated by the European Parliament before it can be adopted. The opinion of the Legal Affairs Committee will be of considerable importance.

Bangeman Initiative

In Lisbon on 25th October 1992 we received for the first time a proposal from DGIII for a new form of joint cross-border practice between professionals. The proposals, as they were presented to us, were not welcomed by the CCBE Delegations who much preferred the CCBE draft Directive. Led by Niels Fisch-Thomsen we produced a detailed submission within the very short three week deadline. The project is not at present being proceeded with by the Commission.

Draft Directive for Defective Services

This draft Directive has given cause for uncertainty as to whether it applies to the legal profession and concern that it would reverse the burden of proof in negligence cases involving damage to persons through injury.

The Secretary of the Legal Affairs Committee of the European Parliament has told us that because of the many proposed amendments to the draft, including those suggested by the CCBE, and the widespread dissatisfaction with it, the Commission has decided to withdraw it for the time being. It may be re-introduced in a completely different form or it may not re-appear at all. It seems to have been accepted, at least for the present, that the legal profession should be excluded from the Directive.

VAT

Following on the CCBE Resolution, passed at Barcelona on 25 April 1992, the question of the possibility of exempting legal services from VAT, or recommending putting them in the lowest possible banding, particularly in relation to legal aid work, was pursued with the Commission.

On 28th October 1992 we received a letter from Sebastian Birch, chef de unité of DG XXI-C3 explaining that the Commission had taken note of the CCBE's views and would take them into account at the first opportunity for review which would be in 1994. Work must be started soon to ensure that we make effective representations in the forthcoming review. One point of principle that has arisen is whether (as in Belgium) it is permissible to charge different rates of VAT for locally qualified lawyers and legal consultants (including those from other Member States).

Lawyers from Countries outside EC

(a) GATT Round

Legal services are included in the GATT Round as an integral part of business services. For the last five years we have been in regular discussion with the EC Commission on this subject .

We have had two meetings with the EC negotiators on 28th January 1993 and 24th March 1993 who maintain the position (which the CCBE has also taken) that discussions should be confined to those services which can be said to be an adjunct to business services, namely the right to give legal advice on the law in which a lawyer is qualified and on international law but not local law. EC law is regarded as part of local law. It is expected that now that Peter Sutherland has taken over as Director of the GATT, these discussions will enter a more intensive phase. Reservations have been maintained for those Member States with particular rules. The discussions are of vital importance because they affect not only the right of access for EC lawyers to practice outside the EC but the right of non-EC lawyers to practise in the EC. I have written formally to Sir Leon Brittan pointing out that at present the proposals for liberalising services only apply to incorporated bodies and not to individuals and partnerships and are therefore ineffective in assisting European lawyers where practices are largely unincorporated. In the United States practices are increasingly being incorporated. I have also pointed out that it was always intended that the GATT Round would not deal with the question of how the right to give legal advice should be delivered and therefore that the Commission's offer was not intended to signify agreement throughout the Member States to MNPs, MDPs or the right of foreign legal consultants to employ locally qualified lawyers.

(b) United States

The CCBE Special Committee met the American Bar Association (ABA) Special Committee in Brussels on 16th January 1993. This, again, is one of a series of meetings that have taken place over the last four years. The policy of the ABA and the US government is to secure increased access for US lawyers in Europe either through the GATT Round or in bilateral negotiations with different Bars or Governments in Europe. Until this meeting there had been no proposals from the United States to liberalise the restrictive position in the United States (access for foreign legal consultants in only 14 states, many with very restrictive conditions, and only 200 foreign legal consultants in the whole of the United States). At this meeting members of the ABA Sub-Committee produced a draft Model Rule which, if adopted, would significantly liberalise the right of foreign legal consultants to establish offices in the United States. 'A considered response was sent to the EC Commission on 23rd June 1993 after a draft had been distributed to all Delegations for comments. These questions will be further discussed at the ABA Meeting in New York in August. The German government decided to discontinue separate negotiations with the US when they realised that they might be inconsistent with the general approach being worked out through the Commission and the CCBE.

(c) Japan

Since 1989, pressure has been put on the Japanese government and the legal profession both by the United States Government and by the EC Commission to liberalise the existing rules on foreign legal consultants. The present round of discussions started in the late summer of 1992. I prepared briefing papers for the Commission in advance of a joint visit by the Commission and the EC legal profession to Tokyo on 16th and 17th December 1992. In two days of discussions with the Japanese government, the Japanese legal profession, and the Independent Study Commission set up by the Japanese government, we made proposals for changes which would enable foreign legal consultants to practice more effectively in Japan. This visit was followed up by a visit from the Japanese to Europe in April/May 1993 in the course of which they met the Presidency of the CCBE and the legal professions in France, Germany, Netherlands, Belgium and the United Kingdom in separate meetings. The Japanese Delegation presented the CCBE with a questionnaire which has been answered. Also a paper analysing the issues was sent to the Commission on 23rd June 1993. The Japanese have made a positive general response to the general negotiating position of the CCBE. The way to make real progress (both in relation to discussions with the United States and Japan) may well be to consider forms of co-operation short of employment and partnership. The particular relevance of these discussions (as with those with the Americans) is that any agreement will affect discussions over foreign legal consultants from all other non-EC countries. There is no general agreement within the CCBE, that within the EC, lawyers from outside the EC should be permitted to enter into partnership with EC lawyers or to employ them.

Legal Aid

This is a subject that affects all lawyers. In most countries the civil courts are simply not available to ordinary citizens to settle their disputes. The remark of the Danish Minister of Justice in Elsinore, that there is no additional money in Denmark for legal aid, is illustrative of a problem which faces governments and legal professions all over Europe. This problem needs to be tackled by Bars and Governments in partnership. The CCBE is involved in preparing a handbook and a technical report on cross border legal aid with funding and the active co-operation of the EC Commission. The project is being undertaken by David Walters for the CCBE and is being looked after on behalf of the CCBE by Peter Baauw from the Netherlands. The work has been completed within the time limit and will be relied on by the Commission in its Green Paper on Access to Justice to be published in the Autumn. It is proposed to hold a debate at the Plenary Session in Brussels so that the CCBE can formulate its own policy on this subject that vitally affects the legal profession. Legal Aid is also the subject of a working group chaired by Peter Baauw.

Access to Justice and ADR/Quality of Service

Aspects of access to justice apart from legal aid are also of the greatest importance to all lawyers and are the concern of a new special working group chaired by Ramon Mullerat from Spain. Their tasks include quality of legal service. The working group is making contact with the new Section of the ABA dealing with Alternative Dispute Resolution. Discussions will take place at the UIA Convention in San Francisco with Robert Raven, Chair of the ABA Section. On 27th March 1993 the Presidency had a very constructive meeting with Mme. Suzanne Jessel, in charge of the unit in DGIII which has been set up in anticipation of the ratification of the Maastricht Treaty, and with Mr Dieter Hoffman of the Consumer Policy Unit. This will be an area of increasing importance once Maastricht has been ratified and one in which the legal profession must play an important role.

The Single Practitioner

This working group is chaired by Sotiris Felios of Greece. It will examine the particular role and problems of small firms and single practitioners who are the majority of the lawyers in each of the Bars in the CCBE. The Consumer Affairs division of the Commission is becoming interested in this subject which is of growing importance.

ECO/Legal Audit

This working group is chaired by Steffen Juul of Denmark. It is becoming increasingly important to protect the environment. One method of achieving this for companies to carry out an environmental audit either as a voluntary or as a compulsory requirement. The role of lawyers in the environmental audit process has not been sufficiently emphasised in either EC legislation or in similar legislation in Norway and Sweden. This working group is in the process of finalising a policy report which will be debated at the Plenary Session in Brussels. The intention is to press for a specific role for lawyers in ensuring that the legal requirements imposed by environmental legislation have been complied with.

The Young Lawyer

The initial task of this working group chaired by John Fish of Ireland is to monitor the EC Diplomas Directive. A number of countries have not yet implemented the Directive under which lawyers who are nationals and members of one Member State can become full members of the Bar or Law Society of another Member State. Within the constraints of very limited resources the Committee will undertake further work relating to the position of young lawyers in our profession. The problems are becoming more acute with the increasing numbers of young people who wish to join the profession and the decreasing amount of work that is available at a time of general recession. A nominated member of AIJA, the worldwide young lawyers association, sits on this Committee. Other important topics to be studied include the need for all lawyers within EC/EEA to be qualified in EC law.

Human Rights/Council of Europe

This special Committee chaired by Louis Schiltz of Luxembourg has had two meetings with the Commission on Human Rights and the Council of Europe. The first task is to make submissions on the reorganisation of the Commission and Court of Human Rights and the new rules of procedure which must follow. The Council of Europe has programmes to assist those living in Central and Eastern Europe including lawyers. I spoke at one of them in Vienna in February 1992. We are discussing with the Council of Europe how the CCBE can best participate in such programmes.

Comité de l'Est

This Committee led by Leo Spigt of the Netherlands has performed a number of important tasks. It has reported on the application for Hungary's admission to the CCBE as a result of which Hungary's application for observer status was approved at the Plenary Session in Manchester. It is considering the application of Poland.

On 18th December 1992 it held a mini-summit in Prague with representatives of Central and Eastern Europe Bars. On 26th March 1993 the Presidency met with Ms. Karen Fogg and Mr Kalbe at the EC Commission to discuss ways in which the CCBE, in partnership with the Commission, can assist the legal professions in Central and Eastern Europe. A pilot scheme for assistance to Estonia and Rumania was approved by the EC Commission at the end of April under the Phare Democracy Programme. In addition the Dutch government has most generously given 50,000 Guilders (about £15,000) so that we can investigate the needs of the legal professions in Central and Eastern Europe and see how we can help. Work has already begun on the projects. The Committee is careful not to duplicate the excellent work done by many Bars and Law Societies in this area.

It will appear from this and the previous item that both the EC Commission and the Council of Europe are active in helping in Central and Eastern Europe. We are surprised that the two organisations have so little contact with each other.

Deontology

The Committee dealing with the CCBE Code of Conduct is led by Heinz Weil, the Second Vice-President. The Common Code, adopted for cross-border activities by the Member States and the Observers in 1988, has been one of the great successes of the CCBE in recent years. The Committee is monitoring the implementation of the Code of Conduct within the Member States and the Observer States. It is also considering whether any more detailed rules can be recommended for lawyers' cross-border advertising. This is an important subject in view of the spread of multinational associations within the Member Countries. The Committee is also maintaining links with the IBA which is working on worldwide rules of professional conduct.

The Special Committee at the Court in Luxembourg

This Committee is chaired by Mary Finlay SC of Ireland. In the past the Committee has had detailed discussions with Judges and officials at the Court of Justice on the setting up and detailed rules of the Court of First Instance and the notes for guidance in the oral procedure. They have also had discussions on notes for guidance on the written procedure. A Committee of the Court of Justice under Judge Zuleeg is completing its draft notes for guidance on the written procedure which will be discussed with the Special Committee. The Committee was involved with the Court in organising a very successful seminar in Luxembourg for young lawyers in November 1992 and the CCBE has been asked to provide judges for a moot competition for students to be organised in conjunction with the Court.

Other Special Committees

The Special Committees on Competition Law chaired by Alain Desmazieres de Sechelles of France and Company Law chaired by Henning Rasner of Germany, have also been working in their specialist areas.

CCBE Meetings

The CCBE held a very successful Plenary Session in Manchester from 23-26 April 1993. We are extremely grateful to the United Kingdom Bars and Law Societies and the Northern Circuit and Manchester Law Society not only for their very generous hospitality and support but also for their participation. I have covered the main subjects discussed and decisions taken elsewhere in this Report. In addition the Heads of Delegation have held four meetings in Brussels to carry forward our work.

Conclusion

We are anxious that the work of the CCBE should be as widely known as possible. It should reflect at European level the wishes and concerns of the profession. It should not attempt to do those things that can best be done by national or local Bars or Law Societies. Nor is it an academic organisation engaging in abstract research. On the other hand the increasing number of decisions affecting the legal profession which are made in Brussels makes it imperative that the CCBE is strengthened in order that the legal profession as a whole can be represented effectively before the EC Institutions and the Institutions in Strasbourg. It has many of the same tasks to perform at EC level that other Bars have to perform in their own areas. It is well understood by a number of Delegations that the CCBE will in due course need additional resources if it is to discharge its responsibilities to the profession effectively.

Inevitably we rely on the Delegations to consult with their Members on important matters of policy and to report to them on the activities of the CCBE. We are always looking for ways in which the work of the CCBE can be made more relevant to the needs and concerns of the Profession and better known to lawyers who are not active in the work of their own Bars and Law Societies. All ideas will be very welcome. There is much to do in the second half of this year and I shall report to you again at the end of my Presidency at the end of the year.

John Toulmin QC
President of the CCBE

Speech to the Deutscher Anwaltstag in Stuttgart, 21 May 1993

It is a very great honour for me as President of the CCBE to represent the European legal profession at this great Anwaltstag. The German legal profession has always played a leading role in the work of the CCBE. I think in particular of the contributions of Dr Heinrich Huchting, former President of the CCBE, and Dr Hans-Jürgen Rabe with whom I have worked closely on the Standing Committee at the Court in Luxembourg and of Dr Heinz Weil, 2nd Vice-President of the CCBE who will be President in 1995, Dr Hans-Jürgen Pohl, Head of the German Delegation and leading member of the Finance Committee and Dr Norbert Westenberger, who has undertaken a number of important tasks including co-ordinating work on the E.C. Diplomas Directive.

I am grateful for the great support which the work of the CCBE receives from the German profession. The work which we do is of increasing relevance to all lawyers. The themes of this year are, first, that we, as lawyers must remain independent, free from unnecessary interference by the State. Secondly, we are increasingly interdependent. Changes which occur in the structure of the profession in one Member State increasingly affect other Member States, Thirdly, we must be concerned at the difficulty of ordinary citizens obtaining justice within a reasonable time and at a price which we can afford and fourthly, we must do what we can to support the emerging legal professions in Central and Eastern Europe.

Lawyers have never been well liked by the public. There is a joke in England that two old people were visiting the churchyard of an old church. They saw a gravestone on which was written "Here lies a lawyer and an honest man". One old gentleman turned to the other and said, "How surprising it is that in this village they have buried two people in the same grave." In the United States I am told that lawyers have a lower status than croupiers in casinos. They are not regarded as being helpful. Two travellers were in a hot-air balloon. They got lost. They saw someone on the ground and asked the person where they were. The person looked up and said, you are in a hot-air balloon", One balloonist turned to the other and said, 'The person on the ground must be a lawyer. The answer was 100% accurate and 100% useless." It is not enough any longer for lawyers simply to claim special rights and privileges. They must be justified. If they are justified lawyers are better thought of and listened to and better able to preserve their independence (which is, in fact, a necessary element in a free society). This applies both at EC and at national and *Länder* level. Our experience has been that if you do produce a reasoned case the Commission will listen constructively and help if they can. This has happened over our draft Establishment Directive. The Directive was passed by the CCBE in Lisbon by ten votes to two. The Commission has adopted it in its work programme for 1993. Dr Christiane Kirschbaum, a *Rechtsanwalt*, is responsible at the Commission for doing the official draft. We hope that it will be approved by the Council of Minsters by the end of this year.

It is now essential that we develop the policy on the establishment of lawyers who come from outside the EC. This is necessary both in the context of the GATT Round and of the bilateral discussions which are continuing with the United States and Japan. It is also necessary because lawyers from outside the EC do want to establish offices within the EC We also need to develop a reasoned policy on cross-border multi-disciplinary partnerships (MDPs). Since lawyers are moving in increasing numbers across EC boundaries we are all interdependent. Changes in one Member State will affect the rest of us. The position of MDPs in Germany is of particular importance in our discussions. We are hoping to discuss policy papers on these issues at the next plenary session in Brussels in November.

Access to justice is also of great importance to us all. Later this year the CCBE will be publishing a comparative study on cross-border legal aid which has been commissioned by the EC Commission. I have no doubt that it will show how difficult it is for ordinary citizens to have access to the Courts. In the debate which is already taking place the legal profession must play a constructive role. Our views must be heard and understood by governments. In reaching our conclusions we must learn from each other's legal systems.

Thirty years ago next month I was in Berlin in front of the Rathaus Schönberg when President Kennedy made his *"Ich bin ein Berliner"* speech (it should, of course, have been *"Ich bin Berliner"*). This was a remarkable occasion. What made an even greater impression on me was my visit to Bernauerstrasse where I saw the flowers marking the places where those had died because they wanted to be free. It is wonderful to me that the wall has come down and that East Germany is part of Germany. We must do all we can to help the others who are also free, the legal professions of the newly independent States of Central and Eastern Europe.

In a few weeks I shall write a fuller account of the work of the CCBE which will, I hope, be translated into German and be available for everyone to read. I have found that during my time in the CCBE, lawyers from the different Member States have drawn increasingly closer together. That gives me great hope not only for lawyers but also for Europe.

Thank you very much for inviting me to this great conference and for giving me the privilege of speaking to you.

Report in 2010 by His Honour Judge John Toulmin CMG, QC on his CCBE Presidency in 1993

(Published by the CCBE ion its 50th Anniversary)

1993 was a significant year. My two Vice Presidents, Niels Fisch-Thomsen and Heinz Weil, to whom I owe a great debt of gratitude, and I worked very closely together. The year started with a planning meeting which included Janice Webster, the tireless Secretary-General. There was a fundamental problem. We had to demonstrate that the CCBE was credible and representative of the European legal profession so that in subsequent years it could be funded sufficiently to carry out its necessary tasks. Thanks to Niels and Heinz, the delegations and many individual contributions we made substantial progress. Control of finance is vital. Heinz Weil and the Finance Committee led by Hans-Jürgen Pohl put proper procedures in place and we ended the year with reasonable reserves.

The immediate task was to progress the Draft Directive on Rights of Establishment agreed in Lisbon on 23 October 1992. We had to ensure that it was approved and adopted by the Council of Ministers as part of the working programme. This occurred at the Ministerial Meeting on 1 April 1993.

The second task was to represent the European legal profession in the discussions on the GATT (Uruguay) Round. I led for the CCBE from late 1989 and had the responsibility for discussions with the EU Commission. Uniquely, at the invitation of the EU Commission negotiators Ambassador Paeman and Arnaud Bordes, the CCBE collaborated closely in the negotiations. In 1992-3 there were meetings in Japan in December 1992, with representatives of the ABA in January and August 1993, a special meeting with the US and Japanese lawyers' delegations and Trade Representatives at Évian-les-Bains in October 1993, and many meetings with the EU negotiators.

I was delighted that, contrary to the wishes of the Japanese, and without any support from the US, legal services were included in the World Trade agreement. This opened the way for lawyers to represent their clients and establish offices worldwide. If legal services had been excluded, this would have encouraged worldwide legal protectionism.

In January 1993 there were 12 Member States and 10 Observer countries in the CCBE. At the Manchester Plenary Session we changed the Statutes and welcomed Iceland and Hungary as Observer members and paved the way for Austria Sweden and Iceland to become full members from 1 January 1994.

There were many meetings with the European Institutions, including the European Court of Justice and the Court of Human Rights, and many others including generous invitations from national Bars and Law Societies. Perhaps the most significant was the European Bar Presidents' Conference in Vienna where for the first time the CCBE was given special precedence as the representative of the European Legal Profession. There were also successful meetings in Barcelona, Paris, Edinburgh, Nicosia, Stuttgart, Elsinore, London, New York and Auckland New Zealand. At the final plenary session in Brussels, after extensive discussions, we approved multi-national partnerships and unanimously rejected multi-disciplinary partnerships. Earlier, Niels Fisch-Thomsen provided a detailed response which helped to stifle a proposal by Commissioner Bangemann for a new form of cross-border practice between professionals.

Legal Aid and Access to Justice was a major priority. In a project masterminded by Janice Webster and Peter Bauuw, and funded by the EU Commission, David Walters prepared a hand-book on Legal Aid. There were successful working groups on Access to Justice, the Problems of the Single Practitioner, Environmental Audit, the Young Lawyer and the Working of the EU Diplomas Directive, and standing committees on the Luxembourg Court, the Strasbourg Court, Competition Law, Company Law, and Deontology.

Leo Spigt's Committee de L'Est secured generous financial assistance from the EU Commission and the Dutch Government to assist legal professions in Estonia and Rumania and to support those in Central and Eastern Europe.

What a privilege it was to be President of the CCBE. My wife Carolyn and I look back on wonderful friendship and hospitality and a very special year in our lives. Congratulations to the CCBE on its 50th birthday!

The Lawyers' Establishment Directive and the GATT

This part of the section on the CCBE is concerned with the detailed negotiations in the GATT Round in which I was involved from 1989 and which were completed in December 1993, and the Lawyers' Establishment Directive which, after a tortuous history starting in 1988 was finally adopted in 1998.

"Avocats sans Frontières" is the speech which I gave at the launch of the European Circuit of the English Bar on 22 March 2001(with minor edits). It sets out the history of the two negotiations, the first being my conduct on behalf of the CCBE of the negotiations in the Uruguay (GATT) Round on behalf of the European Legal Profession and secondly, as a leading participant, in the negotiations on the Lawyers' Establishment Directive. If either had taken a different course, it would have stultified the provision of legal services as a necessary support to the spread of commercial activity within the European Union and worldwide.

The speech, setting out the history of the negotiations, sheds light on the inter-action between a non-government organisation, ie the CCBE, and two different Directorates of the Commission, and also on the differing approaches of the Commission to the GATT negotiations and the Draft Lawyers' Establishment Directive. An interesting sidelight in such negotiations (and other dealings with public bodies) is that it sometimes appears that an official is rejecting the case which you are putting forward because it is not consistent with current EU Commission policy. Sometimes, in fact, the official is delighted to receive the point of view because it strengthens internal arguments in favour of your position. These negotiations were, perhaps, the most important politico-legal tasks that I undertook in my career.

The tri-partite discussions in the GATT Round in Évian-les-Bains on 15-16 October 1993 with representatives of the United States' and Japanese legal professions and the professional negotiators, referred to in section 16 of the speech, came about as the result of positive support from the EC Commissioner, Sir Leon Brittan, and a very senior EC official, John Richardson. The discussions were the subject of a long article in "The American Lawyer" by Karen Dillon in the April 1994 edition. In a very fair report, she emphasised that the purpose of the American delegation was to put pressure on the Japanese delegation to accept multinational partnerships in Japan. It was clear to me at a very early stage in the discussions that there would be no meeting of minds because of the problems which each delegation had, and which I set out in my speech, and which are also set out in Ms Dillon's article. I say in my speech that I did not regard the talks as a failure. In her article Ms Dillon reports my conclusion that the talks "cleared up a lot of misunderstandings" but that the time between the end of the talks and the end of the Uruguay negotiations in December 1993 did not leave enough time to arrive at a consensus. I was not unhappy with the result. I was clear in my own mind that so long as legal services remained in the GATT Round, further liberalisation would inevitably occur in due course.

There were many problems in achieving progress in the Uruguay Round. It was only human nature that lawyers should wish to preserve their own cherished practices while, at the same time, urging others to liberalise theirs so as to give them increased market access as foreign lawyers. A briefing note to the EC Commission, which I wrote on 18 April 1991 (p. 196) sets out a progress report in the GATT negotiations. By then the Commission had been persuaded that court-based legal services should be treated differently to commercial advisory services. Initially there had been those in the Commission who thought that they should be treated the same, and that court-based services should also be included in the GATT Round.

I have also included a paper entitled "Legal Practice for Foreign Legal Consultants in Japan", written on 23 June 1993, i.e. before the meeting in Evian-les- Bains (p.202). The article sets out some of the practical issues relating to Japan and provides a clear picture of the Japanese negotiating position and my responses in our bi-lateral discussions. It also gives important background to the Evian discussions. Our approach to the Japanese position was firm but far less aggressive and confrontational than the United States' approach. The Japanese had done impressive homework on the differences between the rights of foreign lawyers in different Member States (and also in the United States) and this was something we had to take fully into account.

Are there any general lessons for the present and the future? My experience would suggest that most officials at the Commission (and indeed the judges at the Luxembourg and Strasbourg courts) were remarkably open to discussion and persuasion. It could be said that we were lobbying, but once they were convinced that we had genuine points of view which demanded consideration, we were listened to carefully. I felt that the breakthrough in the Uruguay Round discussions really came at the long meeting on 29 January 1991 when most of the time we were making constructive points on the Draft WTO Framework Agreement on which we had no direct interest.

The lessons are clear. There is much more community of interest within the countries of the European Union than some would have us believe. There are, of course, the headline disputes. But otherwise considerable progress can be made in putting forward a country's position (and matters which require special consideration) by participating in EU discussions at all levels. At the level of the Ministerial Councils, I have heard from European friends that two Ministers epitomise this approach (this is not an exclusive list), Kenneth Clarke,

Minister of Justice, and William Hague, the Foreign Secretary. Before he arrived, the appointment of Hague was viewed on the continent of Europe with some fear and trepidation. Now he is spoken of enthusiastically with considerable admiration and respect and is clearly very effective in putting across the United Kingdom's case.

Avocats sans Frontières

Speech at the Inauguration of the European Circuit: 22 March 2001 by His Honour Judge John Toulmin CMG, QC, at the Old Hall Lincoln's Inn.

It is a singular honour to be invited to give the talk at the launch of the European Circuit. May I begin by congratulating all those concerned with the launch. May I also congratulate the Bar Council on recently opening an office in Brussels. I am sure that both ventures will be successful and will benefit the bar as a whole.

It is a particular honour to share a platform with Lord Slynn of Hadley and David Vaughan QC. Lord Slynn was successively Advocate-General and Judge at the European Court of Justice before returning to London as a judge of the House of Lords. He will be regarded as one of the most influential judges of the 20th century. He appears in this story on two occasions.

David Vaughan QC is one of the two leading European practitioners of the last 30 years and is a pioneer of legal practice on the European circuit. It is entirely appropriate that he should become the first leader of the circuit. May I add my warmest congratulations.

Although this is primarily an overview of the developments that have taken place in liberalising European legal practice, I thought it would be interesting to fit into the general picture some events in which I participated personally which appear to be particularly noteworthy. This will give a small taste of the working of the European Institutions and the British Government in practice.

1. The Treaty.

In the background lawyers have had throughout to bear in mind the following provisions of what in 1972 was called the Treaty of Rome but later, as amended, became the Treaty of European Union and subsequently incorporated the Treaty of Maastricht, the Treaty of Amsterdam and the Treaty of Nice. The fundamental principals are set out in the early Articles.

Article 3(c) sets the objective of "the abolition, as between Member States, of the obstacles to free movement of goods, persons, services and capital."

I emphasise removal of obstacles.

Article 5 (now Article 10) requires the Member States to take all measures necessary to ensure the carrying out of obligations under the Treaty. "They shall refrain from any measures likely to jeopardise the objectives of the Treaty".

Article 7 (now Article 6) provides that "within the field of application of the Treaty and without prejudice to the special provisions mentioned therein, any discrimination on the grounds of nationality shall hereby be prohibited."

We were also concerned particularly with the Articles of the Treaty dealing with the right of a lawyer to establish in another member state (Articles 52-58, now Articles 43-48) and the equivalent provisions relating to the provision of services (Articles 59-66, now Articles 49-55).

2. The issues.

Increasingly as legal practice has become more global, we have had to address a number of inter-related questions involving not only the right to practice within the European Union but also the right to practice worldwide.

The range of topics is wide.

1. The right of a lawyer who is a national of one Member State to establish an office in another Member State.

2. The right of such a lawyer to provide services in another Member State from his home office or chambers.

3. The conditions under which such a lawyer is permitted to appear in court in another Member State either as a locally established lawyer or from his or her home state as a provider of services.

4. The rules of professional conduct and discipline to which the migrant EU lawyer should be subject.

5. The requirement that the migrant lawyer should become a full member of the bar or law society in the place where he or she wishes to establish or be required at least to register his presence.

6. The right of the home state lawyer to enter into partnership with (MNPs) or to employ the migrant lawyer.

7. The right of the EU migrant lawyer to enter into partnership in the host state with professionals who are not lawyers (MDPs).

8. The rights of EU lawyers to practice outside the EU particularly in the United States of America.

9. The rights of non-EU lawyers to practice within the EU.

Questions 8 and 9 may also raise the questions in 1 - 7.

As the practice of the law has become more European and more global, the demand from the legal profession itself for answers to these questions has become more intense. Both the legal profession itself, and the regulatory framework which supports it, have changed radically in the last 30 years. Even though this is the case, much legal practice in the European Union is still carried out by single practitioners or very small firms. Many rightly see their traditional forms of practice under threat from large firms and governments. This process of practice by larger firms (and larger sets of Chambers) has gone much further in England and Wales than in many other parts of the European Union. The English Bar has also changed radically over the past 30 years and this process is not complete.

3. The early years.

In 1972 the United Kingdom had not yet joined the Common Market which then had 6 members, all civil law countries with similar systems of law and organisation of their legal professions. Practice was local, the rule of 'unicité de cabinet' prevailed. A group of lawyers or a firm was permitted to have only one office. If the matter required the assistance of a lawyer in another part of the country, or even 10 miles away within the jurisdiction of another Bar, the matter normally had to be referred to another lawyer.

As David Vaughan and I sat in the Bar Council›s offices in Carpmael Buildings in 1972, at meetings of the International Practice Committee, this did not seem very surprising. It was only in the late 1960s that the English Bar had abolished circuit rules which required a QC off-circuit to appear with a junior from the circuit and also required a junior from another circuit to pay a fee to the circuit in order to appear in a case on it. Solicitors had only recently in 1969 been permitted to have more than 19 partners. A few had small offices staffed largely by ex-pats, in Paris and Brussels.

In the United States there were no national law firms, and very few firms had offices outside the state where the main office was established. A few firms had small offices in Washington, a very few had token offices in London Paris or Brussels.

The one major exception to purely local practice was the English Bar practising overseas. English barristers appeared regularly in Hong Kong and Singapore, and in the Caribbean and Bermuda. They were also entitled without examination to become members of the New York Bar. This overseas practice has diminished as local bars have become stronger and the countries concerned more legally independent.

4. The Court of Justice.

Most of the early progress towards freedom of movement for lawyers within the European Union was accomplished by the European Court of

Justice. It is perhaps not surprising that the early landmark cases were essentially local disputes which crossed national boundaries.

In 1974 there were two landmark decisions. *Reyners v Belgium* [1974] ECR 631, [1974] 2 CMLR 305, concerned a lawyer born in Brussels of Dutch parents who retained his Dutch nationality. He was refused permission to be admitted to the Belgian Bar and establish practice in Brussels on the grounds that he was not Belgian and did not come within the exceptions permitting non-nationals to be admitted to the Belgian Bar. Van Binsbergen [1974] 1 ECR 1299, [1975] 1 CMLR 298, concerned a Dutch lawyer who moved his residence to Belgium and was refused permission to provide the service of representing his client before the Dutch court because he was no longer resident in Holland. The issues in both cases may have been local, but the results were far-reaching.

Apart from the fundamental provisions of the Treaty which I have already set out in detail, the Court in Reyners had to consider the title on Establishment and in particular Article 52 of the Treaty. The Article provided that restrictions of the freedom of establishment of nationals of a Member State in the territory of another Member State shall be progressively abolished. "Such progressive abolition shall also extend to restrictions on the setting up of agencies, branches or subsidiaries by a national of any member state established in the territory of any Member State."

Article 52 (now Article 43) made it clear that "freedom of establishment shall include the right to engage in and carry on non-wage earning activities under the conditions laid down by the law of the country of establishment for its own nationals". There are similar provisions in Article 59(now Article 49) in relation to services.

There appeared to be an exemption under Article 55 (now Article 45) which might apply to lawyers. "Activities which in any State include, even incidentally, the exercise of public authority shall so far as that State is concerned be excluded from the application of the provisions of this Chapter" (ie relating to establishment.)

The Court decided in Reyners and Van Binsbergen:

1. Articles 52 and 59 were of direct effect even in the absence of Directives implementing their provisions.

2. The practice of law was not an exercise of public authority under Article 55 and therefore lawyers were not exempt from the provisions of the Treaty.

3. A Member State was not permitted to enact legislative provisions which gave its own nationals privileges over nationals from other Member States - Reyners.

4. Certain restrictions were justifiable if they were for the general good, i.e. those relating to organisation, qualification, professional ethics, supervision, and liability which were binding on any person established in the State in which the service was provided - Van Binsbergen at para 14.

5. By the same token rules to ensure the due observance of rules of conduct and respect for professional ethics might be justified.

The two cases were followed in 1977 by Patrick, an English architect who wished to reside and practice in Paris. The Court of Justice held that where, as in this case, there were bi-lateral conventions between English and French architects, they provided the yardstick by which a court would judge whether a restriction was reasonably justified or not. In this case they held that it was not.

Also in 1977 the European Court held in *Thieffrey v Conseil de L'Ordre de Paris* [1977] ECR 765, [1977] 2 CMLR 373, that a Belgian lawyer who held a Belgian diploma, which had been recognised by the University of Paris as the equivalent of the French diploma, could not be refused admission to practice at the Paris Bar on the grounds that he did not have the French Diploma.

In effect the Court made it clear that the framing of rules in a way which discriminated in practice against foreign EC nationals from taking up and pursuing activities in a Member State was prohibited. The decision in Thieffrey did make it clear that it was permissible for a Member State to retain its own requirements for admission to its Bar or Law Society, provided 4 conditions were met - those requirements were justified in the public interest, were applied without discrimination, genuinely furthered the objective that was being pursued and were proportionate to that objective. These requirements were confirmed in later cases. In Gullung [1988] ECR 111 paras 24-31, the Court held that the requirements could include a requirement that incoming lawyers should register with the host Bar: see also *Kraus v Land Baden-Wurtemburg* [1993] ECR I - 1663 at 1697(para 32).

5. Early Legislation.

By the time of the first Directive relating to lawyers, the Lawyers' Services Directive of 22 March 1977 (EEC 77/249), the European Court had already set many of the parameters of legal practice in Reyners and Van Binsbergen. The requirements of the Council of Ministers to issue Directives to further the objective of abolition as between Member States of obstacles to free movement was contained in the Treaty itself. Little had happened as far as the legal profession was concerned.

Article 57(1) of the Treaty required the Council of Ministers, on a proposal from the Commission, and after consultation with the Parliament, to issue

Directives regarding mutual recognition of diplomas, certificates and other qualifications. Article 57(2) required the Council to issue Directives regarding the co-ordination of legislation and administrative provisions of Member States concerning the engagement in and exercise of non-wage earning activities.

On 7 July 1964 the Council had issued a Crafts Directive providing that in accordance with the principle of free movement, vocational training and participation in a particular branch of a craft or trade (e.g.welding) without interruption for a certain number of years, was sufficient for a person to be entitled to pursue the same activity in another Member State. The Advocate-General in Thieffrey pointed out that cases involving employed persons brought under Article 48 provided useful guidance for the implementation of the Treaty. There are echoes of this concept in the debates of the next 30 years.

In 1969 the Commission published a draft Directive giving lawyers extensive rights to provide services in other Members States by giving legal advice and by appearing in Court in those Member States under the disciplinary rules of the host Member State. It was not adopted by the Council of Ministers. The legal profession relaxed. In the succeeding years little progress was made until in the mid-1970s a somewhat similar Draft Directive was introduced. In 1976 David Vaughan and I, in the Bar's International Relations Committee, saw drafts of the Lawyers' Services Directive and heard reports from John Hall QC, leader of the UK delegation of the CCBE, of its progress. It reached thirteen drafts before eventually the 11th draft was adopted as Council Directive (EEC) 77/249.

It seemed to be modest in scope and, for the United Kingdom at least, not to require any changes in the way law was practised. But it had far-reaching consequences which were not appreciated at the time. It permitted a lawyer established in London to provide services by going to another Member State to advise on any law including local law using the English professional title. The English lawyer was also permitted to appear in court in conjunction with a local lawyer qualified to appear before that court. When the migrant lawyer was doing advisory work he was subject to the rules and discipline of his home state but was required to respect the rules in the host state especially those rules concerning the incompatibility of the exercise of the profession of lawyer with other activities in that state, professional secrecy, relations with other lawyers, conflicts of interest and advertising. For court work the migrant lawyer was subject to host state rules. The only exclusions from the right to provide services related to the notarial activities of conveying land and the winding-up of estates.

The far-reaching consequences were that you could not impose a lesser degree of adherence to rules of conduct of the host state from the migrant lawyer actually established in the host state than were to be imposed upon the lawyer providing services who remained in the home state but went occasionally to the host state. If the migrant provider of services was required to respect host rules as part of his obligation, it was impossible logically to argue that the migrant established lawyer could disregard them at will.

As a post script, in 1988, to the considerable surprise of many lawyers, including I suspect many of those who had approved the provision in 1977, the European Court held in *Commission v Germany* 25 February 1988, [1988] ECR 1123, that acting in court in conjunction with a local lawyer meant no more than that a migrant lawyer must be introduced by a lawyer qualified to appear before that court who could assure the court that the incoming lawyer could conduct the case effectively and would respect the applicable rules of court and professional conduct.

6. Lawyers' Establishment Directive: the early years.

Soon after the 1977 Directive was agreed Comte Davignon, the relevant EEC Commissioner wrote to David Edward QC, as he then was, the current President of the CCBE, and asked the CCBE to work on a draft establishment Directive. It took over 20 years to agree and implement such a Directive. After the initial work there were 2 early drafts known as Zurich 10/80 and Athens/5/82 from the dates and places on which they were completed. These set out alternative proposals and pointed up the fundamental differences of philosophy within the legal professions of the Member states.

The differences included the following mutually conflicting views often held by different Bars and Law Societies as a matter of principle.

1. A reluctance to recognise a category of lawyer other than that of a fully admitted member of the local legal profession. This view was taken particularly to emphasise that all lawyers within a jurisdiction should be subject to precisely the same professional rules and discipline.

2. A reluctance to recognise as a full member of the local legal profession those who were not fully conversant with the national law of the host Member State. Such lawyers, it was felt, should only be able to use the professional title of the state in whose laws they were fully qualified.

3. A reluctance in France and Germany in particular to breach the rule of 'unicité de cabinet'.

4. A fear by migrant lawyers that if migrant established lawyers were subject to host rules and discipline, those rules would be used by the host profession to discriminate against the migrant lawyer.

5. Despite the Lawyers' Services Directive, a feeling that migrant established lawyers should not be permitted to advise on host state law.

JOHN KELVIN TOULMIN
ARMIGER
CONSILIAR: DÑAÉ REGINAE AD LEGEM
JUDEX DÑAÉ REGINAE CURIALIS
PRAESES CONCILII ADVOCATORUM EUROPAEORUM
ORDINIS AUSTRIARUM
LECTOR QUADRAG: 2008

DEUS ROBUR MEUM

Coat of Arms for John Toulmin in the Middle Temple,
a privilege of being Master Reader

Interior of the Temple Church

The Toulmin family: Geoffrey, Hilary, John, Carolyn and Alison
at John Toulmin's swearing-in as an Official Referee on 4 November 1997

The "Clos Toulmin" vineyard in the winter, Auxey-Duresses, Burgundy

John and Carolyn Toulmin in the vineyard

This was the position when I became a full member of the UK Delegation to the CCBE in October 1983. In terms of the real need of the legal profession for rules governing practice in another Member State, the situation had not changed much since 1972. There was little more demand for English lawyers to practice in Paris and Brussels but in any event there were few restrictions there which caused problems. Both the English Bar and Law Society had entered into conventions with the Paris Bar in December 1975 these conventions were terminated by the Paris Bar in 1985 in anticipation of the reforms of the French legal profession - see below). English lawyers in Brussels were permitted to practice under their own title and carry on advisory work. The local situation had not changed in France or Germany either; practice was still local. Similarly there was little demand as yet from US lawyers for additional rights. They practised in a small way in London, Paris and Brussels and were not looking for expansion into other Member States.

7. 1984 - Klopp

Things were about to change. In a landmark opinion in Klopp [1984] ECR 2971, [1985] 1 CMLR 99, delivered on 10 May 1984, the Advocate-General Sir Gordon Slynn declared 'unicité de cabinet' to be unlawful if it prevented rights of freedom of movement secured by the Treaty. A German lawyer who had all the qualifications for admission to the Paris Bar was refused admission because he proposed to retain his professional office in Dusseldorf. Sir Gordon Slynn's opinion was followed by the full Court in its judgment on 12 July 1984. It declared such a refusal to be unlawful because it prevented the lawyer from exercising rights of freedom of movement to which he was entitled. It left open the question of whether or not the migrant lawyer could have not only an establishment in his home state but more than one establishment in France. Soon after the decision in Klopp a court in Marseilles held that the rule that lawyers were permitted to have only one establishment was unlawful under French domestic law.

8. The Diplomas Directive.

On 28 June 1984 at Fontainebleau, the Commission launched the programme entitled "The Peoples' Europe". An important part of it was the programme for the completion of the single market by 31 December 1992. This was initially the responsibility of Lord Cockfield who was called to the Bar by the Inner Temple in 1942. He decided that progress for providing freedom of movement by sectoral Directives for individual professions was too slow and that what was required was a Framework Directive based on mutual recognition of higher education diplomas.This would enable suitably qualified professionals to use their existing qualifications to become full members of the equivalent profession in another Member State, any deficiency would be made up by an aptitude test or a period of adaptation. The original proposal for the Diplomas Directive was published on 16 July 1985. This was a few days before the Council Regulation 2137/85 of 25 July 1985 which set up European Economic Interest Groupings, (EEIGs) which enabled independent firms from different countries to set up a legal structure to pool resources for marketing, libraries and referrals, and was a form of association used by some medium sized firms of solicitors.

At first the legal professions were not fully aware of the determination of the Commission to enact the draft Diplomas Directive. In November 1985 the Bar European Group hosted a meeting in the Inner Temple which was presided over by Lord Justice Goff, at which Lord Cockfield left those present (who included Lord Slynn and David Vaughan) in no doubt that he intended to pursue his objective with determination. He did say, with some reluctance, that the Commission would be prepared to consider pursuing an equivalent Directive for lawyers alone if it was agreed by the European legal profession as a whole and by the Council of Ministers.

The CCBE suspended work on a draft Establishment Directive and worked hard to reach agreement on its own draft Diplomas Directive. It forwarded its own text to the Commission on 31 July 1986. The Commission did not reply until December 1986 when it told the CCBE that it would not propose a separate Directive for the legal profession.

9. 1986 generally.

1986 was an important year. It saw both the Single European Act and the start of the GATT Round which provided the context within which the legal profession would be developed. On 17 February 1986 the single European Act was signed in Luxembourg. It provided a significant step towards European integration and marked the watershed between Europe as a purely economic free-trade entity and one which had as a real goal, rather than a pious hope, the ever-closer union between the Member States. For lawyers Article 8A was important; "the Community shall adopt measures with the aim of progressively establishing the internal market over a period expiring on31December1992...The internal market shall comprise an area without internal frontiers in which the free movement of goods, services, persons and capital in ensured in accordance with the Treaty."

10. The GATT Round - Preliminaries

Also in 1986 a new GATT Round for the liberalisation of world trade was launched at Punta del Este in Uruguay. In early 1987 the American chamber of Commerce on behalf of US lawyers made five demands of the Japanese government.

1. US law firms in Japan should be permitted to have Japanese lawyers as partners.

2. US law firms in Japan should be permitted to employ Japanese lawyers in their offices in Japan.

3. US law firms should be permitted to practice law in Japan under the name by which the firm was generally known.

4. Migrant US lawyers should be able to count practice at their offices worldwide against the requirement that they must have completed five years' practice before they could be registered in Japan as foreign legal consultants.

5. US lawyers should have the right to handle foreign arbitrations in Japan.

These demands reflected a significant change which was starting to take place in American legal practice. Foreign offices were starting to be set up by US law firms in much greater numbers to do full scale legal practice. This process accelerated rapidly. By the early 1990s, for example one US law firm had 50 lawyers in its Paris office alone. A similar change was taking place in European practice. English solicitors were also establishing offices in larger numbers within Europe and also in Hong Kong and Tokyo. Dutch law firms were starting to expand worldwide and also to forge close links with Belgian firms and others on the continent. The demands of the US Chamber of Commerce in Japan were also supported by the European business community in Japan in July 1989.

It was not clear in 1987 whether, despite the US demands, legal services would be included in the GATT Round. In early 1987 the EC Commission retained a firm of accountants as outside consultants to prepare a study which would form the basis of its decision. In due course the CCBE was able to assist in the study.

By early 1988 it was clear that the Commission was determined to include legal services and it was important for the CCBE to co-operate with the Commission in a positive way. I had no doubt that any agreement in the GATT Round on legal services would have an impact on European law practice since a number of Member States did not permit other EC lawyers to establish offices in those States. If as a result of agreements in the GATT Round, US lawyers were permitted to open offices in those Member States even on a limited basis, the same rights could hardly be refused to lawyers from other Member States. For a long time a number of my colleagues were trapped in their own logic. They were unable to believe that the GATT Round had any relevance for lawyers. For them the logic was simple: the negotiations concerned trade, lawyers were not tradesmen so it could not concern them. I shall return to the negotiations later.

11. Diplomas Directive Part 2.

Meanwhile the CCBE having been refused its own sectoral Directive at the end of 1986, had serious problems with the draft Diplomas Directive. There was a local UK concern that it would exclude from its provisions barristers and solicitors who did not have a University law degree. David Vaughan QC played an important part in ensuring that it was the higher professional qualification and not the University degree, which gave rights under the Directive. A more general concern among lawyers was the provision in draft Article 4 which gave the migrant professional not the host profession the right to choose whether the migrant professional must undergo a period of adaptation for not more than three years or to take an aptitude test in order to become a full member of the host profession. The lawyers' argument was that where the system of law and rules of professional ethics were different in the host state, the host state was entitled to satisfy itself that the migrant was competent in host state law and practice. This meant that host state should be able to require the migrant lawyer to take an examination or test in order that it could be so satisfied. Otherwise a migrant lawyer who had spent three years in a branch office in the host state of the firm established in his home state,would have been able to become a full member of the host state profession without any knowledge of local law or ethics.

The CCBE (with crucial assistance from others) secured the following derogation in Article 4; " by way of derogation, ... for professions whose practice requires precise knowledge of national law and in respect of which the provision of advice and/or assistance concerning national law is an essential and constant aspect of the professional activity of the host member state, may stipulate either a period of adaptation or an aptitude test". All states in the end specified an aptitude test. There was endless debate at the time as to what the tests could include. In the event the provision has worked well.

In June 1988 the Council of Ministers agreed a common position including the special provision for lawyers. In October 1988 the Parliament deleted the special provision. They were overruled by the Council in December 1988 and the special provision was restored to the draft. Council directive EEC 89/48 of 21 December 1988 came into force on 4 January 1991 two years after it was notified to the member states.

The insertion of the special provision was a considerable achievement for the CCBE and the legal professions at a time when in the "High Noon" of Thatcherite economics all professions, including the legal profession, were being looked at as traders where the market should dictate the conditions in which those services would be provided. This philosophy was predominant in the general thinking of a large part of the Commission.

Having said that, I should qualify it immediately as far as officials with whom we dealt were concerned. For the GATT Round we dealt with DGI, dealing with external affairs. For the internal market we dealt with DGIII and subsequently with DGXV. In the United Kingdom we dealt with the Department of Trade, which was the lead department for the Diplomas Directive and the GATT Round, and with the Lord Chancellor's Department. The officials at the Commission dealing with the GATT Round, all non-lawyers, were outstanding. None more so than Arnaud Bordes of DGI who was dealing in the later stages of the negotiations not only with legal services but also with audio-visuals, one of the most contentious parts of the Round. We received similar co-operation from most but not all the officials dealing with the internal market in DGIII and DG XV and all those in the Department of Trade and the Lord Chancellor's Department.

12. Lawyers' Establishment Directive Part II.

At the beginning of 1988 work was resumed on the draft Lawyers' Establishment Directive. The President of the CCBE, Denis de Ricci of France, in an effort to make progress, asked for three texts to be prepared reflecting the differing positions of the legal professions in the member states. Michel Gout of France prepared a draft which required the incoming lawyer to become a full member of the host legal profession. This was in line with the law which had been drafted in France whose purpose was to integrate the positions of avocat and conseil juridique and,for the first time, to give the new unified French legal profession a monopoly on the giving of legal advice. I was asked to produce a draft reflecting the view of a number of City of London solicitors that lawyers should be entitled to establish offices in the host Member State using their home state title and subject only to such rules of their home Bar as their home Bar chose to impose upon them. Heinz Weil, a German Rechtsanswalt living in Paris, and Niels Fisch-Thomsen President of the Danish Bar, produced a draft permitting establishment under home State title but subject to all the rules of conduct of the host Bar.

At the plenary session of the CCBE in Copenhagen on 28 May 1988 a vote was taken. The French proposal and the compromise each received four votes, my draft received two votes - the UK and Holland. There were two abstentions. The four authors of the drafts met in a corner of the room and after a short discussion proposed that they should have a short time to see if they could find a way out of the impasse, not acting as members of their respective delegations, but as "experts of the Presidency". We agreed to meet on the weekend of 2/3 July 1988 initially at the house of Michel Gout in Rochefort-en-Yvelines just south of Paris.

I thought that a new approach was needed to avoid the debate being bogged down yet again in what were described as "principles". I went to see

Richard Bain, who had practised for a number of years as a barrister on the Western Circuit and had then emigrated to France and was practising from Linklater's Paris office and was one of the most prominent members of the English legal community in Paris. We devised twenty-five questions which an establishment Directive had to answer if it was to respond to the needs and concerns of both the incoming lawyers and the host Bars. They were designed to deal with practical matters e.g. should a lawyer be required to register with the host Bar? Answer "Yes". Should such a lawyer have a right to be registered subject to a certificate of good standing? Answer, "Yes".

We spent Saturday 2 July 1988 in Rochefort working through the questions and talking around the issues. It became clear that we would be able to reach agreement on a draft. We spent the Sunday in Paris producing the first draft. This required considerable courage on the part of Michel Gout since any acceptance of the right of a lawyer to establish in France without becoming a full member of the local Bar ran contrary to the draft French law which prohibited establishment under home state title and which was in due course enacted and came into force on 1January 1992.

Our joint proposal had a better prospect of success than previous drafts not only because, coming from different points of view, we were all able to subscribe to it as individuals, but also because one area of unease was about to be lifted.

On 28 October 1988 in Strasbourg a common code of professional conduct was adopted by the CCBE after many years of work. lt dealt with a) General principles; e.g. Independence of the lawyer, personal integrity confidentiality and personal publicity; b) Relations with clients; c) Relations with Courts and d) Relations between lawyers. The Code managed to reconcile differences of philosophy between the common law and the civil law. The code owed much to the work of Hamish Adamson, Secretary of the working group, who was also international secretary of the Law Society of England and Wales, and Secretary of the UK delegation to the CCBE. He has, incidentally, written a book entitled "Free Movement of Lawyers" which is the authoritative work on the subject. Originally the CCBE code only applied to cross-border activities between lawyers from different member States.

These rules of professional conduct have since been incorporated into the rules of professional conduct of all the Member States, the countries of the European Economic Area, Cyprus, the Czech and Slovak Republics, Poland and Turkey. The adoption of these rules helped to allay the fears of migrant lawyers that the rules of the host bar would be used to discriminate against them. The Code was amended in Lyon at the CCBE plenary session on 27 November 1998 and is now to be applied to professional conduct between lawyers from the same Member State. It has long been incorporated in the Conduct of the English Bar.

There were a number of important developments in the European legal profession in 1989.

1989 was the year of the White Paper on the reform of the legal professions in the United Kingdom. In Germany the constitutional court on 14 July 1987 had invalidated the German Bar rules as being unconstitutional. In 1988 a German law society committee had decided by an overwhelming majority that national partnerships were permissible. It was in 1989 that German law firms in different parts of the country began to re-organise themselves by amalgamating or by setting up branch offices in other parts of Germany. This enabled the German profession to strengthen itself and thus to play its full part as a leading European legal nation. From this time discussions on liberalising the profession ceased to be largely theoretical but mattered to increasing numbers of practising lawyers in Europe.

13. Lawyers Establishment Directive Part III.

In 1989 and 1990 important progress was made on the experts' draft Establishment Directive. There was an important meeting at the EC Commission on 27 January 1989. A delegation of the CCBE met Herr Martin Bangemann, Commissioner responsible for the internal market, DGIII, and M Beuve-Mery, Head of the Division dealing with legal services. They said that they were reluctant to take up sectoral Directives for professionals particularly since the Diplomas Directive had only just been adopted. They said that would consider doing so only if three conditions were met: a) It enlarged rights recently given to lawyers under the Diplomas Directive; b) it was generally agreed by the legal professions and c) that it was generally agreed by the Member States. During 1989 work on the draft Directive continued. This included meetings with the Commission.

On 25 January 1990 at meetings with Herr Bangemann, M Beuve-Mery and Mme Kirschbaum, the Commission gave the CCBE draft a warm welcome although they recognised that it had not yet been voted upon by the delegations or been considered by the Member States. At the same meeting, they expressed informal objections to the French law which withdrew the right to lawyers from other Member States to establish an office in France using their own professional title, a right which had been exercised by English lawyers since before the First World War.

14. The GATT Round Part II : Substantive Discussions

We must leave the story of the Establishment Directive in 1990 and return to the GATT Round whose discussions were running in tandem. It was clear towards the end of 1989 that in principle the Commission intended to include legal services in the Gatt Round but nothing had been decided beyond that. At a meeting with the Commission, DGI , in November 1989, it appeared that the

EU offer might well include private litigation before the courts and notarial activities in addition to legal advice. Discussions intensified from the end of 1989. The Round was originally due to end in December 1990.

On 21 December 1989 I attended a relatively low level meeting with officials of DGI at the Commission to consider what was described as a "Panorama on Legal Services". I only attended because no member of the Presidency of the CCBE was available. The meeting was, in the event, of considerable significance. The draft Panorama was in tradesmen's' jargon. I managed to introduce a substantial number of amendments, emphasising the overriding duty of lawyers to the court in litigation and the duty of professional responsibility in advisory work which could override the duty to one's client. I based my suggested amendments on the CCBE Code of Conduct. These amendments were accepted. This was the start of my responsibility for the negotiations on the GATT Round on behalf of the CCBE as a whole. It continued until December 1993 when the Round was in fact completed. My continuing involvement was invaluable.

Once the EC Diplomas Directive had been enacted there was intense lobbying by US lawyers to include mutual recognition in the GATT Round. In June 1990 the Commission responded by asking us to provide a list of obstacles for EU lawyers in the rest of the world. This we did. At the same time we amplified to the Commission the distinction between court work which we said was work in the furtherance of justice, and should be excluded from the EU offer altogether, and legal advisory services which we accepted were an adjunct to the furtherance of trade. The distinction had been foreshadowed by the amendments to the Panorama in December 1989. The officials made it clear that they understood the distinction which we were making. We formed the impression that there might well be outside political considerations which would decide whether or not they were able to accept it in practice.

In July 1990 court related services were in fact included in what was called "The Central Product Classification List". For the time being therefore, legal services were included, although the CCBE view that they should be excluded was shared by the relevant committee of the Council of Ministers.

In August 1990 there was meeting of the representatives of the ABA at which they made detailed demands of everyone else to liberalise but made no offer or even acknowledgment that changes needed to occur in the US.

The US Annexe on Legal Services of 3 October 1990 maintained worldwide the demands which had been made of the Japanese in 1987. It also included demands that American lawyers could participate in multi-disciplinary practice outside the US and that there should be no unnecessary barriers to US lawyers becoming full members of the foreign host state legal profession.

It excluded the right of lawyers not admitted in the foreign jurisdiction to appear in court.

At a meeting of the liberal professions in Brussels on 16 November 1990 the attitude of the Commission as a whole still seemed to be that there was little difference between lawyers and tradesmen and that lawyers' services should be treated no differently from other business services. The date for the conclusion of the Uruguay Round passed without agreement. On 7 December 1990 the discussions at government level had been adjourned for the duration of the Gulf War. They were in fact resumed in March 1991.

Work at lower levels continued. We had a long and wholly constructive meeting at the Commission on January 29 1991. It lasted for 2½ hours and was extremely successful. The deficiencies in the US offer which included access for foreign lawyers in only 9 states, was discussed. We also discussed the draft WTO Framework Agreement as a whole.

A follow-up meeting of the liberal professions to the disappointing meeting of November 1990 took place on 11 June 1991. At that meeting I suggested to the Commission officials present that if progress was to be made in the very detailed individual negotiations for each profession, the Commission (who really did not have the manpower to cope on their own) needed the assistance of individual sectors and that the CCBE was prepared to give that assistance. To my surprise and delight my offer was immediately and warmly accepted by the very senior member of the Commission present, Hugo Paeman. [In 2008, I was invited by Professor John Jackson to spend a week at Georgetown University, Washington DC. At a seminar in which Ambassador Paeman was present, he confirmed his general offer and my acceptance. He said that the legal profession was the only one that had taken up the offer.] The Commission's offer for the legal profession proceeded thereafter on the basis of legal advice only in the law in which the migrant lawyer was qualified and international law. This remained the Commission's offer on behalf of the Member States. I return to the conclusion of the GATT Round later.

15. Lawyers' Establishment Directive 1991-1993.

I left the Lawyers' Establishment Directive at the end of 1990 with the draft still under discussion within CCBE but having received a general welcome from the Commission. The year 1991 saw some further progress but no conclusions. The Court of Justice gave important guidance in the case of Vlassoupoulou [1991] ECR 1-2357, [1993] CMLR 221, Opinion of A-G Van Gerven 28 November 1990, Judgment of Court 7 May 1991. The Court made it clear that in judging the equivalence of qualifications, the host Member State, in effect the host Bar or Law Society, must even before the Diplomas Directive took effect, take into account all the knowledge and experience acquired by the migrant lawyer in both the Member State of origin and in the host

Member State when deciding the extent of the deficiency of knowledge which the migrant lawyer must rectify before being admitted as a full member of the host profession.

On 10 May 1991 at the CCBE Plenary Session in Dublin there was a vote on the draft Establishment Directive. The four-four-two split with two abstentions of Copenhagen in 1998 was transformed into eight votes in favour of the experts' draft, three against and one abstention. This was a substantial step forward but was not enough for the draft Directive to be adopted by the CCBE or to satisfy the condition of the Commission that the draft had been generally accepted by the EU legal professions.

Discussions continued. After January 1992 they took place against the background that from January 1992 multinational partnerships were permitted in England and Wales for solicitors. The breakthrough came after a constructive intervention from the Batonnier of Paris, Georges Flécheux, then in his last year of office, at the Plenary Session of the CCBE in Barcelona in May 1992. As a result of minor changes in the draft, the French delegation were able to vote for the draft Directive at the Plenary Session in Lisbon on 23 October 1992. The draft Directive was adopted by the CCBE by ten votes in favour to two against. Spain voted against for the rather strange reason that the draft was not liberal enough. Luxembourg voted against on principle and because it feared that the Luxembourg Bar would be swamped by foreign lawyers.

On 9 December 1992 the members of the Presidency met M Perrissich, the Director of DG III, who warmly welcomed the draft which had been adopted and told us that it would be put into the work programme for the Commission for 1993. It was clear that the Commission accepted that the first and second conditions had been met, i.e. the draft Directive gave new rights over and above the Diplomas Directive and had achieved general acceptance from the legal professions in the Member States.

Some progress was made in early 1993. On 27 March 1993 a delegation from the CCBE saw a senior lawyer in the Legal Services Directorate, M Etienne, from Luxembourg. He congratulated us on agreeing the draft Directive and said it was a model for other professions. He said he would give an unequivocal opinion that the draft complied with European law. Sadly he was about to retire.

On 1 April 1993 there was a ministerial meeting in Brussels to consider whether the third condition had been met, namely that the draft Directive was generally acceptable to the Member States. Thanks, at least in part to very effective representation by the Lord Chancellor's Department, represented by David Gladwell, this was achieved.

There was then a period when nothing appeared to be happening. On 1 January 1993 the dossier had been passed from DG III to DG XV as a result of reorganisation within the Commission. Our draft appeared to have got stuck.

Eventually we asked for a meeting with the Commissioner. On 15 December 1993 we met with M Verderame, the Commissioner's chef de cabinet. He promised us that the Commission Draft Directive would be published in the New Year, 1994. It did not happen. The Commission draft was not finally published until December 1994, two years after the CCBE draft Directive had been presented to M Perrisich.

In the meantime, the French delegation at the CCBE had done a volte- face and was no longer in favour of the Directive.

16. GATT Round: Conclusion.

The EC Commission's offer to give access to foreign lawyers within the European Union (either by way of establishment or services) to advise on the law in which the migrant lawyer was qualified and international law, was challenged by the US lawyers as discussions within the Round were drawn out.

The deadline of 31 December 1990 had been put back to the end of 1992 with the Round due to be completed during the Bush Presidency. It became clear that even that date would not be met, and the date was put back to the end of 1993. From November 1992 discussions on legal services further intensified. In four separate meetings both CCBE and ABA representatives had separate discussions with representatives of the Japanese Bar and with each other. The EC Commission and the US Trade Representation were pressing the Japanese for improved access to Japan for foreign lawyers. The ABA representatives were also concerned that if and when the draft Directive on Rights of Establishment was implemented, it would put US law firms at a competitive disadvantage with their European counterparts.

In November 1992 a distinguished Brazilian lawyer, Dr. Durval de Noronha Goyos Jr., whose firm had and has offices, inter alia, in Brazil, Miami, London and Lisbon, wrote an article in the November issue of the magazine "Lawyers in Europe" entitled "Derisory Progress". In it he set out the restrictions on foreign lawyers establishing themselves in the US as foreign legal consultants. He pointed out that there was no access at all in 34 States, and in the remaining 16 states and the District of Columbia there were only 196 legal consultants of whom 160 were established in New York. He exposed the barely concealed restrictions on practice in California and Texas in the shape of onerous insurance requirements which severely inhibited foreign lawyers from establishing offices in those important States. There were only six registered foreign legal consultants in California and one in Texas. These figures were to be compared with over 1000 legal consultants in London at the time and over 500 in Brussels.

The problems for foreign lawyers in the United States were emphasised by the CCBE delegation at meetings with the ABA Committee. At least partly as a result of this pressure, the ABA Committee drafted a model rule on foreign legal consultants which was adopted by the ABA at its Convention in August 1993. It was described by Steven Nelson, the very able leader of the ABA delegation, as a " goodwill gesture that the US hoped would lead to substantive negotiations". It was certainly a considerable step forward but in practice it could be no more than a goodwill gesture because individual States had exclusive jurisdiction over who was able to practice in that State. The real problem for some States was not as they saw it a few foreign lawyers, but lawyers from other States in the US who would come in in large numbers. My conclusion at the time was that I was rather pessimistic about the chances of the Model Rule receiving general acceptance.

As a result of assistance from the Commission at the highest level, a meeting was arranged at Evian-les-Bains on the shores of Lake Geneva on 15 and 16

October 1993. The delegations from the ABA , CCBE and Japan were accompanied by senior officials concerned with the negotiation of the GATT Round. Delegations had no authority to agree anything, but the discussions might well be reflected in agreements made in the Round. In any event agreements could be made between the Japanese and US governments and the European Union in the Round relating to legal services whether the lawyers agreed or not.

The discussion did not in the event result in agreement. The officials were no doubt much clearer as to the reasons for the sticking points after the intensive series of meetings. The US regarded the talks as a failure; I did not. I was in no position to negotiate away deeply-held views, nor could I properly demand that European lawyers in Japan should have the right to take Japanese lawyers into partnership or employ them in their offices when such rights were not generally available to Japanese lawyers resident in Europe. The US and the Japaneses lawyers also had their difficulties which made a wider agreement impossible.

In the end the European offer made in the GATT Round was a modest one, namely the right of lawyers from other participants in the GATT to establish offices in the Member States from which they could advise on the laws of the countries in which they were qualified and in public international law. Even this modest offer was subject to derogations from some member States including France. The offer did not include the right for non-EC lawyers to practice EC law. EC law was to be treated as part of the domestic law of the

Member States. In the same way that US Federal Law is part of the domestic law of the United States. Negotiations in the GATT Round were concluded on 16 December 1993. The agreement was signed in Marrakesh in April 1994. There were 125 participating countries.

As I have set out in more detail in this Chapter, a few days before the conclusion of the Round, I had been telephoned by M Bordes who was also in difficult negotiations over audio-visuals, to ask what would be my reaction if legal services were dropped from the negotiations. I explained that it would be a disaster for the spread of the legal profession worldwide to provide the necessary support for worldwide commercial activity. He kept faith with my answer which was, in any event, consistent with the EU's ultimate negotiating position.

I felt it was very important that legal services should remain in the GATT Round so that the modest levels of commitment could be built on later. I now believe that with the adoption of the European Directive on Lawyers' Rights of Establishment, the time has come to re-visit these issues. I know that the US is anxious to do so. At the end of 2000 the US Government submitted a paper to the WTO emphasising that legal services are important to the world economy in their own right and underpin commercial activity world-wide. I agree. I note too that bilateral discussions are taking place with the US to try to ease the qualifications required of English lawyers to be admitted to the New York Bar (see Law Society Gazette, 15 March 2001, page 8).

In addition to liberalising access for lawyers the participants in further talks should discuss the adoption world wide of a professional code of conduct similar that adopted by the CCBE in 1988 and amended in Lyon in 1998. Having studied both the US and Japanese codes of conduct I do not see any serious impediment to such negotiations reaching a successful conclusion. The task is obviously not for the exclusive prerogative of these participants, but the lack of difficulty in relation to these codes would no doubt be mirrored by a study of other professional codes.

17. Lawyers' Establishment Directive: Final Phase.

I ended my Presidency of the CCBE at the end of 1993 with a promise from the Commission of a draft Establishment Directive in early 1994. In fact it took the intervention of the Legal Affairs Committee of the European Parliament to achieve progress.

In July 1994 I was with Willi Rothley MEP in Trier after a meeting at the European Law Academy. I complained that the CCBE Draft Directive had stalled in the Commission nearly two years after it had been presented to the Commission by the CCBE, and some months after the Commission draft had been promised. Herr Rothley said that there was a way forward since, at the next meeting of the Legal Affairs Committee of the European Parliament, the Chairman would be away and he, as Vice Chairman of the Committee, would be in the Chair. He would call for the draft from the Commission in advance of the meeting. He did so. The Commissioner said that this would not be possible. In September 1994 Herr Rothley, as temporary chairman of the Legal Affairs Committee, summoned the Commissioner to explain the lack of the Commission Draft. The Commissioner responded by promising a draft by the end of 1994.

Eventually on 21 December 1994 the draft appeared. In an attempt to accommodate the French opposition to the CCBE draft, the Commission produced a proposal which contained the unlawful provision that there should be only a temporary right to establish in another Member State under home state title for five years. At the end of that time, the migrant lawyer would be required either to qualify as a full member of the host legal profession or to go home.

For a long time there was no progress, but in Gebhard [1996] 1 CMLR 603 (Opinion of A-G Leger, 20 June 1995) [1995] -1-4186, Judgment on 30 November 1995, the European Court of Justice came to the rescue. The Court concluded on a reference from Italy that a right of establishment under home title without full integration into the host profession did exist. It defined what was meant by establishment and services, and held that where a national pursued an activity on a stable and continuous basis that should be governed by the title of establishment rather than services. "The temporary nature of the provision of such services is to be determined in the light of the duration, regularity, periodicity and community. However the provider of services may equip himself with the infrastructure necessary to perform the services in question".

At the CCBE meeting in Dresden in November 1995, two weeks before the European Court's decision, but after the Advocate-General's opinion, a further compromise was reached in the Presidency of Heinz Weil, one of the original experts of the Presidency. The five year limitation on establishment under home title was deleted, but admission as full member of the host Bar was made easier. The vote in the CCBE, now enlarged to include the countries which acceded to the European Union in 1994, had France, Spain and Luxembourg voting against, but it was not enough to block agreement. A considerable amount of constructive work was then done by a subcommittee of the European Parliament chaired by Mme Nicole Fontaine, MEP, Vice President of the Parliament, which took note of the ruling in Gebhard and the CCBE proposed compromise in Dresden. The Committee succeeded in agreeing a text to be voted on by the Parliament on 19 June 1996.

On the day before this debate took place, there was a debate in the House of Lords on 18 June 1996 on a report on Lawyers Rights of Establishment by the House of Lords Select Committee on the European Communities, chaired by Lord Slynn of Hadley. The importance of this Committee should be better appreciated. Such is its standing within the European Union that it is one of the very few national bodies before whom EC Commission officials regularly appear. In the past it has produced influential and distinguished reports on among other subjects, the Diplomas Directive, the Court of First Instance and the 1996 Inter-Governmental Conference. I have little doubt that this report played an influential part in the final outcome of the establishment Directive. It was also noteworthy that in the debate introduced by Lord Slynn, Lord Irvine of Lairg, Lord Lester of Herne Hill and the then Lord Advocate, Lord Mackay of Drumadoon, made constructive speeches in support of the concepts set out in the draft Directive as amended. It is interesting that the Lord Advocate stressed the importance of the common code of conduct in imposing standards.

On the following day, 19 June 1996, the European Parliament approved the Sub-Committee's amended text by a large majority. On 24 September 1996 the text was accepted by the Commission subject to a report by a working group of the Council of Ministers, which was set up to look into the economic consequences.

On 25 April 1997 the final text of the Establishment Directive went to the Council of Ministers. Political accord on the text was unanimous except for Luxembourg which remained resolutely opposed. Luxembourg referred the case to the European Court but failed to have the Directive annulled.

On 16 February 1998 the final text was adopted. On 14 March 1988 the text was published in the Official Journal. The Directive came into effect on 14 March 2000 as Directive 98/5/EC.

The underlying principles were not so very different to those discussed in Rochefort-en-Yvelines nearly ten years before. In an excellent article in a Festschrift to Pierre Van Ommeslaghe, Batonnier Georges Albert Dahl of Brussels remarked (page 758) that the long years of controversy had undoubtedly permitted improvements to be made, but had also resulted in many complications". It was appropriate that agreement should have been reached during the Presidency of the CCBE of Michel Gout, one of the original experts of the Presidency.

Put briefly, the Establishment Directive gives a right to lawyers to establish a practice in another Member State and pursue the activities of giving legal advice and representing a client in legal proceedings using their home title provided that where such activity is reserved to lawyers in the host Member State, it shall be undertaken in conjunction with a locally qualified lawyer. The Directive (Article 5) specifically gives Member States the right to lay down specific rules for access to Supreme Courts such as the use of specialist lawyers. The migrant lawyer is required to register with and has a right to be registered by the competent authority of the host Member State with special provisions to deal with Barristers and solicitors in the United Kingdom and Ireland (Article 3). All other states except Denmark have divided professions but Notaries are excluded altogether from the Directive.

There are rules relating to the applicable rules of conduct and requirements relating to professional indemnity insurance (Article 6), Disciplinary proceedings (Article 7) and Salaried practice (Article 8).

Article 10 gives the established lawyer additional rights to be admitted to the host State bar to those given under the Diplomas Directive. This applies once the lawyer has effectively and regularly pursued for at least three years a professional activity in the host Member State.

Article 11 deals with joint practice and Article 12 gives a right to use the name of the firm used in the lawyer's home Member State.

I was asked to chair a Committee of the Inns of Court to advise on the steps which the Inns should take to implement the Directive. David Vaughan was a member of the Committee. We met in a room in Middle Temple less than 100 yards from the room in Carpmael Buildings where we had started nearly 30 years before .

18. Conclusions

Looking at the range of topics with which I started, 1) a migrant EC lawyer who is a national of one Member State, now does have a right to establish an office and practice in another Member State; 2) a migrant EC lawyer has the right to provide services in another Member State; 3) the migrant EC lawyer has the right to appear in the Court of another Member State; 4) the disciplinary rules to which the migrant EC lawyer will be subject have been settled; all Bar Rules must conform to the principles set out in the CCBE Code of Conduct; 5) the migrant lawyer is not required to become a full member of the Bar or law Society of the place where he or she is established; 6) the provision of multi-national practice is governed by Article 11 of the Establishment Directive which has not changed since the Experts' Draft. It is generally permitted except where such a grouping is incompatible with the fundamental rules laid down in the host state. In other words, it is not permitted for barristers in the UK and Ireland because they are not permitted to form partnerships among themselves. Solicitors can form partnerships among themselves so under the Directive (as well as under domestic law) they can form partnerships with lawyers from other Member States.

I should add that one of the guiding principles has been that the division of the legal profession in the UK into barristers and solicitors is an internal matter. Nothing should be done by way of European Directives which would alter the balance between barristers and solicitors by a side-wind. 7) Multidisciplinary partnerships were the subject of a hostile declaration adopted unanimously by the CCBE in Brussels in November 1993 during my Presidency. The subject is not satisfactorily resolved at least as far as accountants and some consumer organisations are concerned. Article 11 (5) of the Lawyers Establishment Directive provides that where a Member State prohibits MDPs it may prohibit lawyers who are part of an MDP from establishing as such within its territory.

There is still much work to be done in developing the legal profession but hopefully the stage is now set for a successful expansion in the practice of barristers on the European circuit now that the basic framework is in place. I congratulate you and wish you every success.

I end with a modest question. Should the Bar and the Inns consider whether there is any way in which the Inns could reflect the new legal order by doing more to welcome lawyers and Judges from other Member States into their midst.

Under the European Communities (Lawyers Practice) Regulations 2000 the matter is regulated for migrant established lawyers but could something be done for those who wish to provide Services and for Judges from other jurisdictions?

Briefing Note on GATT for the European Commission and CCBE 18 April 1991

1. The Council of the Bars and Law Societies of Europe (CCBE) is the professional organisation representing the Bars and Law Societies of the European Communities having consultative status with the Commission, the European Court, and the European Court of Human Rights. It has, as observer members, representatives of the Bars of Austria, Cyprus, Finland, Norway, Sweden and Switzerland. The CCBE worked with the Commission on the Commission's paper on legal services dated 22 December 1989 which set out the sectoral negotiating objectives for the legal profession in the present GATT Round.

2. In its description of legal services the Commission emphasised that "lawyers provide independent and highly specialised services to virtually all persons and bodies in private and public life. In view of the highly responsible tasks carried out by lawyers, the profession is compulsorily organised on a national level and legal services are subject to strict licensing regulations."

3. After the general review, the Paper goes on to set out the issues and objectives as follows:

"(a) A clear distinction should be made between judicial activities (court proceedings etc) which should not be covered by the liberalisation process and legal services in the broad sense including legal advice in the host country which should be progressively liberated, although it must always be remembered that the individual lawyer must remain independent in the giving of legal advice as well as in litigation.

(b) For this and any other profession, the agreement should not apply to employment in the public service (Article 48(4) of the Treaty of Rome,) and activities connected, even occasionally, with the exercise of official authority (Article 55).

(c) It should be accepted that quality of service is the prime consideration and therefore a high level of professional qualification is necessary; at the same time this principle must not be used as an excuse for protectionism.

(d) Mutual recognition of professional qualifications should only be introduced where it is realistic to be assessed on a case-by-case basis (See EEC proposal on non-discrimination)".

4. It is clear that the Commission recognizes the special position of lawyers in society and that lawyers require special treatment in the GATT Round to reflect their particular rights and responsibilities.

It is also clear that the Commission's approach, which the CCBE endorses, is to exclude from the GATT Round judicial activities, activities arising out of employment in the public service and activities connected with the exercise of official authority. The Commission has concentrated on progressively liberalising other legal services including the giving of legal advice while recognising that in these areas a high level of quality of service is necessary for the protection of the consumer in the giving of legal advice just as much as in Court work and that in giving this service the lawyer must remain independent of the client. In order to protect the consumer, all lawyers practising in the EEC (whether from EC countries or not) should he subject to the CCBE Code of Conduct agreed by all Member Delegations which applies to both Court work and to advisory work carried out by lawyers.

5. The original objective of the Commission included the ability to give advice on host State law for those lawyers who are competent to give it. The present proposal of the Commission is that the giving of legal advice on the laws of the place where the lawyer is qualified (the home State) and on international law should be included in the GATT Round but that giving advice on other law should be left to reciprocal agreements.

6. It would be consistent with the Commission's approach if lawyers who wish to establish offices in order to give legal advice in other States should have a duty to register with the local legal authority which should have a corresponding duty to register them provided the incoming lawyers could give proof of dignity, honour and integrity. This proof should be limited to a valid certificate of good standing by the home State Bar or other competent authority that the incoming lawyer is not only a fully qualified member of his or her Bar or Law Society in good standing but is fully covered for professional indemnity insurance and the safeguarding of clients' funds. They may also require from the incoming lawyer proof of his or her call or admission to the relevant Bar or Law Society. Such a right could be withdrawn only for good cause. It would be necessary for the home State Bar, of which the incoming lawyer is a member, to have the right to participate in any disciplinary process in order to avoid any risk of discrimination. In view of the diversity of standards and qualifications that exist in different jurisdictions of the world, all incoming lawyers should be subject to host State standards of practice, conduct and discipline, as applied in accordance with the spirit of this agreement.

7. It would also be necessary for the protection of the consumer that the incoming lawyer should be subject in the host State at least to indemnity

insurance requirements which are broadly equivalent to those to be applied to members of the host State Bar.

8. The CCBE has produced a Code of Professional Conduct (Deontology) designed primarily for cross-border activities for lawyers in EC which was agreed by the Bars of the Member States in Strasbourg in 1988 (and has also been approved by the Observer States). Preliminary discussions with representatives of the American Bar Association indicate that there are no obstacles of principle to its adoption in the United States (subject to minor changes which do not affect the main principles of the code of conduct). It is relevant to point out that only through the GATT mechanism (or other Treaty) can the Government of the United States of America legislate for all the States in America. Discussions should take place with other jurisdictions so that a code along the lines of the CCBE Code could evolve for all cross-border practice. This should form part of a sectoral annex to apply to all cross-border trade in legal services. The CCBE is ready to help the Commission in achieving this goal.

9. The GATT Round is based on the Concept of Most Favoured Nation treatment. It requires, in respect of any measure covered by the agreement, that each party shall accord immediately and unconditionally to services and service providers of any other party, treatment no less favourable than that it accords to like services and providers of any other country (draft Article II). The CCBE welcomes this principle to be applied to the rendering of legal advice on the law in which a person is qualified (home State law) and upon international law. It is assumed that the exclusion for judicial assistance is intended to exclude all those matters encompassed by host state national judicial activities (Court proceedings etc).

10. It is worth noting that in the Commission's draft framework agreement on legal services Article 2 (4) (relating to standstill provisions) is particularly obscurely drafted.

OTHER ARTICLES IN THE DRAFT

11. Generally

Many of the Articles contain square brackets. Until these questions have been resolved it will be impossible to make final comments. However the following points are relevant.

12. ARTICLE 1 - SCOPE OF SERVICES

Occasional services abroad rendered from the office in the home State, questions of rights of establishment of offices in the host State and questions relating to the obtaining of local qualifications to practise as a lawyer in the host State (Diplomas) are all within the scope of the proposed agreement. The draft agreement is not entirely clear on whether restrictions can be imposed on how the services are to be delivered e.g. could a right be given to advise on international law and the law of the home State, but only to those fully qualified in the host State? We assume that this is not the intention of the draft.

13. ARTICLE 5 ECONOMIC INTEGRATION

It is this Article which enables the Member States of the EC to negotiate together through the Commission and prevents Directives agreed by the Member States being automatically extended to third countries through Most Favoured Nation treatment. The draft text says that for Articles-28 and 29 the EEC shall be deemed to be a Government. It is not clearly stated but does this mean that for other purposes such as dispute procedure each Member State remains a separate entity? In relation to any bilateral agreements, does this mean that they must be between the Commission and other States outside the EC, or can they be between individual Member States and non-EC Countries? We assume that the specific reference to Articles 28 and 29 preserves the right of individual Member States of the EC to conclude their own bilateral agreement with Third Countries.

14. ARTICLE 14

Article 14(1)(a) should include measures to be taken to safeguard the quality and administration of justice unless judicial activities are specifically excluded from the agreement.

Article 14 (1) (b) must preserve and extend the separate right of legal professional privilege and confidentiality (*secret professionel*) which exists when lawyers are giving legal advice to their clients. It is to be noted that if this is to be achieved it will alter the position in Europe where, in the A M & s case, the European Court of Justice held that lawyers from outside EEC countries but practising in the EEC were not entitled to claim legal professional privilege.

15. ARTICLE 23 - Dispute Settlement and Enforcement

The CCBE would like clarification of how this would work in practice, and how the arrangements would interact with national or local regulatory procedure. It is understood that the Article must be read along with Article 6(3)(a) which provides for domestic judicial review in the case of a domestic consumer complainant. The CCBE would be concerned if Article 23 provided an alternative route by way of a tribunal which might sidestep the normal domestic forums for the resolution of such disputes and which might deny parties the direct route to the European Court of Justice by way of Article 177 references. It is also concerned that any tribunal set up by the Commission might not have a proper input from the legal profession. The Commission have accepted however that if the Tribunal route is taken in relation to the provision of legal services the CCBE would be involved and would play a significant part in the resolution of the dispute. In the course of recent Hearings in the U.S. Congress, the House Majority Leader, Rep. Richard Gephardt, expressed his dissatisfaction at the procedure for the settlement and enforcement of disputes which is at present proposed.

16. SCOPE OF LEGAL SERVICES

As already indicated, the scope of legal services is extremely wide and it should be noted that lawyers in certain countries have interests under other headings of the subjects for the GATT negotiations, including financial services and the sale of real property.

OTHER OFFERS

17. United States.

In the view of the CCBE the purpose of the GATT Round is to facilitate the widening of choice in the giving of legal services. In those countries which consist of a number of jurisdictions, this rule must apply to all its component jurisdictions. This is particularly important in the United States since legal services are regulated on a State-by-State basis and not by the Federal Jurisdiction. At present the vast majority of States in the United States do not permit foreign lawyers to establish offices for the giving of legal advice and there have been some complaints, even in those States that do, that obstacles have been put in the way of those wishing to set up offices. The giving of the right in some States (subject to stringent conditions) does not represent substantial compliance with the principles of the right of establishment for the purpose of the giving of legal advice. Such a right must exist in all States without any limitations and entry must be subject to a simple procedure e.g. a certificate of good standing from the home Bar together with proof of membership of the Bar and proof of appropriate measures for securing satisfactory indemnity insurance cover. The host Bar or Court authority should not be able to delay establishment of offices by imposing additional requirements.

18. JAPAN

If foreign lawyers are to have a right to establish branch offices in Japan to give legal advice on their own law and international law they must be able to give this advice and be able to run their offices on the same terms as locally qualified lawyers. If locally qualified lawyers are entitled to give legal advice immediately on qualification there is no reason why foreign lawyers should not be similarly entitled to give legal advice although it will be confined to their own law and international law. The requirement for foreign lawyers to have practised for five years before being permitted to establish as a foreign lawyer in Japan must be abolished. Equally it is an unreasonable restriction to prevent a foreign lawyer from practising under his or her firm name.

19. OTHER OFFERS

A number of other offers have been made by various States. Some of these are rather imprecise. The CCBE would welcome a further opportunity to comment on offers from other States as the negotiations develop.

JOHN TOULMIN QC
Second Vice President CCBE

Approved unanimously at the Plenary Session in Dublin May 11, 1991

Legal Practice for Foreign Legal Consultants in Japan: a paper by John Toulmin QC, President of the CCBE 23rd June 1993

On December 15 and 16, 1992 an EC Delegation led by Mr Hoffman and Mr Bronkhorst for the EC Commission met with representatives and Senior Members of the Japanese Ministry of Justice and Department of Trade and Senior Members of the Japanese legal profession. The EC Delegation included officials from the Member States and representatives of the EC legal profession including John Toulmin QC, then 1st Vice-President of the CCBE, and distinguished lawyers from Belgium, France, Germany, the Netherlands and the United Kingdom. The discussions were forthright but extremely friendly.

The Japanese made reference to the five points which the US Government and legal profession and the EC lawyers in Tokyo had raised in relation to foreign legal consultants:

(a) the employment of Japanese lawyers;

(b) entering into partnership with Japanese lawyers;

(c) the five year post-qualification experience and the home state requirement;

(d) the restrictions on the use of the firm name;

(e) representation of clients in international commercial arbitration and before government agencies.

The Japanese handed out a paper saying that employment of Japanese lawyers by foreign legal consultants and partnerships with foreign legal consultants in Japan were not negotiable.

At the meeting the Japanese made the following comments in relation to the five topics:

(a) and (b) Employment and Partnership

The Japanese said that the prohibitions were justified by the need to preserve the independence and the culture of the Japanese lawyer but the Ministry of Justice said that they could be more "creative" in relation to forms of joint working between EC and Japanese lawyers.

(c) Registration Requirements

There was no movement on this subject. It appears from the various law directories, that in fact many US firms register those over five years in practice and bring the others in listed as "lawyers not qualified to practise as foreign legal consultants". They are nevertheless listed in the directories with their US qualifications.

(d) Restriction on the Use of the Firm Name

It was conceded at our meeting on 15th December 1992 that this restriction should be lifted and this was specifically confirmed at the meeting with the Study Commission on the following day.

(e) Restrictions on Foreign Lawyers conducting Arbitrations in Japan

The factual position was not clear. This may be because foreign arbitrations are subject to restrictive Japanese arbitration rules rather than restrictive Bar rules. We emphasised the need for the rules to be both changed and relaxed.

In addition to these issues others emerged as important restrictions for foreign legal consultants.

1. Restriction on scope of practice (for example a Belgian lawyer must refer his client to a Japanese lawyer if his client requires advice on Spanish law even though he could easily obtain the advice from a Spanish lawyer in his Madrid office and give that advice to the client).

2. The difficulty of providing an efficient service to a foreign client investing in Japan. In effect all that could be done was to provide the client with a referral to a Japanese lawyer and accompany the client to meetings.

3. Existing arrangements for co-operation with Japanese lawyers were impractical.

4. Immigration permits for foreign lawyers have to be renewed after one year and not every three years as for other foreigners.

5.(a) An onerous tax questionnaire is circulated periodically and must be completed.

At our meeting with the Japanese on 7th May 1993 discussions centred on

(a) the possibility of partnerships between Japanese lawyers and those from other countries where the non-Japanese members of the partnership would not be permitted to practice in Japan. (There is a similar partnership rule in Florida between Brazilian lawyers and Florida lawyers). We said that this was impractical.

(b) The question of MDPs with accountants. The Japanese were pleased to hear that all Delegations in the CCBE were against cross border MDPs.

(c) The question of closer forms of co-operation between Japanese and non-Japanese lawyers short of partnerships was explored briefly.

(d) In the context of the GATT Round we made it clear that the five year minimum qualification period was as unacceptable in the United States as in Japan.

(e) We emphasised the high standards required for qualification as a lawyer in the EC and also the high standards of professional conduct required of EC lawyers. We said that there was no difference in the approach between Japanese and the EC on these questions.

(f) On arbitration, the Japanese appeared to feel under considerable pressure and here appeared to be some willingness to consider a relaxation of their rules. We made it clear that in our view their restrictive attitude meant that arbitrations would go elsewhere and that the Japanese economy would lose a valuable source of income.

At the meeting, Dr Okaira, of the Japanese Trade Mission in Brussels, told the President of the CCBE how positive the meetings had been in Japan in December 1992. After the meeting he telephoned the Director of the CCBE to thank the CCBE for the discussions that had taken place with the CCBE and a number of national Bars. We understand that the Japanese Study Group was due to report in September 1993 but that the timetable is slipping. In order to take matters forward the CCBE has answered the Japanese Questionnaire, which we received immediately before the meeting, a copy of which is sent with these papers.

We now comment on the various issues in the following order:

1.The Five Year Rule

2. Advice limited to the law of qualification

3.Arbitration

4. Use of Firm Name

5. Code of Conduct

6. Registration Procedures

7. Co-operation between Japanese and Foreign lawyers

8. Partnership between Japanese and Foreign lawyers

9. Employment of Japanese lawyers by Foreign law firms.

We should preface our comments by noting that in many EC jurisdictions there is still a prohibition against even lawyers from other Member States setting up offices as foreign legal consultants. This will change within the EC if the draft EC Lawyers Establishment Directive is adopted. In other Member States e.g. France particular restrictions apply. This serves to emphasise that in many EC countries the present situation is far removed from the situation where law firms are entitled to set up offices anywhere in the world, to employ local lawyers, and take them into partnership. It is also a fact that this is not possible as a general rule in the United States either. We also emphasise that in our view it is not possible to demand relaxation abroad of rules which we are not prepared to relax at home. Finally it is clear to us that the Japanese are extremely well aware of the position of foreign legal consultants throughout Europe and any negotiations must proceed on this basis. We are somewhat concerned that the present stalemate may suit the Japanese. If they are told "it's all or nothing" they will not make concessions even in those areas where changes could be made to the significant advantage of foreign legal consultants in Japan.

1. THE FIVE YEAR RULE

There is a requirement that a foreign lawyer licensed to practice in Japan should have five years experience in the country in which he is qualified.

Commentary

This rule is taken from the rule for foreign legal consultants in the United States. All those states which permit foreign legal consultants (14 in all) have a five year rule (except Michigan, three of the last five years and California, four of the last six years). Some permit the five years experience to he obtained in foreign offices. The purpose of the rule in the United States is (as we understand it) not so much to restrict the rights of the foreign lawyer hut rather those from other US jurisdictions.

Argument for Relaxation

a) It cannot be objectively justified. While there may theoretically be an argument for requiring one lawyer in a foreign office to have this level of experience there can he no justification for such a general requirement (It is not a requirement anywhere in the EC). The clients of foreign legal consultants are sophisticated companies who are able to evaluate the qualifications and expertise of the lawyers who they instruct. If the five year rule is to be retained in any form, the possibility should exist for the foreign lawyer to prove that he or she has had relevant experience in home State law in a foreign office which can he included in the five-year qualifying period. After all, the practice of the law of the home country is all that the foreign legal consultant is at present permitted to do in many countries outside EC (including Japan).

b) The five year rule prevents the rotation of younger lawyers who may be prevented from acquiring the necessary experience in international practice that can best meet the needs of clients in Japan.

c) The rule prevents the firm bringing young staff into the office who command lower fees and thus enable the work to be carried out at less cost to the client. At worst this may prevent a firm for reasons of cost from competing for work that it is qualified to do. Large scale international work requires lawyers of different seniority and levels of experience.

d) The period of five years is in itself a serious disincentive to lawyers moving to Japan. Both in terms of career (the partnership pattern makes it advantageous to be in the home office between five and seven years in practice) and for family reasons (children, schooling etc.) this is often a difficult time to move.

e) It does not sufficiently respect the qualifications obtained in the home jurisdiction or take into account the requirement in Japan of the foreign lawyer to register with the local competent authority and be subject to local Japanese Bar discipline. All EC lawyers have had extensive training in their own law before qualification. All are subject to their own Bar or Law Society's Code of Conduct in addition to the Japanese disciplinary Code. All Bars have incorporated Article 3.1.3 of the CCBE Code of Conduct which states that "a lawyer should not handle a matter which he knows or ought to have known he is not competent to handle without cooperating with a lawyer who is competent to handle it." The lawyer will be disciplined if he or she breaks the rule.

2. ADVICE LIMITED TO THE LAW OF QUALIFICATION

Commentary

This rule exists in many of the State jurisdictions in the US which permits foreign legal consultants. The New York rule excludes advice on US law unless it is based on the opinion of a lawyer qualified to practice in that State. US lawyers have a monopoly in the giving of advice on Federal and State law. The EC Commission's offer in the GATT Round takes a similar position. The offer is confined to advice on the law of the country of qualification and international law but not local law. For this purpose EC law is regarded as law domestic to EC Countries and not as part of international law.

Within the EC, in some countries lawyers have a legal monopoly in the giving of paid advice on law (including foreign law). In other EC countries no such monopoly exists. Where there is no monopoly, anyone, including foreign legal consultants, can give advice on local law. Where there is such a monopoly the giving of advice on local law can be restricted to locally qualified lawyers. This is what happens in Japan. There has not surprisingly been no attempt by the United States to break the Japanese lawyers' monopoly in this area.

Arguments for Relaxation

a) The present rule requires a firm to pass the client to a Japanese lawyer even where the firm has a lawyer fully qualified to give that advice in one of their other offices. For example a firm of French lawyers with a French lawyer in its Japanese office may have a corresponding firm in Hong Kong from whom the relevant advice on Hong Kong law could be obtained. Why should they be required to refer the matter to Japanese lawyers for them to obtain the advice from Hong Kong lawyers?

b) Frequently the nature of international legal practice is such, that, in order to give appropriate advice to the client, it is necessary to obtain advice on law from a number of different jurisdictions. This rule may amount to a very real restriction on the ability of the foreign legal consultants to serve their clients.

c) It may have the effect of inhibiting the growth of Tokyo as an international centre for trade and finance because the ability to obtain the necessary legal advice is so restricted.

3. ARBITRATION

A foreign lawyer is not permitted to appear in international arbitrations which are conducted in Japan (although it appears that he may be permitted to act as an arbitrator).

Commentary

It is clear that the objective of the rule is to increase work for local lawyers by creating a monopoly for local lawyers in the conduct of arbitration proceedings. We suggested that in fact it may have the contrary practical effect of depriving local lawyers of work since there is now in international arbitration a wide choice of places in which to arbitrate and international clients are likely to choose the place where they can instruct the lawyers of their choice. There used to be restrictions on foreign lawyers preparing and appearing in arbitration in London.

When they were lifted the local lawyers found that their arbitration work in fact increased. It is not clear whether the restrictions in Japan are caused by the Bar Rules or the separate Arbitration Statutes or both. On both occasions on which we have met the Japanese government and Bar representatives we have stressed the need for the rules to be changed not only in the interests of the foreign legal consultants but also in the interests of the Japanese public and profession.

Arguments for Relaxation

1. The inability of a client to instruct a foreign lawyer in an arbitration governed by foreign law diminishes the quality of the arbitration and makes it more likely that the parties will arbitrate elsewhere.

2. The monopoly position of the Japanese lawyer would still apply in relation to issues of Japanese law.

3. The rule should be changed to remove the restriction on foreign legal consultants conducting the arbitration even if the rules of procedure of the arbitration are international rules and not those of a particular State. It will no doubt be necessary for the expert evidence on the relevant law of the arbitration to be given by an expert qualified in that law.

4. We understand the ethics in Japan that litigation and arbitration should be a last resort. International arbitration is extremely expensive and is not undertaken lightly. If it has to be conducted by Japanese lawyers who do not have the necessary expertise in foreign l aw it is likely to be more protracted and therefore more costly as well as less effectively conducted than if foreign lawyers are able to take a full role in its arbitration.

4. USE OF FIRM NAME

As we have already indicated the Japanese signalled that they are m principle prepared to agree to make the necessary changes.

5. CODE OF CONDUCT

The question of whether the Codes o f Conduct and discipline m EC Countries are comparable to the Japanese Code was raised m Tokyo in December 1992 and again at the recent meeting in Brussels. Part of their concern is that they do not want as a matter of public policy to import what they see as the over-commercialisation and over litigiousness which they see as having taken hold in the United States. We have assured them that, although expressed differently, the CCBE Code and the Japanese Code are very similar and that the standards of ethics are as high in the EC countries as they are in Japan.

6. REGISTRATION PROCEDURES

Commentary

We are concerned both that in the United States and in Japan the registration procedures are cumbersome and time consuming and can amount to a real disincentive and even an effective barrier to becoming a registered foreign legal consultant. In our view the registration procedures should be transparent and simple. They are neither transparent nor simple either in the United States jurisdictions which admit foreign legal consultants or in Japan. The CCBE draft Directive on Establishment provides a procedure which could form a basis for discussion. It is essential that rules and procedures should be clear, operated fairly and equally in all cases and be processed with reasonable speed. It is also essential that they should not have the effect, as they do in some States in the United States as an effective barrier to entry (for example by imposing insurance requirements on foreign legal consultants but not on local lawyers - one foreign legal consultant only in Texas - or fixing the level of insurance so high that foreign firms cannot comply - only six foreign legal consultants in California.

Argument for Relaxation

1. There is some evidence that the registration process in Japan can take as long as six months. The procedure could be shortened and streamlined.

2. It also appears that applications are delayed or rejected on small and unimportant points of detail e.g that the order of the date month and year is not consistently stated in the application or the punctuation is not that which the registration authority prefers.

7. CO-OPERATION BETWEEN JAPANESE AND FOREIGN LAWYERS

Commentary

The outcome of the CCBE meetings with the Japanese government and legal profession indicates that this is a positive area for further discussions where real progress could be made on practical measures which would greatly assist foreign offices to practice effectively in Japan. These principles could also be developed to provide the basis for a multilateral agreement on legal services within the GATT Round.

Arguments for Relaxation

The JSBA has published some draft rules which could establish a regime for co-operation and joint working between Japanese and foreign lawyers in Japan. The rules are designed to maintain the separate identity of the two lawyers and to ensure that the monopoly of giving legal advice by Japanese lawyers is preserved. However for it to be an effective relaxation further discussions need to take place to secure the agreed objectives.

a) The concept of the practical management of a shared office is not developed in the draft. Such a concept could certainly assist in achieving efficiency and cost saving without compromising the basic principle;

b) There is no reason why suitable arrangements could not be made for sharing office facilities including a receptionist, telephones and faxes whilst firms maintained their separate identities;

c) Further discussions could take place on combined billing of individual clients.

8. PARTNERSHIP BETWEEN JAPANESE AND FOREIGN LAWYERS

Commentary

Here we are not discussing a partnership between a Japanese firm and one or more firms of foreign lawyers where the foreign lawyers are prohibited from practising in Japan. We are concerned with the development of worldwide multinational practice without any restriction on where members of the partnership are established. Such a practice is prohibited not only in Japan but also even in some States in the United States where foreign lawyers are permitted to establish offices as foreign lawyers. It is prohibited at present even for EC lawyers with each other in many Member States. It is permitted in England and Wales but although the law changed on 1st January 1992 there are, as yet, few multinational partnerships. Before the change in the law a number of foreign firms practised side by side with English solicitors without much apparent difficulty.

In the absence of direct experience there is a fear, not confined to the Japanese, but reflected also in a number of contributions at our recent Plenary Session in Manchester in April 1993, that local lawyers of an MNP would find themselves looking to the Head Office outside the jurisdiction rather than to their own professional bodies and would be under pressure to import into their own jurisdiction the professional ethics and method of practice of another jurisdiction. There is a fear that what is seen as the over-commercialisation and over- litigious legal culture of the United States would be imported into the foreign jurisdiction. There is also a fear that the local profession would lose many of their most able practitioners to the large international firms. Others take a different view and say that these fears are substantially unfounded.

Certainly it is appropriate to understand that the legal culture in Japan, and in many other countries, is different to that in the United States and that the fear (whether misplaced or not) is genuine.

Arguments for Relaxation

1. It is suggested that the most efficient way of providing the international service which the clients require is by a partnership.

2. It is said that it is the most cost efficient way of providing the service.

3. The client would know if things go wrong that the responsibility lies with the partnership. They would not have the problem of working out whether the Japanese firm or the foreign firm was responsible for the problem.

4. A partnership would be the best way to bridge the culture gap between Japan and the outside world and the combined law firm would be able to develop a "seamless service" for the clients.

5. The monopoly of the Japanese lawyer in the giving of paid legal advice and the enforceability of the Japanese professional code would safeguard the integrity of the Japanese profession.

9. EMPLOYMENT OF JAPANESE LAWYERS BY FOREIGN LAW FIRMS IN JAPAN

Commentary

In Japan, foreign lawyers are not permitted to employ Japanese lawyers although Japanese firms may employ foreign lawyers (but not take them into partnership). Unequal rules in relation to the employment of foreign legal consultants are not confined to Japan. For example, in England and Wales, solicitors may employ foreign legal consultants without restriction but solicitors (and barristers) employed by foreign legal consultants may advise the foreign firm only and may not advise the clients directly or act as independent lawyers. The difficulty is that only a local lawyer may supervise another local lawyer and it is not possible for a foreign lawyer to carry out such supervision.

Arguments for Relaxation

It is suggested that relaxation of the rule coupled with the relaxation of the partnership rule would provide the most cost effective and efficient service to the client. The fears of those who oppose partnership also apply even more strongly to the employment of local lawyers by foreign legal consultants. They feel that such lawyers as employees would be in a more subordinate and less independent position than partners. We feel that perhaps progress may be made if changes are made more gradually and negotiations take place on the basis of what practical changes can be made to enable the clients to obtain the services which they need.

CONCLUSION

We are convinced that substantial improvements can be made in the course of the current negotiations. Changes in the pattern of international legal practice are taking place very fast and we reject any argument which says that changes made now will be set in tablets of stone for the indefinite future. We think that the logic of the development of international legal services may well require further changes in the relatively near future as experience will show what effect the present round of changes has had. A gradual change may be seen as psychologically more acceptable to the legal professions involved and thus more likely to be accepted. We are concerned that the demand for too great a change now will effectively prevent any changes and will stultify the development of international services, including those in Japan by foreign legal consultants, which is urgently needed.

Worldwide Code of Ethics

Although written in 1992, the topics raised in this article in the *Fordham International Law Journal* remain highly relevant. One of the great achievements of the CCBE was the unanimous agreement in 1988 in Strasbourg on a Common Code of professional conduct. It covers a) the function of a lawyer in society, b) the principle of independence, c) relations with clients, d) relations with courts, and e) relations between lawyers. It was quickly incorporated into the disciplinary codes for lawyers throughout the European Union and has been updated since. It provided a very important plank both in the progress of the Lawyers' Establishment Directive and in the Uruguay (GATT) Round. It was important that this Code had been agreed because if lawyers were to be permitted to establish offices in other member states, local disciplinary rules to be applied to foreign lawyers needed to be formulated in the context of agreed general principles. This made subsequent negotiations a little easier because I could say that this had been achieved within the European Union and that there were no serious obstacles to the agreement of a common code (perhaps with minor amendments) with the United States, Japan and other states worldwide after further negotiations.

In my article in the *Fordham International Law Journal* (with the Code annexed) I explain the Code and in particular how the difference between the common and civil law approaches were resolved. The potential difference of approach in the United States is discussed. There is also a detailed discussion on contingency fees, which is highly relevant to the current discussions following Lord Justice Jackson's report on this subject with whose conclusions I entirely agree. I pose the question now which I posed then, "why cannot the Code (with any necessary amendments) be adopted as a worldwide Common Code of Professional Ethics?" If adopted, it would have the consequence set out in the Law Journal article at p. 216, namely "If a Belgian lawyer wishes to instruct a lawyer from Brazil or a Michigan lawyer wishes to instruct a lawyer from Mauritius, each would know that there was a common set of professional rules which would apply."

The current GATT Round continues without great hope of success. However, it seems recently to have had a fresh impetus. Perhaps the agreement on a worldwide code of legal ethics could become one of its achievements?

I am well aware that this would be no more than an important first step. The question would remain, as it does within the United States, how will these rules be applied in each jurisdiction? Can any mechanism be devised to achieve a reasonable degree of uniformity of approach? I realise that it would be difficult to achieve agreement between autonomous and independent jurisdictions, but until the effort has been made, no one can know that it might not achieve a measure of success.

A Worldwide Common Code of Professional Ethics?

John Toulmin QC *

October 28, 1988 was a landmark day for the Council of the Bars and Law Societies of the European Community ("CCBE").[1] It was on that date in Strasbourg that the twelve Member States of the European Economic Community ("EEC") adopted a common Code of Conduct for Lawyers in the European Community ("CCBE Code" or "Code")[2] as a framework of principles of professional conduct to be applied to all cross-border activities between lawyers in the EEC, including all professional contacts with lawyers of Member States (and other signatories) other than their own, and also to the professional activities of lawyers in a Member State other than their own.[3]

---

* 15 *Fordham International Law Journal* [1991-2] p 673. English Barrister Practicing in Gray's Inn London WCI; First Vice President, Council of the Bars and Law Societies of the European Community [hereinafter CCBE]. A version of this Commentary was presented at the Stein Institute of Law and Ethics Conference on the Internationalization of the Practice of Law at Fordham University School of Law on October 10, 1991.

[1] The title CCBE represents a compromise. The organization was originally called the Consultative Commission of the Bars and Law Societies of Europe. When the name was changed to Council of the Bars and Law Societies of the European Community it was decided to keep the initial letters by which the organization is best known. In the CCBE the delegations represent the legal professions in the Member States. Voting is by country and not by individual delegates. The CCBE has repre?sentative status on behalf of the legal profession before the European Commission, the European Court ofJustice, and the European Court of Human Rights.   The title CCBE represents a compromise. The organization was originally called the Consultative Commission of the Bars and Law Societies of Europe. When the name was changed to Council of the Bars and Law Societies of the European Community it was decided to keep the initial letters by which the organization is best known. In the CCBE the delegations represent the legal professions in the Member States. Voting is by country and not by individual delegates. The CCBE has representative status on behalf of the legal profession before the European Commission, the European Court ofJustice, and the European Court of Human Rights

[2] *Code of Conduct for Lawyers in the European Community* (1988) [hereinafter CCBE Code] The CCBE Code is reproduced in the Appendix to this Essay. The Code has been adopted in different ways in the Member States. For example, the English Bar Council has annexed the Code to its detailed rules. See Bar Council, *Code of Conduct for the Bar of England and Wales* (1990) [hereinafter English Code]. The Law Society of England and Wales has codified articles 2-5 of the CCBE Code in Rule 16 of the *Solicitors' Practice Rules* (1990).

[3] CCBE Code, supra note 2, Rule 1.5. The CCBE's Deontology Working Party prepared an Explanatory Memorandum and Commentary for the Code. Explanatory Memorandum and Commentary on the CCBE Code of Conduct for Lawyers in the European Community, art. 1.5 [hereinafter Explanatory Memorandum] (on file with the Fordham International Law Journal). While it has no binding force, it is useful as a tool of interpretation. The Explanatory Memorandum, with regard to the definition of cross-border activities, stated that such. activities would include contacts in State A even on a matter of law internal to State A between a lawyer of State A and a Lawyer of State B; it would exclude contacts between lawyers of State A in State A on a matter arising in State B, provided that none of their professional activities takes place in

This Code was the culmination of over six years work.

The work started in Athens in May 1982 when the CCBE resolved to consider the feasibility of the establishment of a code of conduct that would act as a set of principles to be translated into a disciplinary code in each Member State. The first very tentative draft was prepared by Lake Falconer, a distinguished Scottish solicitor, in March 1983. There were times during the discussions when the task of reconciling the firmly held views in different countries was very daunting. There was, of course, the considerable task of reconciling common law and civil law systems. There was also the question of what to put into the Code. It was significant that the drafting of different parts of the Code was the responsibility of lawyers from different Member States, and that as the lawyers worked together they were surprised at the extent to which serious differences could be resolved by careful discussion. In their discussions they were assisted by work that had been done by the International Bar Association and the Union Internationale des Avocats, and in particular by work done by the American Bar Association ("ABA") on its codes of conduct.[4]

The CCBE Code has been implemented not only in the twelve Member States but also in the six observer countries to the CCBE: Austria, Cyprus, Finland, Norway, Sweden, and Switzerland, and recently by the newest member, Czechoslovakia.[5] The hope is to build on what has been done and to develop a code of professional conduct that will apply to the cross-border activities of lawyers from all the countries which are signatories to the General Agreement on Tariffs and Trade ("GATT").[6] Thereafter, if a Belgian lawyer wishes to instruct a lawyer from Brazil, or a Michigan lawyer wishes to instruct a lawyer from Mauritius, each would know that there is a common set of professional principles that would apply. The question "Why now?" is simply answered. There has been such an increase in cross-border

State B; it would include any activities of lawyers of State A in State B, even if only in the form of communications sent from State A to State B. Id.

[4] See *Model Rules on Professional Conduct* (Discussion Draft 1983) [hereinafter Model Rules]; *Model Code on Professional Responsibility* (1980) [hereinafter Model Code]. As of December 1990, 34 U.S. states had adopted codes of ethics for lawyers modeled after the Model Rules. See *ABA/ BNA Lawyers' Manual on Professional Conduct* (BNA) POI:3-4. The other 16 states have either adopted versions of the Model Code, or combined 'provisions of both the Model Rules and the Model Code. Id.

[5] Czechoslovakia was admitted into membership at the Plenary Session of the CCBE at The Hague on October 25, 1991.

[6] Opened for signature Oct. 30, 1947,61 Stat. (pts. 5 & 6) A3, 55 U.N.T.S. 187 [hereinafter GATT]. Only in the current Uruguay Round are GATT members considering the extension of GATT principles to services, including professional services. See, e.g., Peter Hansen & Victoria Aranda, "An Emerging International Framework for Transnational Corporations", 14 *Fordham Int'l LJ.* 881, 888 (1990-1991); Terry Smith Labat, "A View of the Single Market: Trade in Services in EC '92", 22 *Case W. Res. J. Int'l L.* 283, 296 (1990).

activity among lawyers generally, not just among the larger firms or the most powerful legal nations, that such a code is becoming essential.

The desire that this may be achieved is not primarily to benefit lawyers but to provide a basis of consumer protection for the clients whom they serve. There is little doubt that in many places lawyers are more and more regarded as businessmen rather than as members of a learned profession. It is clear that the speech of U.S. Vice President Dan Quayle to the 1991 ABA convention in Atlanta, which was highly critical of the legal profession, struck a chord with many outside the legal profession.[7] In Europe there are many who believe that lawyers are an over-privileged group who do not deserve the privileges that as professionals they enjoy. These critics need to be reminded that the lawyer has a vital role to play in the administration of justice and in society. Lawyers for their part have a responsibility to do all they can to improve ethical standards, to reaffirm those values of independence and integrity, which are vital to the proper functioning of a free society, and to show that they are fit to enjoy the privileges that come to them as professionals.

Both the aspirations and the concerns of the CCBE are shared by the ABA. Zona F. Hostetler, the Chair of the ABA Special Coordinating Committee on Professionalism, spoke to the ABA Annual Meeting in Chicago in 1990 on the subject of professionalism.[8] Ms. Hostetler acknowledged the identity of interest between the ABA and the CCBE in emphasizing the independence of the lawyer to act free of the interests of other clients or the lawyer's own monetary, business, or other personal interests. She also noted that the ABA's Committee on Professionalism was trying to cope with the present realities of practice by "adopting new programs such as mandatory professionalism courses, voluntary counselling, and monitoring programs, and Inns of Court programs modelled after the English system."[9] It is in the same spirit that the CCBE seeks with others to develop a uniform code of conduct that could be adopted worldwide. A process of synthesis has already taken place in the

---

[7] See, e.g., David S. Broder & Saundra Torry, ABA President Disputes Quayle on "Litigation Proposals", *Wash. Post*, Aug. 14, 1991, at AI; Julie Johnson & Ratu Kamlani, "Do We Have Too Many Lawyers?", *Time*, Aug. 26, 1991, at 54; David Margolick, Address by Quayle on Justice Proposals Irks Bar Association, *N.Y. Times*, Aug. 14, 1991, at AI. Vice President Quayle stated that

[t]here are stumbling blocks that we can't make excuses for, because, quite frankly, they're our own fault. ... Our system of civil justice is, at times, a self-inflicted competitive disadvantage. . . . Let's ask ourselves: Does America really need 70 percent of the world's lawyers? Is it healthy for our economy to have 18 million new lawsuits coursing through the system annually? Is it right that people with disputes come up against staggering expense and delay?

Margolick, supra.

[8] Zona F. Hostetler, "Professionalism in the American Bar in the 1990's, Remarks at the Annual Meeting of the American Bar Association" (Aug. 4, 1990) (transcript on file with the *Fordham International Law Journal*).

[9] Id. at 7.

CCBE Code, which is an attempt to incorporate the best of existing codes and to resolve problems resulting from the different approaches of the civil law and common law systems.

What subjects does the CCBE Code address? The preamble sets out the function of the lawyer in society. The function

lays on him a variety of legal and moral obligations (sometimes appearing to be in conflict with each other) towards:

– the client;

– the courts and other authorities before whom the lawyer pleads his client's cause or acts on his behalf;

— the legal profession in general and each fellow member of it in particular; and

– the public for whom the existence of a free and independent profession, bound together by respect for rules made by the profession itself, is an essential means of safeguarding human rights in face of the power of the state and other interests in society.[10]

The Code emphasizes that these principles apply not only to lawyers' conduct in court cases, but also to their conduct when they provide legal advice to clients. It recognizes that it is, on occasion, extremely difficult to maintain independence, particularly in times of economic difficulty to give the client the advice that the client does not want to hear, with the risk that the lawyer may lose that client. It also addresses "the nature of rules of professional conduct" and makes it clear that the particular rules in a jurisdiction arise from the traditions of each bar or law society: [11]

They are adapted to the organisation and sphere of activity of the profession in the Member State concerned and to its judicial and administrative procedures and to its national legislation. It is neither possible nor desirable that they should be taken out of their context nor that an attempt should be made to give general application to rules which are inherently incapable of such application.[12]

The purpose of the Code and its scope of application are set out in Rule 1.3. The Code emphasizes that after enforceable rules are adopted in relation to lawyers' cross-border activities, the lawyer remains bound to observe the rules of the bar or law society to which he or she belongs to the extent that they are consistent with the Code.[13]

---

[10]   CCBE Code, supra note 2, Rule 1.1.
[11]   Id. Rule 1.2.
[12]   Id. Rule 1.2.2.
[13]   Id. Rule 1.3.2.

The second section of the Code concerns general principles of independence,[14] trust and personal integrity,[15] confidentiality,[16] and respect for the rules of other bars and law societies.[17] It emphasizes that a lawyer must not compromise his independence to please his client, a court or third parties,[18] and that this necessity for independence is just as important in non-contentious as in contentious matters.[19] It also deals with incompatible occupations,[20] personal publicity,[21] and the client's best interests.[22] Some of these sections caused much debate. There are different rules among Member States with respect to confidentiality, incompatible occupations, particularly the ability to take on directorships in companies, and personal publicity.

The next section concerns lawyers' relations with clients, including acceptance and termination of instructions,[23] conflicts of interest,[24] contingency fees,[25] fee sharing with nonlawyers,[26] clients' funds,[27] and professional indemnity insurance.[28] The provisions relating to contingency fees caused considerable discussion. Those relating to clients' funds[29] and professional indemnity insurance,[30] which respectively require that clients' funds be kept separate from those of lawyers and that lawyers be insured at all times against claims for professional negligence, are significant advances in client protection.

The fourth section concerns lawyers' relations with courts, including applicable rules of conduct and demeanour in court, and the fair conduct of proceedings in court.[31] It extends these rules to arbitrators.[32]

The fifth section addresses relations between lawyers, including co-operation among lawyers of different Member States,[33] correspondence

[14]   Id. Rule 2.1.
[15]   Id. Rule 2.2.
[16]   Id. Rule 2.3.
[17]   Id. Rule 2.4.
[18]   Id. Rule 2.1.1.
[19]   Id. Rule 2.1.2.
[20]   Id. Rule 2.5.
[21]   Id. Rule 2.6.
[22]   Id. Rule 2.7.
[23]   Id. Rule 3.1.
[24]   Id. Rule 3.2.
[25]   Id. Rule 3.3.
[26]   Id. Rule 3.6.
[27]   Id. Rule 3.8.
[28]   Id. Rule 3.9.
[29]   Id. Rule 3.8.
[30]   Id. Rule 3.9.
[31]   Id. § 4.
[32]   Id. Rule 4.5.
[33]   Id. Rule 5.2.

between lawyers,[34] communications with opposing parties,[35] changes of lawyers,[36] responsibility for fees,[37] the training of young lawyers,[38] and the resolution of disputes between lawyers.[39] The drafting committee had the task of reconciling the differing rules in common law and civil law jurisdictions concerning questions of confidentiality of correspondence.[40] It had considerable discussion about the rules relating to the change of lawyer[41] and the extent of the responsibility (if any) for a lawyer to ensure that the lawyer previously representing[42] a client had been paid before the succeeding lawyer undertook the client's work. Finally, there was discussion as to how disputes among lawyers from different Member States should be resolved.[43]

The most difficult questions are also ones that have been raised by our U.S. colleagues in our discussions on specific provisions of the Code. The first is *secret professionnel* (professional secrecy).[44] The purpose of this rule is to emphasize the importance of retaining confidentiality between a lawyer and his client and to alert the public and the profession to the danger that state authorities may seek to erode it. The general rule is that a lawyer must not disclose confidential information given by his client. This principle was recognised by the European Court of Justice in *AM & S Europe Ltd v Commission*.[45] It is well understood that this general principle may have to be subject to the right of a court in the most exceptional circumstances to require the disclosure of information given by a client in confidence. The general principle is regarded, however, as being of the greatest importance.

Another difficult question relates to incompatible occupations.[46] The rules are:

2.5.1 In order to perform his functions with due independence and in a manner which is consistent with his duty to participate in the administration of justice a lawyer is excluded from some occupations.

2.5.2 A lawyer who acts in the representation or defence of a client in legal proceedings or before any public authorities in a host Member State shall there

---

[34]   Id. Rule 5.3.
[35]   Id. Rule 5.5.
[36]   Id. Rule 5.6.
[37]   Id. Rule 5.7.
[38]   Id. Rule 5.8.
[39]   Id. Rule 5.9.
[40]   Id. Rule 5.3.
[41]   Id. Rule 5.6.
[42]   Id. Rule 5.7.
[43]   Id. Rule 5.9.
[44]   45. CCBE Code, supra note 2, Rule 2.3.1.
[45]   Case 155/79, [1982] E.C.R. 1575, 1610-14, [1982] 2 C.M.L.R. 264, 322-25.
[46]   CCBE Code, supra note 2, Rule 2.5.

observe the rules regarding incompatible occupations as they are applied to lawyers of the host Member State.[47]

What is behind this rule is the question of whether a lawyer may serve as a director of a company at the same time that he or his firm represents that company in legal proceedings. In many parts of Europe this is simply not possible, but in the United States it happens all the time. What happens in a large firm is that the litigation department handles the litigation on behalf of the client while one of the partners, who does not handle any of the litigation at all, may very well be on the board of the client company. The CCBE Code tries to reconcile the European and U.S. systems. First, it provides that incompatibility relates to the lawyer rather than to the lawyer's firm. The lawyer who is himself representing the client in legal proceedings must not be involved in incompatible occupations such as acting as a director of the client company. Second, the Code reflects the need for the lawyer to respect the rules relating to incompatible occupations of the jurisdiction where the litigation is taking place.[48]

The third question relates to lawyers' advertising or personal publicity. In many jurisdictions the rules on lawyers' advertising have been transformed in the last ten years. In England and Wales, for instance, while barristers were once prohibited from personally advertising their practices, they may now do so subject only to rules of good taste.[49] The CCBE Code seeks to respect the rules of those countries where it is still prohibited and at the same time make it clear that in the case of advertising in books and journals the test should be whether publication is permitted in the place where it is primarily intended,

---

[47]   48. Id.

[48]   See id. Rules 2.5.1, 2.5.2, 2.5.3. The Explanatory Memorandum states that [t]he general purpose of rules excluding a lawyer from other occupations is to protect him from influences which might impair his independence or his role in the administration of justice ....

Articles 2.5.2 and 3 make provision for different circumstances in which a lawyer of one Member State is engaging in cross-border activities (as defined in Article 1.5) in a host Member State when he is not a member of the host State legal profession.

Article 2.5.2 imposes full observation of host State rules regarding incompatible occupations on the lawyer acting in national legal proceedings or before national public authorities in the host State. This applies whether the lawyer is established in the host State or not.

Article 2.5.3, on the other hand, imposes "respect" for the rules of the host State regarding forbidden or incompatible occupations in other cases, but only where the lawyer who is established in the host Member State wishes to participate directly in commercial or other activities not connected with the practice of law.

Explanatory Memorandum, supra note 3, § 2.5.

[49]   See generally English Code, supra note 2. Advertising by barristers must conform to British Code of Advertising Practice. See id. ~ 307. English solicitors' advertising must also be in good taste. See *Solicitors' Publicity Code* ¶ 1(b) (1990) (Eng.).

and that a lawyer should not be disciplined because of an unavoidable incidental publication in a place where it is prohibited.[50]

Fourth, although the rules of professional conduct in the United States relating to conflicts of interest and imputed disqualification are among the strictest in the world,[51] the Code requirement, which provides that where the lawyer is acting for two clients whose interests are in conflict he must cease to act for either of them (without a possibility of waiver),[52] causes difficulty. It may be that in a code of universal application, this matter can be resolved by adding a clause permitting waiver by the client, provided that such waiver is freely given after the issues have been fully explained to the client.

Devising the rules relating to contingency fees[53] caused a great amount of difficulty. Many in Europe are opposed to the idea that payment of a fee should depend on whether or not a lawyer is successful.[54] Many believe that

---

[50] See CCBE Code, supra note 2, Rule 2.6.
[51] See Model Rules, supra note 4, Rules 1.7-1.9; Model Code, supra note 4, Canon 5. Model Rule 1.7 states a general rule concerning conflict of interest:

(a) A lawyer shall not represent a client if the representation of that client will be directly adverse to another client, unless:

(1) the lawyer reasonably believes the representation will not adversely affect the relationship with the other client; and

(2) each client consents after consultation.

(b) A lawyer shall not represent a client if the representation of that client may be materially limited by the lawyer's responsibilities to another client or to a third person, or by the lawyer's own interests, unless:

(1) the lawyer reasonably believes the representation will not be adversely affected; and

(2) the client consents after consultation. When representation of multiple clients in a single matter is undertaken, the consultation shall include explanation of the implications of the common representation and the advantages and risks involved.

Model Rules, supra note 4, Rule 1.7.
[52] CCBE Code, supra note 2, Rule 3.2.
[53] Id. Rule 3.3. The Explanatory Memorandum states that the CCBE Code's position on contingency fees reflects "the common position in all Member States that an unregulated agreement . . . is contrary to the proper administration of justice because it encourages speculative litigation and is liable to be abused." Explanatory Memorandum, supra note 3, § 3.3.
[54] E.g., Manfred Caspari, "EEC Enforcement Policy and Practice: An Official View", 54 Antitrust LJ. 599, 609 (1985); Werner Pfennigstorf, "The European Experience with Attorney Fee Shifting", 47 Law & Contemp. Probs. 37, 59 (1984). In his dissent in a forum non conveniens case, Lord Denning in the Court of Appeal criticized the extent to which lawyers can take advantage of the relatively permissive U.S. rules on contingency fees, Castanho v Brown & Root (U.K.) Ltd., [1980] 1 W.L.R. 833, 857 (C.A.) (Lord Denning, dissenting), aff'd, [1981] A.C. 557. In the leading British case, Spiliada Maritime Corp. v Cansulex Ltd. ("The Spiliada"), [1987] A.C. 460, Lord Goff gave the leading speech, where he said that a court should not take into account in forum non conveniens cases differences in juridical advantages in different legal systems, such as the more liberal discovery rules in the United States including the taking of pre-trial depositions and the availability of contingency fees or treble damages, none of which is available in England. Ibid. at 482; if. In re Union Carbide Corp. Gas Plant Disaster at Bhopal, India, 634 F. Supp. 842 (S.D.N.Y.

this compromises the lawyer's independence of judgment, but a number of Member States permit a form of contingency fee. In France, for example, the Paris Bar permits a lawyer to charge a larger fee if the client's litigation is concluded successfully. A similar provision prevails in Portugal.[55] Since the Courts and Legal Services Act 1990,[56] it is permissible in England and Wales to charge a conditional fee[57] under which in civil cases the advocate or litigator, by written agreement, may receive a percentage above the normal fee in the event of success, but no fee in the event of failure. The Code provides that the general prohibition on contingency fees does not apply where there is an agreement that the fee to be charged is in proportion to the value of the matter handled by the lawyer and is in accordance with an officially-approved fee scale or under the control of the competent authority having jurisdiction over the lawyer.[58] It may be necessary to go a stage further and say that contingency fees are only permissible when they are in accordance with an officiallyapproved fee scale and under the ultimate supervision of the competent authority having jurisdiction over the lawyer. A rule in this form may be acceptable to jurisdictions in the United States and provide a proper balance by making contingency fees available subject to officially recognized safeguards, thereby ensuring that the client's position is properly safeguarded.

The provisions relating to clients' money and professional indemnity insurance are among the most important in the Code. Rule 3.8 now sets out clear requirements that clients' funds should at all times be kept separate from the lawyers' funds.[59] Likewise, in Rule 3.9, there is a requirement that lawyers should be properly insured at all times against claims of professional negligence.[60] If a lawyer is unable to obtain reasonable coverage he shall take reasonable steps to draw this to the attention of his clients.[61] It is noteworthy that our U.S. colleagues had no difficulty with these provisions. It is to be observed that the imposition of a rule for lawyers in host Member States must imply that coverage is available on reasonable terms and that, where applicable, existing arrangements must be taken into account. It is important that the lack of availability of coverage should not be used as an excuse to prevent a foreign lawyer from establishing an office in the host Member State.

1986) (Keenan, J), aff'd in part and rev'd in part, 809 F.2d 195 (2d Cir.), cert. denied sub nom. *Executive Comm. Members v Union of India (Union Carbide Corp.)*, 484 U.S. 871 (1987).

[55] See *EC Legal Systems: An Introductory Guide* (Maurice Sheridan & James Cameron eds. & John Toulmin QC. consulting ed., 1992) (discussing article 65(1) of rules of Portuguese Bar Association, as well as fee charging in other Member States).

[56] Courts and Legal Services Act, 1990 (Eng.).

[57] Id. § 58.

[58] CCBE Code, supra note 2, Rule 3.3.3.

[59] Id. Rule 3.8.

[60] Id. Rule 3.9.

[61] Id. Rule 3.9.2.4.

The problems in formulating rules relating to correspondence between lawyers are similar to those for *secret professionnel* in that there are significant differences in the rules in different Member States. In Denmark, Germany, the Netherlands, and the United Kingdom (and in the United States), "without prejudice" communications cannot be withheld from the client unless the client agrees.[62] In other jurisdictions such communications must be withheld from the client.[63] The rule in the Code emphasizes the need for a communication to be clearly marked as confidential and imposes the duty on a recipient who cannot guarantee its confidentiality to return it to the sender without revealing its contents to others.[64]

There was much discussion on the rules relating to the change of lawyer and responsibility for the fees of the lawyer who has been replaced. In some jurisdictions a lawyer has a duty before he takes on a case to ensure that a previous lawyer has been paid.[65] In the common law jurisdictions no such duty exists. The compromise is that the lawyer should have some duty to ascertain that arrangements have been made for the settlement of the former lawyer's account.[66]

The provisions relating to responsibility for fees reaffirm provisions contained in the Declaration of Perugia.[67] The provisions make clear that where work is being referred by one lawyer to another it is important that the fee arrangements should be clear at the outset. The rules follow the principle familiar to common lawyers that where a lawyer instructs a colleague to give him advice that will be passed on to the client, the lawyer making the request is liable to pay the fees of the second lawyer.[68] Where the lawyer simply refers his client to another lawyer, he is not liable.

It will have become clear that the Code is the product of discussion both on general principles and on difficult practical questions. A code of general application will need to build on the work that has been done. From helpful and constructive discussions with my US colleagues I am satisfied that there is no fundamental question that will prevent the CCBE Code of Conduct from providing a basis for a cross-border code of universal application.

---

[62] For further discussion on laws concerning correspondence between lawyers, see Serge-Pierre Laguerre, *Lawyers in the European Community* 151-52 (1987).

[63] See Explanatory Memorandum, supra note 3, § 5.3. The Explanatory Memorandum states that "[t]his principle is recognised in Belgium, France, Greece, Italy, Luxembourg, Portugal and Spain." Id.

[64] CCBE Code, supra note 2, Rules 5.3.1, 5.3.2.

[65] See Explanatory Memorandum, supra note 3, § 5.6.

[66] CCBE Code, supra note 2, Rule 5.6.1.

[67] See CCBE, Declaration of Perugia on the Principles of Professional Conduct (Sept. 16, 1977), discussed in Laguerre, supra note 63, at 255-58; see also CCBE Code, supra note 2, Rules 5.6, 5.7.

[68] CCBE Code, supra note 2, Rule 5.7; see Model Rules, supra note 4, Rule 1.5 comment (discussing division of fees).

I know that the US federal system of government poses a particular problem for the United States to adopt such a code. It is the individual states that adopt their own rules of conduct and not the ABA, or the federal government. The ABA is not in a position to deliver the agreement of all fifty states. My proposal is that an international code should be agreed upon as a set of general principles to which individual jurisdictions would be invited to subscribe. In this respect the position is no different to the implementation of the CCBE Code, which has been voluntarily adopted throughout the EEC by jurisdictions no less independent than the states of the United States.

Appendix

CCBE Code of Conduct for Lawyers in the European Community

1 Preamble

1.1 *The Function of the Lawyer in Society*

In a society founded on respect for the rule of law the lawyer fulfils a special role. His duties do not begin and end with the faithful performance of what he is instructed to do so far as the law permits. A lawyer must serve the interests of justice as well as those whose rights and liberties he is trusted to assert and defend and it is his duty not only to plead his client's cause but to be his adviser.

A lawyer's function therefore lays on him a variety of legal and moral obligations (sometimes appearing to be in conflict with each other) towards:

– the client;

– the courts and other authorities before whom the lawyer pleads his client's cause or acts on his behalf;

– the legal profession in general and each fellow member of it in particular; and

the public for whom the existence of a free and independent profession, bound together by respect for rules made by the profession itself, is an essential means of safeguarding human rights in face of the power of the state and other interests in society.

1.2 *The Nature of Rules of Professional Conduct*

1.2.1 Rules of professional conduct are designed through their willing acceptance by those to whom they apply to ensure the proper performance by the lawyer of a function which is recognised as essential in all civilised societies. The failure of the lawyer to observe these rules must in the last resort result in a disciplinary sanction.

1.2.2 The particular rules of each Bar or Law Society arise from its own traditions. They are adapted to the organisation and sphere of activity of the profession in the Member State concerned and to its judicial and administrative procedures and to its national legislation. It is neither possible nor desirable that they should be taken out of their context nor that an attempt should be made to give general application to rules which are inherently incapable of such application.

The particular rules of each Bar and Law Society nevertheless are based on the same values and in most cases demonstrate a common foundation.

1.3 *The Purpose of the Code*

1.3.1 The continued integration of the European Community and the increasing frequency of the cross-border activities of lawyers within the Community have made necessary in the public interest the statement of common rules which apply to all lawyers from the Community whatever Bar or Law Society they belong to in relation to their cross-border practice. A particular purpose of the statement of those rules is to mitigate the difficulties which result from the application of "double deontology" as set out in Article 4 of the E.C. Directive 77/249 of 22nd March 1977.

1.3.2 The organisations representing the legal profession through the CCBE propose that the rules codified in the following articles:

– be recognised at the present time as the expression of a consensus of all the Bars and Law Societies of the European Community;

– be adopted as enforceable rules as soon as possible in accordance with national or Community procedures in relation to the cross-border activities of the lawyer in the European Community;

– be taken into account in all revisions of national rules of deontology or professional practice with a view to their progressive harmonisation.

They further express the wish that the national rules of deontology or professional practice be interpreted and applied whenever possible in a way consistent with the rules in this Code.

After the rules in this Code have been adopted as enforceable rules in relation to his cross-border activities the lawyer will remain bound to observe the rules of the Bar or Law Society to which he belongs to the extent that they are consistent with the rules in this Code.

1.4 *Field of Application Ratione Personae*

The following rules shall apply to lawyers of the European Community as they are defined by the Directive 77/249 of 22nd March 1977.

1.5 *Field of Application Ratione Materiae*

Without prejudice to the pursuit of a progressive harmonisation of rules of deontology or professional practice which apply only internally within a Member State, the following rules shall apply to the cross-border activities of the lawyer within the European Community. Cross-border activities shall mean:

(a) all professional contacts with lawyers of Member States other than his own; and

(b) the professional activities of the lawyer in a Member State other than his own, whether or not the lawyer is physically present in that Member State.

1.6 *Definitions*

In these rules: "Home Member State" means the Member State of the Bar or Law Society to which the lawyer belongs. "Host Member State" means any other Member State where the lawyer carries on cross-border activities.

"Competent authority" means the professional organisation(s) or authority(ies) of the Member State concerned responsible for the laying down of rules of professional conduct and the administration of discipline of lawyers.

2 General Principles

2.1 *Independence*

2.1.1 The many duties to which a lawyer is subject require his absolute independence, free from all other influence, especially such as may arise from his personal interests or external pressure. Such independence is as necessary to trust in the process of justice as the impartiality of the judge. A lawyer must therefore avoid any impairment of his independence and be careful not to compromise his professional standards in order to please his client, the court or third parties.

2.1.2 This independence is necessary in non-contentious matters as well as in litigation. Advice given by a lawyer to his client has no value if it is given only to ingratiate himself, to serve his personal interests or in response to outside pressure.

2.2 *Trust and Personal Integrity*

Relationships of trust can only exist if a lawyer's personal honour, honesty and integrity are beyond doubt. For the lawyer these traditional virtues are professional obligations.

2.3 *Confidentiality*

2.3.1 It is of the essence of a lawyer's function that he should be told by his client things which the client would not tell to others, and that he should be the recipient of other information on a basis of confidence. Without the certainty of confidentiality there cannot be trust. Confidentiality is therefore a primary and fundamental right and duty of the lawyer.

2.3.2 A lawyer shall accordingly respect the confidentiality of all information given to him by his client, or received by him about his client or others in the course of rendering services to his client.

2.3.3 The obligation of confidentiality is not limited in time.

2.3.4 A lawyer shall require his associates and staff and anyone engaged by him in the course of providing professional services to observe the same obligation of confidentiality .

2.4 *Respect for the Rules of Other Bars and Law Societies*

Under Community Law (in particular under the Directive 77/249 of 22nd March 1977) a lawyer from another Member State may be bound to comply with the rules of the Bar or Law Society of the host Member State. Lawyers have a duty to inform themselves as to the rules which will affect them in the performance of any particular activity.

2.5 *Incompatible Occupations*

2.5.1 In order to perform his functions with due independence and in a manner which is consistent with his duty to participate in the administration of justice a lawyer is excluded from some occupations.

2.5.2 A lawyer who acts in the representation or the defence or [sic] a client in legal proceedings or before any public authorities in a host Member State shall there observe the rules regarding incompatible occupations as they are applied to lawyers of the host Member State.

2.5.3 A lawyer established in a host Member State in which he wishes to participate directly in commercial or other activities not connected with the practice of the law shall respect the rules regarding forbidden or incompatible occupations as they are applied to lawyers of that Member State.

2.6 *Personal Publicity*

2.6.1 A lawyer should not advertise or seek personal publicity where this is not permitted.

In other cases a lawyer should only advertise or seek personal publicity to the extent and in the manner permitted by the rules to which he is subject.

2.6.2 Advertising and personal publicity shall be regarded as taking place where it is permitted, if the lawyer concerned shows that it was placed for the purpose of reaching clients or potential clients located where such advertising or personal publicity is permitted and its communication elsewhere is incidental.

2.7 *The Client's Interests*

Subject to due observance of all rules of law and professional conduct, a lawyer must always act in the best interests of his client and must put those interests before his own interests or those of fellow members of the legal profession.

3 Relations with Clients

3.1 *Acceptance and Termination of Instructions*

3.1.1 A lawyer shall not handle a case for a party except on his instructions. He may, however, act in a case in which he has been instructed by another lawyer who himself acts for the party or where the case has been assigned to him by a competent body.

3.1.2 A lawyer shall advise and represent his client promptly [sic] conscientiously and diligently. He shall undertake personal responsibility for the discharge of the instructions given to him. He shall keep his client informed as to the progress of the matter entrusted to him.

3.1.3 A lawyer shall not handle a matter which he knows or ought to know he is not competent to handle, without cooperating with a lawyer who is competent to handle it.

A lawyer shall not accept instructions unless he can discharge those instructions promptly having regard to the pressure of other work .

3.1.4 A lawyer shall not be entitled to exercise his right to withdraw from a case in such a way or in such circumstances that the client may be unable to find other legal assistance in time to prevent prejudice being suffered by the client.

3.2 *Conflict of Interest*

3.2.1 A lawyer may not advise, represent or act on behalf of two or more clients in the same matter if there is a conflict, or a significant risk of a conflict, between the interests of those clients.

3.2.2 A lawyer must cease to act for both clients when a conflict of interest arises between those clients and also whenever there is a risk of a breach of confidence or where his independence may be impaired.

3.2.3 A lawyer must also refrain from acting for a new client if there is a risk of a breach of confidences entrusted to the lawyer by a former client or if the knowledge which the lawyer possesses of the affairs of the former client would give an undue advantage to the new client.

3.2.4 Where lawyers are practising in association, paragraphs 3.2.1 to 3.2.3 above shall apply to the association and all its members.

3.3 *Pactum de Quota Litis*

3.3.1 A lawyer shall not be entitled to make a *pactum de quota litis*.

3.3.2 By *"pactum de quota litis"* is meant an agreement between a lawyer and his client entered into prior to the final conclusion of a matter to which the client is a party, by virtue of which the client undertakes to pay the lawyer a share of the result regardless of whether this is represented by a sum of money or by any other benefit achieved by the client upon the conclusion of the matter.

3.3.3 The *pactum de quota litis* does not include an agreement that fees be charged in proportion to the value of a matter handled by the lawyer if this is in accordance with an officially approved fee scale or under the control of competent authority having jurisdiction over the lawyer.

3.4 *Regulation of Fees*

3.4.1 A fee charged by a lawyer shall be fully disclosed to his client and shall be fair and reasonable.

3.4.2 Subject to any proper agreement to the contrary between a lawyer and his client fees charged by a lawyer shall be subject to regulation in accordance with the rules applied to members of the Bar or Law Society to which he belongs. If he belongs to more than one Bar or Law Society the rules applied shall be those with the closest connection to the contract between the lawyer and his client.

3.5 *Payment on Account*

If a lawyer requires a payment on account of his fees and/or disbursements such payment should not exceed a reasonable estimate of the fees and probable disbursements involved.

Failing such payment, a lawyer may withdraw from the case or refuse to handle it, but subject always to paragraph 3.1.4 above.

3.6 *Fee Sharing with Non-Lawyers*

3.6.1 Subject as after-mentioned a lawyer may not share his fees with a person who is not a lawyer.

3.6.2 The provisions of 6.1 above shall not preclude a lawyer from paying a fee, commission or other compensation to a deceased lawyer's heirs or to a retired lawyer in respect of taking over the deceased or retired lawyer's practice.

3.7 *Legal Aid*

A lawyer shall inform his client of the availability of legal aid where applicable.

3.8 *Clients [sic] Funds*

3.8.1 When lawyers at any time in the course of their practice come into possession of funds on behalf of their clients or third parties (hereinafter called "client's funds") it shall be obligatory:

3.8.1.1 That client's funds shall always be held in an account in a bank of similar institution subject to supervision of Public Authority and that all clients' [sic] funds received by a lawyer should be paid into such an account unless the client explicitly or by implication agrees that the funds should be dealt with otherwise.

3.8.1.2 That any account in which the client's funds are held in the name of the lawyer should indicate in the title or designation that the funds are held on behalf of the client or client's [sic] of the lawyer.

3.8.1.3 That any account or accounts in which client's funds are held in the name of the lawyer should at all times contain a sum which is not less than the total of the client's funds held by the lawyer.

3.8.1.4 That all client's funds should be available for payment to clients on demand or upon such conditions as the client may authorise.

3.8.1.5 That payments made from client's funds on behalf of a client to any other person including

a) payments made to or for one client from funds held for another client and

b) payment of the lawyer's fees, be prohibited except to the extent that they are permitted by law or have the express or implied authority of the client for whom the payment is being made.

3.8.1.6 That the lawyer shall maintain full and accurate records, available to each client on request, showing all his dealings with his client's funds and distinguishing client's funds from other funds held by him.

3.8.1.7 That the competent authorities in all Member States should have powers to allow them to examine and investigate on a confidential basis the financial records of lawyer's client's funds to ascertain whether or not the rules which they make are being complied with and to impose sanctions upon lawyers who fail to comply with those rules.

3.8.2 Subject as after mentioned, and without prejudice to the rules set out in 3.8.1 above, a lawyer who holds clients [sic] funds in the course of carrying on practice in any Member State must comply with the rules relating to holding and accounting for client's funds which are applied by the competent authorities of the Home Member State.

3.8.3 A lawyer who carries on practice or provides services in a Host Member States [sic] may with the agreement of the competent authorities of the Home and Host Member State concerned comply with the requirements of the Host Member State to the exclusion of the requirements of the Home Member State. In that event he shall take reasonable steps to inform his clients that he complies with the requirements in force in the Host Member State.

3.9 *Professional Indemnity Insurance*

3.9.1 Lawyers shall be insured at all times against claims based on professional negligence to an extent which is reasonable having regard to the nature and extent of the risks which lawyers incur in practice.

3.9.2.1 Subject as aftermentioned, a lawyer who provides services or carries on practice in a Member State must comply with any Rules relating to his obligation to insure against his professional liability as a lawyer which are in force in his Home Member State.

3.9.2.2 A lawyer who is obliged so to insure in his Home Member State and who provides services or carries on practice in any Host Member State shall use his best endeavours to obtain insurance cover on the basis required in his Home Member State extended to services which he provides or practice which he carries on in a Host Member State.

3.9.2.3 A lawyer who fails to obtain the extended insurance cover referred to in paragraph 3.9.2.2 above or who is not obliged so to insure in his Home Member State and who provides services or carries on practice in a Host Member State shall in so far as possible obtain insurance cover against his professional liability as a lawyer whilst acting for clients in that Host Member State on at least an equivalent basis to that required of lawyers in the Host Member State.

3.9.2.4 To the extent that a lawyer is unable to obtain the insurance cover required by the foregoing rules, he shall take reasonable steps to draw that fact to the attention of such of his clients as might be affected in the event of a claim against him.

3.9.2.5 A lawyer who carries on practice or provides services in a Host Member State may with the agreement of the competent authorities of the

Home and Host Member States concerned comply with such insurance requirements as are in force in the Host Member State to the exclusion of the insurance requirements of the Home Member State. In this event he shall take reasonable steps to inform his clients that he is insured according to the requirements in force in the Host Member State.

4 Relations with the Courts

4.1 *Applicable Rules of Conduct in Court*

A lawyer who appears, or takes part in a case, before a court or tribunal in a Member State must comply with the rules of conduct applied before that court or tribunal.

4.2 *Fair Conduct of Proceedings*

A lawyer must always have due regard for the fair conduct of proceedings. He must not, for example, make contact with the judge without first informing the lawyer acting for the opposing party or submit exhibits, notes or documents to the judge without communicating them in good time to the lawyer on the other side unless such steps are permitted under the relevant rules of procedure.

4.3 *Demeanour in Court*

A lawyer shall while maintaining due respect and courtesy towards the court defend the interests of his client honourably and in a way which he considers will be to the client's best advantage within the limits of the law.

4.4 *False or Misleading Information*

A lawyer shall never knowingly give false or misleading information to the court.

4.5 *Extension to Arbitrators Etc.*

The rules governing a lawyer's relations with the courts apply also to his relations with arbitrators and any other persons exercising judicial or quasi-judicial functions, even on an occasional basis.

5. Relations between Lawyers

5.1 *Corporate Spirit of the Profession*

5.1.1 The corporate spirit of the profession requires a relationship of trust and co-operation between lawyers for the benefit of their clients and in order to avoid unnecessary litigation. It can never justify setting the interests of the profession against those of justice or of those who seek it.

5.1.2 A lawyer should recognise all other lawyers of Member States as professional colleagues and act fairly and courteously towards them.

5.2 Co-operation Among Lawyers of Different Member States

5.2.1 It is the duty of a lawyer who is approached by a colleague from another Member State not to accept instructions in a matter which he is not competent to undertake. He should be prepared to help his colleague to obtain the information necessary to enable him to instruct a lawyer who is capable of providing the service asked for.

5.2.2 Where a lawyer of a Member State co-operates with a lawyer from another Member State, both have a general duty to take into account the differences which may exist between their respective legal systems and the professional organisations [sic] competences and obligations of lawyers in the Member States concerned.

5.3 Correspondence Between Lawyers

5.3.1 If a lawyer sending a communication to a lawyer in another Member State wishes it remain confidential or without prejudice he should clearly express this intention when communicating the document.

5.3.2 If the recipient of the communication is unable to ensure is [sic] status as confidential or without prejudice he should return it to the sender without revealing the contents to others.

5.4 Referral Fees

5.4.1 A lawyer may not demand or accept from another lawyer or any other person a fee, commission or any other compensation for referring or recommending a client.

5.4.2 A lawyer may not pay anyone a fee, commission or any other compensation as a consideration for referring a client to himself.

5.5 Communication with Opposing Parties

A lawyer shall not communicate about a particular case or matter directly with any person whom he knows to be represented or advised in the case or matter by another lawyer, without the consent of that other lawyer (and shall keep the other lawyer informed of any such communications).

5.6 *Change of Lawyer*

5.6.1 A lawyer who is instructed to represent a client in substitution for another lawyer in relation to a particular matter should inform that other lawyer and, subject to 5.6.2 below, should not begin to act until he has ascertained that arrangements have been made for the settlement of the other lawyer's fees and disbursements. This duty does not, however, make the new lawyer personally responsible for the former lawyer's fees and disbursements.

5.6.2 If urgent steps have to be taken in the interests of the client before the conditions in 5.6.1 above can be complied with, the lawyer may take such steps provided he informs the other lawyer immediately.

5.7 *Responsibility for Fees*

In professional relations between members of Bars of different Member States, where a lawyer does not confine himself to recommending another lawyer or introducing him to the client but himself entrusts a correspondent with a particular matter or seeks his advice, he is personally bound, even if the client is insolvent, to pay the fees, costs and outlays which are due to the foreign correspondent. The lawyers concerned may, however, at the outset of the relationship between them make special arrangements on this matter. Further, the instructing lawyer may at any time limit his personal responsibility to the amount of the fees, costs and outlays incurred before intimation to the foreign lawyer of his disclaimer of responsibility for the future.

5.8 *Training Young Lawyers*

In order to improve trust and co-operation amongst lawyers of different Member States for the clients' benefit there is a need to encourage a better knowledge of the laws and procedures in different Member States. Therefore, when considering the need for the profession to give good training to young lawyers, lawyers should take into account the need to give training to young lawyers from other Member States.'

5.9 *Disputes Amongst Lawyers in Different Member States*

5.9.1 If a lawyer considers that a colleague in another Member State has acted in breach of a rule of professional conduct he shall draw the matter to the attention of his colleague.

5.9.2 If any personal dispute of a professional nature arises amongst lawyers in different Member States they should if possible first try to settle it in a friendly way.

5.9.3 A lawyer shall not commence any form of proceedings against a colleague in another Member State on matters referred to in 5.9.1 or 5.9.2 above without first informing the Bars or Law Societies to which they both belong for the purpose of allowing both Bars or Law Societies concerned an opportunity to assist in reaching a settlement.

Ethical rules and Professional Ideologies

In 1997 it was appropriate to look back over the transformation of legal practice during the previous thirty years since I started to practice law and to consider particular contentious issues of practice, many of which remain current fifteen years later. I had the opportunity to do so at a Cornell University Law School Seminar in Paris on 4-5 July 1997. The speech was subsequently revised for publication as Chapter 14 of *Lawyers' Practice and Ideals, A Comparative View* published by Kluwer Law International in 1999. I have made minor amendments to avoid repetition.

The chapter explains the changes in the practice of law and the expansion in the number of lawyers in England and Wales and the United States from the 1960s when I was called to the Bar and worked for a New York law firm. These crucial events transformed legal practice from individual practice on a lawyer's own, or within a relatively small firm to large corporate law practice with a partner heading teams of more junior lawyers and paralegals who would do the dull, time-consuming but extremely lucrative research, drafting and document review work. The changes accelerated during the 1980s and the 1990s. They led to fat years for the civil and commercially based legal profession. Michael Trotter's thoughtful book *Profit and Practice of the Law*, referred to at page 241, is re-published and is available at www.amazon.com. Trotter is a prominent corporate lawyer from Atlanta, Georgia.

This period may be ending, not least with the advent of strong company in-house legal departments led by the equivalent of successful partners in major law firms, the advent of sophisticated computers and the publication of templates for an increasing number of relatively routine but otherwise time-consuming (and extremely profitable) legal tasks. These factors will eliminate much of the profitable and time-consuming work by middle-rank associates and paralegals which has fuelled the large fees of law firms and firms of solicitors. Real value-added work will continue, rightly, to attract high fees. Michael Trotter is following up his previous book by another, also to be available at www.amazon.com, with the title *Declining Prospects: How Extraordinary Competition and Compensation Are Changing America's Major Law Firms*.It is a sobering book which analyses carefully and in depth current and likely future trends in the legal profession in the United States. These same trends can be expected for the major English solicitors' firms and other comparable firms around the world.

The article also considers the cost of litigation. The refrain is a familiar one - "Going to law is too expensive and too protracted both for ordinary litigants and for large corporations". It also addresses the question of multi-disciplinary practices, still a current important topic. Although I have not included the contributions of the two Professors whose points I am addressing, the points emerge clearly enough. Finally it addresses the question of professional ethics with further reflections on the CCBE Code.

I analyse what I saw then, and still see, as very real practical problems in permitting multi-disciplinary partnerships between lawyers and accountants. Even with the relative commercialisation of large firm legal practice, the ethos of legal practice and accounting practice remains a distance apart. I found this on the two occasions when firms of accountants were retained to report on the legal profession and I observed their work. On neither occasion did the accountants have a real and instinctive understanding of the professional duties and obligations of the legal profession.

To those who see "one stop shopping" as a panacea, I still say "Beware". This topic has international relevance since, if multi-disciplinary practices are permitted in one country and the legal entity sets up a branch office in a state where it is prohibited, it is impossible to prevent the entity from referring work offshore to the office in the country where it is permitted.

Ethical Rules and Professional Ideologies

John Toulmin CMG QC *

INTRODUCTION

It is a great privilege to be invited to speak at this fascinating seminar.

I led for the CCBE[1] in discussions between the European, American, and Japanese legal professions on the free movement of lawyers and a common code of professional ethics. I also led for the CCBE on discussions with the European Community (EC) Commission on a draft directive on the right of lawyers to establish offices in other Member States using their existing home qualification[2] and on negotiations relating to the services of lawyers in the GATT Round where I was involved in formulating the European Union (EU) Specific Commitment to Market Access under Article XVI of the General Agreement on Trade in Services (GATS).[3] I am presently a nominated member of service panels of the Dispute Settlement Body of the World Trade Organization. Although there are important differences between professional ideologies in the legal professions of the United States and Western Europe, lawyers from the two regions have much more in common than divides them. They are like two trains on the same tracks going in the same direction with the US train in the lead. Many in Europe see in the United States what lies ahead for them and are concerned at what they see. This is not the only perspective. I suspect, too, that the ideology of a large firm in New York or Chicago has more in common with that of a large firm in London or Brussels than with the single practitioner in Ithaca, New York. Although there are differences in the ethical rules in different parts of the world, the rules have much in common. If the will existed to do it, a worldwide code of ethical principles could be agreed based on the U.S.Model Rules, the Japanese Code, and the

---

* At the time that this paper was prepared Judge John Toulmin was a practicing Queen's Counsel. Since November 1997 he is a Judge of the Technology and Construction Court of the High Court. This paper was prepared for the Cornell Law School seminar in Paris, 4-5 July 1997, and was revised after the seminar.

[1] Council of the Bars and Law Societies of Europe

[2] A final text COM(96)446 Final was published by the EC Council on 25 April 1997.It is based on the draft agreed to by the CCBE by a majority of 10-2 and presented to the EC Commission in November 1992. For an authoritative commentary on the Directive see Adamson, *Free Movement Of Lawyers*, 2nd ed, 1998. The Directive was adopted 14 March 1998 to come into force on 14 March 2000. Council Directive (EC) 98/5 CDJ L77 14/3/98 p. 36.

[3] See 1995 Documents Supplement to Legal problems of International Economic Relations 3rd Ed by Jackson, Davey & Sykes.

CCBE Code, which has been adopted in all the countries in the European Union. I shall deal with this later. It is also largely the subject of the paper by Professor Leubsdorf.

Speed of Change

I am acutely conscious of how difficult the task of the comparative lawyer is today. The speed of change in the worldwide legal profession, particularly in Europe, has accelerated in the last ten years so that statistics of even four years ago are out of date and conclusions drawn from them are liable to be misleading. There are two major causes of change. First, commercial legal practice has become global. The legal professions from Germany and France were at first slow to respond to change but are no w doing so along with others in Europe. Second, the influence of the development of a European-wide legal order both through the European Union and the European Court of Human Rights is having a significant effect. These are broad enough topics in themselves to be the subject of separate papers.

Professional Ideologies – A Concern

I should like to start with professional ideologies. There can be no disguising the fear, particularly in civil law countries and Japan, that they will be overrun by common law practices and that the low esteem in which lawyers are held in the United States will spread to other countries.

It seems that the larger and more powerful the law firms in the United States have become, the lower lawyers have fallen in public esteem. The perception that lawyers are no longer in a unique profession with overriding responsibilities to the system of justice has encouraged the large accounting firms to campaign for the inclusion of lawyers in accountant-led M D Ps. I shall comment later on Professor Wolfram's Paper on multi-disciplinary practices.

The Historical Perspective- United States

The practice of law has changed radically in the United States since I was in New York in 1965. Many of these changes are identified in *Profit and the Practice of Law* by Michael H.Trotter, a partner in the Atlanta law firm of Kilpatrick and Stockton[4] (with offices in Augusta, Brussels, Charlotte, London, Raleigh, Washington, D.C., and Winston-Salem, a commentary on change in itself). The changes in law practice have been much greater in the last thirty years than in the previous seventy years.

---

[4] See Michael H. Trotter, *Profit and the Practice of Law- What's Happened to the Legal Profession?* University of Georgia Press, 1997.

In 1891 Henry L. Stimson, having passed the New York Bar exams, spent a year in Articles.[5] The great change that occurred in New York in the 1890s was that he was paid during his articles. He joined with Bronson Winthrop in 1893 as a junior partner in the firm led by Elihu Root.[6] Winthrop was the trusts and estates lawyer, and Stimson was the litigator involved in general but important litigation. The firm prospered. Stimson had a most distinguished public career. Winthrop recruited like-minded individuals including Albert Putnam and George Roberts, who formed the backbone of a firm whose members not only regarded individual professional integrity and service within the firm as paramount but also felt it important that the lawyers in the firm, both partners and associates, should have a home life and interests outside the la w. On arrival at the firm in 1965 I was told firmly by the managing partner, James W. Husted, that the hours of the firm were 9:30 to 5:30 and although I was expected to do so whenever necessary, I would receive no brownie points for staying late unnecessarily. Winthrop Stimson Putnam and Roberts then had eighty-five lawyers, of whom twenty-five were partners, and prided itself on the fact that everyone including unqualified staff was part of the firm's family.[7] [The firm has now merged with a west coast law firm and is called Pilsbury Winthrop. I have no specific knowledge of Pilsbury Winthrop, but for most firms of comparable size this ethos has long gone – see Trotter, *Declining Prospects*, page 58.]]

In his informative book, Michael Trotter looks back to the 1960s[8] and notes that then the largest firm in New York had one hundred twenty-five lawyers[9] and the largest in Atlanta had twenty-one. Firms normally had only one major office although some firms outside Washington DC may have had small offices there and some had one or more small overseas offices.

There was only a small number of associates in relation to the number of partners. The largest firm in Atlanta had seventeen partners and four associates.

The firms maintained the highest standards in recruitment, but one of the criteria that would be thought in the 1990s to be potentially discriminatory was whether the lawyer would "fit in" with the ethos of the firm. Firms were

---

[5] See *Turmoil and Tradition -A Study of the Life and Times of Henry L. Stimson* by Elting E. Morison, published by Houghton Miflin Company Boston Chapter 6, 1960. I am honored that my copy has the inscription from George Roberts: ◊As a memento of his (my) association with the law firm of Henry L. Stimson whose character and force have exerted a continuing influence on our practice of law".

[6] In 1901the firm name was changed from Root and Clarke to Winthrop and Stimson. Root had left in 1899 to become Secretary of War.

[7] In the *History of Winthrop, Stimson, Putnam, and Roberts* (privately printed) the firm is described as it expanded in the 1920s as a "fellowship of lawyers." This spirit was certainly present in the 1960s. I believe, contrary to what is said in this paper, that it has been largely retained.

[8] Trotter, supra, Chapter 1,note 5.

[9] Shearman and Sterling. It now has over fifty lawyers in its Paris office alone.

experimenting with billable hours, but it was felt that if hours were used as the sole measure of charging, it did not give a fair indication of value for money. Learning time should be discounted. Particular expertise should be charged at a higher rate. No billing targets were set for partners or associates. Partners were normally paid equal shares of the profits once they had paid for their share of the goodwill [or paid on a lockstep incremental basis]. This did not depend on performance criteria. Clients were loyal to the law firm and often paid a substantial part of their fees by an annual retainer. Large corporations had only small in-house legal departments. Marketing was prohibited by the bar associations in all states. Public service was one of the few ways in which a lawyer could make him or herself more widely known. Lawyers did not specialize beyond very broad areas. Lawyers were loyal to their firm and did not move to another firm except in unusual circumstances. There were only primitive photocopiers; no fax, only telex; no word processors, only type writers; no video conferencing, only primitive telephone conference facilities.

This situation contrasts greatly with that of the 1990s.[10] A number of US law firms have over five hundred lawyers in offices worldwide. Many firms in the U S regard themselves as national law firms rather than New York or Los Angeles or Chicago law firms. Much of the work requires very skilled lawyers, but much is routine and can be done by permanent associates or people in their early years of practice. Billable hours are of paramount importance for partners and associates: associates are often expected to achieve over two thousand billable hours and partners eighteen hundred hours. In addition, they are expected to spend significant additional time on practice development in promotion and advertising. Partners who fail to meet the required objectives will not only suffer a cut in their share of the partnership profits but may be prematurely retired. In any event, the normal retirement age in large firms has been significantly reduced and many in their forties and early fifties suffer burnout. Many marriages or other close relationships fail because the lawyers are never at home. Clients are fickle and shop around between law firms. Many corporations now have in-house staffs the size of large law firms. Public service is regarded, except in a few exceptional cases, as a distraction from the business of making money out of the law.[11] The marketing department, often led by non-lawyers, is regarded as crucial to the success of the firm. Lawyers, including partners, move freely from one firm to another. The firms have to have the latest technology. The legal profession has become the law business. The practice of the law seems to have become less distinct from other professions or businesses. From my own perspective this picture, expressing a view commonly held by those inside

[10]   These comments are based on comments in Mr Trotter's book and my own observations. They were in general supported at the seminar.
[11]   A notable exception is the recent trend in a number of large U.S. firms to encourage pro-bono work.

and outside the law, may be a little exaggerated. Nevertheless, there has been a significant change in the attitude of lawyers and in the functioning of their firms in the last forty years.

The Historical Perspective- England and Wales and Other Parts of Europe

The shape of the solicitors' profession in England has changed dramatically in the last thirty years. Until 1969[12] partnerships were limited to under twenty members. Since that time solicitors' firms have grown in size and number of offices worldwide so that the largest firms rival the largest U.S. firms in a global market.[13] Regional firms from Birmingham, Bristol, Manchester, and Leeds have amalgamated and expanded into London (and abroad) to compete with the firms from the City of London.[14] The recent removal of the restriction on multinational partnerships has meant that, starting with Coudert Brothers, some US law firms have recruited English solicitor partners and provide a full service in London, including advice on English law. London solicitors have taken the lead elsewhere in Europe in opening foreign offices and forging alliances with lawyers from other parts of the world. A notable change that has accompanied these developments is that restrictions on advertising for solicitors and barristers have been largely removed.

There has also been a significant change in the pattern of practice at the Bar of England and Wales. It is clear that the rules under which English barristers operate are little understood in the United States. The English Bar in private practice in the U K has grown in size to 9,698 barristers on October 1, 1998.[15]

---

[12]   1969 Companies Act.
[13]   In 1996 Clifford Chance had 1,418 lawyers worldwide, 907 in London, Freshfields 741, Alien and Overy 697, Linklaters and Paines 640, Simmons and Simmons 615, and Slaughter and May 600.(Figures taken from European Legal 500, 1996.)
[14]   For example, in 1997, Hammond Suddards had 302 lawyers, with offices in Bradford, Brussels, Leeds, London, and Manchester. Osborne Clarke had 183 lawyers with offices in Bristol, Barcelona, Brussels, Frankfurt, Copenhagen, Lyon, Paris, and Rotterdam.
[15]   See General Council of the Bar, Annual Report, 1996. There are 1005 barristers in the Crown Prosecution Service and the Government Legal Service. Id.

	Total	Women	Women as Percentage
October 1973	3,137	239	7.61
1974	3,368	252	7.48
1984	5,203	641	12.31
1985	5,367	696	12.97
1994	8,093	1,763	21.78
1995	8,498	1,900	22.36
1996	8,935	2,115	23.67
1998	9,698	2,410	24.85

Women barristers provide 39.7 percent of the increase between 1985 and 1996 and 41.81 percent

As can be seen from the figures below, one-third practice from Chambers (offices) outside London. Increasing numbers in London practice from chambers located outside the Inns of Court. Barristers join together to share expenses but may not share fees and so must be separately instructed. Nevertheless, frequently in complex cases two or more barristers appear together in court to represent a single client, often, but not invariably, from the same Chambers. Barristers' Chambers have increased in size so that many now have over forty members. Professional expenses of chambers are usually graded so that the more senior and higher earners pay a greater proportion than those starting in the profession. It has not been the case for many years that a young barrister in good Chambers will spend some years without being able to provide for himself out of his or her earnings.[16] Barristers are entitled to receive referrals direct from foreign lawyers, other professionals, and even lay clients outside the United Kingdom.

Partnerships between barristers are prohibited and the Bar cherishes its independent role, which includes supporting the individual against the state. In the last thirty years it has been in the forefront (with the judges) in developing judicial review (in the Administrative Court) as a means of providing redress for individuals against administrative decisions of the state, including local government. Barristers are not free under their ethical rules to refuse to accept cases in the areas in which they practice provided they are available to do so and an appropriate fee is offered.[17]

In other parts of Europe, the changes have been more recent but no less profound. The amalgamation of the professions of avocat and conseil juridique in France from 1 January 1991 will no doubt be discussed by Batonnier Ader.

---

of the increase between 1994 and 1996.

Barristers practicing from chambers outside London

1973	883
1974	941
1984	1,505
1985	1,552
1994	2,719
1995	2,88 7
1996	3,052

Id. The percentage practicing from chambers out of London has risen slightly from 28 percent in 1973 to 34.15 percent in 1996.

[16] Many young barristers in good chambers earn as much in their early years as their colleagues in firms of City solicitors and sometimes more.

[17] This is well demonstrated by barristers who defend members of the IRA charged with terrorist activities and the fact that in 1997 the prime minister's wife, Cherie Blair, appeared against the government in a case before the Luxembourg Court.

France now has law firms of significant size, including some that were directly affiliated to accountants until January 1, 1997.[18]

In Germany the removal of the prohibition on a firm having more than a single office has led to the formation of firms with national and international offices.[19]

In the Netherlands and Belgium there are large Anglo-Saxon-style firms such as De Brauw, Blackstone, Westbroek with 274 lawyers[20] in 1996 and Nauta Dutilh with 390 lawyers.[21]

Stibbe, Simont is an amalgamation of Dutch, Belgian, and French firms with offices in France, Belgium, the Netherlands, London, and New York. Significantly, the working language of the partnership is English.

There has been significant growth in the size of firms in Spain but less in Italy and Greece. Some firms have used the European vehicle of EEIG (European Economic Interest Grouping) which enables firms to pool their resources for marketing, libraries, and referrals while remaining individual firms.

Firms in Scandinavia are growing by amalgamation, internal growth, and association. Vinge, the Swedish firm (108 lawyers in 1996), share offices in London with a Danish firm, Kromann and Minter (ninety-six lawyers), and a Norwegian firm, Thommessen Krefting and Greve (seventy lawyers). The legal landscape in Europe is changing at a fast rate as Europe draws closer together politically and economically.

The Cost of Litigation

What do the clients think of the cost of litigation? At least in the United States and the United Kingdom there is a serious problem over access to the Civil courts.[22] Going to law is too expensive and too protracted both for ordinary litigants and for large corporations. In the United States and, to a

---

[18]　See *European Legal 500*, 1996. For example, Fidal had 1,024, Ernst 204, Gide Loyrette 204, Archibald 220, Francis Lefebvre 192, and Stibbe Simont 100.
[19]　Oppenhof and Radler, about 220 lawyers with offices in Berlin, Brussels, Frankfurt, Leipzig, Munich, London, New York, and Prague and the Pünder Group with over 180 lawyers in offices in Frankfurt, Düsseldorf, Berlin and Leipzig, Moscow, New York, Warsaw, and Beijing and associate firms with offices in Brussels, Vienna, Paris, Zurich, Geneva, and The Hague. There are over 360 lawyers in the group.
[20]　Offices in Amsterdam, Brussels, The Hague, Eindhoven, London, New York, Prague, and Rotterdam.
[21]　Offices in Amsterdam, Breda, Brussels, Eindhoven, Madrid, New York, Rotterdam, and Singapore.
[22]　See Treaty on European Union and Final Act, Feb. 1, 1992, art. 3, 31 I.L.M. f24 [hereinafter Maastricht Treaty]. Access to justice in the European Union became an area of competence of the EU under the Maastricht Treaty. Article three provides that "Member States shall inform and consult one another with a view to coordinating their action." Id.

lesser but increasing extent, in the United Kingdom, this has led to the rise of alternative dispute resolution ("ADR").[23]

At one end of the economic scale, major corporations are deciding increasingly that the way to resolve disputes is to bypass the courts and rely on organizations like the CPR in New York and CEDER in London to provide trained mediators and arbitrators skilled in bringing parties together to reach an acceptable solution. At the other end of the economic scale, small claims courts are being established where legal representation is not encouraged. In civil law countries the development of A DR is viewed with some suspicion. Lawyers are concerned that this is an attempt to import alien procedures from common law countries into civil law procedure. They do not see the need for it. They feel that the resolution of civil disputes in civil law countries is less expensive and less confrontational than in common law jurisdictions. They have no wish to embrace pre-trial depositions and elaborate document discovery into their own procedures.

Multidisciplinary Practices

Finally, there is the question of the effect of multidisciplinary practices on the practice of law, discussed in detail by Professor Wolfram in his excellent paper. I can only offer a few observations that may provide a different focus. I agree with him that there is a widespread fear that the major accounting firms may try to take over the worldwide provision of corporate legal services, including major corporate litigation, by incorporating legal services as an important but minor part of their overall business. There are other forms of multidisciplinary practice, and in discussing this issue there are traps for the unwary. In some countries lawyers have a monopoly in the giving of legal advice which offers the lawyer some protection even within a multidisciplinary practice. In other countries, like the United Kingdom and the Scandinavian countries, there is no such monopoly. There is no legal prohibition against accountants giving legal advice.

A multidisciplinary partnership may range from a partnership between two branches of the legal profession such as advocates and notaries to a partnership including lawyers and accountants in which the accountants predominate. In some countries a qualified tax adviser may be a partner in a law firm. This will have no adverse effect on the independent practice of law. On the contrary, it enables the lawyer to provide specialist accounting or tax advice as an adjunct to law practice. This is quite different in scale from one of the big five worldwide firms of chartered accountants having a law firm in its partnership.

---

[23] Following a report by Lord Woolf, Master of the Rolls and the Presiding Judge of the Court of Appeals, the British Government introduced on 24 April 1999 a radical reform of the Rules of Civil Procedure which it hopes will reduce the cost of dispute resolution for ordinary litigants.

In Germany, historically, multidisciplinary partnerships have been predominantly partnerships of lawyers who have taken tax advisers or accountants into partnership to assist them in the provision of legal services to their clients.[24] The lawyers remained responsible for the acts of the partnership. In 1993 the German Constitutional Court held that a lawyer who was an employee of a firm of chartered accountants was entitled to be a member of the bar. This opened the way for the worldwide accounting firms. There is some safeguard for the individual lawyer in Germany in that legal advice must be given under the name of the qualified lawyer rather than the firm's name. I should emphasize that this safeguard does not exist in the United Kingdom.

In most countries in Europe multidisciplinary practices are prohibited, although this prohibition is under attack. The test ultimately to be applied is whether such restrictions can be objectively justified in the public interest. In France, the accounting firms have become among the largest providers of legal services, although some ground that was lost to the accountants has been recovered by the lawyers in that since December 31, 1996, shares in French law firms must be owned exclusively by lawyers.[25]

There is a widespread fear among European lawyers that when lawyers are in the minority in partnerships with accountants, the traditional values of lawyers looking toward the courts and the spirit of the profession rather than simply carrying out the wishes of the clients within the letter of the law will be eroded. Two questions arise. First, is it a real fear? Do accountants have lower or different professional standards than lawyers? Second, is the fear based on more than a sentimental view of a golden age harking back to the time when law was less complex or a desire by lawyers to defend their territory?

The objections to multidisciplinary practices relate primarily to conflicts of interest, the independence of the lawyer, and legal professional privilege. These would seem at first sight to be likely to have a better hearing in the climate of the 1960s than in the consumer-oriented 1990s, but with the growth of mega firms they may in fact have at least as much substance now. Conflicts of interest are described as "skewed incentives" in Professor Wolfram's paper. Rules relating to conflicts of interest are often more strictly observed in the United States than in many other countries where "Chinese walls" enable lawyers to avoid potential conflicts of interest. Put strictly, there is a conflict of interest in permitting accountants to draw up accounts and then to certify them as correct. Where the lawyer, either employed by or a partner of a firm of accountants, has given legal advice in relation to the same accounts it is easy to see that in theory there may be a further conflict of interest. There is also a

---

[24] Based on information provided by the CCBE in 1997.
[25] See supra note 17.

significant reduction in consumer choice if an accountant has given accounting advice to one party and an opposing party is unable to use the legal services of the same firm because of a conflict of interest. The seriousness of this must be tested not only in relation to big cities and major litigation but also small towns with few law firms and accounting firms. A further objection is that by tying agreements the client may be forced to use the accountant's services as well as the lawyer's or vice versa ("bait-and-switch tying agreements") and the lawyer will obtain expensive accounting advice that is not necessary (or the accountant will obtain expensive legal advice). I have in the course of practice seen the amount of money spent on complex accounting advice to support simple and in some cases self-evident propositions of damages in personal in jury cases, and know this risk is a real one. The danger is greater if the lawyer and the accountant are under pressure to meet targets for billable hours. The multidisciplinary partnership may on the one hand provide the advantage of one-stop shopping but on the other will reduce consumer choice if conflicts rules are properly observed.

The comments of both Professor Leubsdorf and Professor Wolfram on the independence of the legal profession in the United States and Europe are very revealing. It would appear that in Europe the independence of the lawyer now has a significantly higher value than in the United States.[26] It seems that more weight would attach in Europe than in the United States to the argument that if the lawyer is to be truly independent he or she must be able to give advice without obtaining a benefit from those drawing up the accounts or certifying them as correct. There is also a real concern that if the partnership is funded by capital from an accounting firm, that adversely affects the lawyer's independence.[27]

It may be difficult to disentangle what is privileged and what is not. In the United Kingdom the privilege is confined to communications between the lawyer and the client in the giving of legal advice. If the lawyer is a partner

---

[26] It may be that the general reputation of lawyers in the United States has led other American academic lawyers to the general approach that lawyers are concerned only with their own self-interest. European lawyers would say that the approach was unduly cynical. Like the rest of humanity, no doubt lawyers' motives are mixed. To assess them it is necessary to analyze the values that underlie their actions; which are positive as well as negative. Conclusions based on the purely cynical approach are frequently inaccurate.

[27] See *Bulletin of the European Union*, 1998 EC Directive Art. 11(5). The EU Directive on the rights of establishment for lawyers entitles a host member state, insofar as it prohibits lawyers practicing under its own professional title from doing so, to prohibit lawyers from other member states from practicing in association with nonlawyers. Id. The grouping is deemed to include nonmembers of the profession if the capital of the grouping is held entirely or partly, or the name under which it practices is used, or the decision-making power is exercised de facto or de jure by persons who do not have the status of lawyers. Id. Where the fundamental rules governing a grouping of lawyers in the home member state are incompatible with the rules in force in the host member state the host member state may oppose the opening of a branch or agency within its territory without these restrictions.

of or employed by the accountant it may be difficult to decide whether the privilege exists.

Professor Wolfram refers in his paper to the arrangements between accountants and firms of English solicitors. It appears that although the relationships are close, they are still not multidisciplinary partnerships. There is a clear distinction between a firm of solicitors that derives its fees largely from one client but maintains an entirely separate existence, and one that is part of the same partnership, particularly if the dominant part are nonlawyers.

Professor Wolfram also discusses the problem of inconsistent professional regulations. It may be possible to deal with this potential problem by requiring all members of the partnership to adhere to the professional rules of both lawyers and accountants, but the particular problems should be investigated and resolved before and not after multidisciplinary practices are permitted.[28]

Professor Wolfram raises the concern that unless M D Ps are permitted in the United States, American law firms will be at a serious disadvantage in the global market. This remains to be proved. Corporate clients are very sophisticated users of legal and accounting services. They are well aware of potential conflicts of interest. If the restriction can be justified in the public interest, it should remain.

The Consequences of Change: General Comments

Until ten years ago, the legal profession in Europe, including particularly the United Kingdom, had much in common with the legal profession in the United States in the 1960s. In some countries European lawyers would have understood most easily the U.S. legal profession in the late nineteenth century.

Many do not like the changes that have recently taken place. Current U.S. law practice gives less individual freedom to practice law as the individual wishes and less freedom to practice independently of colleagues in the same firm. In the 1990s there has been more competition but for lawyers in the larger firms more money, more stress, less time with family, and less time to pursue outside interests. Law at its best is practiced to the highest standards but at a cost that few can afford. In Europe, access to justice is assuming an increasing importance at the Community level. It is necessary in an increasingly complex world to make the law more accessible and cheaper. Unless the lawyers take

---

[28] At the World Trade Organization (WTO), a ministerial decision established a working party on professional services to ensure under Article VI.4 of the GATS that regulatory requirements are not more burdensome than necessary and do not constitute unnecessary barriers to trade; to monitor international standards; and to establish guidelines for the mutual recognition of qualifications. See Ministerial Decision on Professional Services (1994), reprinted in *Law & Practice Under the Gatt*, at 17-18 (Kenneth R. Simmonds ed.) (1994). They have taken the accountancy profession as their first priority. At this stage they are concentrating on single professions starting with the accounting profession. The legal profession was expected to be considered at a relatively early stage.

the lead in this process, procedures will be introduced for the resolution of disputes which will bypass them. Computers will be harnessed to set out the law to be interpreted by lay people. Lawyers will be excluded from representing clients in a range of civil cases.

Professional Ethics

With the globalization of legal practice the need for a worldwide common code of professional ethics becomes greater. On October 28, 1988, the representatives of the legal professions of the twelve member states of the European Union agreed unanimously to adopt a common code of professional conduct.[29] It was a signal success. It was achieved only after much discussion over six years between representatives of countries operating different legal systems. The United Kingdom and Ireland represented the common law system, Denmark the Scandinavian legal system, and France and other countries the civil law system.[30] The code has been implemented not only in those twelve countries but also in the countries that have since joined the European Union and the observer countries of the CCBE, which include the Czech and Slovak Republics, Hungary, and Poland from the former Eastern Europe.

The code applies specifically to cross-border activities between lawyers and seeks to restate what would be regarded by some U.S. commentators as the traditional values of the 1960s in a way that is relevant to practice at the end of the twentieth century.[31] It would be interesting to know whether they would be more in tune with the philosophy of the U.S.legal profession of 1960 or even 1900. This assertion of individual independence emphasized by Professor Leubsdorf in his excellent paper is well understood in England and forms the cornerstone of the English legal profession. The English Bar also asserts that the duty to carry out instructions from clients is subject to the duty to observe the profession's ethical rules and the duty to the court. The difference between the perception of French avocats and many American

---

[29] See John Toulmin CMG QC, A Worldwide Common Code of Professional Ethics, I5 *Fordham Int'l L. J.* 673 (1992) (providing a detailed commentary on the CCBE Code). The most recent changes were adopted by the CCBE at its plenary session in Lyon in November 1998. They do not affect the analysis set out below.

[30] See Laurel S. Terry, An Introduction to the European Community's Legal Ethics Code Part I: An Analysis of the CCBE Code of Conduct, 7 *Geo. J, Legal Ethics* I (I 993) (hereinafter Analysis); Laruel S. Terry, An Introduction to the European Community's Legal Ethics Code Part II: Applying the CCBE Code of Conduct, 7 *Geo. J. Legal Ethics* 345 (1993). This includes the Common Code and Explanatory Memorandum. It is also available from the CCBE Offices at rue Washington 40, B-1050 Brussels, Belgium.

[31] See e.g., Analysis, supra note 31, at 55 (Professor Terry interestingly comments, in relation to the absence of detailed rules, that "[t]he silence of the CCBE Code (in relation to conflicts of interest) reflects more confidence in the judgment of the lawyer and the lawyer's ability to resist temptation:'); see also CCBE Code, supra note 2, at Para 3.2 (general principles).

lawyers is that, like English barristers, French avocats have historically been a court-based profession. This leads to the conclusion that the lawyer has an overriding responsibility to the court in any work he or she does because the lawyer is conscious that any advice she or he gives may be tested later in court. I agree entirely with Professor Leubsdorf's comments that the avocats' profession in France has moved from one of single practitioners to one of firms but has at the same time impressively sought to preserve the requirements of individual responsibility that were necessary in a historically predominantly advocacy profession.

As I set out in more detail in the Fordham International Law Journal article in Chapter 17, several difficult topics appear to reflect differences between the United States and the civil law system. In some cases the only way they could be resolved was by providing essentially conflict of law provisions in the explanatory memorandum. These are professional secrecy[32] discussed in Professor Leubsdorf's paper (I suspect that the differences are greater in theory than they are in practice); incompatible occupations,[33] in particular whether a lawyer may be a director of a company at the same time that his firm is representing the company in legal proceedings; lawyers' advertising rules;[34] conflicts of interest;[35] contingency fees;[36] confidentiality of correspondence between lawyers[37] (in civil law countries confidentiality exists between lawyers to the exclusion of their clients; in common law countries there is a duty to disclose communications to the client; this issue is also discussed comprehensively in Professor Leubsdorf's paper); and the duty of the incoming lawyer to see whether arrangements have been made so that the previous lawyer in the case has been paid his or her fees.[38] The explanatory memorandum makes it clear that the duty under the code is limited to making the inquiry. In some member states the duty goes further. The differences in approach to each of these questions is reflected in the CCBE explanatory memorandum and is capable of solution within a single code. In the case of the former prohibition against advertising, the rules have changed in many countries, including the United Kingdom, as Professor Leubsdorf explains. Equally, variations on contingency fees are now permitted in France and the United Kingdom, where previously they had been prohibited. Comparisons have also been made with the Japanese code of professional conduct. Its provisions are also reconcilable with the European and U.S. Codes. It is important that the work is undertaken to achieve a worldwide common code

---

[32]   See CCBE Code, supra note 2, at para 2.3 (confidentiality).
[33]   See CCBE Code, supra note 2, at para 2.3 (incompatible occupations).
[34]   See CCBE Code, supra note 2, at para 2.6 (personal publicity).
[35]   See CCBE Code, supra note 2, at para 3.2 (conflicts of interest).
[36]   See CCBE Code, supra note 2, at para 3.3 (pactum de quota litis).
[37]   See CCBE Code, supra note 2, at para 5.3 (correspondence between lawyers).
[38]   See CCBE Code, supra note 2, at para 5.6 (change of lawyer).

of professional responsibility and that it is then enforced in the different jurisdictions. Once disciplinary action has been taken in one jurisdiction that decision should be taken into account in other jurisdictions where the lawyer has established an office. The recent draft European Directive on lawyers' rights to establish an office under home title could serve as a precedent for this.

A Last Thought

In conclusion, I should like to thank Cornell University for organizing this important seminar. These are difficult issues. The legal profession-practitioners, academic lawyers, judges, and regulators on both sides of the Atlantic - will need to show foresight and wisdom if change is to be carried forward positively. I do not take a negative view of the changes that have taken place nor think the legal profession needs to be defensive. The key for the legal profession is to involve itself in a positive way. My experience has been that the best way forward is the constructive and positive approach of identifying problems and seeing how they can be solved in the public interest.

The European Court of Justice

I was the Chairman of the CCBE Consultative Committee of the European Court of Justice, the Luxembourg Court, from 1986-1992. I have retained a close interest in the development of the Court, and I gave evidence to the House of Lords Select Committee on the Inter-Governmental Conference in 1995 making various proposals relating to the future of the European Court of Justice (ECJ). My written evidence to the Select Committee remains relevant to the current discussion on the role of the ECJ. It is too long to reproduce here, but many of the points are summarised below.

In 2008 I was invited to Brazil by Dr Durval de Noronha Goyos to give three lectures which he had organised as part of the 30th anniversary celebrations of his international law firm, Noronha Advogados, one of the very few international law firms which come from Latin America.

On 16 June 2008, at a special sitting of the Justice Tribunal of São Paulo, the largest province of Brazil, presided over by the Chief Justice. I gave a lecture charting the history of the ECJ which raises many of the issues which are the subject of the current debate. It is reproduced here with minor amendments.

My written evidence to the House of Lords Select Committee is to be found in 1996 Inter-Governmental Conference (IGC) Minutes of Evidence 18, Report Session 1994-5, HL Paper 88. My evidence is summarised in the House of Lords Select Committee Report on the Summary of Evidence, Session 1994-1995, 21st Report HMSO Paper 105 of 3rd November 1995. I am reported accurately as commenting that "In the absence of clear Treaty provisions, the Court has no option but to be activist... para 156", "that national courts should be encouraged to interpret basic Community law themselves...para 159".

I also suggested that "consideration should be given to permitting dissenting opinions in the ECJ where central questions of interpretation of the Treaty were in issue"... para 163.

The topic of dissenting opinions was taken up by Judge Dr Josef Azzizi, judge of the EU General Court, in his very thoughtful chapter in the Liber Amicorum(page 49). In a chapter entitled "Unveiling the EU Courts' Internal Decision-Making process: A Case for Dissenting Opinions?" After a detailed examination of the issues, he concludes (page 66) that " from a merely intellectual point of view, unveiling through dissenting opinions the fact that in the course of deliberations different positions have been taken by members of a judicial panel, would not be shocking". However he concludes that EU law is still in a phase of consolidation and it would not seem advisable to abandon, at least in the next decades, the secrecy of deliberation.

This subject is also taken up by Lord Bingham in his forward to "The Essays in Honour of Sir Francis Jacobs", former advocate-general at the ECJ. Those comments are referred to in my lecture at page 268 below.

At paragraph 213 of the Summary of Evidence, detailed reference is made to my proposal that there should be amendments to the Treaty to clarify the areas of competence of the European Union and the member states, the precise delineation of the areas of shared competence. The Summary noted my proposal that a specialist committee of the Council of Ministers (perhaps of the Justice Ministers) could be set up to consider whether existing Commission programmes were properly matters of Community competence. These are ideas which, in the less febrile atmosphere away from negotiations over the dinner table at a European summit, might find some support among other member states. In 1995 I also wrote an article on the ECJ for The Times in which I concluded in that "the debate needs light not heat". This approach is at least as important now as it was then.

In my São Paulo lecture, I followed the development of the ECJ and the Court of First Instance, now the General Court. I concluded, then as I had also concluded in 1995, that the history of the Court in accurately interpreting the relevant EU Treaty explained its judicial activism. Put bluntly, if there is a desire among the Member States that the court should adopt a different general approach, the Lisbon Treaties need to be amended. I suggested in 1995 that a more restricted approach might, in the alternative, be achieved by better drafted legislation which more closely defined the division of powers, between the European Union and the Member States. This has not happened. It may still be worth considering.

I also raised future problems which the ECJ will encounter as its workload increases. I emphasised more generally that, in my view, as the world grows smaller, the aim should be to achieve not just regional but wider global agreements, and to bring together judges and lawyers from different parts of the world to discuss common problems.

Are there any more general lessons? The answer is the same as at page 170. The CCBE Committee established a rapport with the Luxembourg Court judges which meant that we had genuine discussions. They asked for help over legal aid (one case had taken up their allotted funds for the year) and I wrote a paper which they found helpful. They modified their original ideas for the Notes for Guidance for Oral Hearings, particularly in relation to time limits for oral presentations, to take account of points which we had made.

We also had meetings with the Strasbourg Court, and were able to make suggestions to ease a little the seemingly hopeless congestion of cases. Sadly, this currently seems to be a systemic problem which may lead to wholesale reform of the Court which is felt, by many countries including the United

Kingdom, to be exceeding its powers by taking marginal cases and making adverse decisions on issues which should be within the margin of appreciation, i.e. decisions left to the national courts in the Member States. These cases should be filtered out at the preliminary stage, perhaps by an initial reference by the Strasbourg Court to a designated national court for a reasoned opinion which would include a statement that the case was, or was not, in the view of the designated national court, within the margin of appreciation or otherwise inadmissible. If the Strasbourg court accepted this opinion, the case would fail at that stage. I should also note that the media often confuse the two courts, all too often the Luxembourg court is blamed for decisions made by the Strasbourg court.

The European Court of Justice

Speech at the Justice Tribunal of São Paulo by HH Judge John Toulmin CMG QC on 16 June 2008

It is a very great pleasure and privilege to speak to such a distinguished audience of judges and lawyers on the subject of the European Court of Justice. I should emphasise at the start that I am speaking in my personal capacity and that the views expressed without attribution are entirely my own.

The European Court of Justice has for over 50 years, from the very beginning, been at the heart of the development of what used to be called the European Community and is now called the European Union.

My interest in the European Court of Justice, and European law generally, goes back to 1964. It was when I was at the University of Michigan in 1964 that I took a course entitled " Law and Institutions of the Atlantic Area" taught by Professor Eric Stein, then a pioneer in European law teaching who was still teaching at the age of 95.[He died in 2011 at the age of 98] At that time there were no similar courses in the United Kingdom, and only one other in the United States. The course included an examination of the institutions of the fledgling European Economic Community, including the Court of Justice, and other Institutions in the Atlantic area.

From 1984 - 1993, I was a member of the CCBE's Delegation to the European Court of Justice and for 6 years I led the Delegation. By then the Judges of the Court consisted of 19 members, 13 Judges (expanded from the original six, one from each Member State) together with six Advocates General who have equal status with the Judges. It was, and is, the function of the Advocates General, to deliver a detailed, substantive, and individual opinion on the case before the Judges of the Court give their collective opinion. As a member of this committee, I drafted a paper on Legal Aid before the Court, and participated in the drafting of the Notes for Guidance in the written and oral procedure to assist parties who were appearing before the Court.

I can well remember Delegation meetings at the Court in Luxembourg. About half the Judges came. Like the deliberations of the Court itself, our meetings were conducted in French. They were always friendly, constructive and relatively informal. Such a discussion today would inevitably be different. There are now 27 Judges, one from each Member State, together with 8 Advocates General (and the number of Advocates General is likely soon to increase). The volume and subject matter of cases before the Court (and the Court of First Instance) has expanded vastly.

Out of the vast canvas of the last 50 years or so of the European Court, I have pondered as to what might be of the greatest interest to this distinguished audience. The European Court of Justice has been a key institution from the start of the setting up of the Coal and Steel Community in 1951 and the Common Market in 1957. I start by charting the progress of the European Union and how that has impacted on the Court. I then consider what type of cases come before the Court of Justice and the Court of First Instance, then I discuss the procedure of the Court. Having in mind that, in an oral hearing which I witnessed in the Commercial Court in Sao Paulo, the lawyer came in and set his time-clock to 15 minutes and the Court turned over the hour-glass designed so that in 15 minutes the sands of time would run out, I shall mention the time limits of the hearings at the European Court of Justice. I shall then explain the role of the Advocates General. Finally, I offer some thoughts on the future.

In 1945 much of the mainland of Western Europe had been bombed and occupied twice in 30 years. It was clear that Western Europe, exhausted by two world wars, was immediately confronted with another threat. At the end of the Second World War, the Soviet Union had occupied Eastern Europe. Berlin, surrounded by Eastern Europe, was occupied by four powers, the United States, the United Kingdom and France in West Berlin, and the Soviet Union in East Berlin. East Germany, a satellite state of Russia, extended west almost to Hamburg. The Soviet Union had threatened to cut off West Berlin by closing the land corridor to the West provided by the autobahn. In 1948 the West mounted a massive air-lift of vital supplies to preserve their presence in West Berlin. At his speeches in West Berlin in the summer of 1963, President Kennedy underlined the Soviet threat to the West. (I was present at President Kennedy's famous "Ich bin ein Berliner" speech.)

What was called the European Economic Community and is now called the European Union was born under the twin beliefs that never again should Western Europe tear itself apart and that Western Europe needed to come together to combat the threat from the East. That last threat was recognised by Sir Winston Churchill in his famous speech at Fulton, Missouri, in the United States in 1946 when he said that " an iron curtain had descended over Europe". Sadly the United Kingdom, which could have had such a decisive role in shaping the future of Western Europe, opted out at the beginning and did not join the European Union until 1973.

The first initiative towards what is now the European Union was taken by the French Foreign Minister, Robert Schuman, who announced on 9th May 1950 that he proposed to place the whole of French and German coal and steel production under a Common High Authority. The organisation would be open to the participation of other European countries. Significantly he proposed that the new Authority would be subject to the control of a court of justice.

On 18 April 1951, the forerunner of the European Economic Community, the European Coal and Steel Community, was established by a Treaty signed in Paris. The institution, heavily influenced by French administrative law, included the High Authority, a Council of Ministers, a General Assembly and, most significantly, the Court. The six founding Member States, Belgium, France, Germany, Italy, Luxembourg and the Netherlands, had all suffered from the ravages of war. The preamble of the Treaty hinted at further closer co-operation, " to lay the foundations for Institutions which will give direction to a destiny henceforth shared".

On 25 March 1957, the same six states signed the Treaties of Rome establishing the European Economic Community and the European Atomic Energy Community. Each of the two communities had a Court of Justice, a Commission (rather than a High Authority), a Council of Ministers and an Assembly. The Court of Justice became the Court of Justice of the European Communities.

Article 2 of the Treaty of Rome referred to the task " by establishing a common market, and progressively approximating the economic policies of the Member States to promote throughout the Community a harmonious development of economic activities, a continuous and balanced expansion and increase in stability, an accelerated raising of the standard of living and close relations between the states belonging to it." This declaration was important because it looked beyond the initial purpose of the Treaty, which was to secure the fundamental freedoms of the European Economic Community (currently set out in Article 3(1)(c) EC) - freedom of movement of goods capital and workers, freedom of establishment and provision of services throughout the Member States. From the start, the Court of Justice has had well in mind the Treaty objective of closer relations between the Member States - later "ever closer union". It is these words which have been crucial to the way in which the European Court has interpreted successive treaties. So long as this overriding objective remains, the Court is bound to continue to interpret the Treaty in a way which many would call "activist".

The supremacy of Community Law over National Law was established early by the Court. In *Costa v ENL* [1964] ECR 585 in 1964, the Court was concerned with a challenge to the legality of Italian nationalisation measures. The sum involved was the lira equivalent of £1 sterling. The principal at stake was enormous. The Court of Justice said this:

"By contrast with ordinary international treaties the EC Treaty has created its own legal system which on the entry into force of the Treaty became an integral part of the legal systems of the Members States and which their courts are bound to apply.

By creating a Community of unlimited duration having its own institutions, its own legal capacity, and capacity of representation on the international plain, and more particularly real powers stemming from a limitation of sovereignty, or a transfer of powers from the States to the Community, the Member States have limited their sovereign rights albeit within limited fields and thus created a body of law which binds both their nationals and themselves".

Later, in Simmenthal [1976] ECR 1871, the Court went further and declared in unequivocal terms that " A National Court which is called upon within the limits of its jurisdiction to apply provisions of Community Law is under a duty to give full effect to those provisions, if necessary refusing of its own motion to apply any conflicting provision of national legislation, even if adopted subsequently, and it is not necessary for the Court to request or await a prior setting-aside of such provisions by legislative or other constitutional means".

In other words, the Court of Justice was confirming, at an early stage in the development of the European Union, the supremacy of Community law over national law and, at a relatively early stage, that the provisions of Community law had direct effect over national legislation. Normally Community Directives do not come into effect immediately but provide a period of time in which they can be implemented by detailed national legislation.

The accession of Denmark, Ireland and the United Kingdom on 1 January 1973 did not significantly affect the structure of the European Economic Community.

After the initial enthusiasm, progress towards achieving the four freedoms had slowed. Much of the progress in the years immediately before 1984 was provided by decisions of the European Court of Justice. A fresh impetus was needed and the Heads of Governments' meeting at Fontainbleau in 1984 provided the impetus. This led to the White Paper, "Commissioning the Internal Market" by Commissioner Lord Cockfield (COM 85/310) and to the Single European Act which was signed in February 1986 and came into force on 1 July 1987. Its main purpose was to ensure progress towards the completion of the internal market, i.e. the effective guarantee of the four freedoms, by the 31 December 1992.

The Single European Act also introduced tentatively the concept of a European foreign policy - " European co-operation in the sphere of Foreign Policy". At this stage there was no active role for the European political institutions, the Council of Ministers and the European Commission. They were merely entitled to be informed of the decisions of the Member States.

The harmonisation of Community legislation was made easier by changes from unanimous to qualified majority voting. Additional competences added at European level were the environment and technological research. Also the concept of monetary co-operation was introduced. Article 20.1 of the Single European Act provided that the Member States should co-operate to ensure convergence of economic and monetary policies for the further development of the Community.

Finally, and most important for this lecture, the Single European Act provided for the establishment of the Court of First Instance in Luxembourg. This came about for a number of reasons. First, the case load of the Court which had been light in the early years after it had been set up, had increased in the late 1970s and 1980s so that there was an unsatisfactory backlog of cases. Secondly, the Court was ill-equipped to deal with cases which involved the detailed examination of vast numbers of documents and complex factual situations as occurred in anti-dumping, state aids and competition infringement cases. Thirdly, the Court of Justice's time was being taken up with employment cases, disputes between officials of Community institutions and those institutions in their capacity as employers.

I well remember the delicate negotiations which took place over the transfer of business to this new Court. It was not until 1994 that anti-dumping cases were finally transferred. Furthermore, cases brought by natural or legal persons (rather than references by the courts of the Member States) were also transferred.

The next move forward came in the Treaty of Maastricht, which came into force on 1 November 1993. The Treaty was called " the Treaty of European Union" (TEU) reinforcing the concept of progress towards closer political union of the Member States. It introduced the concept of the Three Pillars - the European Community and two new pillars, the Common Security Policy and Justice and Home Affairs. Symbolically, the Treaty removed the word "economic" from what was from then on to be called "The European Union".

The Treaty widened the areas of Community competence into education, public health, culture, consumer protection, industrial and developmental co-operation. It highlighted the importance of the environment. The Treaty also had a "Social Chapter" from which the United Kingdom opted out.

Of particular importance juridically, was that the Treaty of European Union introduced into the Treaty the concepts of subsidiarity and proportionality.

Article 3(b) the TEU defines subsidiarity as follows:

"In areas which do not fall within its exclusive competence the Community shall take action in accordance with the principle of subsidiarity only if and in so far as the objectives of the proposed action cannot be sufficiently achieved by the Member States and can therefore by reason of the scale of effects of the proposed action be better achieved by the Community".

The principle of proportionality had been developed by the European Court much earlier. Paragraph 8 of the judgment in Fromancais [1983] ECR 395 defines it as follows: " In order to establish whether a provision of Community law is consonant with the principle of proportionality, it is necessary to establish in the first place whether the means it employs to achieve the aim correspond to the importance of the aim and, in the second place, whether they [the means] are necessary for its achievement".

By the time of the Treaty of Amsterdam, signed on 2 October 1997, the European Union had been enlarged to 15 Member States. This necessitated a further shift from unanimity to qualified voting in the Council of Ministers. The Treaty introduced the concept of the following fundamental principles throughout the European Union - liberty, democracy, respect for human rights and fundamental freedoms, and the rule of law. It developed the Social Chapter to which the United Kingdom was now a party having given up its opt-out. It is obvious how far the aims of the Union had progressed beyond the original four freedoms, whose purpose was to facilitate free movement within the territory of the European Union, to the aim of ensuring fundamental rights for its citizens.

This transformation is further underlined by the move of the majority of the Member States to monetary union. The Euro became the currency of account of those Member States participating in monetary union in 1999. Bank notes in Euros were issued on 1 January 2002 and after the six month change-over period the national currencies ceased to be legal tender. The United Kingdom has opted out of the Eurozone.

In October 1999 at Tampere in Finland, the Council of Ministers of the European Union agreed a far-reaching declaration on the creation of an area of "freedom, security, and justice " within the European Union. This was to be built on the protection of human rights and the combatting of discrimination; an area of security combatting terrorism, trafficking, corruption and fraud; and enhanced co-operation between the judicial authorities of the Member States. This agenda drove much of the work in the European Union in the following years.

The Treaty of Nice followed in 2001 and came into force on 1 February 2003. It was concerned with institutional changes - further moves from unanimous to qualified majority voting, the weighting of votes in the Council of Ministers etc. It extended commercial policy to cover intellectual property and it extended co-operation to cover the development of common foreign and security policy. It also introduced the concept of judicial panels, attached to the Court of Justice, to make the main court freer to deal with the more important cases.

By 2005 the European Union had expanded to 25 Member States with a further expansion to 27 Member States in 2007.

It is not surprising that many thought that the logical next step was to have a formal Constitution for the European Union. After all, what had been developed in a series of Treaties since the Treaty of Rome amounted, in effect, to a Constitution which also formed part of the constitutional arrangements of each Member State. However the draft Constitution, signed in October 2004, was rejected in 2005 by France and the Netherlands, and has been replaced by the Treaty of Lisbon. This Treaty has re-enacted most of the provisions of the draft Constitution. The Treaty of Lisbon was signed by the Heads of Governments on 13 December 2007 and is due to enter into force on 1 January 2009.

It can be seen from this that the areas of competence at European level have grown from relatively small and hopeful beginnings to ones which encompass the fundamental rights of the nationals of the Member States.

The European Court of Justice under Articles 220, 221, 222, and 234 of the Treaty of European Union, (Article 19 of the Treaty of Lisbon) has the task of ensuring that in the interpretation and application of the Treaties, the law is observed.

Under the Treaty of Lisbon (Article 19) the Court of Justice of the European Union encompasses the Court of Justice itself, the Court of First Instance, renamed the General Court, and new specialised courts.

Under the Treaty of Lisbon, the historic methods of bringing actions before the Community courts will be preserved. Under article 19(3) of the Lisbon Treaty, " (3) The Court of Justice of the European Union shall in accordance with the Treaties

(a) rule on actions brought by a Member State, an institution, or a natural or legal person;

(b) give preliminary rulings at the request of a Court or Tribunals of the Member States on the interpretation of Union law or the validity of acts adopted by the institutions;

(c) rule in other cases provided for in the Treaties."

This latter category includes, most significantly, appeals to the Court of Justice on points of law from the Court of First Instance.

There is an important distinction between cases described as "direct actions" and those which are "preliminary rulings".

Direct actions may be divided into a) actions against Member States and b) actions against EU institutions, including staff cases. Actions for preliminary rulings relate to cases which are being heard in the national courts of the Member States, which in the course of the litigation are referred by the national courts to the European Court of Justice for a preliminary ruling on questions of EU law. These are points which are relevant to the issues to be decided in the litigation and on which there is no clear answer as a matter of EU law. Under the Treaties, the national court is required to refer questions on the EU law to the ECJ unless the answer is clear under established EU law.

I need to say a little more about each category. If a Member State is in alleged breach of its obligations under EU law, for example for failing to implement an EU Directive, the EU Commission will bring the alleged breach to the Members State's attention and ask for comments. Most frequently the matter will be resolved at this stage. If matters cannot be resolved, the next stage is to bring the matter before the Court. There is usually further discussion between the EU Commission and the Member State. If matters cannot be resolved at this stage the Court will proceed to judgment.

Examples of actions brought by the EU Commission against Member States are the Commission's action against Denmark for failing to observe EU Rules on public procurement in connection with a major bridge-building project linking Denmark and Sweden, and against the United Kingdom for failing to implement the EU Directive on the purity of drinking-water.

An alternative route for a direct action is that an individual with a sufficient interest may bring proceedings against its government for damages in respect of an alleged breach of EU law.

A State may also bring proceedings against another State for failing to fulfill its Treaty obligations.

In certain circumstances, eg where aid which is given by the State to an enterprise distorts competition within the European Union, the Commission may decide that the State concerned must abolish (or modify) the State aid within a specified time. If the State fails to do so, the Commission (or another Member State) may refer the matter direct to the European Court of Justice.

The second category of direct actions relates to actions against EU institutions. The first area of challenge is an action to annul, that is to set aside Regulations, Directives, recommendations or opinions which are intended to impose binding obligations on the ground that the imposition of such obligations is unlawful under EU law. A further area of challenge is an action for inactivity. The allegation here is not that the EU institution has acted illegally, but that it has failed to act when it should have acted. The third area of challenge is that the decision of the EU Institution, is, in the particular case, unlawful under EU law.

The purpose of the referral for a preliminary ruling under EU law is different. It is to ensure the uniformity of application of EU law in the Member States. Generally, but not invariably, the proceedings in the national court are adjourned pending the ruling of the European Court. The first stage in this procedure is the decision of the national court to refer the question. It must also formulate the terms of the reference. Once it has formulated its reference it is referred to the ECJ and the ECJ will rule upon it. Once the ECJ has given its ruling, it is binding on the national court.

How does the European Court of Justice reach its decisions? As I have said, the Court of Justice currently consists of 27 judges, one from each Member State, and 8 Advocates General. The Court rarely sits as a full court of all 27 Judges. If it does so, the decision is valid if 15 judges are sitting. The Treaty of Nice introduced the "Grand Chamber" of 13 Judges. Its decisions are valid if 9 judges are sitting. The Grand Chamber must sit when a State or a Community institution that is party to the proceedings so requests. Otherwise the Grand Chamber only hears cases of particular difficulty or importance. A 5 Judge Chamber hears most of the cases. A Chamber of 3 Judges hears the most straight-forward cases. Decisions of 5 and 3 Judge Chambers must be taken by at least 3 Judges.

The judgment of the Court is a single judgment of the judges taking part in the decision. The deliberations of the judges take place in secret. The language of the deliberations is French, the language of the Court. Each judge will be required to state his or her opinion and the reasons for it, starting with the most recently appointed Judge. In the event of dissent, the judges will attempt to reach a consensus which may involve compromise but in the end the opinion of the majority will prevail. Secrecy extends beyond the deliberations and the judgment. Judges will not thereafter disclose the substance of the deliberations or whether there was, or was not, dissent.[I have already indicated that there may be room for at least one dissenting judgment to encompass the opinion of the minority. This view was also supported by Judge Sir Gordon Slynn, later Lord Slynn of Hadleigh.]

Before judgment, the case will have gone through a written procedure followed by an oral procedure and, in most cases, an opinion from the Advocate General before the period of deliberation by the Judges. For each case one Judge will be designated as Juge Rapporteur (The Reporting Judge). He or she will be responsible for carrying through the procedure to its conclusion. The procedure is based on the French legal system, but the practice in the United Kingdom and Ireland has in the last 35 years had an influence which many of the Judges trained under the Roman Civil Law system have found to be beneficial, particularly in the oral procedure.

The written procedure follows the familiar pattern of applications, statements of cases, defences and replies. The court provides strict time limits for the lodging of the written pleadings. A party which fails to meet the time limits does so at its peril. The court will not normally extend the time. The pleadings will form the cornerstone of each party's case. The court is extremely reluctant to permit parties later to go outside the pleaded case. The written pleadings must set out a full statement of the relevant arguments of law and fact and append relevant documents which, if of particular importance, must be included in the body of the pleadings. Parties must remember that this is a multi-language court and all written documents must be translated into at least one other language.

The Reporting Judge will draft a report summarising the issues of fact and law and the arguments of the parties. This constitutes the Report for the Hearing and will be sent to the parties. He will also draft a Preliminary Report for the other Judges hearing the case.

The written procedure is followed by the oral hearing. The Notes for Guidance provided by the Court say that it is not necessary for a party to take part in the oral procedure but, in practice, most do. Since the accession of the United Kingdom and Ireland introducing the oral tradition of pleading by barristers as specialist advocates, its effectiveness has been demonstrated. Counsel must make persuasive submissions in a very short period of time, bearing in mind the need for all submissions to be interpreted by one or more translators, normally no more than 30 minutes (15 minutes for interveners) or 15 minutes before the three Judge Court.

In the oral hearing, an advocate may submit new arguments only if they are prompted by recent events since the close of the written procedure. He or she may be required to highlight the most important points of the case and explain the most difficult points. Finally he or she must answer questions asked by the Judges. He or she should not repeat arguments set out in full in the written brief. The advocate is not permitted, unlike the United Kingdom jurisdictions, to provide the Court with a written skeleton of the oral submissions.

The oral procedure was developed significantly after the arrival of British and Irish barristers used to thinking on their feet. The Judges of the Court started to ask searching questions of counsel when they thought they might obtain clear answers. Judge Pescatore from Luxembourg and Judge Mancini from Italy were two Judges trained in the different Civil Law tradition who, in the 1980s, were most prominent in developing judicial questioning as part of the oral procedure.

In an article in the Columbia Journal of European Law in 1995, Judge Mancini said, speaking of the arrival of the English and Irish Judges, charmingly described as the two insular Judges, how " their colleagues [the civil law judges] loved their refusal listlessly to accept the kind of assistance which the lawyers were prepared to give them and they [the civil law judges] started to act in a similar fashion. As a result, interruptions are now more frequent and a question period has become a permanent feature of the hearings, much to their advantage in terms of usefulness and liveliness."

I recall the oral hearing in the case of Gullung in 1986 at which I was present representing the UK Delegation of the CCBE. John Mummery QC (now Lord Justice Mummery), intervening on behalf of the United Kingdom government, had hardly presented three sentences of his submissions before he was interrupted by the Court with a question. Many other questions followed. The Judges enjoyed themselves so much that his submissions took over one hour. I have, of course, no means of knowing definitively, but I shall always believe that it was the brilliant way in which he answered the many questions that turned the case in favour of his clients. The Court, somewhat unusually, disagreed with the contrary opinion from Advocate General Darmon. The Court's decision was vital in preserving the right of a lawyer from one Member State to establish an office in another Member State using his own home title.

I deal now with the role of the Advocates General. As I have said, the eight Advocates General have equal status with the Judges of the Court. One each comes from the five largest States, and the remaining three rotate from among the other Member States. Their numbers have not been increased to keep pace with the recent enlargement of the European Union. In 2003 there were 15 Judges and eight Advocates General, at present there are 27 Judges but still eight Advocates General. It has become clear that the present number is not sufficient to keep pace with a work load which it seems will inevitably increase. In her article on the role of Advocates General in the book of "Essays in Honour of Sir Francis Jacobs", one of the most distinguished Advocates General who served from 1988 - 2006, Judge Eleanor Sharpston, from the United Kingdom, a relatively recent appointment as Advocate General, confirms the need for additional Advocates General. I understand that it is likely that in the near future the number of Advocates General will indeed be increased.

While the Advocate General must be appointed in every case, the Treaty of Nice introduced the possibility of dispensing with the Advocate General's formal opinion on the merits where the Court considers, after hearing the Advocate General, that the case raises no new point of law.

On the other hand, the Treaty of Nice has introduced two new areas of work for the Advocates General. The first is that the Advocate General may propose that judgments of the Court of First Instance should be reviewed by the Court of Justice where the First Advocate General considers that there is " a serious risk of the unity and consistency of the Community being affected". This requires that Judge to read all the judgments of the Court of First Instance. Secondly the Court now has a new obligation, to hear references for a preliminary ruling from national courts in the area of freedom, security and justice.

In his foreword to "Essays in Honour of Sir Francis Jacobs", Lord Bingham of Cornhill, the senior judge in the House of Lords, the highest court in the United Kingdom, refers to the need for the Judges of the Court on occasions "to struggle to find words which will satisfy the majority perhaps reflecting the doubts of some and the reservations of others".

Lord Bingham goes on to contrast this with the position of the Advocates General " who speak with their own voices not through the medium of a Committee". He goes on to say that while the Advocate General is bound to show respect for existing case law... "the opportunity exists to nudge the Court towards new conclusions, to raise new ideas , to throw doubt upon accepted orthodoxy and to bring a single judgment, coherent and informed, to bear on the complex and varied problems which confront the Court".

The Court is not bound to follow the opinion of the Advocate General and in a significant number of cases does not do so. However, the opinion of the Advocate General may be of great importance even when it is not followed. It is published along with the judgment of the Court and will be discussed by academic lawyers and commentators. Even if ideas do not find favour with the Court in the particular case, they may be taken up by the Court in future cases.

I offer some conclusions. The Court of Justice has had to respond to the changing nature of the European Union. In 1988 when Sir Francis Jacobs arrived at the Court, the Court of Justice consisted of 19 Members, 13 Judges and six Advocates General. By 2007 there were three Courts, the European Court of Justice, the Court of First Instance and the EU Staff Tribunal which, taken together, had 67 judicial members.

The average duration of proceedings before the Court of Justice is less than in many Member States, but remains far too long. In "The European Union and the Court of Justice" by Professor Anthony Arnull, 2nd ed (2006), p 139, he notes that the average duration of proceedings is over 20 months and just under two years for references for preliminary rulings from national courts. It is expected that the new accelerated procedure for preliminary rulings and the substantially increased jurisdiction of the General Court will not only speed up the procedure for preliminary rulings, but will also alleviate much of the immediate pressure on the Court of Justice. It remains to be seen to what extent, in the longer term, the time taken for references will be shortened.

Initially the Court of First Instance dealt only with competition and staff cases. By 1994 all direct action, anti-dumping and subsidy cases had been transferred to the Court of First Instance. In 2005 a separate tribunal was set up to deal with staff cases, the European Civil Service Tribunal.

In the 1990s, as a result of the expansion of the areas within the competence of the European Union, there was a need fundamentally to re-think the division of competences of the Luxembourg Court. The Nice Treaty of 2001, in article 225 EC, gave the Council of Ministers power to create new specialised courts under the umbrella of the Court of First Instance to hear certain categories of direct action cases. From these decisions on matters of law an appeal would lie to the Court of First Instance. The Court of First Instance was to be treated as an independent court under the EU Treaties with its own separate responsibilities rather than as an appendage to the European Court of Justice.

The first proposal for a specialised court was the constitution of a court to deal with staff cases in the European Atomic Authority (EURATOM). The new court began work in December 2005.

It seems likely that this does not go far enough. It is clear that there may well be a need for further action to relieve the predictable pressure on the European Court of Justice and, in particular, on the Court of First Instance (now the General Court) with its already very heavy and increasing case load. The most obvious possibilities for further specialist courts would be a specialised European Trade Mark Court to hear appeals from the Office of the Harmonisation of the European Market in relation to Community Trade Marks, a Community Patent Court and a Court dealing exclusively with Competition cases, although this is an area where Judges of the Court of First Instance have themselves specialist expertise.

Even these changes may not go far enough. On 12 December 2007 the Charter of Fundamental Rights was signed in Strasbourg. Its provisions have been incorporated into the Treaty of Lisbon. It is already being cited by the Court of Justice as reflecting established EU law.

The Charter will seem to some merely to ensure individuals rights which have already effectively been granted under successive Treaties. When the European Convention, whose work was concluded with the Draft European Constitution, was set up on 4 June 1999 at the Cologne European Ministerial Council, its stated task was to formulate a Charter of Fundamental Rights with the aim of giving transparency to the fundamental rights which already existed at the level of the European Union.

To others, the Charter will seem like a large extension of the power and competences of the European Union which is unnecessary, particularly since all Member States subscribe to the European Convention on Fundamental Rights and Human Freedoms. They are concerned that the provisions of the Charter go far beyond what could properly be called "fundamental rights". Whatever views one may have on the merits or otherwise of the substantially expanded rights in the Charter compared to the European Convention, it seems inevitable that its implementation will add substantially to the work of the Court of Justice.[The substantially expanded rights may be an area for further inter-governmental consideration. The Charter embodies some cherished concepts of social Europe which may not properly be regarded as fundamental rights and which a number of Member States can no longer afford.

A further source of increasing litigation relates to cases involving the external relations of the European Union, both in relation to international agreements and, in particular, decisions arising out of the disputes procedure of the World Trade Organisation (WTO). The Marrakesh Treaty signed in April 1994 was, of course, negotiated by the European Commission on behalf of the Member States. This difficult subject is addressed in the recent book by Professor John Jackson entitled "Sovereignty, the WTO and Changing Fundamentals of International Law".

Taking into account the further likely increases in the workload of the Court of Justice and the Court of First Instance, I am by no means convinced that any of the current proposals for reform will provide more than a short-term solution to a long term problem. The longer term solution to the question of the appropriate distribution of cases at European level may well need to be much more radical than anything that is at present being proposed.

In thanking you for the great privilege of inviting me to address you, I should emphasise that, in my view, as the world grows smaller our aim should be to achieve not just regional but wider global agreements. This requires detailed discussion and understanding. Over time it must be possible for wider rights to be spelt out of what is at present contained in regional agreements like those of Mercosul and the European Union.

On another level we need to bring together Judges and lawyers from different parts of the world to discuss common problems. I am Chairman of the Trustees of the European Law Academy in Trier (ERA), a city in Germany but very close geographically to the European Court in Luxembourg. ERA is a European Institute which brings together Judges, practising lawyers, lawyers employed in industry, and academics from the different states of the European Union and outside, to discuss different areas of the law. As recently as March 2008 ERA held a conference on the external competence of the European Union. I am also a member of the Middle Temple, one of the ancient Inns of Court. In a few days Her Majesty the Queen will honour us by attending a service in the Temple Church in a service to commemorate the 400th anniversary of the granting of the Royal Charter to Middle Temple and Inner Temple. Both ERA and the Inns of Court are conscious that we are all part of a legal world which is getting smaller and where co-operation on as wide a basis as possible is essential at all levels. Both ERA and the Inns of Court already have substantial world-wide contacts.

I am also a member (until 2009) of the Council of King's College London, a prestigious university of over 20,000 students with premises in the City of London, which has the only Institute in any university in the United Kingdom devoted to Brazil and Portugal. King's College London's Law School is anxious to forge closer mutual links with lawyers and judges in Brazil and is taking active steps to see how co-operation can best be developed for our mutual benefit. Perhaps also we should all be thinking about how we can, as individuals and as groups, take practical steps to increase understanding and co-operation internationally between Judges and lawyers. Speaking personally, I can think of no more positive step than to develop this dialogue between Brazil and the United Kingdom, and Brazil and the European Union.

Once again thank you very much for inviting me.

Academy of European Law, Trier (ERA)

The third Institution with which I have been involved is the Academy of European Law (Europäische Rechtsakademie), ERA. This section contains three articles. The first is my history of ERA in the 2010 ERA Annual Report. The second is a short introduction which I wrote for the July-December 2010 ERA Programme. The third is a "Dinner Speech" at ERA on 25 March 2011.

Some of the outline of the history of ERA has already been set out in Dr Heusel's chapter in the *Liber Amicorum* (p.21). It has been an extraordinary experience to watch ERA develop from a fledgling organisation to one firmly established within the European Union and a great privilege to have had a part in achieving it.

In the 2010 Annual Report, at page 53, I was given the opportunity to write a full, if relatively brief, review the history of ERA, with particularly emphasis on the period from 1997 – 2010 when I was Chairman of the Board of Trustees.

The article charts the development of ERA from its beginnings. Even in 1997 it had no premises of its own, whereas by 2010 it had acquired and was using a third building on its site, previously occupied by the Bundesbank. The other two buildings are the ERA building and a hotel, which is run independently of ERA but is used by ERA for its conference guests. The story of the development of ERA from its modest beginnings to its present position, as the pre-eminent provider of European legal education, is an inspiring one. The article also looks forward to the future of legal education for judges and practitioners within the EU and the role which ERA could play within it. These questions remain to be settled, as does the precise role which the European Union will take in legal education under Articles 81ff of the Lisbon Treaties. The answers to these questions will be relevant not only for ERA, but will impinge upon the domestic rules in the Member States. A current example of this is the aspiration of the EU Commission to train a substantial number of judges from the Member States in EU law by 2020.

Dr Heusel has identified the important changes which took place in the years 1998-2000. At a time of uncertainty for ERA, when it was necessary for the Chairman of the Board of Trustees to take positive steps to ensure its future, Dr Heusel is correct to say that I was largely responsible for some, and with him for other, important changes in that year. Among these changes were; the changes to the Foundation Statute to guarantee ERA's independence; the appointment of Dr Heusel as Director; the establishment of a Management Board; the discussion and implementation of a medium term strategy and the placing of financial reporting on a business-like basis to the Governing Board (which includes representatives of those who provide much of the funds for ERA).

The following years after 2000 may have seemed to those at ERA as years of consolidation. My perception as Chairman of the Board of Trustees was different. What was regarded by some as "consolidation", I regarded as considerable forward progress towards maturity, excellently led by Dr Heusel with the considerable assistance of the deputy Directors and the staff. An important innovation, with which I was much involved, was the obtaining of recognition by regulatory authorities in the Member States that ERA's courses qualified as satisfying the requirements to be counted towards the annual points required by practitioners for continuing professional development (CPD).

I also include both my brief introduction to the programme for July – December 2010 (p. 283) to give a flavour of ERA's programme, and my "Dinner Speech" on 25 March 2011(p. 285) when I attempted to answer the question why ERA as an institution is regarded with affection by so many people. This affection is also evident in my references to ERA in my "Reader's Speech" (see p. 332 and following).

ERA Annual Report 2010
A brief history of ERA

By John Toulmin CMG QC
Chairman of the ERA Board of Trustees 1997-2010

I became Chairman of the Board of Trustees at the Trustees' meeting of 19 June 1997. I handed over to my successor, Pauliine Koskelo, Chief Justice of Finland, on 1 January 2011. When I started, ERA only had a small office next to the Nell's Park Hotel. What is now ERA was a building site, the foundation stone of the new building having been laid by Minister Peter Caesar and the then President of the Governing Board Horst Langes, on 18 March 1996. By the end of 2010, the building recently acquired from the Bundesbank had been re-furbished and was fully operational. In 1997 ERA was 5 years old, now it is soon to celebrate the 20th anniversary of its foundation.

In 1997 there were 15 Member States, Austria, Finland and Sweden having joined as recently as 1 January 1995. In 2011 we have 27 Member States. The European Union has developed at considerable speed. In 1997 Monetary Union was still some years away. Justice and Home Affairs were part of the Third Pillar of the Maastricht Treaty, and the EU's role was limited to promotion of co-operation between the Member States. The 2009 Lisbon Treaties, incorporating the Treaty for the Functioning of the European Union (TFEU), enlarged the competence of the EU in criminal matters and confirmed the increased competence in civil matters set out in the Treaty of Amsterdam. The competences in civil and criminal matters are set out in Articles 81 and 82 of the TFEU. Commissioner Reding is working very actively to fulfil the new mandate. I shall return to this topic and the new opportunities which it presents at the end.

It is clear that both the European Union and ERA have been transformed since June 1997. It is the genius of the founders and those working at ERA that ERA has been able to evolve to the changing needs of legal Europe while keeping faith with the original purpose for which ERA was created, and for which it was initially so generously supported (and continues to be supported) by the state of Rhineland-Palatinate, the Federal Republic of Germany, the City of Trier and the European institutions – the European Commission, the Court of Justice and the Parliament.

I start with a brief history of ERA in the period before 1997.The idea which Horst Langes MEP and a few of his fellow members of the European Parliament put to Peter Caesar, Minister of Justice of Rhineland- Palatinate in the late 1980s, was " the ever-greater need for individuals and authorities involved in the application and implementation of European Law to gain a wider knowledge of European law and in particular Community law and its application and to have increasing opportunities for a mutual and comprehensive exchange of experiences".

On 8 and 9 November 1991 ERA was formally inaugurated at a conference in the Electoral Palace in Trier.

On 22 June 1992 the Academy of European Law Foundation was established jointly by the Grand Duchy of Luxembourg, the State of Rhineland-Palatinate, the City of Trier and the Association for the Promotion of the Academy.

On 12 March 1992 ERA held the first of seven seminars that year on the topic of asylum and immigration policy. In 1993 it held its first full programme of 26 seminars.

The governance of ERA is carried out by a Governing Board, an Executive Board and a Board of Trustees, and, since 2000, a Management Board consisting of the Director and up to three deputy directors of the Academy, a modern structure for the administration of an increasingly complex organisation. At different times individual members of the three external Boards have played crucial roles in the development of ERA.

The Board of Trustees held its first meeting on 5 July 1993 with Willi Rothley MEP as the first Chairman. The Board of Trustees consisted of a wide representation of nominated representatives of the Member States and the European Institutions, and judges, lawyers practising independently and in companies, and academics from the Member States appointed by the Governing Board. Its task was primarily to assist Wolfgang Heusel, then the Director of Programmes, and the legal staff in the development of the training programmes of the Academy. From the start it had a considerable input into the particular courses and it chose the topic for the Annual Congress and helped in its preparation in co-operation with the ERA lawyers.

In addition, since the Governing Board was concerned primarily with financial matters, the Board of Trustees gave advice on strategy and on topics like marketing the Academy and publicity. A Marketing Committee was set up in which Sir Thomas Macpherson, former President of the European Association of Chambers of Commerce and Industry Eurochambres, and Heinz Weil, Avocat à la Cour de Paris, a German Rechtsanswalt and also President of the CCBE in 1995, have played particularly important roles from the beginning in advising on how ERA should be presented and marketed to the outside world. Because the advice of the Trustees was valued and acted upon appropriately by the staff at ERA, the level of attendance of trustees at the Annual Meetings was and is very high, an average of over 40 participants.

The concept of the Annual Congress was and is to provide a platform for discussion of European legal policy by considering in depth a subject which combines aspects of European-wide policy with questions of law. The first Conference in 1993 was on "The Future of Europe – Centralised and De-Centralised approaches". ERA's position, to which it has always adhered, is that it acts as a facilitator devising programmes to enable the issues to be elaborated by experts and participants. ERA must not take sides but ensure that the issues are presented fairly and comprehensively. The detailed work of preparing the courses and the legal policy conferences is carried out by the staff lawyers.

The members of the Board of Trustees have continued to play an important part in the development of the programmes both through the annual Trustees' meetings and in direct contact with the ERA lawyers responsible for the particular course. At the start, the programmes were divided into foundation programmes, programmes for experts and special programmes on demand. As EU lawyers have acquired a greater knowledge of European law, and as the law itself has impinged more and more on the everyday life of its citizens, the programmes have become more sophisticated. The composition of the Board of Trustees has changed to meet this need with more experts in particular areas of the law, and the Trustees' Meetings provide an intensive and informed scrutiny of the proposed programmes for the coming year.

Coming to 1997, when I became Chairman of the Board of Trustees, ERA was still an organisation trying to establish itself. It had done well in the early years but questions were still being asked about its direction and why its existence was necessary when there were, albeit with different purposes, institutes with a European-wide mission in Florence, Bruges and Maastricht. Trier was thought to be relatively inaccessible and the three buildings on the site, for the Academy, the Bundesbank and the Hotel, were still over a year from completion.

The subject for the Annual Congress in 1997 was "The Legal Limits for a Geometrically Variable and Multi-speed Europe", continuing the debate on major topics in the development of the European Union. This was then a fundamental issue concerning the development of the European Union. Other important seminars in that year included the impact of European consumer protection legislation on domestic civil and contract law, the first ERA seminar on Media Law and the first ERA seminar in Estonia.

The ERA Congress Centre was opened by Jacques Santer as President of the European Commission on 11 September 1998. This was followed by an inspiring symposium on Monetary Union in which the keynote speakers were Pierre Werner, former Prime Minister of Luxembourg, and "Father of Monetary Union", Lord Howe of Aberavon QC, former Foreign Secretary and

Chancellor of the Exchequer in the United Kingdom, and Alain Lamassoure, former French Minister for European Affairs.

In 1998 ERA opened a small office in Brussels and participated in two important initiatives. In the first, ERA participated with the TAIEX office in Brussels in the organisation of 22 further education courses for judges in the then-associated countries in Central and Eastern Europe with a further 16 to follow in 1999. The second related to the PHARE follow-up project on the approximation of legislation in Hungary with EU law. This followed pervious PHARE projects in Hungary and Bulgaria.

1999 saw further recognition at European level. In July 1999 the ERA library was awarded the status of an EU documentation centre. On 8/9 November 1999 ERA put on the first seminar on request for the European Parliament, an exercise which was to be repeated annually until 2008. Also in 1999 ERA developed its own website. The Annual Congress was on the Eastern Enlargement of the European Union-strategies for optimising the accession of the Candidates from Central and Eastern Europe.

However 1999 was primarily a year of change for ERA. Very sadly, Peter Caesar, who had done so much to establish and develop the Academy, fell ill and died on 30 December 1999. Ernst Merz, who had been Director since 1 October 1992, left to return to his Social Affairs Court in Koblenz.

It was time to assess the future of ERA. It had come a long way since its foundation, but it was still not well-known among the lawyers and judges in the European legal profession. In the year 2000, ERA was still a fledgling organisation. By December 2010 it had become an established and important provider of legal education in the rapidly developing European Union. Wolfgang Heusel was appointed Director on 1 January 2000 and it is largely his vision which has taken ERA forward to its present position.

A crucial factor in ERA's development has been that the staff, currently from 13 different countries, have stayed much longer and many have established careers at ERA. This has improved the quality of the courses. On a personal note, I can say that the Annual Congresses and the courses which I have attended have been outstanding both in the organisation of the courses and the preparation of the accompanying documents.

In 2007 ERA celebrated its 15th anniversary with an important conference on "The Future of Legal Europe". In 2010 there were 128 events with 7,487 participants. About one third of the events took place outside Trier or Brussels. By then, ERA had organised over 1000 events with nearly 60,000 participants, not only in Trier, but in more than 100 cities in 31 different European countries. It is impressive that despite the difficult economic conditions, ERA was in 2010 able to attract almost the largest number of participants in its history, and was able in financial terms to break even. This demonstrated the careful financial management at ERA.

Since 2000, ERA's position as a European institution has been further recognised in a number of important respects. Starting with the accession of Ireland as a Patron of the Academy in the year 2000, 22 Member States, Croatia as an acceding State and Scotland, have also become Patrons.

Since 2005, starting with the Luxembourg and UK Presidencies, ERA has, at the Presidencies' request, put on seminars to explore important issues, which were priorities of that Presidency. The Luxembourg Presidency's topics included Mutual Trust in the European Criminal Law Area, and Free Movement in the Schengen Area. In 2011ERA organised a conference on Data Protection Measures at European level, international challenges and directions of future movements, for the Hungarian Presidency. It has also become involved in the legal training for the staff of incoming Presidencies, in particular in preparation for the Polish Presidency from July 2011. In addition ERA co-operates with large numbers of Ministries of Justice in the Member States in organising training events.

EU institutions have continued to commission seminars from ERA for their own staff and for third parties. These have included seminars on anti-discrimination Law, EU law on equal treatment between men and women, telecommunications, and combating fraud.

Judges of the Court of Justice and members of the European Commission and Parliament have continued to be most generous with their time and support as members of the Executive and Governing Boards, and the Board of Trustees, and in participating in ERA events.

ERA has also co-operated increasingly with organisations at European level and at national level. These have included not only the European institutions, but also, amongst others, the Council of the Bars and Law Societies (CCBE) and the European Company Lawyers Association (ECLA), emphasising ERA's role in providing legal training and the opportunities for lawyers in private practice and in business to meet together. As a former President of the CCBE I was very honoured, as my last act as Chairman of the Board of Trustees, to chair and sum up the conclusions at a joint CCBE/ ERA Conference on 26th November 2010 to celebrate the 50th anniversary of the CCBE. The topic was "Legal Aid, a Fundamental Right for Citizens – Effective Access to Justice in the European Union". The keynote speech from Commissioner Reding made it clear that she was proposing to issue a White Paper on Access to Justice in the EU in 2012 and on Legal Aid in 2013.

In 2010 ERA, in addition to co-operation with the institutions of the Union, had about 60 co-operation partners . This number has been increasing steadily.

In a further development, many Member States require their practising lawyers to undertake annually continuing compulsory profession development (CPD) and ERA has been recognised as an approved provider. Attendance at a two-day ERA seminar enables lawyers in most jurisdictions to meet their annual CPD requirements.

As the legal world has become smaller, ERA has extended its training beyond the EU. Between 2000 and 2005, ERA organised a series of ten training workshops for Chinese judges and prosecutors. ERA is an associate partner of the China-EU School of Law. In 2009 and 2010 ERA, with the City of Trier and Beijing Normal University, was involved in a project supported by the Chinese and German Ministries of Education, to bring European and Chinese perspectives on how to identify the causes of disparities of wealth and how they can be overcome, through better infrastructure, planning and disaster prevention and management. In 2010 ERA organised a two week information and training seminar for Chinese officials on behalf of the European Commission DG for Regional Policy.

On 18 February 2004 ERA organised a one week programme for Chilean lawyers. Since 2008 ERA has been implementing a three year project aimed at strengthening international co-operation in criminal matters in Ukraine, Georgia and Moldova. ERA has also held seminars on the WTO (World Trade Organisation) in Brussels, participated in by eminent lawyers and academics from other countries including the United States.

On the basis of three successful annual European Traffic Law Congresses organised by ERA since 2000, also in 2004, the Institute of European Traffic Law was launched with the support of ERA, which provided its secretariat until 2009.

Within its core purpose, ERA has been expanding its services since 2000 to fulfil the increasing needs of the European legal community. In 2000 it launched its quarterly publication *ERA Forum*, with a distinguished editorial board, as a serious legal journal with articles on important European law topics, and a summary of European Court decisions. In 2007 Springer took over its production and marketing. Since then the journal has been available on the internet and has been particularly successful in this format. In 2010 the number of successful full text downloads was 23,807.

The Brussels office has become of central importance to ERA as a result of the entry into force of the Lisbon Treaties and the adoption of the Stockholm programme. It focuses on three key areas – ERA's role in providing judicial training, contacts with European institutions, legal bodies and national representation based in Brussels, and in updating staff in Trier on the latest developments at European level. Its "ERA Briefings" organised about once a month on topical developments in the EU are particularly successful.

Since 2007 ERA has developed a series of e-learning modules in different areas of EU law and has recently used video conferencing as an inter-active method of training lawyers.

It is recognised that coming to legal conferences is expensive, particularly for young lawyers from new member states, and ERA has set up the Peter Caesar scholarships, named after the former Minister for Justice in Rhineland-Palatinate. ERA awarded 25 scholarships in 2010 and would like to do much more if it could raise the necessary funding.

Finally the three buildings which have been integrated on the ERA site since the autumn of 2010, the two ERA buildings and the Hotel, provide substantially increased space, able to accommodate much larger ERA conferences (as well as providing much needed increased space for staff), are available to outside bodies on occasions when ERA is not holding its own conference.

In view of the increased competences for the European Commission and the Parliament and its impact on the increased opportunities for ERA, it is necessary to follow the founding and subsequent history of the EJTN, (the European Judicial Training Network). In October 2000, ERA became a founding member of the EJTN and has been a driving force in its development. EJTN's aim been to co-ordinate and develop judicial training in the European Area of Freedom, Security and Justice, in particular in view of the growth in judicial co-operation between the Member States. On 29 March 2001 ERA was appointed as the Secretariat for the EJTN.

On 29 June 2006 the Commission issued a communication promoting judicial training at European level, and mentioned ERA as one of the key institutions at European level organising seminars for practitioners. In July 2008, the European Parliament called for the creation of a European Judicial Academy "which shall include EJTN and ERA". In October 2008 the Justice and Home Affairs Council in Luxembourg called for stronger support of judicial training activities and requested the development of common European training programmes by the EJTN and its members, including ERA as the only European training institute.

In May 2010 the EJTN General Assembly elected ERA as the convenor of the working group on Programmes and as a member of the working group on Technology. Also in 2010 ERA led a consortium together with EJTN which is conducting a study for the European Parliament on judicial training in the EU. ERA has for many years organised seminars for the judiciary in the Member States focussing on practical training involving case studies mainly derived from the practice in the participants' home countries. In 2010 more than 1400 judges and prosecutors from all over Europe took part in ERA training events, most of the events being in conjunction with EJTN.

In relation to civil law, Article 81(e) and (h) of the TFEU amplify the general provisions in Article 81 requiring the European Parliament and Council to adopt measures for the proper functioning of the internal market aimed at ensuring "(e) effective access to justice" and "(h) support for the training of the judiciary and judicial staff".

In relation to criminal law, Article 82 of the TFEU confers in Article 82(c) the obligation on the European Union to support the training of the judiciary and judicial staff. Under Article 82(2) it confers wide powers on the EU to establish minimum rules to facilitate mutual recognition of judgments and judicial decisions. Police and judicial co-operation in criminal matters may also be the subject of minimum community rules under Articles 83-86.

To ensure effective access to justice through the Courts of the Member States by competent judges at a reasonable cost and within a reasonable time is one of the greatest challenges for the Member States and the European Union's Institutions. The training of the judiciary and judicial staff is a small part of that problem. Fundamental change is required to the system of delivering justice in many Member States if anything approaching effective access to justice, certainly in civil cases, is to be achieved through the Courts.

The Stockholm programme places great emphasis on training and e-learning and in paragraph 3.2.1 states that " Training of Judges (including administrative courts) prosecutors and other judicial staff is essential to strengthen mutual trust... the Union should continue to support and strengthen measures to increase training in line with articles 81 and 82 TFEU". It is not clear whether it is intended that this would include only those who exercise a judicial function, or whether it will include all those including practising lawyers who are involved in the process of justice. In either event, without being complacent about it, ERA is well-placed in terms of expertise and facilities to meet the future training needs of lawyers, judges, civil servants and academics and to continue to develop programmes to help to provide effective access to justice in the Member States (and in the wider world) both within the framework of EU legislation and within its traditional activities.

I cannot end this survey without a special personal tribute to Dr Wolfgang Heusel and all the staff during my time as Chairman of the Board of Trustees and, in particular, among those who have left, Ernst Merz the former Director, Fabian Pereyra and Sarah Jund, former Directors of Programmes. Since 2000 Wolgang Heusel has been Chairman of the Management Board which since 2006 has consisted of him and three Deputy Directors of ERA, Jean-Philippe Rageade (Director of Programmes), Luc Doeve (Director of Finance and Conference Services)and John Coughlan (Director of Corporate Communications). They have headed a dedicated staff of lawyers and support staff who embody the spirit of ERA. They succeed in giving an air of relaxed informality and warmth at the same time as being very professional. They are joined by a team of interpreters led from the beginning by Wolfgang Fehlberg. They interpret in English, French, German, Italian and other languages with great skill and their work has been invaluable.

It has been a great privilege to serve as Chairman of the Board of Trustees during these 14 years of extraordinary change. I thank most warmly my fellow Trustees for their contributions, encouragement and support both in the annual meetings and in advising and assisting the staff on other occasions. I thank in particular my Vice Chairmen, Francesco de Angelis, Walter van Gerven, Josef Azizi and Péter Köves. It is a great pleasure to hand over the chairmanship to Pauliine Koskelo who is ideally equipped to chair the Board of Trustees in the next stage of ERA's development. As I have said, ERA has the staff, the organisation, the capacity and the support from the Governing Board, the Executive Board, and the Board of Trustees to embrace the new opportunities and challenges in European legal education, which arise both as a result of the Treaty of Lisbon and naturally as European law grows to be more and more a part of the law of the Member States, and also to play a wider role in the development of legal education world-wide.

Preface to the July – December 2010 ERA Programme

The main task of the Board of Trustees, whose names are listed in this booklet, is to assist the Director of Programmes and the permanent staff in developing the programme of events which ERA offers to promote training in European law and practice. This work is carried out at the day long annual meeting of the Trustees, attended normally by over fifty Trustees, and by informal contacts between the staff and individual members. In the past all the Trustees considered the future programme together at the annual meeting, but recently the Trustees have split into groups to consider in depth particular areas with the legal staff. Together with ideas from participants, the open programme of events has been developed under the guidance of Jean Philippe Rageade, as Director of Programmes, to respond to the developing needs of legal Europe as it expands and develops. Participation in ERA's activities is widely recognised in the Member States as fulfilling the requirements for individual professional development.

ERA provides courses on specific aspects of law and practice both in Trier, easily accessible via Luxemburg, and throughout the European Union; intensive English language courses; and briefings in Brussels which provide topical analysis of important developments relating to the constitution and laws of the EU. *ERA Forum*, available online, is recognised increasingly as a valuable source of in-depth articles on aspects of EU law and practice.

Participants in ERA's activities include lawyers in private practice, in-house counsel, judges, prosecutors, academics, representatives of EU and national governments, law enforcement agencies and NGO's. An important benefit is the opportunity for the interaction of participants from different countries, legal backgrounds and experience.

ERA's programme for the 2nd half of 2010 reflects the new competencies of the EU under Articles 81 and 82 of the Treaty of Lisbon relating to judicial co-operation in civil and criminal matters. This has been reinforced by the Stockholm Programme adopted by the European Council on 10th and 11th December. This will require the development of new initiatives as the European Union seeks, while respecting the legal sovereignty of the Member States, to provide for better understanding by lawyers and judges of law and procedure at EU level and to enhance the level of knowledge and co-operation between the lawyers and judges in the Member States and their legal systems.

There is a more fundamental problem which will have to be addressed both at European and national level. This is how to develop appropriate yardsticks by which the EU and national systems should be judged to ensure that citizens in the EU have access to justice, so that criminal and civil cases are resolved by competent judges within a reasonable time and at reasonable cost. Related to this is a question which the 2008 Mediation Directive (2008/52 EC) seeks to address, and to which the Stockholm Programme refers, namely what part mediation and other forms of Alternative Dispute Resolution should play in the legal process. A seminar to be held at ERA in March 2011 is very relevant to this topic.

While ERA's mission to organise courses, conferences, seminars and specialist symposia for continuing vocational training, and to provide a forum for discussion, has not changed since 1992, the way it discharges its duties has been transformed over the last eighteen years. From 1992 to 1998 ERA had no conference centre of its own. In September 1998 the Conference Centre in Trier was opened by Dr Jacques Santer as President of the EU Commission. In order to respond to the expanding needs of training in a Union of twenty seven Member States, ERA has acquired the third building on the Trier site. Although it will not be opened formally until Spring 2011, it is now available for the first time for use for the current programmes and will enable ERA to continue to develop and enhance its services.

As a Member of the Board of Trustees since ERA's foundation, and its President since 1997, I am honoured to be asked to commend the current Programme. I am sure that you will find the programmes in this booklet, organised by ERA's experienced and dedicated lawyers, both stimulating and enjoyable.

Speech given at the Dinner to celebrate the opening of the new building at the European Law Academy, Trier, Friday 25th March 2011

This is billed as a "Dinner Speech"[1]. Originally I had in mind a very different type of speech to the one I shall make - perhaps a half-an-hour panorama of recent EU law, or the differences between civil law and common law. When Wolfgang Heusel explained to me how this evening would work, and that it was to be an informal evening, it seemed to me to require a very different approach! I was put in mind of the fact that when I was President of the CCBE, I explained, quite dishonestly, that there was a tradition in England that all speeches should take place before, not after, dinner. It makes the speeches much shorter. This is a celebration party and I shall not detain you for long.

What a wonderful building this is! Well worth celebrating. I saw the building before work started. The transformation is remarkable. It looked like the Lubianka. Indeed there are vaults below which, if you stray into, you may only be found in 30 years' time! I was at the hotel opposite on the last night that the Bundesbank was here. It may have been a dream, but I was sure that I could see the fire and smell the burning bank notes!

I pose the question, why are we all here? I suppose the obvious answer is that we were all lucky enough to be invited to this splendid occasion. But I pose the question again. Why are we all here? What is it that attracts us to ERA? Why do we feel part of the ERA family?

In a short and very selective history of the last 19 years, we have some clues. In the late 1980s, Horst Langes and Otto Theissen put a proposition to Peter Caesar, Minister of Justice of Rhineland Palatinate, for the setting up of a new Institution " ... to enable individuals , and others involved in the application and implementation of European Law, and in particular Community Law, to gain a wide knowledge of European Law, and in particular Community Law and its application, and to have increasing opportunities for a mutual and comprehensive exchange of experiences".

---

[1] Published as an end piece to the *Liber Amicorum*, supplement to vol 12, *ERA Forum*, May 2011.

This was particularly far-sighted when you think that there were then 12 Member States and many of the countries now part of the European Union were recently freed from totalitarian regimes. So this is the first clue: the importance of the work which ERA undertakes. We are all engaging in an enterprise which has as its object something which we believe in.

No one should underestimate the importance in the founding and continuing support of the institutions from the Parliament, Court of Justice and Commission, and from the Federal Republic of Germany, the state of Rhineland Palatinate, and not forgetting the city of Trier, which gave the land upon which these buildings stand. Without their active support, ERA could not have achieved anything. So we have a second clue: not only are ERA's aims worthwhile, but they are capable of being realised.

The first meeting of the Board of Trustees was on 5 July 1993. The Board of Trustees was from the first broadly based and drawn from all the Member States, with representatives of the different branches of the legal profession. In the early years it played a vital part in helping to develop the programmes in conjunction with Wolfgang Heusel as Deputy Director and Director of Programmes. It also discussed issues of broad strategy. Because there were no resources for it, the Board was also involved in questions of marketing. From the earliest times it was made clear that all ideas would be listened to and considered. The Trustees were genuinely participating in the development of ERA. It was the opposite of the meeting where a few speak all the time and busy people, many of whom have come from a long way away, feel that they have been unable to contribute and that no one would have been interested in any event in what they had to say. If you do not feel included, you do not come back next year. If you are valued, you give willingly of your time. So we have another clue: we feel valued and this makes us feel part of ERA.

For a long time it was doubtful whether ERA would survive. After all, people would say "We have Institutes at Bruges, Florence and Maastricht, why do we need ERA and where is it anyway?"

Until 1998 ERA had no permanent home, only small offices near the Nells Park Hotel. Meetings took place in the Ramada Hotel.

I arrived for the 1997 Trustees Meeting rather less prepared than I would have liked. Willy Rothley, the Chairman, took me on one side. He said, "The organisation is too German. We need to widen participation in order to demonstrate the European nature of ERA. I am going to propose you as Chairman of the Board of Trustees". I agreed to do it, but only if he agreed to be one of the Vice-Chairmen. There began my 14 fulfilling years as Chairman of the Board of Trustees. It has been a very great privilege. This provides the next clue: ERA is a genuinely European organisation.

In 1998 the new building was inaugurated, but there were still worries about ERA's survival. The staff came and went, They did good work but provided little stability. There were worries about ERA's future direction. Even with the new building there was no guarantee that ERA would survive. Indeed if Wolfgang had not been confirmed as Director, I am not at all sure that ERA would have survived.

The period since 2000 has seen the transformation of ERA from infancy to maturity. The first sign of this was that the staff stayed for much longer. This demonstrated that it was worthwhile staying because of what ERA had become. Secondly it indicated that it was a great place to work. It has meant that the quality of ERA's conferences have improved to a very high level. The staff do outstanding work. This provides the next clue: when we come to ERA we are immediately aware of the good atmosphere.

This loyalty is shared by the rest of the staff and by others who come to ERA including the interpreters, led from the beginning of ERA by Wolfgang Fehlberg. During my time as Chairman I had a running game with the interpreters as to whether I could tell a joke in English which was wholly untranslatable into any other language. I must find out one day whether or not I succeeded!

In 2006 a management board was created with Jean-Philippe Rageade, Luc Doeve, and John Coughlan. A management board to share the task of the direction of the Academy was a vital tool of management if ERA was to move forward. By this time a proper management structure had become essential, and I acknowledge the part which Jean-Phillipe Rageade, Luc Doeve and John Coughlan have played. This brings us to the next clue: which is that ERA is equipped in organisational terms to meet future challenges.

It has been very important to me after 14 years as Chairman of the Board of Trustees, to have the right successor. It is time to move on. We need new skills for new times and so I am very happy to hand over to Pauliine Koskelo, Chief Justice of Finland, who is my ideal successor and so wonderfully equipped in so many ways to take the participation of the Board of Trustees forward.

Well there we have it! This brief summary provides part of the answer to the original question "Why are we here"? What is it that binds us to ERA? And makes us feel part of the ERA family. We think of the importance of the work which ERA undertakes, the fact that our contributions are valued, and the good atmosphere, but I don't think that that is the whole story. There is a special chemistry which binds us together. I think it comes back to Wolfgang Heusel himself. There is an air of informality and unstuffiness, coupled with the pursuit of excellence, which is not found in many European institutions and which is the hall-mark of Wolfgang and of ERA. It is part of the special chemistry which Wolfgang has created in ERA and which he is carrying on with the help of the management board and of the staff. We feel included and are delighted to be part of ERA's family.

I have spoken for long enough. There will be no more speeches. This is a party and the evening is yours!

Institute of Psychiatry - Internal and External Collaboration at King's College London: The Law School and the IoP and the Health Schools

The fourth institution is the Institute of Psychiatry (IoP). The fifth institution is King's College London.

"Pursuit of Excellence" covers my period of particularly close association with the Maudsley and Bethlem Hospitals Management Board and its successor bodies, and the IoP between 1979 and 2002. "Internal and External Collaboration" brings the history of the merger between the IoP and King's College London up to date, and considers the question of cross-departmental collaboration within King's and internationally, and then focuses on the relationship between the IoP and the Law School.

After I retired as chairman of the Management Advisory Committee, I gave a lecture on 5 February 2003 setting out the history of the IOP from the time when I joined the Hospital Management Board of the NHS Maudsley and Bethlem Hospitals in May 1979 until my retirement from the Chairmanship of the IoP Advisory Committee in May 2002. This period had not been covered in any current history. It was a time of turbulence both for the NHS Hospital Trust and for the IoP. The IoP has been for many years and is one of the world's leading institutions for the research and treatment of mental health and its history is therefore of particular importance. It is not generally known that in the 1980s and early 1990s the IoP had to transform itself not merely to flourish but even to survive. The good health of the IoP in 2002 was not achieved without considerable pain. I also describe the negotiations leading up to the merger with King's College London and the early difficult period after the merger in 1997. While giving the general history I have also included some reference to the part which I played in particular events.

While some progress has been made since 2003, the challenges for mental health to which I refer at the end of my IoP lecture remain. There is the continuing problem of mental illness within the population and the problem that much of the service at GP level remains inadequate. However, much work has been done, particularly at the IoP to reduce the stigma attaching to mental illness. A further breakthrough has occurred in that the current Health Services Bill recognises for the first time that mental illness is of equal importance to physical illness.

As I set out in "Internal and External Collaboration", I joined King's Council in 1997 and retired in the summer of 2009 after 12 years as a member and latterly as Chairman of the Governance Committee. I was honoured with a Fellowship of King's College in 2006. In my time as a member of Council, King's had, under Professor Arthur Lucas as Principal, assimilated the IoP and the medical schools (Guy's ,King's, and St Thomas'(GKT)) and moved forward under Professor Sir Richard Trainor to be rated one of the top 25 universities in the world. This rather inspiring story, which I have been fortunate to see as a member of King's Council, is too recent for me to attempt to chronicle it. One important recent step forward has been the grant to King's of a long lease of the East Wing of Somerset House, which was occupied by King's in early 2012. Part of the space is taken by the Law School which, for the first time for 50 years, has appropriate accommodation.

My association with the IoP did not in fact end in 2002. I remained a member of its Advisory Committee until 2009 and retain close links with the IoP.

"Internal and External Collaboration" brings the history of the integration of the IoP within King's up to date. It was on the nomination of the IoP that, originally, I became a Member of the Council of King's College London when the IoP merged with King's in 1997, although my membership was subsequently renewed by King's from 2003. In 2006 I was a member of the interviewing committee which appointed Professor Peter McGuffin as Dean from 2007-2009 and Professor Shitij Kapur from January 2010. The tensions between IoP and King's College London, evident when the IoP joined King's in 1997, had eased considerably by 2002. There were still occasions thereafter when I was able to assist both parties in avoiding or resolving potential misunderstandings. As I explain in the chapter, this period of transition has been completed. The IoP, as part of King's, has enhanced further its reputation as a pre-eminent institution worldwide.

What follows thereafter arose out of a recent initiative of mine, born out of my experience at the University of Michigan. My theme of interdisciplinary co-operation and collaboration coincided with initiatives which were already under way not only to link individual faculties at King's, including the Law School, other institutions worldwide, but also to promote co-operation at all levels between departments and faculties within the university.

The article sets out dynamic developments that are taking place at King's, including those between the IoP and the Health Schools, and goes on to suggest further areas of collaboration between the Law School and the IoP and GKT.

As I completed this book I heard of the very recent large donation to the Law School announced on 19 March 2012, which will enable the Law School most significantly to enhance its worldwide reputation. It can look to the precedent of the IoP in the 1990s for the creation of a pre-eminent Law School.

In Pursuit of Excellence

Lecture by H H Judge John Toulmin CMG QC

Institute of Psychiatry, 5 February 2003

When I told the Dean that I planned to retire from the Chairmanship of the Management Advisory Committee of the Institute of Psychiatry (The Institute) and the Joint Committee with the South London and Maudsley Trust (The Trust), he very generously said that the Institute wished to mark the occasion by giving me a party. I was asked what form I should like it to take. I reflected that although three histories came out to celebrate the 750th anniversary of the founding of the Bethlem Hospital, they concentrated inevitably on the earlier history and in any event did not cover the major developments of the association of the Institute with Kings College, London (KCL), the development of the Maudsley & Bethlem Trust into the South London and Maudsley NHS Foundation Trust (SLAM) and the buildings of the last few years which have transformed the Maudsley site. I wanted to step back and try to put the events since the start of my association with the Maudsley and the Institute into some kind of perspective.

My association with the Institute and The Trust started with my appointment to the Maudsley & Bethlem Hospital Management Board in March 1979. My first meeting was on 9 April 1979. I remained a member of the Hospital Management Board and it successor, the Special Health Authority, until 1987. In 1982 I became a member of the Board of Trustees of the Institute first as a nominee of the Special Health Authority and then in my own right. My first meeting was on 16 June 1982. In 1994 I became Chair of the Joint Committee of the Maudsley and the Institute and in 1997, on the Institute's entry into KCL, I became a member of the College Council.

In November 1999, at the request of the Dean, I agreed to chair the Management Advisory Committee for two or three meetings as an interim measure. After three years it was time to stand down.

How I Came to be Involved - Normansfield

The first question to answer is how I came to be involved at all. I started as a barrister in 1965 in Chambers that did a great deal of Medical work including what is now called clinical negligence, appearances before the General Medical and General Dental Councils, Hospital Enquiries and Administrative law cases i.e. challenging Government and local authority decisions in the civil courts on the grounds that civil servants, in taking decisions, were acting unreasonably. My pupil master with whom I shared a room after I was taken on as a full member of Chambers was Eric McLellan, one of the leaders in this field and later a Judge. Across the corridor was another expert in the field, Geoffrey Howe QC. I learnt a great deal from them and gradually acquired a practice in this field.

In 1977 I was asked by the then Attorney-General, The Rt Hon Sam Silkin QC, MP, to be junior counsel to the Normansfield Hospital Enquiry. Leading Counsel to the Enquiry was Philip Otton QC, later to be a Judge in the Court of Appeal. The Chairman of the Enquiry was Michael Sherrard QC, one of the leading QCs of the day, who sat with a leading Psychiatrist, an administrator and a social worker. The Enquiry into the conduct of Dr Lawlor, the Consultant Psychiatrist in charge of this 270 bed hospital at Teddington was extended to the conduct of those responsible for the management of the hospital at District and Regional level and also to the role of the Department of Health. It was particularly concerned with Dr Lawlor's use of seclusion and his drug therapy as a method of controlling difficult patients. This was, and is, a fundamental moral and ethical issue which is much easier to answer in theory than in practice. At the end of the Enquiry I was asked by Sam Silkin if I would like to be a member of the Hospital Management Board of the Maudsley. He said that before he went into politics he had been on the Maudsley & Bethlem HMB and had found it a rewarding experience.

During the Enquiry I met Dr Ivan Clout who as a GP member of the Regional Hospital Board was the only person who had foreseen in advance the trouble which would occur. at Normansfield. Six months before the nurses walked out of the hospital and refused to return unless Dr Lawlor was suspended indefinitely, he wrote with characteristic bluntness, "There is a time bomb under Normansfield". No one took any notice.

Although a lay member, I came to the Maudsley with a background of having been involved in medical cases acting both for and against medical practitioners and with the experience of the Normansfield Hospital Enquiry which in the end had lasted for a year.

My association has spanned nearly 24 years. I have seen many changes both in psychiatry and associated disciplines and in both the Maudsley and the Institute. The History is of necessity incomplete. It is my perspective from the standpoint of a lay member not a professional. It does not attempt to cover in detail the Maudsley after 1987 nor the Institute before 1982.

Some things have not changed.

First, the core values have not changed. This is best summed up by the title of this lecture and in the Joint Statement of Common Purpose, agreed through the Joint Committee of the two Institutions which sets the current Agenda. "The Institute of Psychiatry and the South London and Maudsley Trust work together to establish the best possible care for people who experience mental health problems. A key joint aim is promoting excellence in research, development of teaching in the sciences and disciplines key to the understanding of the treatment of mental disease and related disorders of the brain. The knowledge and skills thus gained will be applied to prevention of these disorders, finding the most effective treatment and developing the best service models for the community". The pursuit of excellence is the golden thread that runs through the modern history of both Institutions. I take the modern history to start with the opening of the Maudsley Medical School in 1923 and its recognition by the University of London in 1924. On the Hospital side Bethlem moved to its present site at Monks Orchard Road in 1930.

Second, the Institute and the Maudsley have always had a worldwide reputation in the world of psychiatry. This has enabled them to attract and retain outstanding staff and to retain to an extraordinary extent the affection and loyalty of those who work here. Its modern reputation started with Professor Edward Mapother and Professor Sir Aubrey Lewis 70 years ago. The Institute and the joint hospitals have attracted to what, even 40 years ago, was still the fledgling speciality of psychiatry outstanding individuals who were, and are, pioneers in their fields.

Third, the Maudsley has had and still has trust funds which are independent of the NHS. The joint hospitals were formed as Professor Sir Dennis Hill who was Professor of Psychiatry when I joined the HMB graphically described it, "The one Bethlem, was very old and very rich. The other, the Maudsley was very young and very poor".The fact that the joint hospitals have significant trust funds is a continuing and important part of the story that follows. By 1947 Bethlem trust investments excluding land amounted to £276,233(about £7m in today's money) with an annual income of £36,000 (£900,000). Among the land which it owned and owns is part of the South Side of Piccadilly including the land on which Fortnum & Mason stands. In 1949 the Trustees of the Bethlem endowment took the crucial decision that any improvement to the Institute of Psychiatry housed in the hospital buildings constituted an improvement to the joint hospital, and trust funds could be used for this purpose.

Fourth, they have attracted outstanding men and women to lead the Institutions. In particular during my time there have been 4 Deans: Jim Birley 1971-82, Robin Murray 1982-89, Stuart Checkley 1989-2001 and George Szmukler since 2001. The Maudsley and its successor the South London and Maudsley Trust (SLAM) has had only three heads of administration, Nicky Paine 1962-85, Eric Byers 1985-99 and Stuart Bell since 1999. Their leadership has been crucial.

Fifth, in my time both institutions have been lucky with their lay members of the Hospital Boards and the Trustees of the Institute who have made outstanding contributions. This has been particularly true of the Chairs of the Institutions who, in the case of the Institute have been unpaid, and in the case of the Maudsley have been paid at a very modest level, starting with the Chairs Gordon Wixley, Ivan Clout, Trevor Owen, Bernard Williams and Madeliene Long for the joint hospitals and SLAM, and Sir Roger Ormrod, Gordon Wixley, David Maitland, Trevor Owen and Bernard Williams for the Institute.

Sixth, it is noticeable that when one or other Institution is going through difficult times, it is the ordinary lay members who have a particularly important role to play. They have come from different backgrounds, and, almost without exception, they have brought considerable added value to the Institutions. Good examples are Mary Appelbe in the earlier period, and Margot Croft who were involved with the charity, Mind, and gave outstanding service to the Maudsley and the Institute. Others have included, for example, the trade unionist David Basnett, the former Secretary of State for Health Lord Ennals, and the journalist Polly Toynbee at a critical period for the Institute in 1986.

Seventh, and most importantly, the reason why the Maudsley and the Institute have survived as recognisably separate institutions is that they have pursued the highest standards together. They realised long before I arrived that this close co-operation was essential. The history of the Institutions since 1979 has been dominated by reorganisations and threats of reorganisation. In any one of these, decisions could have been taken which would have destroyed or damaged one, or both institutions. It was only the excellence of the Joint Hospitals which preserved it as a unit in the 1980s and 1990s and transformed it into something better with the advent of SLAM. It was only because of its international reputation that the Institute was able to survive as an entity and to preserve a substantial degree of autonomy after it joined KCL in 1997. It was the joint reputation of the two Institutions which has secured the new buildings, costing about £40m, which have been developed in the last 5 years.

Lay Members at the Maudsley.

Before going to the general history, I should like to say a little about my personal involvement in the work of lay members at the Maudsley. A lay member in 1979 had a number of tasks. First he or she contributed to the discussions over the policy for the running of the hospital at Board meetings. Secondly, the lay members formed the Patients Discharge Committee to which a patient had a right of appeal against compulsory detention other than detention by the Courts. If that appeal was unsuccessful there was an appeal to a Mental Health Review Tribunal. Thirdly, in conjunction with a staff member of the Management Board the lay member was expected to undertake two formal visits to different parts of the Bethlehem & Maudsley in the course of a year so that over the whole year the whole of both hospitals was visited. A detailed report with recommendations was submitted to the

Committee after each visit and was followed up by the management. This was not only valuable in its own right but it was invaluable in getting to know the hospitals and understanding their problems. Finally, lay members often participated in ad hoc committees consisting of professionals and lay people.

Seclusion - Joint Committee

There are two topics to which I should refer in more detail. They are illustrative of co-operation between lay and professional members. The first, seclusion, arose out of my hospital visits in company with professional members of the Authority. The second, the setting up of a Joint Committee of the Maudsley and the Institute of Psychiatry, was a special ad hoc committee involving professionals and lay people. They are examples of particular subjects in which I personally was involved.

Seclusion at the Maudsley & Bethlem

I have already said that this was a crucial topic in the Normansfield Hospital Enquiry. Defined as "confinement in a space from which the patient had no means of egress", I assumed that it was not used at the Maudsley. I was clear that such actions by staff represented potentially a serious infringement of the civil liberties of the person confined and that the policy of seclusion was open to serious abuse. On a visit to Normansfield we saw one patient who was routinely confined in a locked space in the evening because, so it was said, of shortage of staff and not because there was any risk that the patient would harm himself or others. If seclusion was used at all, and I recognised that it might be necessary in extreme circumstances where there was a risk that the person might otherwise injure himself or herself or others, it was essential that it should be meticulously recorded in accordance with a protocol which was laid down by the hospital and which enabled others to check to ensure that it was only being used when and to the extent that it was necessary and justified.

I discovered on an early visit with Dr Raymond Levy, soon to become the Professor of Old Age Psychiatry that seclusion was being redefined at the Maudsley so that it did not include exclusion from a building or time out for positive reinforcement. I was told that this last was a form of punishment as part of a treatment programme and since it had been agreed with the patient it did not count as seclusion.

I raised the matter at a meeting of the Hospital Management Board on 6 April 1981 when it was resolved to ask the Medical Executive Committee to set up a working party to look at the possibility of producing rules governing 'time-out' patients which took into account medico-legal and ethical considerations.

We raised the subject again after a visit to Bethlem with Dr Peter Noble, the then Chair of the Medical Executive Committee, in October 1981 and again in relation to 111 Denmark Hill in March 1982 with Professor Cawley, where we insisted that exclusion to an area within the grounds amounted to seclusion and required clear documentation.

A Report from the Medical Executive Committee in May 1982 produced a new seclusion policy for the Joint Hospitals. Seclusion was defined as the containment in a room or other enclosed area of which that patient has no means of egress. The person imposing the seclusion was required to record the date, name, legal status of the patient, the duration of the seclusion, the reason for the seclusion and the frequency of the observations. The form was required to be countersigned both by a responsible Medical Officer and a nurse with the rank of Nursing Officer.

This did not end the discussion on what is a very difficult and sensitive subject. In May 1985 it was reported to the Board that the Medical Executive Committee had resolved that "Preventative segregation is an emergency procedure". The need to segregate violent patients was only to be appropriate for certain units which would apply to the Committee to approve the procedure - approval was granted to the Interim Service Unit, the Intensive Care Area, Fitzmary 2 and the Villa. I felt that this represented substantial progress.

This is a difficult and sensitive issue. The lay members, representing the public have an important part in resolving it. Each generation must review the policy of restraining or controlling patients including the use of drugs for restraint rather than treatment in the light of what is regarded as acceptable at a particular time. These days, service users must, rightly, be made fully aware of their rights. This adds a further dimension to this discussion and to the policies which must apply to the whole hospital.

The Joint Committee

An important initiative, carried through by an ad hoc committee, was the setting up of the joint committee of the Maudsley and the Institute. It first met on 9 May 1990 and had its 50th meeting last October 2002. I took over the Chairmanship in 1994 and have chaired well over half the meetings.

Although there was close co-operation between the officers of the two bodies, I was concerned during the 1980s that no formal joint committee existed. There were many issues concerning the development of the cramped Maudsley site, the future of the two institutions, the development of local services and the working of the internal market for health which I felt made such a committee essential. The objection was always that it would be impossible to reach agreement on the membership of such a committee unless it was so large as to be unwieldy and ineffective.

On 15 March 1989 the Institute proposed that I should chair a small group to look at the possibility of setting up a joint Committee. A similar proposal was made by the Special Health Authority.

The fears of those who thought we had been given an impossible task were wholly unfounded although there was, of course, discussion over the membership. We were able to put positive proposals before both bodies including suggested membership. At the meeting of the Institute in December 1989 the case for a joint Committee was accepted in principle. At the meeting in January 1990 the Special Health Authority formally agreed to the setting up of the Joint Committee. On 21 March 1990 the Institute formally adopted the resolution "that a joint co-ordinating and strategy committee be set up in line with the Government's report on arrangements for improving relations between Universities and the NHS".

As it turned out, we were not doing anything very revolutionary. On 14 February 1914, in a letter to the London County Council, Dr Henry Maudsley had proposed the establishment of a joint hospital - university organisation. Eighty years later we had managed to establish a committee.

On 9 May 1990 the Joint Committee held its first meeting.

Its terms of reference were and are wide. They included the drawing up of a mission statement for the two bodies: planning, particularly on the Maudsley site; development of services in Camberwell; academic developments and the public relations of the two institutions.

The Committee has been useful to the Maudsley and the Institute. Its existence was affirmed in 1997 with the approval of the Principal of KCL, Professor Arthur Lucas after the merger with KCL had taken place. After the South London and Maudsley Trust had taken over in 1999, I asked, as Chair, whether they would like it to continue and they said emphatically that they would.

The Partnership agreement between the Institute and SLAM confirmed the role of the Joint Committee which as the Joint R + D research strategy puts it "exists to ensure a close and productive relationship between SLAM and the Institute of Psychiatry for the benefit of health care, research and teaching in all disciplines applied to mental health. It is regarded as an important element in the management of both bodies".

Government Policy in Health and Education 1979-90

a) Health.

Very shortly after I became a member of the Hospital Board, the Conservatives came into office on 3 May 1979. The history of the Maudsley and the Institute from 1979 - 1990 must be seen against the background of the Thatcher government's determination to make radical changes in the National Health Service and to make policy changes in education, including diverting money from London to the regions.

In 1979, the incoming government was concerned at the cost and inefficiency of the National Health Service and was determined to do something about it. Health Service spending had been rising fast and continued to rise between 1979 and 1983. During this period it went up from £9.5 billion in 1979 to £15.5 billion in 1983. Against this rise it must be remembered that the country was in a period of high inflation, amounting in total to over 40% in the four years. Government policy had a number of strands. It promoted the contracting out of services. It took measures to curb the drug bill. It changed the structure and management of the Health Service. It sought to promote efficiency by making deductions from annual budgets as efficiency savings. From the late 1980s it piloted and then introduced the internal market for health.

Its policies were opposed by the Unions, who said incorrectly that the Conservatives wished to privatise the National Health Service. Their suspicion was fuelled in 1982 by what they regarded as a manifest injustice over pay compared with others in the public sector and also by a leaked document from the Central Policy Review Staff, a think-tank set up independently of the government which proposed a move to a health service paid for by private insurance. There was a long general strike of NHS workers in 1982. There was also a strike at the Maudsley and Bethlem in 1986 as a result of what they regarded as the unfair effect of government cuts on services.

The Government also turned its attention to the structure and management of the NHS. Change took place in two stages: first, after a brief consultation, it decided on a new structure for Health Authorities in the NHS. On 5 April 1982 the new Health Authorities came into being including the Maudsley and Bethlem SHA.

Second, the Government asked Roy Griffiths, the Chief Executive of Sainsbury's, to investigate the management within the Health Service. He reported in the autumn of 1983. He said that every service shared a number of common problems even if the service was different to making cars or selling goods. Retail industry had lessons to teach the NHS.

He concluded that there must be a more efficient management structure within each Health Authority which required the decision-making process to be pushed downwards. He also concluded that there should be a general manager for each hospital responsible for securing the best service for the patients. He also took the view that there should be much greater involvement of clinicians in the management process. The proposals caused resentment, particularly in the nursing profession, which saw the measures as weakening the advances which nurses had made in participating on terms of equality with doctors and administrators. He also recommended the introduction of efficiency savings which were effectively cuts in funding and caused particular difficulties in times of financial stringency. The strategy was to provide annual increases in government funding of Health authorities but these increases would not match pay awards or increased costs caused by inflation. The balance of the costs had to be met out of savings in the hospital budget. In practice this required recurring savings in both clinical and non-clinical support services. This problem was compounded for the Maudsley by a shift of resources away from the South East which progressively reduced the allocation of funds to the South East Thames Regional Health Authority.

These policies were, by their nature, blunt instruments which did not differentiate between the relatively efficient and less efficient authorities. They led to the serious unrest among the staff at the Hospitals in 1986.

The final stage was the introduction of the internal market for health. The 1988 Health and Medicines Act launched the first steps towards the internal market. The Act created a split between purchaser and provider aimed at removing the traditional restrictions on annual budgets. It also emphasised the importance of patients being cared for in the community and of transferring resources from the NHS to local authorities. It continued the policy of squeezing resources in the name of efficiency. Authorities were expected to make efficiency savings to the value of a 0.5% annual increase. This required all hospitals including the Maudsley to go through the painful task of evaluating its services to see if any could be dispensed with and whether cuts were required in the services which were retained. This was followed by the setting up of the internal market for the NHS in 1990 and the reforms of the 1990s.

b) Education.

The Department of Education was pursuing somewhat similar policies. The Institute of Psychiatry received its state funding through HEFCE (the Higher Education Funding Council). There were threats in 1979, at the time when I joined the Maudsley that the funding formula would change in a way that would be disastrous to the Institute largely as a result of shifting resources away from the south of England. In fact, between 1979 – 1986 the allocation rose from £1.5m to £2.6m but this was in a period of high inflation. The under-funding did result in acute financial difficulties for the Institute by 1986.

The Government was also concerned to promote efficiency in the use of educational resources. After effective cuts in earlier years, in 1986 it commissioned a senior industrialist, Sir Alex Jarratt, to investigate the possibility of a 2% reduction in funding to promote efficiency – unfortunately for the Treasury, Jarratt reported that he was unable to find quantifiable savings from efficiency in University budgets. An enforced reduction of 2% in the Institute's budget at that stage might have prevented its survival.

The Institute, in common with other institutions engaged in research, has always received some funding from the private sector. As a result of Government policy these additional monies which were desirable in 1979 had become by 1990 essential for survival. This resulted in a change of culture at the Institute as departments had to compete with other Institutions for research grants.

The Maudsley & the Institute. Introduction

Almost as soon as I became a member of the Maudsley & Bethlem Hospital Management Board in 1979 we had to grapple with the consequences of the Government's health policies and were well aware of the problems which the Institute was encountering.

For the period to 1986 the three R's, two of which I have already touched on when giving the brief overview of Government policy, occupied much of the time of the Maudsley.

These were reorganisation, rebuilding and revenue. Although each impacted on the other and was relevant to the very difficult year of 1986 I shall deal with them separately. The Institute had its own problems in the same period and I shall deal with these before turning to 1986 and beyond.

Reorganisation to 1986

The Government's policy of reorganisation started with the paper on Structure and Management in the NHS, which we considered in June 1980. It was followed by 'Towards a more responsive service' which considered restructuring in the S.E. Thames Region. In September 1981 proposals were put forward for the future governance of the post-graduate hospitals and they included the abolition of the Hospital Management Board of the Joint Hospitals and its replacement with a Special Health Authority (SHA) with a new Chairman and a new membership. Following this, as with each reorganization, there was a period of uncertainty with the possibility that the Authority would be abolished altogether. This was followed by a further period of uncertainty as to who would be reappointed and what new people would be brought in.

The new Chairman, Dr Ivan Clout, was one of the last Chairmen of the new Authorities to be appointed before the new Authority took over on 5 April 1982. The story of his visit to Normansfield with his conclusion that "There is a time bomb under Normansfield" encapsulates him rather well. He was a shrewd GP with a manner which was forthright. Some called it abrasive. He was perceived by many including the Unions, I think wrongly, to be unsympathetic to psychiatry. There was a feeling that Dr Clout had been sent in to sort out the Maudsley and he was quickly resented by many of the staff. Their view was unfair but understandable.

Almost immediately Dr Clout was faced with national industrial action which started on 5 July 1982 in support of the nurses' pay claim. It lasted until December 1982 when the government agreed to a statutory pay review body for nurses. This dispute was nationwide and not of his making. Although there was some serious disruption at the Maudsley, the general level was comparatively low which was a considerable tribute to all concerned – staff, management and unions.

The Griffiths Report on management in the Health Service, published in the autumn of 1983, was considered by the SHA on 9 January 1984 during the short period allowed for consultation. The main recommendation was that a General Manager should be appointed to replace the House Governor. In its response, the SHA expressed concern at the effect that such an appointment would have on the duties and responsibilities of the Chairman, the members of the Special Health Authority and the members of the Management Team of Officers.

The Government went ahead with its proposals. The SHA thought that this would involve relatively little change since the roles of House Governor and administrator member of the Management Team of Officers could be merged and Nicky Paine who had been House Governor since 1962 could continue in the enlarged role of General Manager for the last three years before his retirement.

This was not to be. Nicky Paine was forced to retire prematurely on 6 October 1985. Many in the joint hospitals felt that Paine who had been appointed OBE in 1981 in the New Year's Honours List for his outstanding service to the Health Service had been badly treated.

Eric Byers, a member of the British Institute of Management and District Administrator for the Tunbridge Wells Health Authority was appointed as General Manager from October 1985. He gave outstanding service until his retirement in 1999 but he had a difficult start.

The serious unrest of 1986 was faced by the Special Health Authority with a Chairman widely thought to be unsympathetic to the Maudsley and a Chief Executive newly appointed who was felt to have supplanted a much loved and generally effective predecessor. This was a difficult position for both of them and also for the SHA

Rebuilding to 1986

It was clear to anyone visiting the Maudsley in 1979 that extraordinary work was being done by staff in buildings which were very run down. In order to make progress, the Maudsley was using Trust funds to fund building projects. Substantial sums were provided out of endowment funds (nearly £1m) for the District Services Centre which was opened in 1982.

An opportunity arose to make substantial progress in raising the funds necessary to rebuild the main wards at the Maudsley. In April 1979 an approach was made on behalf of Garfield Weston whose family owned Fortnum & Mason that they wished to extend the lease of 181- 4 Piccadilly. The rent negotiated under the long lease granted at the start of the 20th Century was nominal. The lease was due to run out within about 20 years and substantial capital expenditure on the building was needed. Such expenditure would not be financially viable unless the lease was substantially extended.

Surveyors were instructed to negotiate on behalf of the Maudsley and in April 1981 they came up with a proposal which was considered by the Management Committee. There was further consideration at the May 1981 meeting when the lessees made it clear that they were proposing to spend £¾m on refurbishing the store. The Management Committee considered at that meeting, at my instigation, that the sum offered was insufficient and the surveyors were instructed to continue the negotiations. On 6 July 1981 the Board agreed to a new extended lease on payment of £1¾m. Later the Weston Trust made a substantial gift to the Bethlem Trust. We all thought that this substantial injection of funds earmarked for capital projects would provide the trigger for early refurbishment of the hospital wards. This was not to be.

This was not the fault of the Hospital Management Board or its successor the Special Health Authority. On 5 April 1982, on reorganisation, the endowment funds were transferred to the new Health Authority. The outgoing Authority at its last meeting expressed the view that the highest priority for capital development was the refurbishment or rebuilding of Maudsley Wards 1-6 and the Villa. It considered what part of the additional funds from the Piccadilly Estate should be invested for the benefit of future generations and concluded that the whole of the liquid funds which had accrued to the Board in those transactions should be held available for capital developments. The incoming SHA took a similar view.

There was considerable wrangling with DHSS over the use of the money and whether or not it was to be available as a sum additional to the sum to which the Maudsley was entitled by way of capital allocation. The planning procedures were grindingly slow. At the meeting on 11 March 1985 the SHA complained that approval in principle had not yet been given by the Department of Health. By May 1986 matters had progressed to the stage where a project manager needed to be appointed. The cause of the delay at the DHSS was reported to have been that the relevant official did not have authority to approve applications which did not fit into his written guidelines so he had done nothing.

Only in July 1987 did work start on the first replacement Ward Block and a new front entrance for the Maudsley.

To complete the saga, the first ward block, due for completion in November 1988, was occupied in early March 1989. Permission for the rebuilding of the second ward block was then given by the DHSS. Tenders for the second ward block were received by November 1989. The building work was started in January 1990 with completion of work in July 1991 and occupation of the building in November 1991.

Sadly the hope that the Trust funds would be able substantially to rebuild the main wards of the hospital had long gone. The money had been carefully invested by the Trustees but the accumulated profit was lost in the Stock Market crash of 1987.

A similar and even more lengthy saga of uncertainty attended the building of the Regional Neuroscience Centre at Denmark Hill although unlike the rebuilding of the Maudsley this did require strategic decisions by the DHSS and the Regional Health Authority. The delays caused uncertainty not only in the siting of the Centre but in the future of Neurosciences at the Maudsley. Without Neurosciences it was doubtful whether the Institute and the Maudsley were viable entities. The issue was discussed by the RHB as early as July 1980. The state of uncertainty lasted until 1995 when Mrs Virginia Bottomley as Secretary of State for Health, took the decision personally that the project should go ahead at Denmark Hill. The building was completed in 1997.

Looking at the building projects through the lens of January 1986, the rebuilding of the Maudsley which was urgently needed had not started and there was uncertainty over the siting of the Regional Neurosciences Centre which was regarded as vital for the future of the Maudsley and the Institute. Of course when the projects were eventually completed they played an important part in transforming the morale of both institutions.

Revenue 1979-85 – The Maudsley

Although reorganisation and rebuilding (or lack of it) were of considerable importance, the greatest problem for the Maudsley in the years up to 1986 centred around the effect of the Government's across-the-board revenue cuts. These problems led directly to the widespread industrial action at the Maudsley in 1986.

This compounded the other major source of difficulty which was the transfer of resources away from the South East. This resulted in a progressive reduction in the sums available for the Region from 10% of the total revenue available in 1979/80 to 3% in 1987/8. This caused serious problems for many hospitals in the Region including the Maudsley. This was not immediately offset by the enhanced priority of the Government for Mental Health because the additional government money went into care in the community rather than care in hospital. Aspects of the policy of care in the community still remain to be tackled in 2003. The numbers of mentally ill patients who live on the streets of London without treatment are an urgent reminder to us all that the problem remains unresolved.

These financial problems became evident in 1982-3 and acute in 1983-4.

The government's requirement for loss of staff and the general financial situation were sufficiently serious for the SHA on 9 January 1984 to endorse the action of the Management Team of Officers to stop recruitment until the end of the financial year except for the Interim Secure Unit.

The financial problems also inhibited the possibility of developing a local service in South East London. A Report of the Health Authority Service endorsed the Health Authority's view that the Maudsley could not run a satisfactory level of service for East Lambeth on the funds available and any question of taking on the service for the whole of Camberwell must depend upon its being fully funded.

There were growing difficulties in the financial year 1984-5 when there was a serious shortfall of revenue against expenditure. By November 1984 there had been a net projected overspend of £108,800 on the 1984-5 budget. In November 1984 a freeze of 1% of the Exchequer Revenue Cash limit for 1985-6 was proposed as a first step towards reversing the erosion of the Maudsley's finances. The news was also given at the November 1984 meeting of the SHA that there would be no increase in the research allocation for the following year 1985-6 to meet the additional cost of pay awards.

The overspend for 1984-5 was in fact reduced by a grant of £89,500 from Exchequer funds to allow for management budgeting.

The news for 1985-6 was gloomy. The squeeze was tightened. Exchequer funds provided for a 3% increase in salaries, a 4½% increase in prices and no allowance for development. It was expected on all sides that wages and prices would increase by significantly more than these amounts. The revenue to be received from the Exchequer represented a cut in real terms. In fact the inflation rate reduced from 6.1% in 1985 to 3.4% in 1986 so the settlement was less harsh than anyone anticipated.

When Mr Byers took over as General Manager in October 1985 he heard that the projected shortfall on the budget for 1985-6 would be £350,000 as a result of pay awards which had already been announced. It was clear that a deficit of this magnitude could not be met out of efficiency savings.

The Authority entered 1986 concerned not only with the deficit for 1985/6 but also whether the increases in wages and prices would be fully funded in 1986/7.

The Authority was well aware that the Institute was in the middle of its own financial crisis. There was one area which threatened to sour relations between them namely what the SHA should pay for services provided for it by the Institute.

The Institute 1979-85 – Finance

There were two major financial problems at the Institute, the threatened reduction of the HEFCE grant and the imprecise way in which resources used by the SHA were paid for.

As early as 1976 and 1977 the Institute was experiencing financial problems. For example, the grant for 1977/8 was 2.8% less than for 1976/7. In June 1980 there was a serious threat that as a result of the new proposals for funding higher education, the Institute's grant would be reduced to 50% of its 1979 level by 1982.

At the meeting of the Maudsley and Bethlem Hospital Management Board in February 1981, we were told that there was a long-standing problem about the level of payments made between the Hospital and the Institute in respect of services provided by the other. This was not even partially solved long term until 1990 when with the good offices of the then Chairman of both bodies, Trevor Owen, it was agreed that the SHA would transfer a monthly sum to the Institute on the basis of an agreed budget for the year subject to periodic adjustment .

In 1981-2, the Institute, along with other higher education institutions, suffered a severe cut in its funds from the British Post Graduate Medical Federation (BPMF) which had very severe consequences at a time when costs were rising sharply. The extent of the problem which the cuts were anticipated to cause can be gauged by the fact that the Federation made a special allocation of £3m to London University to pay for the consequent cost of voluntary retirements and redundancies in its constituent institutions which were expected to result from the reduction of funding.

In December 1981 the Institute decided to charge a tuition fee of £100 pa for all students registered for higher degrees from January 1982. A further cut in University grant income was expected to be 2.8% in real terms for 1982-3.

In fact the Institute managed to be in surplus for 1981-2. It then benefitted from a new system for formula funding introduced in 1982 which favoured Institutions with a large research income. By the standards of those days, the Institute had done well in securing outside funding for research. It also benefitted in 1983-4 from an improvement in the income from Students fees.

Nevertheless a deficit for 1983-4 was expected. An appeal from alumni and staff raised £30,000.

At the meeting on 3 January 1984 Dr Clout took the initiative and suggested that the Maudsley might make an additional contribution for 1983/4 for services provided by the Institute to the joint hospitals. This was the first of a number of payments for services which were made from trust funds on an ad hoc basis.

It was at the following meeting in March 1984 that David Maitland former Managing Director of Save & Prosper became Treasurer and Chairman of the Finance and General Purpose Committee. His inheritance was not promising. His contribution over the next twelve years can hardly be overstated.

By June 1984 the financial situation was even more serious. The deficit was £150,000. The SHA provided a special grant of £60,000, for 1984/5 only, in recognition of the provision of general clinical services provided by the Institute at the Maudsley. An additional payment of £19,000 was received to pay for the cost of maintenance of the neurology extension leaving a projected deficit of £70,000.

The Institute decided that the only way out of the recurring crisis was to look for ways of generating large amounts of additional income. To this end they investigated co-operating with a US company, Charter Medical, to open a Clinical Research Unit for NHS patients with addiction problems. These discussions continued from the end of 1984 to the end of 1986 but were ultimately unsuccessful.

Meanwhile the financial problem was becoming more acute. In December 1984 the figures for 1984-5 projected a deficit of £256,000. A negative cash flow was expected from February 1985. The position was exacerbated by the gap between an increase in the recurrent grant allocation of 3% and actual pay awards of 5%-6%. There was an immediate need to reduce expenditure. It was agreed to freeze expenditure which was inessential or not urgent and to examine ways of reducing budgets. A working party was set up to report in March 1985. At the meeting in April 1985 Dr Clout was again extremely constructive. He suggested that a reasonable amount of income could be generated annually by research for the Trust which would be carried out by the Institute. Such funds could be paid for by the Trust out of endowment funds earmarked for research.

The Working Party produced an ambitious target for additional fee income. Whilst noting the close relationship between the Institute and the Joint Hospital, the Working Party also noted that the Institute recovered hardly any of the recurring costs of facilities provided for the SHA. In particular it identified for recovery

1.   Recovery of overheads £25,000

2.   Savings on Departmental Maintenance £60,000

3.   Savings on Staff and Wages £300,000

It considered radical options such as closure of departments, a reduction in the amount of annual research and changes in departmental structures. A final report was requested for June 1985.

By the meeting on 17 July 1985 the prospects for the future had worsened. Recruitment to posts falling vacant continued to be frozen. Dr Clout was again constructive. Although the talks about payment by the SHA for services provided by the Institute staff were unlikely to be resolved he said that the projected deficit for 1984-5 which had been reduced to £65,000 would be covered by the SHA. He hoped that they would be able to help in future years by applying on a non-recurring basis funds from the Trust.

In 1985-6 there was a serious financial deficit. A reduced budget was to be implemented based on an 18% cut in expenditure of the Institute's departments and the dispute with the SHA over the latter's payments for the Institute's services had not been resolved.

1986 and beyond.

The year for the Maudsley opened with an impending financial crisis on current account and the threat of curtailment of major capital projects. An alternative which was being pursued was to sell off land at Bethlem and use the funds for later stages of the development of the Maudsley site. Another alternative, which offered hope for the future, was that the boroughs of Bromley and Croydon had expressed an interest in developing joint services in mental illness and mental handicap using the Bethlem site. The immediate problem was serious. In March 1986 the projected deficit for 1985/6 was £380,000. This would increase to £417,000 for 1986/7 if services were maintained. It was clearly essential to bring the finances into balance and the only way to do so was to make recurring savings on both clinical and non-clinical services. A plan was required before the May meeting of the SHA.

The SHA did not have time to wait until then and in March 1986 Mr Byers announced proposals for ward closures and restrictions of service and indicated the possibility of some nurses being downgraded. An action committee was formed consisting of junior doctors and nurses. The anger of the staff was fuelled by a perception (not correct) that the cause of the financial problem was waste and poor management by clinical teams at the Maudsley.

The March proposals provoked a vigorous Parliamentary campaign led by local MPs Harriet Harman and Simon Hughes. On 6 May 1986, in a written Parliamentary question, Harriet Harman asked the Secretary of State bluntly if the Government had any plans to abolish the Maudsley. She received an unequivocal denial. On the Institute side, George Walden MP, then Minister for Higher Education, said in a written answer that the Institute, in association with the Maudsley, provided clinical training in psychiatry and psychology. He said that the Institute was a major centre for research into mental disorder.

At the SHA meeting of 12 May 1986 the atmosphere was angry. There was a rumour that the SHA planned to reduce the clinical staff by between 45 and 60. The Chairmen of the JCR (Junior Doctors) and the Medical Committee protested at the underfunding of the service both in terms of revenue and capital. They said that the shortfall in revenue was due to the underfunding of pay awards and the growing deficit on certain agency payments and not to overspending by the Authority. Before the meeting were proposals for serious curtailment of services. Dr Clout (who may well not have been in personal sympathy with the Government's position) had to make it clear that the Authority had no option but to make cuts to return the budget to balance.

On 15 May 1986 Ray Whitney MP, the responsible junior Minister in the Department of Health, met the staff at the Maudsley. This was followed by a meeting on 12 June 1986 between the senior members of the Trust and Mr Whitney. It yielded some benefits on the capital side. He confirmed that DHSS would underwrite the cost of the re-building of the second ward block. It yielded no improvement in the financial position on current account. The DHSS was not prepared to provide additional revenue towards the shortfall between government allocation and cost of increased pay awards. The DHSS was also not prepared to write off the deficit incurred in previous years. The furthest the government would go was to keep the capital and revenue position under review.

The SHA meeting on 8 September 1986 took place unusually in the Gymnasium at the Maudsley in order that staff could attend. Strong opposition to the proposed cuts was expressed. Nevertheless there was no alternative but to agree a freeze on recruitment and a curtailment of estate management work. A proposal was adopted to rationalise the training of nurses.

There was some improvement in the financial situation in the coming months as a result of outside factors. There was a reduction in the rates payable to the Local Authority. Fuel prices reduced thus reducing the cost of heating. The DHSS made an additional contribution of £366,000 for the medium secure Dennis Hill Unit at Bethlem which went a long way to offsetting the deficit of £433,000.

The longer term financial position then began to improve a little and the crisis between management and staff abated although the dispute left its scars. There was, as a result of the emergency cuts, a shortage of trained nursing staff which led to some ward closures, and a shortage of beds for emergency admissions. There was also a shortage of social workers as a result of cuts by Southwark Council. As a result the Maudsley lost 50% of its social workers.

By January 1988 the finances had been brought into balance and cash overdrawings were being repaid. This was only achieved by means which provoked a protest from the Management Team of Officers that the series of cuts had reduced nursing to a dangerously low level. There were Union demonstrations and for a period of 6 weeks from the end of March 1988 there was an overtime ban. The only growth was in designated project funding.

The improvement in the financial situation nevertheless was a considerable achievement with which Dr Clout was able to end his chairmanship of the SHA. It was brought about at considerable cost within the organisation. In 1988 Professor Russell, the Professor of Psychiatry, asked plaintively "When will there be an improvement in services?" In fact the way forward for the Maudsley had been signalled. In 1987 the SHA accepted in principle, and subject to funding, the earlier recommendation in 1984 that the SHA take over and manage all Camberwell psychiatric services.

The Institute

Lord Ennals and Ms Polly Toynbee attended for the first time as Members of the Committee of Management at the meeting on 19 March 1986. They heard that the deficit for the year 1985/6 was expected to amount to £67,062 after taking into account receipts of £49,000 in tuition fees and the Library contribution from the SHA of £19.594. This was a substantial underestimate. The projected deficit was quickly increased to over £200,000 and was then revised down to £125,145 in June 1986.

There was one piece of very good news at the March 1986 meeting. The Institute, in what was the forerunner to the Research Assessment Exercises, was rated by the University Grants Commission as "outstanding for research activities". This was the highest possible rating. It was only achieved outside London by Oxford University and within the BPMF (British Postgraduate Medical Foundation), also only by the Institute of Neurology for its Clinical Neurology. It was hoped that this affirmation of the excellence of the Institute's work would enable the BPMF to be more generous in its support of the Institute. It was, but not for another year. The meeting also welcomed Sir Alex Jarratt's Report that there were no obvious quantifiable savings in efficiency in Universities which would compensate for an annual 2% cuts in Government funding for higher education. If this cut had been imposed, I doubt that the Institute would have survived.

It was at the meeting in March 1987 that it was announced that the Institute was to receive a large non-recurrent allocation of up to £400,000 in view of its 'outstanding' academic rating. By June 1987 the Institute also received a grant of £88,550 for repairs and maintenance to the roof of the Institute. It also received a special allocation of £390,000 for equipment. In December 1987 the deficit for 1986-7 on current account was reduced to £15,115 as a result of an increase in fee income.

The budget for 1987-8 showed an estimated surplus of £13,200. This was the first time a surplus had been shown since 1981-2. The heavy cloud, which remained temporarily, was that the BPMF threatened in June 1988 to top slice the grant. This proposal was quickly withdrawn after vigorous protests.

The meeting of the Institute Committee of Management on 21 September 1988 announced that a small deficit of £22,200 was projected for 1988/9 and that even without top slicing the deficits were likely to continue. The meeting agreed that to carry on as at present would mean that the Institute would continue to live from hand to mouth. It was resolved that there was a need for initiatives to generate new sources of income. This process had in fact already started and was a turning point in the fortunes of the Institute.

The year 1988 showed a dramatic rise of 21% in research income from £4.06m in 1987 to £4.92m in 1988 coinciding with the arrival of Professor Anderton and his team of neuroscientists from St George's. It took time to change the mind set of some who were used to depending upon funding from the BPMF and now needed to find other sources of funding. There was only a small percentage increase in institutional funding for 1989 and 1990.

At the meeting in March 1990 the need for the generation of new sources of income was again emphasised. It was clear that without substantial additional funding the Institute was facing a bleak future or no future with declining grants from the BPMF and declining income from overseas students. The Institute would have increasing deficits and might well not survive.

The Dean and the Chairman of the Committee of Management retired at the end of 1989 and April 1990 respectively. It is not surprising that the tributes to them emphasised their contributions in the face of adversity

1979-89 Other Developments

To portray the period from 1979-89 solely in terms of serious problems is to fail to do justice to the significant developments that did take place during this period. These developments were at the start of a process which enabled the Maudsley and the Institute to take advantage of the opportunities for development which took place in the 1990s.

Significant efforts had already been made to raise funds from other sources although they had not yet been successful enough. In 1979 the amount of outside funding of the Institute equalled the funds provided by HEFCE. By 1986 the amount received from HEFCE had reached £2.6m while income raised from outside sources had risen to £3.9m. The respective figures for

1989 and 1990 were £3.2m and £3.4m from HEFCE funding and £5.0m and £5.4m from Research Income.

In addition, the Psychiatry Research Trust set up in 1985 had raised over £700,000 by 1989 and was supporting two research projects, two annual public lectures, a number of student scholarships and was contributing towards the cost of the Addiction Research Unit.

Among academic developments, the Chair in Old Age Psychiatry was established in 1983 supported by a senior lecturer. Professor Jeffrey Gray from Oxford University was appointed Professor of Psychology in 1984 and brought with him a significant team.

As I have already noted, Professor Brian Anderton from St George's Hospital was appointed to the new Chair of Neuroscience in 1988 and with his team has developed an important and distinguished new department concentrating in particular on work on Alzheimer's disease.

A move had been made towards a more effective organisation of research. In 1989 preliminary bids were made to the MRC for funding leading to the setting up of Interdisciplinary Research Centres (IRCs) in brain and behaviour and neuro-degenerative disorders. This was an early forerunner of the IRGs (Interdisciplinary Research Groups), the pattern of organisation on an interdisciplinary basis which exists today and contrasts with the rather rigid departmental basis which was current in the 1980s.

There was one very significant disappointment. The research assessment which in 1986 had been regarded as "outstanding", only attracted a rating of 4 out of 5 in 1989. This was explained, rather complacently, as being attributable to the facts that the Chairs of Neurology and Neuroscience were vacant at the time. It was a setback which could have had serious consequences. The immediate consequences were serious enough. The Assessment meant that the Institute had less money and less prestige than before.

The overriding task which faced Dr Stuart Checkley as the new Dean and Trevor Owen the relatively new Chair of the Special Health Authority, who took over the Chair of the Institute from David Maitland in 1990, was to change the culture of the Institute to one where Departments needed to raise substantial income from research if the Institute was to survive as an independent and largely self governing body. This was in line with the development of the Government's internal market in the National Health Service which also required the Maudsley to be more commercially orientated.

After 1989. The Background

A logical extension of the Government's policy of privatisation of the ancillary services and the promotion of efficiency was the launch of the Government's initiative "Working for Patients". The White Paper in 1989 led to the 1990 National Health Service and Community Care Act. The purpose was to create an internal market in health where money would follow the patient and providers would compete with one another to deliver the service at the lowest reasonable cost.

The policy was produced in the middle of one of the regular funding crises and was criticised as being motivated not by a wish to provide a better service but to save money. The Government replied that there was everything to be gained from spending scarce resources as wisely as possible.

Under the 1990 Act, large hospitals were encouraged to opt out of direct control by the Department of Health and run themselves as independent Trusts competing with other hospitals for patients and resources. The internal market required managers to contract annually with health providers at District or Special Health Authority level.

The policy was strenuously opposed at first and later reluctantly accepted. The Maudsley was fortunate that Eric Byers realised early that, as a centre of excellence which was efficiently run, the Maudsley was in a position to compete successfully within the internal market and to flourish under the new arrangements. This was not immediately evident to everyone. It was a considerable achievement for both Institutions to survive the new challenges which were about to occur.

Changes in Personnel

In June 1989 Dr Stuart Checkley was appointed Dean from 1 October 1989. He came to the job with a fresh mind and a clear set of objectives. He stayed until the end of April 2001 and worked at a breathtaking pace until the day of his retirement. His last act, on his last day in post, was to submit the material for the Research Assessment Exercise which resulted in the Institute receiving its 5* rating. His mind set would be described as result orientated

In 1993, when Professor Gerald Russell retired as Professor of Psychiatry, the Committee of Management acknowledged, what had been evident for some years, that the Institute had developed beyond the point where one Professor could attempt to provide leadership for others outside his department. Such a policy would have been likely to discourage academic stars used to running their own departments from coming to the Institute. It was as Director of Research and Development rather than as Professor of Psychiatry that Professor Sir David Goldberg had such an influence on the Institute. He came from the University of Manchester at a time when many in his position would have been winding down in their last years before retirement. He pursued his tasks at the Institute with the enthusiasm and vigour of someone thirty years younger in the six years until his retirement in 1999.

One key figure, Eric Byers, who had been appointed as General Manager of the Trust in 1985 on a five-year contract remained until 1999. On his retirement, in paying tribute, I said that "It was impossible to overstate the importance of the relationship between the Trust and the Institute and of the part played by Eric Byers in developing that relationship for the mutual benefit of both organisations".

The 1990s: Uncertainty for Both Institutions.

I ceased to be a member of the Maudsley & Bethlem Special Health Authority in 1987. Since then I have not been directly involved although since 1994 I have seen changes from the vantage point of the Chair of the Joint Committee. The most recent period is too close to put into historical context but there are specific aspects which I want to discuss.

From the start of my involvement, the continuing independent existence of the Maudsley & Bethlem Trust had been in doubt. There was always a case for saying that the services at the Maudsley & Bethlem Hospitals could be subsumed within their respective catchment areas. There was also a feeling by some that the Special Health Authorities and Trusts were in a privileged position which should not be allowed to continue. This discussion also formed the backdrop to the 1994 reorganisation. There was a considerable threat that the Maudsley SHA would be abolished as part of that reorganisation. Likewise the Institute was conscious that even after having overcome its acute financial problems of the 1980s, its independent existence remained under threat.

There were three specific threats to the Maudsley and the Institute. The first was from the Tomlinson Committee, which was set up by the government in 1990 and reported in 1992. Tomlinson recommended that the NHS should only pay for the cost of clinical services which were both excellent and useful to the NHS. Some in the Department of Health said that the Institute's research was not relevant to the NHS. The Dean submitted a paper arguing that the research was relevant. This was followed by an investigation into the extent to which the research was directed to R and D. A group of external assessors appointed by the DHSS agreed at the end of 1994 that the research was indeed relevant. This resulted in an agreement that the NHS should pay properly for such research and an income stream of £14m per annum was created, which has formed the basis of the NHS research and development contract with the Maudsley. It is now worth £20m. It has to be acknowledged that much more research at the Institute is relevant to the NHS now than it was in 1992.

The second threat was the exposure of the Maudsley's services in the internal NHS market. Despite Eric Byers' positive attitude, there was a real fear that other hospital trusts would not pay for the Maudsley's specialised services. In fact the specialsit services thrived under the internal market and were able to generate growth.

The third threat was to neuroscience services. The saga of the 1980s continued into the 1990s. After the decision had been made in 1987 that the Regional Neuroscience Centre should go to Denmark Hill, the project went to sleep. Tomlinson recommended that the Centre should be sited elsewhere. In announcing her decision to overrule the recommendation in 1994, Mrs Bottomley gave as her main reason the need to support the research of "the Institute of Psychiatry at the Maudsley". The decision was vital to the future of the Institute.

Reorganisation at the Maudsley from 1990

In the result, despite considerable pressure to the contrary, the Special Health Authority survived the 1994 re-organisation, and on 1 April 1994, became the Maudsley & Bethlem Trust under a new Chairman. This change did not affect the close working relationship of the Maudsley and the Institute. Both Chairmen were members of and regularly attended the Joint Committee.

In April 1999 a new Trust was created. It was responsible for the mental health services in the catchment areas of the Bethlem, Maudsley, Lewisham and Guys and West Lambeth NHS Trusts and covered the Boroughs of Lambeth, Lewisham, Southwark and Croydon, including some of the most socially deprived areas in the country. There were fears at the Institute that the merger would result in loss of synergy between the Institute and it new body. To the credit of those concerned this is not what happened. The new Chair, Madeleine Long, and the chief executive, Stuart Bell, made it clear that they regarded the maintenance and, if possible, the strengthening of links between SLAM and the Institute as essential. [Their role in the continuing development of those links with King's and the IoP has been outstanding.]

The Institute from 1990

The change of personnel at the Institute at the end of the 1980s was beneficial. It enabled a new team to make a new start. Particularly after the arrival of Professor Goldberg in 1993, a new spirit and renewed self-confidence became apparent.

The policy of the new Dean was to react positively to the situation. He had a clear strategy in pursuit of excellence. From the outset he was insistent that each part of the Institute should achieve its maximum potential. He was determined where possible to ensure that each raised as much research income as it could. He was anxious to restore to the Institute its top research rating. This would enable the Institute to recruit academic stars. He understood that more needed to be done to promote the Institute's achievements to the outside world. He realised very early that the quality and clarity of submissions to outside bodies whether in relation to the Research Assessment Exercise or later JIF(Joint Infrastructure Funding) bids for new buildings was crucial to achieving the best possible advances for the Institute and the Trust in the interests not only of the Institute but of psychiatry as a whole.

In June 1990 he introduced a policy that headship of departments should be for fixed terms of 5 years renewable, and that the appointment should be made by the Committee of Management on the advice of the Academic Board and with the recommendation of the Dean. This ensured that people did not stay too long as heads of departments and that those who did not want to undertake the additional responsibilities were not forced to undertake them merely because of seniority.

Part of the strategy was to continue to ensure that, when additional services were undertaken, they were properly funded and did not put in jeopardy the Maudsley's international status. In the course of 1990 the Dean was able to announce to the Committee of Management that the transfer of the Camberwell Services to the SHA would take place on 1 April 1991 and that the SHA had received assurances from the Department of Health that specialist national services would not be eroded. The Addiction Science building at Bethlem was completed at the end of 1990. The running costs would add an additional annual burden on the Institute's budget. This provided an example of potential problems with new buildings. The Bethlem Trustees required an annual rental of £168,000 to cover the capital contribution of £2.1m. Together with running costs this meant the Institute needed to find £250,000 annually in order fully to occupy the building. These problems were solved and the National Addiction Centre was launched in July 1991. The recurrent funding of the running costs of major buildings is, of course, always a significant cost which must be covered.

In June 1994 Stuart Checkley was re-appointed as Dean for 5 years from 30 September 1994. The appointment was against the background of the approval of Heads of Agreement for the merger with King's, an association which started on 1 August 1994. The atmosphere was very different to that of his appointment in 1989. The Institute had a new self-confidence and was making substantial progress. The part that the Dean personally played in this success was huge.

Institute Research Funding from 1990.

The raising of outside funding for the Institute, which was such an important theme in the 1980s, was crucial in the 1990s to the Institute's survival.

From 1991-1992 the Institute increased its income from research by 14.6% from £5.4m to £6.2m. Before it could congratulate itself Mr Alford, Treasurer of the BPMF, told the Committee of Management in June 1992, bluntly and helpfully, that it must increase its grant income faster than it was doing. The Committee of Management fully supported the Dean in requiring increased targets for outside funding from each Department.

The most important news of the year came in December 1992 when the Institute received the highest rating of 5 in the Research Assessment Exercise. This was crucial to the financial well-being of the Institute as well as to its academic standing.

Between 1991-2 and 2001/2 both the Government grants and the research grants showed impressive increases in a period when average annual inflation was under 3%. Government grant rose from £3.65m in 1991/2 to £9.6m in 2001/2, an increase over the period of 116%. Income from research grants rose from £6.2m in 1991/2 to £18.3m in 2000/1. The period from 1991/2 to 1995/6 accounted for a substantial part of the increase from £6.2m to £10.78m or 73.9%. Taken together income had risen from £9.85m in 1991/2 to £34.8m in 2000/1 of which research grants and contracts accounted for 52%, HEFCE grants 25% and academic fees from Health Authorities 16%. Taught programmes accounted in 2000 for just under 10%. This pure teaching component related almost entirely to specialist postgraduate courses.

Recruitment of Academic Stars and Research Assessment Exercise.

The top research rating had been crucial for the Institute's survival in 1986. The loss of the top rating in 1989 was detrimental to the Institute in finance and prestige. Once the academic rating was restored in December 1992, academic stars could be recruited to work at the Institute. They would not only enhance the prestige of the Institute, but they would also bring with them substantial research grants and would further the aim of the achievement of excellence on which the Institute prided itself.

Although an undoubted academic star, Sir David Goldberg's strength lay in management as well as research. His recruitment in 1993 as Professor of Psychiatry and Director of Research and Development was a crucial development. He brought with him a formidable record from Manchester. A reflection of his pre-eminence in the profession and his service to psychiatry and the Maudsley was acknowledged publicly both by his Knighthood and by the naming of the Health Service Research Building as the David Goldberg Centre.

In 1994 the Maudsley was able to recruit two Academic stars from the University of Pennsylvania, Professor Robert Plomin and Professor Judy Dunn. The MRC funded the package which included a team of support staff. Their roles were to be interdisciplinary and they would play a major role in the MRC Centre in social generic and developmental psychology. I well remember the feeling of excitement when their appointments were announced. Their arrival led to a significant growth in research income..

In 1996 Professors Caspi and Moffit were recruited from the University of Wisconsin at Madison to chairs in Social Genetic and Developmental Psychiatry.

These changes contributed to the achievement of a top 5* rating in the Research Assessment Exercise whose results were announced in December 1996. The RAE was led by the Dean and Professor Goldberg but involved all departments of the Institute. The result confirmed the excellence of the research at the Institute and generated significant additional income for further recruitment of academic stars.

In July 1998 Professor Peter McGuffin was recruited to be Director of the Social Genetic and Developmental Psychiatry Research Centre to succeed Sir Michael Rutter. The MRC Child and Adolescent Psychiatry Unit to be completed in 2000 would form part of the Centre.

In 1999 it was announced that Professor David Clark, Professor Anke Ehlers and Professor Paul Salkowskis would come from Oxford in October 2000. Professor David Clark was to be the Professor of Psychology and the others would have chairs in the Department. They were and are regarded as pre-eminent in their field. The new team would need an additional 560 sq metres of accommodation. This was achieved by a new construction on top of the West wing. The Bethlem and Maudsley Trustees committed £1.2m towards the cost. Additional facilities were found at 99 Denmark Hill for work in Cognitive Behavioural Therapy. This enhanced the standing of the Department which was already outstanding into the front rank in the world. The new Psychology Building was started on 12 June 2000 and was occupied at the end of November 2000.

Also in 1999 it was announced that Professor Peter Huxley from Manchester would be appointed to the new Chair of Social Work from 10 October 1999. In 2002 Professor Sheila Hodgins from Montreal was appointed as the new Professor in Forensic Psychiatry.

These appointments were balanced by appointments from within of persons of great distinction. First and foremost was the appointment of Robin Murray [now Professor Sir Robin Murray] as Professor of Psychiatry from 1 October 1999. Although he had been appointed to a chair at King's College Hospital in 1989, he had maintained his links with the Institute. Other appointments included Dr Steve Williams as Professor in Neuro-imaging, Professor Eric Taylor to be Head of Department of Child Psychiatry and Professor Kevin Gournay to be the first Professor of Psychiatric Nursing in 1995; Professor Graham Thornicroft became Professor of Community Psychiatry in 1996, Director of Research and Development in 1998 on the retirement of Sir David Goldberg and Chairman of the new Health Service

Research Department from October 1999. In 2001 Professor Simon Wessley became director of the Clinical Trials Unit.

In December 2001 it was announced that the Institute had again achieved a 5* rating in the Research Assessment Exercise. This was a very considerable achievement for the Institute as a whole . 82% of all staff were included. This underlined the Institute's position as a world leader in the field of psychiatry.

Interdisciplinary Research Groups (IRGs) and Departments.

The size of the Institute and the scope of the work it undertakes has been transformed in the last 30 years.

In 1965 the Institute of Psychiatry had seven departments and six Professors - Psychiatry, Biochemistry, Biometrics headed not by a Professor but by a Reader, Experimental Neurology, Neuro-endocrinology, Neuro-pathology and Psychology. By 1997/8 the Institute had 9 IRGs and 40 Professors.

Development of Local Services.

The development of local services alongside international and national research was an important development. Although a start had previously been made in the provision of local services, it was only after the integration of the Camberwell service in 1991 that the Maudsley and the Institute became fully involved in local services. The period of negotiation before the terms of transfer were agreed was a difficult one. The problems centred on funding. In particular, there was a concern that as a result of poor funding the standards then provided would be below those which the Maudsley was prepared to accept. The Maudsley continued to insist that each local project was fully funded for care to the appropriate standard before it was prepared to take over the service.

In March 1995 the Maudsley agreed to take on Croydon local services. It was agreed that Warlingham Park would close and the services would be transferred to Bethlem. The Trust was also to take on services when the Brook Hospital at Greenwich closed. This prompted the Institute to consider appropriate academic initiatives within the enlarged catchment area and to see how academic input could be best provided. The Institute entered into discussions with Croydon over the establishment of a Chair in Community Psychiatry.

The Croydon project led to the appointment of Professor Graham Thornicroft to head a new section of community psychiatry in the Department of Psychiatry based at Bethlem in space made available by the NHS Trust (another example of excellent co-operation). He was to be supported by a Senior lecturer and a Lecturer.

These developments were important in themselves and made possible the formation of SLAM. If the Maudsley and Bethlem Hospitals had not provided services rooted in their own communities it is unlikely that they would have survived as the nucleus of a separate health authority providing psychiatric and related services.

In 1999 the new South London and Maudsley Trust's catchment area was a reflection not only of the development of local services at the Maudsley and Bethlem Hospitals but also of the changes that had taken place on the academic side as a result of the high level of co-operation between the Institute and KCL in the provision of mental health and related services. This followed the merger of the Institute as part of KCL and included the merger a year later between KCL and UMDS.

Estate Strategy.

Perhaps the most obvious change in the Institute and the Maudsley has been the change in the buildings. Until 1988 there was little change apart from the District Services Centre and the Medium Secure Unit. Then the rebuilding of the main wards of the Maudsley took place. In 1989 the South Wing of the Institute was substantially redeveloped to provide new laboratories for Neuroscience. The Addiction Sciences building was added in 1990. In 1991 the Institute received a programme grant and a building grant of £1.2m from the Wellcome Trust for the construction of a new floor on the East wing of the Institute.

The academic Neurosciences Building was opened in 1997.The Henry Wellcome building for Psychology was opened in 2001. The David Goldberg Centre for Health Services Research was also opened in 2001. Payment for the building included a specific contribution by the NHS under the present government of £1.5m. The Magnetic Resonance Imaging building will be opened formally in 2003. The CCIB Centre for Cell and Integrative Biology comprising the Institute of Psychiatry Centre for the Cellular Basis of Behaviour and the King's Centre for Cardiovascular and Endothelial Biology (CVEB) is in the planning stage.

A major concern for much of the period was what to do with Princess Marina House which had been used to house nurses. It stood empty for many years as a magnificent reproach to us all on a site which was otherwise thoroughly congested. The problem was solved when the Institute made a successful bid to the Joint Infrastructure Fund (JIF) to house the new Social Genetic and Developmental Research Centre. The Institute was awarded £14.6m and work on the new centre started in December 2000. The Centre was occupied last month, January 2003.

These changes in themselves represent an extraordinary success which will carry the Institute forward as a successful world leader in the field of psychiatry and related disciplines.

The Merger with KCL.

At the end of 1992 the Committee of Management concluded with great reluctance that the status quo was not an option. It considered the possibility of linking up with other institutions in the BPMF, for example with the Institute of Neurology. It came to the conclusion that although the SHA might have the ability to survive as an entirely separate entity, it was clear that the Institute would not.

A London Implementation Group, which was set up in 1993 to consider specifically the implementation of the Tomlinson report in London, seemed to be pursuing its own agenda. There was a fear that it would recommend that the Institute should be split up between different institutions across London. Because of its proximity to King's College Hospital, it seemed logical for the Institute in the first instance to have preliminary discussions with Professor Arthur Lucas, the Principal of KCL.

There were three principles which the Institute considered vital: a) that it should preserve its integrity; b) that it must preserve its close relationship with the Maudsley and c) that no association should put at risk the construction of the Regional Neuroscience centre at Denmark Hill.

The Committee of Management endorsed these principles. They said that there was a need to develop an academic rationale for close ties with KCL. The scope and life-expectancy of the guarantee of the retention of the Institute's integrity needed to be explored. Any merger with KCL would have to take account of the fact that any financial problems at KCL must not adversely affect the financial position of the Institute.

After negotiations, general heads of agreement were approved subject to the siting of the Regional Neurosciences Centre at Denmark Hill. The period of association with KCL started on 1 August 1994. It was understood that, if it was successful, the association would lead to merger. From that date, the Dean attended a number of KCL Committees as an observer.

The association was taken forward in late 1995. KCL made it clear that it understood the importance of the Research strategy of the Institute on which by then 70% of its funding depended. It was essential that the Institute should retain academic coherence and an appropriate degree of autonomy. The Institute would join KCL as a school and would remain as a separate school. It would have a substantial degree of financial autonomy and would retain local administrative support.

By then the proposed merger of KCL and UMDS (the United Medical and Dental Schools of Guys, Kings and St Thomas' Hospitals was in a relatively advanced stage of planning. They would have five health related schools across the hospitals - medicine, dentistry and bio-medical sciences, health and life sciences, nursing and midwifery.

By March 1996, the Committee of Management decided that an early merger with KCL would be in the best interests of the Institute because it would end the period of uncertainty.

In June 1996 the method of joining was discussed. The Institute also decided that the NHS Trust should be more closely involved in the process. Before taking the final decision to join it was agreed that there were two key conditions on the Institute's side. First, the Institute must be and must remain a separate school of the College, independent of the five schools of the UMDS merger. Secondly, the financial arrangements must not to be to the detriment of the Institute. These were not to be mere transitional arrangements but to continue in perpetuity unless both sides agreed to a change.

There were still important negotiations to take place but by March 1997 agreement had been reached with KCL which gave the Institute a secure future with an appropriate degree of autonomy. It was agreed on both sides that this was an agreement in perpetuity and not merely a transitional arrangement. The Institute had secured a greater degree of independence and devolution of administrative services than was then available to other schools. Its funding position was also protected in perpetuity. The merger took place on 1 August 1997. On merger, I was nominated by the Institute's out-going Committee of Management as a member of the Council of KCL for six years.

At the start, both sides had reservations. The Institute chaffed at a certain loss of independence and being, to some extent, dependent on KCL's bureaucracy. The reticence on KCL's side stemmed from the fact that it did not fully understand how hardly won the Institute's prestige and relative financial prosperity had been. There was a questioning as to why the Institute should have a special position within King's. The problem was reflected in small things like the fact that the map of the KCL Denmark Hill site did not, for a time after the merger, include the Institute of Psychiatry.

The initial period was bound to be difficult because the merger of KCL and UMDS did not take place until a year later in 1998. This process had also to be worked through before the real benefits of the merger could be seen.

This has now happened and from the perspective of 2003, I judge the merger to have been a success, although there are still some difficulties. I have witnessed the evolution not only from my position at the Institute but also as a Member of the Council of KCL.

Professor Stuart Checkley as Dean not only joined the KCL College Committee on merger but also the Board of Management of GKT. The Dean attends all KCL Council Meetings as a Head of School and also the Academic Board. Professor Stuart Checkley took a full part on these activities and Dr George Szmukler, his successor as Dean, has done the same. As the merger has progressed KCL has understood more fully why the Institute insisted on the special conditions for merger. The atmosphere has changed on the part of KCL from a certain reticence to a much more positive welcome.

Looking Back and Looking Forward.

In looking back over the last 24 years I have seen many changes. First, there have been enormous developments in psychiatry. In many of these the Institute and the Maudsley have been in the forefront. Second, the range of research at the Institute has been transformed. Third, there has been a significant change in the status of patients. Twenty four years ago it would have been unthinkable to regard patients as service users and to involve them fully in aspects of research. The difference is illustrated in the SLAM Annual Report for 1999-2000. A service user in Lewisham wrote: "In Lewisham we are treated as service users with a vested interest in service delivery, not patients to have things done to us without any consultation or explanation". Fourth, the status of nursing has been significantly enhanced. Nursing is properly now regarded as an academic as well as a professional discipline. Fifth, research is now organised by IRG on an interdisciplinary rather than on a departmental basis. Sixth, the re-building that has taken place has transformed both the Maudsley hospital and the Institute of Psychiatry. Seventh,both the Maudsley and the Institute, while maintaining and enhancing their international reputation, now provide a service firmly rooted in the local community. The direct responsibility of SLAM for the mental health of 1 million people in the four local boroughs has been achieved without detriment to the Institute's or Maudsley's national and international position. Eighth, the pattern of the funding of services has changed with the internal market for health. The balance of funding at the Institute has changed. Whereas the Institute was predominantly funded by the government in 1979, it was 70% privately funded in 2002.Ninth, both the Maudsley and the Institute have become part of larger units. This has not affected their close collaboration.

All these changes have to be seen in the context of urgent national and international challenges which existed in 2003 and which need to be addressed. One third of the population of the United Kingdom will suffer from some form of mental disorder or depression at some time in their lives. Many will need active treatment. There is a need to address problems resulting from the ethnic diversity of the population. Services at GP level for mental disorder or depression are woefully inadequate. One aspect of this should be a review of the way in which psychiatry is taught to ordinary medical students. We have still not begun to solve the problems of those on the streets, many of whom need treatment for mental illness or mental disorder. There is still a stigma attached to mental illness and mental disorder which leads to serious problems of discrimination.

On a local level, the Institute needs to implement its dissemination strategy. Much important and valuable research does not reach service users, carers, mental health organisations or the media and other audiences outside the Institute and the academic community.

There is a need for an improvement in mental health services worldwide. Work needs to be done to develop services within a European Union soon to be expanded to the East. The Institute and the Maudsley should be at the leading edge of the many developments which need to take place.

Conclusion

There is a wider issue with which I must conclude. There has been much talk recently in the Press and elsewhere comparing UK educational institutions adversely with American universities, and particularly Harvard. For most of the period since 1945, the Institute and the Maudsley have been amongst the top 5 Institutions in the world for the treatment of mental illness and mental disorder. It is undoubtedly the case that this is so in 2003. One yardstick is the fact that articles written by those at the Institute are among the most quoted by their fellow academics in journals worldwide. It is impressive that the Maudsley and the Institute should exist and care for people in one of the poorest parts of London. The Institute, SLAM and now KCL have the awesome responsibility of ensuring that the Institute remains one of the top five institutions in the future. The reputation of the Maudsley as the Harvard of world psychiatry has been achieved primarily by those who work in those institutions, but credit must also be given to those outside who have enabled it to flourish. They include those in the past who made the decisions in government to preserve the Maudsley's independence; Mrs Virginia Bottomley who overruled Tomlinson so that the Regional Neuroscience Centre finally came to Denmark Hill, and those at KCL who had the wisdom to understand that although the Institute is proud to be part of KCL, it would flourish best with an appropriate amount of independence.

My last word is one of gratitude. I have found my association with the Maudsley and the Institute and those who have worked here both in a professional and lay capacity to have been one of the most fulfilling parts of my life. I am both proud and grateful to have had the opportunity to be involved with two institutions whose watchword has been the pursuit of excellence.

Internal and External Collaboration at King's College London – the Law School, IoP and GKT

The Institute of Psychiatry (IoP) merged with King's in 1997. The Medical Schools of Guy's Hospital, King's College Hospital and St Thomas' Hospital (GKT) together with the Dental Schools, collectively known as UMDS, merged with King's in 1998. These mergers effectively created a new University. The mergers of Queen Elizabeth College and Chelsea College with King's in 1986 had created a university of 6,000 students. The mergers in 1997/8 created a university of over 20,000 students.

Although King's was in effect a new university, it was not a new university from scratch. The mergers brought together institutions with their own proud traditions and energies, The task of the two Principals, Professors Arthur Lucas and Sir Rick Trainor (and Professor Barry Ife who was acting Principal in 2003/4) was to harness the skills, energies and traditions of the joining institutions to the existing traditions of King's, which was, itself, a proud and successful institution founded in 1829. Before the new King's could go forward in its new clothes, each constituent part of King's had to be convinced that, far from detracting from its former prestige, the new King's would enhance it.

The completion of the process of assimilation was a necessary pre-requisite for a successful fully integrated King's, which would be in the best position to enhance its standing in the world community of universities. A successfully integrated organisation would, in turn, be in the best position to recruit world- class staff and to collaborate with other universities and institutions which would want to collaborate with King's.

The process of merger was a gradual one. In the early years it took most of the energy of senior management and, as I remember, a considerable amount of the time and energy of King's Council. The fact that the IoP and the Medical Schools were pre-eminent in their own fields made the process not easier but more difficult. During this phase it was necessary to retain an unwieldy King's Council of over 50 with many observers from different faculties, in order that information and reassurance could be disseminated. Baroness Patricia Rawlings, as Chairman of King's Council, played an important part in this process, and also in choosing new members of Council from outside King's who would themselves enhance the prestige of King's and harness their own energies to the development of the College.

By the time Rick Trainor arrived in autumn 2004 and certainly by the time Baroness Rawlings retired in 2007, the most difficult phase of consolidating the merger was over, and Professor Trainor (knighted in 2010) and the Marquess of Douro, as the new Chairman of Council, were able primarily to devote their energies towards developing the new King's into a great university.

The change manifested itself in a number of ways. Although I had already served on the Council for nine years, I was in 2006 asked to stay for another 3 years to chair the Governance Committee whose main task was to reform the Charter, the Statutes, the Ordinances and the Regulations of the College so that the governance infra-structure was fit for a 21st university. This also involved carrying through a fundamental reform of King's Council, reducing it in size from over 50 to its present size of 21.

Second, the Principal and his team have been able to harness the energy within King's released, after coping with the merger, into more productive areas which has helped King's to move forward as a leading university.

One area which has blossomed in the new King's environment has been the inter-disciplinary collaboration between departments and the collaboration between departments and outside institutions. I shall later relate this to the IoP and the Law School, and make suggestions as to how such co-operation could be enhanced, but the Department of English, part of "old King's", provides a striking illustration of the types of collaboration which transform a university and are illustrative of the change from previous traditional attitudes.

The English Department has a well-established link with the Royal Society of Literature, providing King's students with an opportunity to participate in Masterclasses. It also has a relationship with the writer's society, English Pen. The London Shakespeare Centre, the Centre for Humanities and Health, the D'Oyly Carte Professor of Medicine and the Arts, and the Centre for Life Writing are all based in the English Department. Collaborative work includes master's degree programmes with the British Library, the British Museum and the Globe Theatre. The Department also has collaborative doctoral programmes with the Imperial War Museum, the Museum of London and the National Portrait Gallery. At a recent seminar which I attended, King's was investigating how it can widen and deepen such collaborations. In addition the Department has links with overseas institutions, including universities in Kolkata, Cape Town, New York and Canberra.

A new innovative appointment, related to but extending beyond English, is that of Deborah Bull, the former prima ballerina of the Royal Ballet, and, since 2008 Creative Director of the Royal Opera House, who joins King's in the newly created role of Director of King's Cultural Partners, a cross-disciplinary teaching and research initiative looking for innovative collaboration between arts institutions and King's.

A separate initiative has been the creation of institutions focusing in a multi-disciplinary way on Brazil, India and China, and, most recently, Russia. The purpose of each Institute is to act as a leading international centre for the contemporary study of that country, focusing on a range of academic, cultural and practical disciplines and involving close collaborations with institutions in the relevant country. I was involved in the early stages of setting up the Brazil Institute. When I visited Brazil in 2008, to give three lectures, including the one at the Supreme Court in São Paulo (see Chapter 19), I also had meetings with the British Council and various universities to see how the King's project could be taken forward. At that stage King's was perceived, despite its long history in Portugese and Brazilian Studies, to be one of a number of UK universities, albeit it an important one, which were expressing an interest in Brazil. In 2011 the Brazil Institute was launched with its own space on the King's site and with a distinguished Director and staff.

When I was in Brazil, the judges and the legal profession as well as academics, showed a great interest in having greater contacts with British legal academics, practising lawyers and judges, and I hope that this may be taken forward by the Brazil Institute in conjunction with the Law School as well as the increased contacts which I know are taking place at student level.

With this background in mind, I concentrate on the two faculties at King's which I know best, the IoP and the Law School. I remained a member of the IOP advisory committee until 2009 and I am still in close touch. The terms of the merger left the IoP with a considerable measure of autonomy as a separate school in the university. By 2003 many of the difficulties on merger had been resolved, in large measure due to the efforts of Professor Stuart Checkley as Dean, but collaboration with other parts of King's was not yet whole-hearted and there remained occasions when it was necessary to act as a bridge between the IoP and King's.

The transition was gradual, but the change was signalled in 2006 with the appointment of Professor Peter McGuffin, the distinguished director of the MRC Centre for Social Genetic and Developmental Psychiatry at the IoP, as Dean for the following three years to the end of 2009, followed by Professor Shitij Kapur from the University of Toronto who moved immediately to act as Professor McGuffin's Deputy. As a member of the interviewing panel, I am pleased that these appointments have been very successful. A signal that whole-hearted integration had been achieved came when Professor Kapur was appointed as the Deputy Vice-Principal for the Health Schools from 1 January 2012 while remaining Dean of the IoP.

There is no doubt that the IoP continues to be a success story. An index of success frequently used by academics is the number of citations of IoP staff in other publications. In 2011 the IoP came second in the world using this measure, with only Harvard University ahead of it.

At the level of research, co-operation within the IoP and the Health Schools, and also with military research, has been very impressive. There has also been close co-operation for many years between the IoP and SLAM (the South London and Maudsley NHS Foundation Trust) and between the medical schools and their equivalent NHS Trusts. There is also substantial collaboration between the Cecily Saunders School of Palliative Medicine and other parts of King's Health Schools.

In the last few years, through King's Health Partners, which includes all the King's College medical schools and the IoP, impressive collaboration has developed internationally with other bodies. King's Health Partners, which is a consortium between the College (including the IoP), SLAM and the acute NHS Trusts of King's College Hospital and Guy's and St Thomas' hospitals, is organised into 21 clinical academic groups (the successors to inter-disciplinary research groups- IRGs). Each is charged with achieving excellence in research, teaching and clinical practice. There are two over-arching groups, the Basic Science Institute and the Health Policy and Evaluation Institute. It is the task of the latter (chaired by Professor Graham Thornicroft) to co-ordinate inter-disciplinary research, to extend world-wide networks, to foster excellence, to bring together knowledge and policy research implementation, and to act as a forum for imaginative and creative ideas.

There are many collaborations between the IoP and other agencies advising on mental health, including countries in central and eastern Europe and elsewhere in the world. A recent important collaboration, including research relevant to both mental and physical health, is that between King's, University College and Imperial College in forming the Francis Crick Institute. An important change in the current Health and Social Care legislation is the recent amendment giving mental health an equal importance to physical health.

The Law School has suffered for many years by being housed in increasingly appalling accommodation on the Strand Campus. Rightly, one of the major priorities after the acquisition of the lease of the East Wing of Somerset House, formally opened by HM The Queen on 29 February 2012, has been to house the Law School in appropriate accommodation.

Despite its problems, the Law School has had impressive collaborations with a number of the world's leading law schools. It is part of a consortium on transnational law also including nine overseas universities in London, led by Georgetown University, where King's undertakes a substantial part of the teaching. The Law School also uses the services of the practising legal profession. Leading barristers teach a course in arbitration as part of the LLM programme. I have taught a course on Dispute Resolution in the same programme. Other judges and barristers are also engaged in Law School teaching. Associated with the law school are separate courses in Construction Law which are taught in part by distinguished practitioners.

The position of the Law School has been transformed by its move to the East Wing of Somerset House, which at last gives it the facilities appropriate to a leading law school. There has been a further very recent development which will transform the School of Law, now re-named the Dickson Poon School of Law. On 19 March 2012 a most munificent donation to the Law School by the Hong Kong philanthropist Mr Dickson Poon was announced. This gift will provide scholarships for 75 students including 15 from Hong Kong or China. It will also endow 8 new Distinguished Chairs in the Law School and 7 further posts for rising legal academic stars. The Law School will increase its strengths in law reform, legal policy development and commercial and transnational practice. The aim is to build on the existing excellence in the Law School and also to give students the best possible experience as they prepare for the very competitive world after university.

These are clearly very exciting developments. They put me in mind of the University of Georgetown Law School in Washington DC. That university was transformed many years ago by a substantial endowment from a provincial law school into one of the leading law schools in the United States, pre-eminent in a number of subjects including World Trade Law led by Professor John Jackson. Like Georgetown University, King's College in London has the great advantage of being located in a city at the heart of government. King's has the additional advantage in being located in one of the great commercial and financial centres in the world. It is also located close to legal London with ready access to judges, barristers and solicitors in major world-wide firms. A pre-eminent law school can capitalise on these advantages. During my week at Georgetown University I gave a seminar on the World Trade Organisation. The United States member of the Disputes Settlement Appellate body had heard of the seminar and came along at short notice to participate, along with Ambassador Paeman with whom I had worked on the Uruguay Round 15 years before. Such ease of access is an important plus for the Law School. These contacts will enhance the experience at the law school for students, an important consideration at a time when substantial fees are being charged to students for the Law School experience. It will also widen the horizons of the Faculty.

The very generous gift from Mr Dickson Poon does not detract from my thesis that there is a need for increased collaboration between the Law School and the Medical Schools including the IoP, rather, it underlines it.

This has very recently been acknowledged by the Dickson Poon School of Law and the IoP, who have signalled their intention to set up a collaborative relationship to promote research and teaching between the schools, and, more generally, between the fields of law and psychiatry. This is a ground-breaking development. It will further the already considerable co-operation between the law school and the IoP. However, there is further potential for direct co-operation between the Law School and the IoP and the School of Medicine. There are at present no links at Master's degree or undergraduate level. The Law School has a Centre for Medical Law and Ethics. The interests of members of the faculty, all lawyers, set out on the Law School web site, include mental illness, the human genome project, ethical issues in psychiatry, allocation of resources for health care, and autism. The Centre has no medically qualified staff on its faculty.

There is a wider public need for lawyers and doctors not only to carry out joint research projects, but also at undergraduate and post-graduate level to understand the interaction between law and medicine. The two disciplines are closely connected but have very different ways of looking at common problems.

At various times during my association with the IoP, I suggested that forensic psychiatry was an obvious subject for joint teaching and research. After all, the treatment and proper disposal by the courts of offenders suffering from mental illness or disability would, I thought, improve sentencing practice, produce better outcomes and thus benefit the whole community. This topic would be equally relevant as a research project or as a seminar at undergraduate or graduate level. I never had any success in progressing such a project.

I remain convinced that there are many medico-legal subjects that would benefit from joint collaboration at undergraduate, graduate and research levels.

I will illustrate this from an innovative project at the University of Michigan in 1993, set out at pp 24-25 of the same issue of The Law Quadrangle Notes as Chapter 10 above. The topics covered would also provide valuable areas of research and collaboration but the project was at senior undergraduate level in the University of Michigan law school and the medical school.

The course was entitled "Law, Medicine and Society." It was taught jointly by Professor Carl Schneider, a law school professor specialising in medical law, and Professor Joel Howell, an Associate Professor of Internal Medicine. It was the first course fulfilling the grade credit requirements in both schools.

The course was a series of seminars. It started by considering the legal basis of the doctor-patient relationship including patient autonomy and issues of confidentiality. It went on to consider particular topics such as assisting suicide and terminating medical treatment. Finally the Seminar considered various aspects of medical malpractice.

At Professor Schneider's suggestion, the students teamed up in pairs, one medical student and one lawyer, in their joint preparations for the Seminar. The law students gave the medical students the basics of the law, and the medical students gave the law students the basic medical knowledge. In the practical exercises the medical students argued the legal case, and the law students argued the medical case. By putting the law students and the medical students together, and reversing their roles, the law students and the medical students were freed to educate each other. In this way future lawyers and doctors were able to learn how differently the other discipline approaches the same medico-legal problem. Professor Schneider said that this was a chance to experience a new way of thinking and that all, including the professors, gained significantly from the course.

An important spin-off from such a course would be improved teaching at the medical schools on how to deal with practical problems when doctors encounter the law in their practice. This involves not only dealing with patients, but also such topics as what to write in patients' notes, how to write witness statements and what to expect in giving evidence to a court.

A number of the medico-legal subjects which I have touched on would also be appropriate subjects for collaborative multi-disciplinary research. These topics would take in welfare and discrimination legislation as well as the common law. A general list might also include the human rights of those who are mentally and physically ill. As an example, I referred in the previous chapter to seclusion (the confining of an individual to a particular space from which there is no means of egress). This remains a difficult topic. Other topics could include Mental Health Act certification (with input from the European Union); stigma and discrimination against those who are mentally ill (with input from MIND); discrimination in the allocation of medical resources in the NHS; withdrawal of treatment from seriously disabled babies and adults; the human genome; use of compulsion in the treatment of anorexia (can some treatments ever be legitimised by consent?; are some treatments unlawful as breaching human rights?); compulsory treatment in the context of UK and international legislation.

An earlier innovation at the University of Michigan could also be considered. The Law Faculty had a Professor of the Faculty of Medicine as an Honorary Professor in the Law Faculty. A member of the Law School and a member of the IOP could both be appointed as an honorary professor in the other institution to develop links and increase collaboration between the two faculties. A better alternative might be to create a new academic post to co-ordinate collaboration between law and the health schools (including the IoP), and to co-ordinate collaborative research both within King's and outside. The project might progress to an Institute for Law and Medicine which would develop collaboration at all levels both between the law school and the health schools, and, more generally between King's and leading institutions worldwide.

Middle Temple

The sixth Institution is the oldest. The history of the Middle Temple goes back to the late 14th or early 15th century. In Sir John Baker's fascinating Chapter 1, page 31 ff, of the *History of the Middle Temple*, he examines the evidence which does not lead to a precise date. It could even have been earlier (see p. 37).The role of the Inns is changing. It was this subject that I addressed in my Lent Term Reading in 2008 (p. 332). I have edited the Reading in a few places to avoid duplication with matters dealt with elsewhere. I also include my Lent Reader's Report in *The Middle Templar*, 2008 Autumn edition (p. 344).

Before being elected Reader, I had had extensive experience of the workings of the Inn. In the years since my election as a Bencher in 1986, I had been very active, having sat on many Committees of the Inn including the Executive Committee. My experience as a barrister for 32 years and a member of the Bar Council for 16 years, including two years as Chairman of the Young Barristers' Committee, were also very relevant to understanding students' problems. It also provided part of the background for the Reading.

I was elected to the ancient office of Master Reader of Middle Temple for the first six months of 2008. Master Reader is primarily concerned to support the education and activities of students in the Inn. The two Readers for the year combine to discharge this function for the whole year. By tradition each Reader presides at a Reader's Feast which takes place in the beautiful Hall built about 1570. The Reader gives his reading at the Feast on a subject of his choice. This can be a legal subject like advocacy and the courts, a subject removed from the law like the music of the Elizabethan composer John Dowland, or, the Autumn Reading in 2011, a comparison between the functions of judges in courts and umpires on the cricket field.

In view of my general background and my international experience, I decided to talk on "The Middle Temple and the Future". In addressing this subject I was particularly concerned with "destiny" (how we should be planning for the future). In his chapter in the *Liber Amicorum*, Dr Heusel (who was present) rightly says that I used the occasion to remind my fellow lawyers of the international and European challenges for the legal profession. I also suggested initiatives which the Inn should take to develop its role as a forum of ideas, capitalising on its historical strength. The Inns of Court can lay claim to be the cradles of the Common Law "from whence all our traditions on both sides of the Atlantic stem", as Lord Rawlinson put it in his inspiring address in Atlanta in 1976. This is demonstrated in the *History of the Middle Temple*, edited by Richard Havery and published by Hart Publishing in 2011. The chapters on the history of the maritime connection by Richard Hill, pages 111ff, and the

American connection by John Colyer, pages 239ff, are particularly relevant. This is not just an ancient, but a living, concept since many barristers are trained in the Inns and return to their countries overseas to practice and each of the four Inns of Court has many links through its members overseas.

There are parallels with the Temple Church which, rightly, lays claim to be "the Mother Church of the Common Law". The question is how these concepts, recognised by many, can be developed in the future. This is only one strand. In my Reading, I suggest a much wider role for the Inn. Some steps have been taken in the direction that I suggested, but many of the topics which I raised remain on the agenda.

I also include, the Lent Reader's Report published in the *Middle Templar* which sets out the activities of Master Reader during my period of office and explains the difference between history and destiny.

Finally, in relation to my Lent Term Reading, I should explain that, on formal occasions, such as my Reading, Benchers of the Middle Temple, irrespective of sex, are described as "Master". For ease of identification I have put in the title "Master" followed by the names by which those Benchers were ordinarily known at the relevant time.

The Middle Temple
and the Future

Lent Reading by HH Judge John Toulmin CMG QC FKC

19th February 2008

It is a very special privilege to be Lent Reader in the year when we are celebrating the 400th Anniversary of King James I's grant of the Royal Charter to Middle Temple and Inner Temple. The grant was made for the housing of the profession and students and their education in the laws of the realm.

Much of the year, rightly, will be spent in commemorating the 400th anniversary but it should also be a time for reflection and renewal of our purpose, hence the title of my reading "The Middle Temple And The Future".

I recently met Sir Humphrey Appleby of "Yes, Minister" fame, now Lord Appleby, former Cabinet Secretary, aged nearly 80, still the consummate Civil Servant. I told him the subject of my reading. " A very bold choice, if I may say so, Master Reader," he said. He had retained his habit of formality. "Couldn't you think of something less contentious?" He paused and thought. Paraphrasing a former Home Secretary of the 1980's, he went on," Master Reader, I thought the task of the Reader during his time in office was to go round the Inn stirring up apathy". He paused again and said with a characteristic grin, "You are a Judge of the Technology and Construction Court, couldn't you instead tell jokes about technology and construction ?" With little thought I replied, adopting the words of a tennis player famous at the time when Lord Whitelaw made that remark, "Man you can NOT be serious".

Historically, Master Reader was required to give an account of himself at Reader's Feast. I have endeavoured to discharge this obligation by drawing on my own experience in the Inn, as a long-standing former member of the Bar Council, and in outside organisations with which I have been closely connected – the Institute of Psychiatry and King's College London; the European Bar Council, also known as the CCBE; and the European Law Academy in Trier, also known as ERA. Through them I will foreshadow the suggestions, which I will make later, on the direction the Inn should take.

In the 18th century it was ordained that there should be some innovation at Reader's Feast. This obligation I have attempted to discharge. The red Burgundy is a gift from our very modest vineyard in Auxey-Duresses, 7 kms from Beaune. The white Burgundy comes from the vineyards in and around

Meursault, 1 km away, of Bruno and Christine Févre, the young couple who look after our vineyard.

After school I went to Cambridge University with an award which happily required me to become a member of Middle Temple, so I joined the Inn in 1960.

In the summer of 1963, just after I had left Cambridge, I went on an Anglo-German conference in West Berlin. It coincided with the visit of President Kennedy and I stood in front of the Rathaus Schönbrunn when President Kennedy made his "Ich bin ein Berliner" speech. It wasn't the fact that President Kennedy called himself "ein Berliner" (a doughnut) which disappointed the crowd, but rather that he did not pledge that the United States would fight for West Berlin. He gave this pledge at the Free University in the afternoon. In history the two speeches have been elided.

The visit, which included the moving sight of crosses in Bernauerstrasse commemorating those who were shot while escaping over the Berlin wall, helped me to understand the motivation of those in the European Union who were and are determined that arrangements must be in place so that Europe will never tear itself apart again.

In October 1963 Michael Howard and I, representing Cambridge, went on a debating tour of the United States: 40 Colleges and Universities in 50 days west of the Mississippi. We went to San Francisco and Los Angeles, but we also went to colleges in small towns like Crete, Nebraska and Yankton, South Dakota. We were in Moscow, Idaho on 22nd November 1963 when President Kennedy was shot. Three weeks later we were in Dallas and saw for ourselves the Texas Book Depository from where the shots had been fired. It was an extraordinary time to be there.

I remember the tour vividly now over 40 years later. It gave me a detailed insight into what the United States was like and an enduring love for the American people, although not always their politicians. Master His Honour Alan King Hamilton QC now aged 103, our senior Bencher, has similar fond memories of the first such debating tour over 80 years ago in 1927.

For me it was the start of a connection with the United States, which took me to the University of Michigan Law School to take an LL M, to work for a New York law firm, Winthrop Stimson Putnam and Roberts, and then on to many cases with United States lawyers, including both litigation and arbitration, and to many close and enduring friendships.

I was called to the Bar in November 1965, on the same night as my wife, Carolyn, who reports for the Law Reports. We were married in May 1967 in the Temple Church and one of the great blessings of my life is that since then we have made the journey together.

Carolyn's pupil master was Michael Sherrard QC. My pupil master was Eric McLellan of Inner Temple in the same chambers as Geoffrey Howe QC. Both Geoffrey Howe, now Lord Howe of Aberavon, and Michael Sherrard and their wives, Elspeth and Shirley, have given us wonderful inspiration, support and friendship over now more than 40 years.

In 1969 Geoffrey Howe QC was called to the Bench of the Middle Temple. The rules for guests in those days were strict. Only with special permission could a guest be invited by a member of Hall, and then only by someone of the same sex. Carolyn invited Elspeth Howe to join our mess in Hall, just as later she invited Shirley when Michael Sherrard became a Bencher. At Master Howe's Bench Call, the food was memorable for all the wrong reasons. The meal consisted of leek soup (burnt), followed by steak pie (burnt), and Elizabethan pudding (burnt) left over from the reign of Elizabeth I. I am sure that everyone has done much better this evening!

The reference to the food gives me an opportunity to pay a special tribute, not only to the catering staff, but to all the staff of the Inn led by the Under Treasurer. We have a staff, at least as devoted to this Inn and this Hall, as we are.

A remarkable demonstration of this was last month's Open Weekend when 25,000 visitors came to the two Inns and the Church. On that occasion the staff, led by Peter Blair and Colin Davidson, demonstrated devotion beyond the call of any duty. So did Master Paul Darling QC and many others.

So also did Master Treasurer (Michael Blair QC). He spent a substantial part of each day in this Hall selling the Inn's merchandise. On one occasion, having persuaded someone to buy rather more bottles of the Inn's port than they had intended by offering to autograph each bottle, he was not satisfied with his work. "Won't you be wanting an Inn tea towel for drying the glasses?" he asked. The buyer meekly agreed.

In 1971 I was elected a member of the Bar Council under 10 years call and was a member of the Bar Council in various capacities for sixteen of the next twenty two years. In 1974 I became the first young barrister to be Chairman of the Young Barristers' Committee. The problem of obtaining pupillages has become even more acute now than it was thirty odd years ago, and it remains one of the most important topics with which the Inn and the Bar has to grapple. Perhaps a solution worth exploring is that the Inns themselves should provide pupillage scholarships for some of those who do not have pupillages funded by chambers. These would also count as funded pupillages.

I have been most impressed with the students I have met as Reader. Some of them have already added greatly to the prestige of the Inn in international Debating and Mooting competitions. They deserve better than the current arrangements.

As chairman of the Young Barristers' Committee, I was a member of the Executive Committee of the Bar Council. In 1974, I wrote to the then Master Treasurer, Lord Diplock, unlike you, Master Treasurer a rather austere figure, to ask if the members of the Inn who were members of the Executive Committee of the Bar Council could meet with the Treasurer, perhaps once a year, so that they would know what the Inn's policy was. I was invited with two other non-Bench members of the Executive Committee, John Griffiths and Kenneth Richardson to meet Master Treasurer. After we had sat down, Lord Diplock held up my letter and said, "This is not good enough". I wondered what I had done. He went on: "This is not good enough. Members of the Inn who are members of the Executive Committee of the Bar Council should be co-opted onto the Executive Committee of the Inn". This happened with Bench domestic business being taken separately. At the first two meetings Lord Diplock invited each of us to give our views before asking the Benchers.

In August 1976 I was lucky enough to be included as the young barrister among 40 barristers and solicitors invited to the American Bar Association Convention in Atlanta, Georgia, to mark the 200th anniversary of the signing of Declaration of Independence. The format was that on each topic there were speakers from both the United States and England and Wales. The initial speeches were followed by a panel discussion. The overall theme was Common Faith, Common Law. The specific topics which were addressed have a familiar ring – they included The Crisis in Criminal Justice; Litigation Today; the Law and the Press; Cost, Delay and other problems.

At the opening session, the Chairman of the Bar gave a welcome on behalf of the English Bar in words which link our distinguished past with the present and the future. Lord Rawlinson said " I represent the ancient Inns of Court and the Bar from whence all our traditions on both sides of the Atlantic stem. Six members of the Inns of Court signed the Declaration of Independence and it is only fitting on an occasion like this that the roll should be called". Five of those were members of this Inn. We have a proud history in upholding the freedoms on which the United Kingdom has been built, and of exporting them to many other parts of the world. How we can translate this dynamic into the world of 2008 is a question I shall attempt to answer.

I was a member of the Supreme Court Rules Committee from 1977-1980 when I took Silk. I was very honoured to be called to the Bench of this Inn on 24 June, 1986.

In 1997 I was attracted to become what turned out to be the last Official Referee, because my jurisdiction in construction and technology cases would be the exact equivalent of that of High Court Judges in the Commercial Court. My hope was that the Court would become the court of choice for international construction cases.

It is not only my activities at the Bar or on the Bench which inform my thoughts on the Middle Temple and the future but also my outside activities.

In 1977, led by Phillip Otton QC, I was nominated as junior counsel to the enquiry into Normansfield Hospital in Teddington, a hospital for those with mental disabilities. When it was over, the then Attorney General, the Rt Hon Sam Silkin QC, asked me to join the Hospital Management Committee of the Maudsley and Bethlem Hospitals of which he himself had once been a member.

In 1983 I became a trustee of the Institute of Psychiatry with which the joint hospitals were associated. In 1997, on its merger, I became a member of the Council of King's College, London on the nomination of the Institute of Psychiatry. I have remained a member of the Council ever since, and I chair the Governance Committee. The current arrangements for governance at King's have developed piecemeal and it has become necessary to review the way in which the College is governed. This has given me insights which are relevant to the governance of the Middle Temple. Some of the problems of King's are entirely different, but some are very similar.

It has been very rewarding and instructive to work with two world class institutions not connected with the law. The Institute is now one of the top five institutions in the world for the investigation and treatment of mental disorders. After mergers with the Institute of Psychiatry and the Guy's, King's and St Thomas's Medical Schools, King's has emerged as a fully fledged and unified university. Under the Principal, Professor Rick Trainor, King's is ranked this year 6th in the United Kingdom and 24th in the world, having been 73rd in the world two years ago.

In each case the success has been achieved by having clear objectives which have been carried through by people of extraordinary quality and vision.

My other main strand of activity relates to the European Bar Council, CCBE, of which I was President in 1993 and which led to my involvement with the European Law Academy in Trier, ERA.

From 1986 - 1991 the CCBE had a triumvirate of Past President, President and Vice-President. This was very unsatisfactory. The Vice-President did not tend to be fully involved until the moment when he became President and the Past President either did too much or was hardly involved at all. The system was changed so that there was a President, first Vice- President and second Vice-President. They formed a triumvirate to carry through a smooth transition from one Presidency to the next and to provide a consistency of policy. The Vice-Presidents were fully involved with the President in the work of that year. It meant that initiatives could be carried forward over a period of years and that, for example, the second Vice-President could take a major responsibility for particular issues which would come to a head in the future. This also meant that the burden on the President could be reduced. This worked extraordinarily well during my time as President with a Danish and a German Vice-President. This is a precedent that the Middle Temple could well follow. [In practice it has done so.]

In the course of the years between 1989 and 1993, as a member of the CCBE, and particularly as a result of conducting the GATT negotiations and being President of the CCBE, I visited China, Japan, Brazil, New Zealand and the United States as well as travelling extensively within Europe and I acquired a unique perspective on the delivery of legal services worldwide.

I have no doubt that the Inn can and should play a more prominent and constructive role in the developing legal world.

In 1993 I became a member of the first Board of Trustees of ERA. In 1995 I became Vice-Chairman and in 1997 Chairman, a post which I still hold. In 2002 Lord Irvine of Lairg, as Lord Chancellor, signed the accession of the United Kingdom to the Foundation and it became a member of the Governing Board of ERA. Based on my personal experience, I would hope that future historians will treat Lord Irvine more kindly than contemporary commentators have done.

In addition to its nominated members, the Board of Trustees has as members leading members of the Court of Justice, the European Commission, judges from the Member States, academics and practitioners.

Even though the Inn is not in the business of conference organisation, the objects of ERA have direct lessons for us since they are based upon a wide concept of education which embraces continuing education for all lawyers. The objects are "to enable the individuals and authorities involved in the application and implementation of European law in the Member States, and in other European States interested in co-operation with the European Union, to gain a wider knowledge of European law, in particular Community law and its application, and to make possible a mutual and comprehensive exchange of experiences". It is the words "to make possible a mutual and comprehensive exchange of experiences" which I wish to underline and to which I will return.

ERA's great strength is that it is not a political or a lobbying organisation. ERA makes it clear that in organising seminars and other specialist symposia, it cannot express any view of its own. But it can and does promote discussion and debate. Middle Temple is in a similar position.

At its 15th Anniversary Congress in September 2007, Judges and former Judges of the European Court of Justice, leading practitioners and academics discussed a number of questions including the following:

As a matter of legal analysis, do we have a European constitution already? And if so, how does it relate to National constitutions?

How in principle does the Court approach the question of opt outs?

One former judge of the Luxembourg Court said that there had been, in effect, a European constitution in existence for the United Kingdom since its accession. I rather agree.

At the conference, the judges of the Luxembourg Court were prepared to explain in general terms how the Court had approached in the past, and how it would approach in the future, any question of law that involved a Member State which had opted out of a relevant part of a Treaty.

Is it not remarkable that we, as lawyers, have had no similar discussions here analysing the constitutional position of the Treaty of Lisbon, or considering how effective in legal terms the United Kingdom opt-outs are likely to be? Such discussions, involving experts, ought, surely, to be informing the current debates which are taking place in the national Parliament. Sadly the debates in Parliament seem to be designed to send the subject to sleep.

In relation to the European Union, of which we are a leading member state and whose law forms so much a part of our law, all we have managed as an Inn in recent years is two dinners to which distinguished European Lawyers and Judges have been invited. Surely we need to do better than this?

I now address the position of the Middle Temple directly. I start with the Temple Church which, as you all know, is owned one half each by this Inn and Inner Temple. The Charter requires the Inns to maintain the Church and the Master's House, to maintain the Master and to provide for services in the church. Ian Garwood, our Director of Estates, has looked after the fabric of the church for a number of years. He has not always had an easy task. We owe him a considerable debt of gratitude for the current good state of the fabric.

Since 1999, the Master of the Temple Church, the Rev Robin Griffith-Jones, an honorary Bencher, and the Directors of Music, Stephen Layton, also an honorary Bencher, and James Vivian, with help from the Reader of the Temple Church, the Rev Hugh Mead, the Verger and many others, have not only performed the Church's traditional functions but have also taken both the speech and the music at the Church to a wider audience, and in the process have transformed the life of the Church. This has been consistent with the aim of the Inns to connect much better with individual members of the Inns and the wider public.

I have only to mention in this connection Sir John Tavener's Veil of the Temple, heard not only in the Temple Church in 2003 but also at the Proms and the Lincoln Centre in New York and on CD, and the Master's hugely popular talks on the Da Vinci Code.

In the last two months alone, I think of the three Carol services last Christmas attended by over 1800 people, the Open Weekend when the Church was packed with visitors throughout the two days and most heard at least one of the Master's talks, and 500 people came to Morning Service on the Sunday. The 2008 Festival has been a wonderful collaboration between Middle Temple, Inner Temple and the Church where the Church with its combination of words and musical is playing a pivotal role. Our choir contains a number of international soloists. If you have not already had an opportunity to do so, do go and hear them in concert.

I should also mention the Master's important series on Islam and the Law which has got off to such an explosive start. I suspect that almost whatever the Archbishop of Canterbury had said would have caused a furore. At the moment there is so much suppressed anger in this country on this and many other topics. What is needed desperately is constructive discussion and wise leadership.

What of the Middle Temple itself?

The excellent new booklet on Middle Temple by our archivist, Lesley Whitelaw, describes the Inn's primary role as promoting the profession of barrister through the provision of education and advocacy training, and support to students and barristers through the provision of collegiate facilities for its members, and professional and residential accommodation.

These are very important obligations which are carried out by the Inn with dedication and largely with success, but the Inn also has a wider role which is of the greatest importance. I return to Lord Rawlinson's phrase 'the ancient Inns of Court and the Bar from whence all our tradition stems'. The Inns of Court stand for the enduring values to which all systems of law should subscribe and which are embedded in the United States' and many other countries' constitutions. The Inns are known and respected throughout the world and have the potential through their links to bring closer together all those involved in the delivery of justice and the rule of law. Further development of these links is a proper part of the Inn's educational mission. They are valuable for judges, practitioners and academics meeting separately and together. Their development should not be confined to common law jurisdictions or to members of the Inn. They are also very valuable for those with whom we establish links.

The Inn should enable dialogue to take place between judges, practitioners and academics from different countries who wish to have discussions with each other. They may take the form of seminars, formal visits, lunches or dinners in the Inn, or informal contact where the Inn provides a common link.

Already we have established links within the Inn between judges, barristers in private practice, academics, those in commerce and those in the public service, which are replicated in few other jurisdictions. We already have an important dialogue in the annual meeting between the Middle Temple, the two other home jurisdictions and Ireland involving judges and barristers. But we lack sufficient links with some important groups both here and abroad.

One way of widening these links is to use our existing contacts, including our Honorary Benchers. Another way is to identify a limited number of individuals who would be asked to help us to develop links with a particular jurisdiction or institution, some of whom might become Honorary Benchers.

I start at home. We have no Honorary Bencher who is a practising solicitor [We now have one, Fiona Woolf, who will become Lord Mayor of London]. Other Inns, including Inner Temple, have found that this contact is invaluable. There is now a network of foreign lawyers established in London virtually all of whom have joined the Law Society. We ought to forge better links with them - perhaps an Amity dinner, a debate. We are proud that His Honour Judge Sir Gavyn Arthur was the first practising barrister to become Lord Mayor of London and we should maintain and improve our links with the City. Law after all is one the United Kingdom's biggest invisible exports.

We are an important part of the European Union yet we have no Honorary Benchers from among the judges or practising lawyers from any Member State other than Ireland, apart from Master Michel Van Doosselaere. [We now have a member of the German Constitutional Court as an Honorary Bencher.] We have strong links with the European Court of Justice through our own Benchers but no Honorary Benchers from other member states among the judges or former judges of the Luxembourg Court, apart from Master, Justice of the Supreme Court of Ireland, Niall Fennelly, and none from the Strasbourg Court.

We have especially close links with the United States particularly through the Chief Justice, Master John Roberts. But even these links need to be strengthened and deepened. Perhaps we should take a greater interest in the work of the American Inns of Court.

In some ways it is even more important that we should forge new links at different levels with legal professions in countries which are fast emerging as world powers - China, India, Brazil and South Africa. The first three are now regarded as so important as to merit permanent seats on the United Nations Security Council. In the case of China we may be able to develop more permanent links through Middle Templars in Hong Kong. I am sure there are also good links with India which can and should be developed further. If we can forge enduring links with Brazil that will help also in relation to the rest of Latin America. I have some links with Brazil and believe that a more enduring contact would be welcomed both by Brazilian judges and the Brazilian Bar.

The development of closer links with South Africa would no doubt lead to better links with many other countries on the African continent.

Once the overall policy has been agreed, we need to set up an international committee to carry the process forward, to set priorities, and to co-ordinate the contacts.

As a separate obligation, we, as lawyers and as individual members of the public have a duty to inform ourselves and the public on legal subjects of general importance. Although it is vital that the Inn remains strictly neutral, the Inn should, itself, organise from time to time seminars or debates on important topics in addition to, or in substitution for, our guest lectures. I can cite two precedents for this approach: the first is the American Bar Convention in 1976, to which I have already referred, and the second is a remarkable debate held in this Hall between Masters Mark Littman QC and Christopher Greenwood QC on the legality or otherwise of the Iraq War.

I have used the current Treaty of Lisbon as a specific example of a topic which we should debate. What about other topics, including those which potentially impinge on our civil liberties? e.g. detention for 28 or 42 days without charge, indeterminate prison sentences, the use of ASBOS, whether the current provision for legal aid provides proper access to justice, legal aspects of global solutions to the environment, and multidisciplinary practices with accountants and others.

This last subject reminds me of a meeting with senior officials from the Commission in Brussels in about 1990. The head of the Belgian Bar said to the official, "I think you regard lawyers as no different from sellers of tomatoes from a market stall". The official nodded and said "Yes". This tendency sadly is alive and well in 2008.

I have one modest practical suggestion. In each period of six months as part of his educational function, Master Reader would chair a debate on a subject of his or her choosing, to be called the Reader's Debate, perhaps taking the place of one of the guest lectures, to be followed by a buffet supper for those who wish to continue the discussion.

Finally, I turn to governance. I was as sceptical as anyone as I read the various notes of guidance in connection with the good governance of Universities but many of the ideas make sense. I am considering them in detail in conjunction with my work at King's and I have taken them into account in what follows.

The debate on governance is on Master Treasurer's agenda for the year. Here are three suggestions. The first is that the immediate past Treasurer should cease to be one of the three officers in the Treasurership. He should be replaced formally by the person who is at present merely ear-marked to succeed the Deputy Treasurer. [This has happened]

Secondly, there is a case for saying that Inn committees should have an Honorary Bencher member of equal distinction to other Honorary Benchers but who is chosen because he or she can provide an independent view. This is particularly the case for Finance and Estates and perhaps also for the Executive Committee. There is a precedent for this too. In past years Master Sir Christopher Benson, who was Chairman for the development of Canary Wharf, has been of immense assistance to the Estates Committee. [Equally, we now have a formidably distinguished group of Honorary Benchers who are actors or directors who might help with advocacy training. We could go further and have an advocacy day open to all with Honorary Bencher participation.]

Thirdly, as I have foreshadowed, in the course of this year we may be able to identify a small number of individuals who can assist us in various capacities, either by providing stronger links internationally, or with the Law Society, or with particular expertise perhaps in finance or property. If that can be done, the 400th anniversary year would be an appropriate time to elect a small number of additional Honorary Benchers who would then be able to help us in carrying forward the task of renewal which is such an important part of 2008.

Finally the position of Master Reader: In his reading in 1982 Master Sir Ralph Kilner Brown wrote, "Together with the Master charged with student affairs and the Master of Moots, [the Reader] should involve himself with student activities at universities and in the Inn, and preside in Hall when moots and other student activities take place". I have only been Reader for six weeks, but it is already clear to me that this does represent a substantial part of the duties of Master Reader and it should be formalised as such in the Inn's constitution.

I looked at the recent portrait outside the Parliament Chamber which includes eight of our most distinguished judges. To their number I add Master Sir Francis Jacobs, one of the most distinguished former judges of the European Court. Master Lord Nicholls and Master Sir Christopher Rose have been Master Treasurer. None has been Master Reader. [Happily Sir Francis Jacobs has since become Reader]. Now that the Reader in one half of the year can substitute for the Reader in the other half, if necessary, I would hope that, even if they cannot undertake the very onerous duties of Treasurer,[happily Master Igor Judge is to be Treasurer for 2014], some of those and others of similar eminence would be able to follow Masters Lord Wilberforce, Lord Scarman, Lord Howe and Lord Mayhew as Reader. Further, being an Honorary Bencher should not be a bar to being elected Master Reader.

When a vigneron in Burgundy tastes wine at a dinner party, if he says "C'est interessant", that really means "It is undrinkable". If he says "Ce n'est pas mal", that means "It is barely drinkable". If he says "C'est tres bon", that means that it is enjoyable. For the rare special bottle of wine which he will always remember, he says simply "Merci". To you all I simply say "Merci".

Lent Reader's Report 2008

It has been a very special privilege to be Lent Reader in this 400th Anniversary year.[1] The celebrations have been hugely enjoyable and rewarding and there are many good things still to come in the Inns and Temple Church. I have been a privileged spectator at the major celebratory events but I will concentrate here on those events specifically connected with my Readership.

In his Lent Reading in 1982, Master Kilner-Brown described the Readers' duties as " together with the Master charged with student welfare and the Master of the Moots, [the Reader] should involve himself with student activities at Universities and in the Inn and preside in Hall when Moots or other student activities take place". In addition, Master Reader gives a reading at his Feast.

As I prepared my Reading, I became aware of a wider responsibility. No one becomes Reader without a lengthy career as student, member of Hall and Bencher. Each is able to bring his or her unique and wider perspective of the Inn unencumbered by day-to-day responsibility as Treasurer or Chairman of a Committee. Master Reader should be expected to reflect this perspective in positive proposals or ideas for discussion. It will then be for others to decide whether and if so how they should be implemented. Master Treasurer has been most generous in his response to this approach.

During my Readership, mostly in company with my wife, Carolyn, I participated in two student weekends at Cumberland Lodge, the Northern Advocacy weekend in York, the Nottingham Bar Vocational Dinner, the Oxford and Cambridge dinners, a Saturday New Practitioners' course, and various MTSA debates. Each event was most enjoyable but the underlying mood of concern amongst students and young entrants was in sharp contrast to the 400th anniversary celebrations. The overwhelming majority of students will not find a pupillage, let alone a tenancy: those that have gone into criminal practice are now so badly paid that a significant number are finding it difficult to remain in the profession.

Part of the Inn's task is to get across the real problems which the Bar is facing. In April I participated in a very important initiative of Master Bernard Richmond and Christa Richmond, an Open Day for schools and Universities with tours of the Inn, lectures and a Mock Trial. The day left those who came in no doubt of the hurdles to be overcome.

---

[1]   Published in *Middle Templar*, Autumn 2008

For any Reader, the Reader's Feast is a unique occasion. Master Reader chooses the dinner and at its end gives his Reading. In the 18th century it was ordained that there should be some innovation - we have a very modest vineyard in Burgundy which produces 1500 bottles a year. We were able to offer Benchers, Members of Hall and Students red wine from our vineyard.

My Reading was entitled "The Middle Temple and the Future". Master Chartres (Dean of the Chapels Royal, Bishop of London and an Honorary Bencher), when dedicating the 400th Anniversary window in the Temple Church, made the distinction between "history" (what we can learn from the past) and "destiny" (how we should be planning for the future). We are joyously celebrating our history. I suggested that we needed urgently to think about our destiny.

My perspective is not only that of student, practising barrister and judge, but also of a former Chairman of the Bar Council's Young Barristers' Committee and President of the European Bar Council (CCBE) and current Chairman of the Board of Trustees of the European Law Academy.

I suggested two initiatives which would be in keeping with the historic role of the Inn.

I noted that Members of the Inn include judges, private practitioners, academics, practitioners in industry, and government lawyers who have opportunities to mix freely which are not available in many jurisdictions where they would be members of separate professions. I suggested that the Inn, free from regulatory responsibilities, could develop its role as a market place of ideas in line with its traditions going back to 1608. It is from the ancient Inns of Court and the Bar that common law traditions worldwide stem. I asked if we were doing enough to ensure that ancient freedoms were not being eroded. In this context, I suggested that possible subjects for debate might include detention without charge, the use of ASBOS, whether the current legal aid provisions provide adequate access to justice, and the plight of the Criminal Bar. In the wider context, I added as examples multi-disciplinary practices and the Lisbon Treaty. I made the proposal that a Reader's Debate should be instituted. Master Reader would organise and Chair a debate on a topic of importance to the Inn or the legal profession, or related to the Rule of Law.

My second theme was that the Inn is part of the world-wide legal profession, known and respected throughout the world. It should develop its important role in bringing together those involved in the delivery of justice and the Rule of Law through further links, not only with common law jurisdictions but also with the European Union and with countries like China, Brazil, India and South Africa. Part of the plan would include the election of Honorary Benchers who would be working Benchers in the sense that they would assist us in developing those links.

The celebrations themselves will I am sure have a lasting effect. The various concerts and lectures and especially the Open Weekend when over 25,000 visited the two Inns, will have helped to de-mystify the Inns and the Temple Church. These events have also helped to bring us closer together as an Inn and have contributed to a sense of community which is the envy of other professions. Perhaps most important of all , Middle and Inner Temple have come much closer together. This will be important in the difficult times which undoubtedly lie ahead. We owe an enormous debt of gratitude to all those who have made possible this year's wonderful events.

The Temple Church

The seventh and last Institution, although very closely linked to the sixth, is the Temple Church. Our family has worshipped in the Church since we were married there in 1967. From 1990-2010 I was a member of the Church Committee which is a joint committee of the two Inns of Court which own the Church, the Inner Temple and the Middle Temple. I was Chairman of the Committee in 2003. Since 1990 I have been a trustee of the Temple Music Trust and its chairman since 2002. The Trust's object is to assist in the promotion of music in the Temple Church and to support its outstanding choir.

I was delighted to be asked to contribute the chapter on the Temple Church to *The History of the Middle Temple*, published by Hart Publishing in June 2011. The whole chapter is too long to reproduce here, but the period from the 1960s is part of my story.

The *History* starts with the Knights Templar in the 12th century and ends in the present century. It is very readable and will remain the definitive history of the Middle Temple for many years to come.

The Church was bombed on the night of 10 May 1941. Much of the Church was gutted and the Father Smith organ, installed in 1685, was destroyed. The new organ, given by Lord Glentanar, was installed in haste. When it was dismantled in 2011 for extensive renovation, it was discovered that many of the pipes had a green coating on the outside as a result of smoking sixty and more years ago in the Ballroom of Lord Glentanar's castle.

The chapter which follows starts with the installation of the new organ and the re-opening of the Church after the repair of war damage. The chapter ends with a salutary warning from Canon Ainger (Reader from 1866 and then, after a short break, Master until1904) that no institution will survive without regular renewals of the spirit. Others may use a different form of words, but the substance contains a universal truth.

I also refer to the international aspiration of the Temple Church to be regarded as the "Mother Church of the Common Law", which fits into the international theme of this book. This theme is closely linked to that of the Inns of Court, and, in this context especially, Inner and Middle Temples (two of the four Inns), as the cradles of the Common Law. In one sense, the Temple Church is both "Cradle" and "Mother Church" through its connection with William Marshall, Earl of Pembroke, and Magna Carta in 1215. The challenge is to transform this aspiration into a living reality.

The Round Church was consecrated in 1185 and the nave in 1240 and, ever since lawyers arrived in the Temple in about 1340 as tenants of the Order of St

John, many have worshipped in the Church, and indeed all members of the two Inns were required to do so in earlier times.

Members of Inner and Middle Temples played a leading part in discovering the New World. Three among a number of explorer members were Drake, Raleigh and Somers. Six members of the two Inns were signatories to the US Declaration of Independence and many more fought on both sides in the American Wars of Independence, see references to *The History of the Middle Temple* in my Lent Reading above.

As I observed in the previous chapter, both Inner and Middle Temples include many members and benchers practising from other Common Law countries, having obtained their legal education in London. Many will also have worshipped in the Temple Church.

Others of different faiths and none will understand that, although times have changed, the Church can justly claim to be the Mother Church of the Common Law, inextricably bound to the two Inns. This is the case, not least because the Royal Charter of King James I of 1608 granting the land to the Inner and Middle Temples, renewed by Her Majesty the Queen in 2008, requires the Inns, as a condition of the grant, to provide "for the celebration of divine service and the sacraments and sacramental offices and ecclesiastical rites whatsoever henceforth and forever as is befitting and hitherto accustomed". The Inns were also required to provide a house for the Master of the Temple, and a stipend of £17.6s.8d (still paid separately, but now supplemented by a sum befitting the Master's senior standing in the Church of England).

The material exists to make the claim "the Mother Church of the Common Law" a living reality, just as it exists to develop further the notion of the Inns of Court as the "cradles of the Common Law".

In each case this may be only a part of the picture. Like the Middle and Inner Temples, the Temple Church could well concentrate not only on its historic role in the Common law, but a wider role. In the case of the Temple Church it could be a force for good in fostering a better understanding of the law and its relationship to different religions.

The Temple Church[1]

The restoration work was undertaken by the firm of Carden and Godfrey, Architects. In 1949 the work of rebuilding began. Dove Brothers of Islington (Builders) had carried out the restoration of Middle Temple Hall. They now undertook the restoration of the Church overseen on behalf of the two Inns by Master Kenneth Carpmael, Master of the House at Middle Temple. The quarries at Purbeck were re-opened to provide the marble columns which were needed to replace those that had been damaged.

Soon after the destruction of the Father Smith organ, Thalben-Ball started the search for a new organ. In Feb 1950 Master Lord Glentanar offered to give the Church an organ built by Harrison & Harrison in 1927/8[2]. Thalben-Ball described it as better than anything that could be obtained new at that time and in many respects equal and in a few respects superior to the old organ[3].

The new organ was brought down from Scotland in 1953 and reassembled in the Church. The work took six months, in fact a very short time for such an instrument. It had to be ready for the service of re-dedication of the chancel on 23 March 1954 in the presence of Master Her Majesty Queen Elizabeth the Queen Mother.

Canon Anson, devoted to the Church, lived just long enough to know of the re-dedication of the Chancel. He died on 31 March 1954. In his book of reflections he said, "I can only say that with most loyal and friendly cooperation of the Reader at the Temple, the Treasurers and Masters of the Bench, the Organist, choir and the surveyors I have never had so happy a post or one which gives greater opportunities to anyone ready to take account both of its limitations and its openings"[4].

This quotation encapsulates the traditional view of the Church centred around the Benchers of the Inns which continued until the late 1990's.

The Round Church and Triforium were rededicated on 7 November 1958 in the presence of the Queen, the Duke of Edinburgh and Master Her Majesty Queen Elizabeth the Queen Mother.

Regular Sunday morning services had started again in January 1955 [using, as we do now, the *Cathedral Service* and the *Book Of Common Prayer*].The boys

---

[1] Extract from the *History of the Middle Temple* (Hart Publishing, 2011)
[2] MT.15/FIL No. 16.
[3] Rennert, p 108; Lewer and Dark, p 157; MT.15/FIL no 19 contains a letter from Thalben-Ball urging the Choir Committee to accept the gift as "a noble successor to the famous 'Father Smith' Church Organ."
[4] Harold Anson, *Looking Forward*, Heinemann, 1938, p 282.

sang again with the choirmen for the first time on 30 October 1955 when the choir included, as a baritone, Ernest Lough [who, as a fifteen year-old boy treble, had made the famous recording in 1927 of Mendelssohn's "Hear My Prayer" ("Oh for the Wings of a Dove")] and his son Robin as a treble. His other two sons also sang as boy choristers. Ernest Lough[5] died in 2000 and his and his wife's ashes rest in the Triforium.

One of the earliest choristers after the war was Ian le Grice who became a chorister in 1957. He has given unbroken service to the Church since that date. After acting as unofficial assistant organist to Dr. Thalben-Ball, he was formally appointed Assistant Organist in 1982. In 2007 he was presented with a scroll of appreciation by the two Inns to mark his 50 years of service to the Inns and to the Church. To celebrate the event, he composed a setting for Holy Communion which is much appreciated.

Canon Firth (1954-57)[6], Canon Milford (1958 – 1968), Dean Milburn (1968-80) and Canon Joseph Robinson (1980-1999) all gave devoted service to the Church. It will be remembered that authority for the conduct of Church affairs rested with the Church Committee who were not enthusiastic about change. The Masters of the Temple presided over the traditional activities, services on a Sunday, weddings and memorial services of Benchers and the annual Carol Service. They visited the sick and cared for those who lived in the Inns. In an unusual and well merited mark of his service, Canon Robinson was elected an Honorary Bencher of Inner Temple. The author remembers Dean Milburn's sermons set in the context appropriate to an eminent ecclesiastical historian[7] and Canon Robinson's wonderful Lenten Addresses and his sermons debunking the radical views of the then Bishop of Durham, Dr David Jenkins.

Dr Thalben-Ball continued as Organist until 1981 when at the age of 85 he retired. He had been made an Honorary Bencher of Inner Temple[8], and was knighted in 1982. He was succeeded by Dr John Birch, Organist of the Royal Philharmonic Orchestra and formerly Organist of Chichester Cathedral. On his retirement in 1997 he became an Honorary Bencher of Middle Temple.

By the early 1990s, it was apparent to the author and others that unless we did something to renew the spirit of the Church it would gradually fade away as an institution. On reflection there were a number of problems. The Church was regarded too much as a preserve of the Benchers of the two Inns. At Sunday Services the whole of the area between the choir and the altar on both sides was set aside for Benchers although, except on special occasions,

---

[5]   1911-2000.
[6]   Canon Firth died in September in 1957. The Rev W. D. Kennedy-Bell, as Reader, was Acting Master until the arrival of Canon Milford.
[7]   Dean Milburn's speech in October 1973 to celebrate the 50th anniversary of Dr. Thalben-Ball's appointment as Organist of the Church is in File Treasury Ref 1108.
[8]   For a list of his recordings, see Rennert p. 151.

relatively few attended. From the 1970s, the vast expansion of the Bar meant that residential chambers in the Inns had to be converted into professional chambers and the Church lost a significant part of its congregation. The congregation rarely included children or young persons and was growing ever more elderly[9].

There was a further problem over taking new initiatives. While the troubles in Ireland were continuing, security in the Inns was of the greatest importance. It had been tightened in the 1970's. There was a risk in encouraging new people to come into the area of the Church. While Master Diplock was alive, there was a constant reminder of the security problem. Master Diplock, founder of the Diplock Courts in Northern Ireland, sat in Middle Temple Benchers' pews for Sunday morning services. Opposite him, on the Inner Temple side, was an armed security guard. This security threat had become less acute by the middle 1990's.

The Church needed a new focus, one where it was made evident that it was there primarily to serve the members and staff of the two Inns and their families and not merely the Benchers. A start was made in the mid 1990's. Master Butler-Sloss of Inner Temple and the author formed a sub-committee with the Master to review those who could be married or have memorial services in the Church or whose children could be baptised in the Church. Canon Robinson was enthusiastic about relaxing some of the limitations confining these privileges to Benchers and their families and some modest changes were made.

When Dr Birch decided to retire in 1997, the interviewing committee, comprising representatives of the two Inns, together with the distinguished organist and choirmaster Christopher Robinson as adviser, wanted to create a new tradition which took account of the developments in choral music in the last 70 years. Some of the candidates, however, thought that the committee would want to try to recreate the time of Ernest Lough and George Thalben-Ball in their heyday. In the view of the committee that was in any event an impossible task. Stephen Layton, Assistant Organist at Southwark Cathedral, the youngest candidate, was appointed by the Inns on the recommendation of the Committee. It is interesting to note that Stanley, Hopkins, Walford Davies, Thalben-Ball, Layton and subsequently James Vivian, were all appointed when under 30 years of age.

Immediately after his appointment, Layton recruited James Vivian, recently down from Cambridge, as Assistant Organist. When Layton left for Trinity College Cambridge in 2006, having been elected an Honorary Bencher of Middle Temple, Vivian succeeded him as Director of the Choir. Although

---

[9]   The author and his wife, also a Middle Templar, have worshipped regularly in the Church since 1967. Frequently theirs were the only children in the Church.

each has his own distinctive style, this made for an easy transition. They have indeed created the new tradition which the Church Committee had hoped to achieve. Greg Morris from Blackburn Cathedral was appointed as Associate Organist to succeed Vivian.

In 1998 Canon Robinson became seriously ill. It was agreed at Christmas 1998 that he would formally retire and become Master Emeritus, although he would continue to reside in the Master's House and perform such duties as he could. The Reader, Hugh Mead, was appointed Acting Master. Canon Robinson's last service was in May 1999 and he died five weeks later[10]. Master Ian Kennedy provided considerable support as Chairman of the Church Committee.

In 1998 the status of the Church was called into question by an opinion that the Temple Church was not a Royal Peculiar. The historical position was vigorously asserted by Master Boydell, an eminent ecclesiastical lawyer and former Treasurer. The matter was happily resolved[11]. The Queen confirmed that the appointment of Canon Robinson's successor would be a Royal appointment and she decided to confer her Visitorial powers on the Dean of the Chapels Royal. The present Dean, Master Chartres, is, of course, also Bishop of London (who has no jurisdiction over the Church) and an Honorary Bencher.

The Choir Committee decided to look for someone younger to be Master. The thinking was that he could relate more easily to the problems of those starting at the Bar and in mid-career and in this way the pastoral duties of the Master could be widened. The Choir Committee (with the Dean of St Paul's as adviser) was permitted to interview two candidates, and Her Majesty was then graciously pleased to appoint the Rev. Robin Griffith Jones as Master for 10 years from 1 September 1999. (His term has since been extended). The new Master's father had been Master Reader of Middle Temple. The Master had been brought up in the Middle Temple and was a student member of the Inn. Although he has pursued a very different career, he has the Temple in his bones.

On appointment the Master was aged 43. It is a measure of his success that he has been elected an Honorary Bencher by both Middle and Inner Temples. His extraordinary skill, energy and enthusiasm have enabled him to reach far beyond those who come to services on a Sunday morning. He has fulfilled the hope that pastoral duties would be extended to younger members of the Inns.

The Master has written scholarly books on the Four Gospels, St Paul's Journeys and Mary Magdalene. In 2002 Dan Brown wrote the world best

---

[10] It is a pity that Canon Robinson's last sermons were not preserved and published.
[11] MT.15/FIL55.

seller "The Da Vinci Code" which features the Temple Church. The Master has given many lectures on the Code to admiring audiences from this country and around the world and his book on the subject has been a best seller. In 2010 with David Park he edited an important book, "The Temple Church: History, Architecture and Art". In 2008 he promoted an important series of lectures on Islam, including a thought provoking lecture by Dr Rowan Williams, Archbishop of Canterbury, in the Great Hall of the Royal Courts of Justice. In the lecture, entitled "Civil and Religious Law in England: A Religious Perspective", the archbishop discussed a number of topics including the place of religious courts in the English legal system.

An important innovation in 1999 was the establishment of a Sunday school during morning service. The Temple Church owes a great deal to the Chartres family. They had two sons in the Temple Choir and it was Master Chartres's wife, Caroline, who established the Sunday school and ran it for a number of years. This meant that families could come and enjoy the service. Children could offer the results of their labours at the altar. The choir parents have made a significant contribution, not only in relation to their own children, but to the well-being of the choristers as a whole. They have been supported for many years by Liz Clarke, the parents' co-ordinator.

The words, the music and the more inclusive family atmosphere have combined to increase very substantially the congregation in the Church both at Sunday services and at the additional services of Evensong, supported by the Temple Music Trust. It has been necessary once again to issue tickets for the annual Christmas Carol Services, now three in number. At the great festivals the Church is full. For other services the average congregation is now over 150. With the encouragement of the Choir Committee, the Master has instituted bi-annual celebrations of baptisms and marriages and for families who have held memorial services in the Church, followed by an informal lunch.

Layton and Vivian, supported by the Master, have transformed not just the musical life of the Church but also the musical life of the Inns. Two Middle Temple Benchers have also had pivotal roles. Master Christopher Clarke was Chairman of the Church Committee from January 2005 to January 2011 and Master Richard Aikens has been the Chairman of the Temple Music Foundation since its launch in 2002. The Temple Music Foundation has promoted concerts by the choir and the newly formed Temple Players in the Temple Church, as well as other concerts in the Church and song recitals in Middle Temple Hall by internationally known singers accompanied by Julius Drake.

Since 1999 the choir has also taken part in a performance of the Dream of Gerontius with the London Philharmonic Orchestra, the boys have provided backing for the film Gormenghast, and the choir has toured Brazil for the British Council. In 2009 the choir recorded on Signum Records a successful

CD[12] "The Majesty of Thy Glory" which was launched in 2010. This was the first recording by the choir alone since 1979. Also in 2010 James Vivian made a recording of English Organ Music[13]. The men of the choir are singers in the front rank of the profession and include a number with international solo careers. The boys' singing and musicianship has steadily improved with additional teaching supported by the Temple Music Trust. The choir is now acknowledged as one of the three best in London.

In addition there have been visiting choirs, particularly Layton's two choirs Polyphony and the Holst Singers, and Canticum conducted by Mark Forkgen, a former head chorister. The Church has been used regularly for classical recordings. The boys sang at the Lord Mayor's Banquet when Master Gavyn Arthur became Lord Mayor of London and the Master was his Chaplain for the year.

Perhaps the most remarkable musical event has been the commissioning and performance of "The Veil of the Temple" by Sir John Tavener[14]. Tavener was recording another of his works, "Eternity's Sunrise", in the Church in June 2000. He was invited with Layton and others to tea in the Master's House. The author was among those present. Tavener suddenly mused, "It is a pity that this is 2000 and not the year 1900. The Temple Church would be a wonderful place for an all night vigil." The idea was taken up immediately. Layton expressed the hope that the choir of the Temple Church might have the opportunity to recover the stature that it had had in the 1920's. The Master hoped that such a piece would bring the sanctity of the Round Church to life. What we had in mind was a relatively simple project of music and readings throughout the night. What Stephen Layton received in March 2002 was one of Sir John Tavener's greatest works which provided unforeseen challenges in its length and complexity. The Vigil would last from 10 p.m. until 5a.m. and the music would be continuous. It would cost substantially more to stage than had been budgeted.

It required the dedication of Layton, Vivian and The Master to bring the project to fruition. In addition to soloists, the performance required a choir of 140 drawn from the Temple Church choir, Polyphony and the Holst Singers, and organ, Indian harmonium, duduk, a Tibetan horn five feet in length, Tibetan temple bowls, tubular bells, a tam-tam and brass. There were two all-night performances on 27 June and 4 July 2003 and a shortened evening performance on 1 July 2003. The performances used the whole of the Church, including the Round and the Triforium, and received excellent reviews and

---

[12]   SIGC D225.
[13]   On Signum Classics: the recording was released in November 2010.
[14]   See also *Lifting the Veil, a biography of Sir John Tavener* by Dean Dudgeon, 2003: Portrait, an imprint of Judy Piatkus Publishers Ltd., London.

publicity for the choir and the Inns[15]. Thereafter the shortened version of The Veil[16] was performed at the Proms and, in the following year, the full version at the Lincoln Centre, New York. In New York, breakfast was served at the end of the performance.

A large part of The Veil was recorded successfully on to two compact discs. None of this could have been achieved without the most generous financial support from Middle and Inner Temple, the GC Baker Family Trust and the Temple Music Trust which had been set up by members of the two Inns in 1979 to promote Temple music[17]. There were many others whose financial and practical support was vital. Penny Jonas has been responsible for coordinating the finances and raising the necessary support for "The Veil of the Temple" and for many subsequent musical projects connected with the Church and with Middle Temple through "Temple Song". Since then there have been many highlights. The year 2008 was a year-long celebration in words and music of the 400th Anniversary of the granting of the Charter led by the two Treasurers, Master Michael Blair of Middle Temple and Master Anthony May of Inner Temple. The two Inns achieved a degree of amity which has by no means always been evident throughout their history. The Anniversary was marked by a commemorative window on the south side of the Church, the first since the Church was re-built after the Second World War.

The Church has, over the years, had remarkable support from the Royal Family. In most recent times the Prince of Wales acted as patron for "The Veil of the Temple". Her Majesty the Queen and the Duke of Edinburgh attended a service in 2008 for the re-dedication of the two Inns and the presentation of a new Charter and in 2009 Master H.R.H. Prince William of Wales attended Evensong in the Church before being called to become Middle Temple's most recent Royal Bencher.

There have been major changes in the appearance of the church since 1997. Ian Garwood, employed by Middle Temple since 1978 and currently the Director of Estates, has been responsible for many years on behalf of the two Inns for supervising the substantial works of renovation and renewal. Among the many changes in the last 10 years, in 2001 and 2002 the outside of the Church was cleaned, clearing away the grime of war. In 2003 and 2004 the vaulted ceiling of the Church was re-decorated. In 2008, after many difficulties, the lighting of the Church was transformed. The gloomy chandeliers were

---

[15]   Richard Morrison's review of 30 June 2003 is at www.timesonline.co.uk/tol/comment/columnist/richard_morrison/article11465. In the course of a review full of superlatives, he said that "It was wonderfully and generously eccentric of the usually hard-nosed lawyers of Inner and Middle Temple to raise nearly half a million quid to get it commissioned, rehearsed and performed".

[16]   The shortened version of The Veil was issued on two CDs RCA 82876661542; it was an "Editor's Choice" of *The Gramophone* magazine.

[17]   See Rennert, p. 173 for the setting up of the Trust.

removed. The new lighting shows off the wonderful colours of the stone. The current task of refurbishing the organ, which has had only minor repairs since it was hastily installed in 1954, is a considerable current challenge for the Inns and their members.

Canon Alfred Ainger, then Reader of the Temple Church and subsequently Master, at the celebration of the 700th anniversary of the consecration of the Round Church on 10 February 1885, said in his sermon[18]:

"The Templars have bequeathed us, as a legacy, this lesson which we must not forget in the hour when we would fain recall the days of their grandeur and fresh enthusiasm: there is no promise of continuance for any institute, any party, any church, any creed, out of which the Spirit shall have departed.... after 700 years the truth remains unchanged for all who pass to worship through the nobly beautiful building that, on this day, was consecrated."

Looking back over the history of the Church, one can only echo the wise words of Canon Ainger, devoted servant of the Church and of the Inns, that any institution needs regular renewals of the spirit, otherwise it will die. One of the most remarkable public contributions of the Middle and Inner Temple is their continuing and generous support for the Temple Church which has enabled this to happen. They have amply fulfilled their obligations under the Royal Charter of 1608 and have received a remarkable heritage in return.

---

[18]   Lewer and Dark, p. 9.

Epilogue: The Vineyard

Throughout the Valedictory Sitting there were references to our house and modest vineyard in France. On 31 January 1997 we bought a virtually derelict 15th century house, with its small vineyard planted in 1974 with pinot noir. "Clos Toulmin" is in the wine village of Auxey-Duresses, one kilometre from Meursault in the Côte de Beaune in the heart of Burgundy. We have been made most welcome by the village for which we are very grateful. It was also a delight to discover that the house is in range of BBC Radio 4 long wave and therefore cricket's Test Match Special. The house and the vineyard have been a very special part of our lives ever since and have widened our horizons in different ways. First we had never renovated a house before. Like all such projects, this had its difficulties. It was also a good background for any judge trying construction cases.

Second, we have learned at firsthand something about the whole process of work in the vineyard from pruning the vines short for quality, to selecting only the best grapes at harvest time. We have also learned about making the wine, although, as we have been told by many "vignerons", no one person could ever learn it all!

Third, we have also learned at firsthand that humans cannot control everything. Vignerons are much more philosophical than lawyers. If the weather is ideal, you have a good harvest: if it hails before the harvest, those vines seriously affected could bear no fruit at all that year. One year the temperature on 24 December dropped to -20c and we lost 10% of our vines. We know that there was nothing we could have done about it.

On a more positive note, we, like everyone else, had the widest of smiles in 1999, 2002, 2005 and 2009 – wonderful years, and in 2008, 2010 and 2011 difficult years when we were able to make good wine after a poor summer because the weather relented in time for the harvest.

Sir Konrad Schiemann, United Kingdom Judge at the European Court of Justice and a friend for 50 years, and his wife have stayed with us in Auxey-Duresses. This very charming and touching contribution to the Liber Amicorum provides a fitting end-piece to the book, combining, as it does, warm friendship, wine and food - and European law.

Wine and Food in European Union Law

Konrad Schiemann *

1 Introduction

Last year Quentin Letts wrote[1] of the Right Honourable Kenneth Clarke QC sitting in the House of Commons "His countenance is seldom less red than a tumbler of Campari but at this point it turned to something more approximate to the scarlet of Clos Toulmin Pinot Noir 2004". I mention this not to launch a discourse on the physiognomy of the present Lord Chancellor but rather to indicate that the vinous products of John Toulmin – vigneron d' Auxey-Duresses – are as well known as the judicial products of John Toulmin QC, sitting in the High Court or England and Wales. I am in the happy position of having more than sampled both.

It is something of an achievement for an Englishman to set himself up as a vigneron in Burgundy. Hugh Johnson, who has a farm in central France, reveals in his delightful "Wine: a life uncorked", that "Riesling I had first thought would be the grape to plant in my vineyard, simply because I like the taste. It might ripen well in our spells of late sunshine. Luxembourg can sometimes do it, and that is far colder and further north. At any rate it was only for the family, many kilometres from any recognised region, so why would anyone mind? I had underestimated your French bureaucrat. "Pas autorisé, Monsieur" means "Just you try it, son". If I'd said Sauvignon Blanc and planted Riesling (and burned the dockets) would they ever have known? The police don't knock when they wander about our land with binoculars looking for poachers. Not worth the risk." John, so far as I know, has followed this cautious approach -as befits anyone who has more than a passing acquaintance with the complexity of the European Union's regulations governing wine.

When the European Economic Community was formed each member nation had its own regulations. Not that each nation had merely one set of regulations. Far from it. Many had a multitude and for many of the rules in each regulation there was, a whole host of exceptions. Yet each provision was in some sense a barrier to trade and thus had to be justified if it were to pass the scrutiny of the Court of Justice. This was potentially extremely tedious and so attempts have been made over the past 50 years by politicians to establish

---

* Sir K. Schiemann M.A. LLB, Judge at the Court of Justice of the European Union. "Wine and Food in European Union Law", by Judge Sir Konrad Schiemann, at p 241 *Liber Amicorum,* supplement to 12 *ERA Forum,* May 2011.
[1]   Daily Mail 20 January 2009.

European wide rules. The rules cover a large variety of fields -including various measures which try to match supply and demand so as to avoid wine lakes and eliminate wasteful public intervention in the markets and redirect spending so as to make European wine more competitive. For those who have a taste for the complexities of this kind of exercise I would recommend a perusal of the pertinent regulations as amended. Their titles give one the general feel.[2] Like all such regulations they are the result of political compromises, reached after years of negotiations, between conflicting aims resulting in texts of mind numbing complexity. The end result is a broad structure which for labelling purposes divides wines into two categories -wines with geographical indications and wines without geographical indications – and divides the former into two subcategories, namely, wines with a protected designation of origin (PDO and its equivalent in other languages) and wines with the slightly looser protected geographical indication (PG! and its equivalents). However, in substance the use of the new terminology appears to be optional and so the old regimes may well carryon in parallel.

Actually reading the regulations is something I personally only do in the line of duty.[3] Since food and wine are an important part of life, and the Common Agricultural Policy consumes some 40% of the European Union's budget, it is not surprising that a significant part of the caseload of the Union's Court has concerned such matters. Late one evening as I was reading my way through one such regulation with a glass of Clos Toulmin in my hand I fear I fell asleep. I found myself dreaming that I was attending a picnic in Burgundy with John and a French friend. I noticed that all the food and drink which John had unpacked from his rucksack brought to mind some case or other elucidating the principles of European Union law.

2 Protected Designations of Origin, Fundamental Rights and Trademarks

Happily I had momentarily forgotten about the regulation which I was trying to construe with the aid of the Court's dense case law. Instead I was introducing the Frenchman to the easy judicial style of Lord Denning with

---

[2] Commission Regulation (EC) No 43612009 of26 May 2009 laying down detailed rules for the application of Council Regulation (EC) No 47912008 as regards the vineyard register, compulsory declarations and the gathering of information to monitor the wine market, the documents accompanying consignments of wine products and the wine sector registers to be kept; Commission Regulation (EC) No 60612009 of 10 July 2009 laying down certain detailed rules for implementing Council Regulation (EC) No 47912008 as regards the categories ofgrapevine products, oenological practices and the applicable restrictions; and Commission regulation (EC) No 60712009 of 14 July 2009 laying down certain detailed rules for the implementation of Council Regulation (EC) No 47912008 as regards protected designations of origin and geographical indications, traditional terms, labelling and presentation of certain wine sector products.

[3] A more agreeable read is an article by Julia Harding, Master of Wine, dated 3.11.2010 which can be found at JancisRobinson.com -which she suggests can best be appreciated glass in hand.

which I grew up. Here are the opening paragraphs of his judgment in *H.P Bulmer v J Bollinger SA.*[4]

"In France the name Champagne is well protected by law. It denotes a sparkling wine produced in a well favoured district of France, called the Champagne district. The vineyards are about a hundred miles east of Paris, around Reims and Epernay. The wine has a high reputation all the world over. In England, too, the name Champagne is well protected by law when used for wine. As far back as 1956 some intruders brought into England a somewhat similar wine. It had been produced in the Costa Brava district of Spain. They marketed it under the name 'Spanish Champagne'. The French growers and shippers brought an action to stop it. They succeeded. Mr. Justice Danckwerts held that the French growers had a goodwill connected with the word Champagne: and that the Spanish intruders had been guilty of dishonest trading, see *Bollinger v Costa Brava* (1960) Ch 262 .... That case in 1960 concerned wine -wine made from grapes -for which the French are so famous. Now we are concerned with cider and perry. Cider from apples. Perry from pears. We English do know something about these. At any rate, those who come up from Somerset or Herefordshire. For many years now some producers of cider in England have been marketing some of their drinks as 'champagne cider' and 'champagne perry'. When it started the French producers of champagne took no steps to stop it. It went on for a long time. But in 1970 the French producers brought an action against an English firm, claiming an injunction. They sought to stop the use of the name Champagne on these drinks. To counter this, two of the biggest producers of cider in England on 8th October, 1970 brought an action against the French producers. They claimed declarations that they were entitled to use the expression 'Champagne cider' and 'Champagne perry'. They said that they had used those expressions for 70 or 80 years in England; that many millions of bottles had been marketed under those descriptions; and that the Government of the United Kingdom had recognised it in the various regulations. They said further that the French producers had acquiesced in the use and were estopped from complaining. In answer the French producers of Champagne claimed that the use of the word 'Champagne' in connection with any beverage other than Champagne was likely to lead to the belief that such beverage was or resembled Champagne, or was a substitute for it, or was in some way connected with Champagne. They claimed an injunction to stop the English producers from using the word 'Champagne' in connection with any beverage not being a wine produced in the Champagne district of France. Thus far it was a straightforward action for passing-off. It was to be determined by well-known principles of English law. But on 1st January, 1973, England joined the Common Market. On 26th March, 1973, the French

4   [1974] *EWCA Civ* 14.

producers amended their pleading so as to add these claims: '9A Following the adhesion of the United Kingdom to the European Economic Community the use of the word 'Champagne' in connection with any beverage other than Champagne will contravene European Community Law.' They relied on Regulation 816176/Article 30 and Regulation 817170 Article 628/12 and 13.... "The French producers claim that, under those regulations, the name Champagne is their own special property. It must not be applied to any wine which is not produced in the Champagne District of France. So much the English producers concede. But the French producers go further. They say that the name Champagne must not be applied to any beverage other than their Champagne. It must not, therefore, be applied to cider or perry, even though they are not wines at all. The English producers deny this. They say that the Regulations apply only to wines -the product of grapes -and not to cider or perry -the product of apples and pears. This is obviously a point of the first importance to the French wine trade and to the English cider trade. It depends no doubt on the true interpretation of the Regulations. It seems that three points of principle arise:

First. By which Court should these Regulations be interpreted? By the European Court at Luxembourg? or by the national Courts of England?

Second. At what stage should the task of interpretation be done? Should it be done now before the case is tried out in the English Court? or at a later stage after the other issues have been determined?

Third. In any case, whichever be the Court to interpret them, what are the principles to be applied in the interpretation of the Regulations? Ifwe were to interpret the Regulations as if they were an English statute, I should think they would apply only to wines, not to cider or perry. But, if other principles were to be applied, the result might be different. That is indeed what the French producers say. They contend that the European Court can fill in any gaps in the Regulations. So that the words can be extended so as to forbid the use of the word 'Champagne' on cider or perry. That is, no doubt, the reason why the French producers want the point to be referred here and now to the European Court."

The conclusion of the court of appeal was that the first instance judge had been entitled to refuse to refer.[5]

John had of course produced some excellent champagne and we talked of the many attempts which had been made to share in the glow of champagne by those outside the region. To regulate this the Community had made some

---

[5]   The case was referred back to the trial judge to try the issue whether there had been a passing off under English domestic law. He found that there had been. However this finding was reversed, so far as champagne perry was concerned, by the Court of appeal: [1978] RPC 79.

regulation restricting the use ofthe phrase "methode champenoise". The validity of this was challenged by the makers of a German sparkling wine in *SMW Winzersekt GmbH v Land Rheinland-Pfalz*.[6] The Court considered the extent of the right to property and the freedom to pursue a trade or profession, the extent of the discretion vested in the Commission, the nature of the control of proportionality applied by the Court to restrictions of those freedoms and the purpose behind the wine labelling regulations. The Court said this:

"19 It follows from the documents on the case-file and the arguments before the Court that the validity of the second and third subparagraphs of Article 6(5) of Regulation No 2333/92 has been challenged in the light of two principles or groups of principles: on the one hand, the right to property and the freedom to pursue a trade or profession and, on the other, the general principle of equal treatment.

The right to property and the freedom to pursue a trade or profession

20 Winzersekt takes the view that the contested provision adversely affects both its right to property and its right freely to pursue a trade or profession, which form part of the general principles of Community law. It submits in that connection that the designation 'methode champenoise' is of fundamental importance for its commercial activity in so far as that designation enables it to make the public aware of its method of production.... 21 It should be pointed out in this respect that in matters concerning the common agricultural policy the Community legislature has a broad discretion which corresponds to the political responsibilities given to it by Articles 40 and 43 of the Treaty and that the Court has, on several occasions, held that the lawfulness of a measure adopted in that sphere can be affected only if the measure is manifestly inappropriate, having regard to the objective which the competent institution is seeking to pursue ....

22 Account must also be taken of the Court's case-law to the effect that the right to property and the freedom to pursue a trade or business are not absolute but must be viewed in relation to their social function. Consequently, the exercise of the right to property and the freedom to pursue a trade or profession may be restricted, particularly in the context of the common organisation of a market, provided that those restrictions in fact correspond to objectives of general interest pursued by the Community and do not;.. constitute a disproportionate and intolerable interference, impairing the very substance of the rights guaranteed....

23 With regard to the infringement of the right to property alleged by Winzersekt, the designation 'methode champenoise' is a term which, prior to the adoption of the.regulation, all producers of sparkling wines were entitled to

---

[6]   Case C-306/93 [2004] ECR 1-05555.

use. The prohibition of the use of that designation cannot be regarded as an infringement of an alleged property right vested in Winzersekt.

24 So far as concerns the impairment of the freedom to pursue a trade or profession, the second and third subparagraphs of Article 6(5) of Regulation· No 2333/92 do not impair the very substance of the right freely to exercise a trade or profession relied on by Winzersekt since those provisions affect only the arrangements governing the exercise of that right and do not jeopardise its very existence. It is for that reason necessary to determine whether those provisions pursue objectives of general interest, do not affect the position of producers such as Winzersekt in a disproportionate manner and, consequently, whether the Council exceeded the limits of its discretion in this case.

25 It should be noted in this regard that among the objectives pursued by Regulation No 2333/92, that of the protection of registered designations or indications of the geographical origin of wines is an objective of general interest. In order to achieve that objective, the Council was entitled to regard it as essential, on the one hand, that the final consumer should receive sufficiently accurate information to enable him to form an opinion of the products in question and, on the other hand, that the producer should not derive advantage, for his own product, from a reputation established for a similar product by producers from a different region. This implies that a wine producer cannot be authorised to use, in descriptions relating to the method of production of his products, geographical indications which do not correspond to the actual provenance of the wine.

26 That objective is implemented in particular by Article 6 of Regulation No 2333/92, which provides that the use of terms relating to a production method may refer to the name of a geographical unit only where the wine in question is entitled to use that geographical indication.

27 It follows that the prohibition laid down in that provision is not manifestly inappropriate in relation to the objective of the regulation at issue.

28 Furthermore, by adopting transitional arrangements such as those set out in the third subparagraph of Article 6(5) of the regulation and by allowing producers who, like Winzersekt, used the designation 'methode champenoise' to have recourse to the alternative expressions contained in Article 6(4) of Regulation No 2333/92, such as 'bottle-fermented by the traditional method', 'traditional method', 'classical method' or 'classical traditional method' and any expressions resulting from a translation of those terms, the Council took account of the position of those producers. In those circumstances, the contested provision cannot be regarded as disproportionate.

29 Itfollows that the second and third subparagraphs of Article 6(5) of Regulation No 2333/92 pursue objectives of general interest and cannot be regarded

as constituting a disproportionate interference with the position of producers such as Winzersekt. In those circumstances, it must be held that the Council did not exceed the limits of its discretion in adopting those provisions.

The general principle of equal treatment

30 In this regard, the Court has consistently held that the principle of equal treatment requires that similar situations should not be treated differently and that different situations should not be treated identically unless such differentiation is objectively justified ....

31 In the present case, the second and third subparagraphs of Article 6(5) of Regulation No 2333/92 apply to all producers of sparkling wines in the Community with the exception of those who are entitled to use the registered designation 'Champagne'. The fact of entitlement to use that registered designation is an objective matter which can justify a difference in treatment. In those circumstances, a difference in the treatment of each of those two groups of producers is justified.

32 The reply to the national court must accordingly be that examination of the question submitted has not revealed any factor of such a kind as to affect the validity of the second and third subparagraphs of Article 6(5) of Council Regulation No 2333/92."

We agreed that it must not be thought that the ECl would uphold the wine regulations come what may. This is shown by *Codornfu SA v Council of the European Union*[7] which has been referred to in innumerable cases and articles thereafter. Codornfu successfully challenged the validity of a regulation which allowed the use of the word "Cremant" only in respect of sparkling wines from France or Luxembourg and thus forbad its use in respect of wines emanating from Spain. The case raised two issues. The first concerned the standing of Cordonfu to apply for such an annulment. The second the legality of the discrimination between France and Luxembourg on the one hand and Spain on the other.

As to admissibility the Court said this:

"19 Although it is true that according to the criteria in the second paragraph of Article 173 of the Treaty the contested provision is, by nature and by virtue of its sphere of application, of a legislative nature in that it applies to the traders concerned in general, that does not prevent it from being of individual concern to some of them.

20 Natural or legal persons may claim that a contested provision is of individual concern to them only if it affects them by reason of certain

---

[7]　Case C-309//89 [1994] ECR 1-01853.

attributes which are peculiar to them or by reason of circumstances in which they are differentiated from all other persons ...

21 Codornfu registered the graphic trade mark 'Gran Cremant de Codornfu' in Spain in 1924 and traditionally used that mark both before and after registration. By reserving the right to use the term 'crem/lnt' to French and Luxembourg producers, the contested provision prevents Codornfu from using its graphic trade mark.

22 It follows that Codornfu has established the existence of a situation which from the point of view of the contested provision differentiates it from all other traders.

23 It follows that the objection of inadmissibility put forward by the Council must be dismissed."

As regards the plea of unlawful discrimination the Court said this:

"26 It is appropriate in the first place to point out that under the principle of non-discrimination between Community producers or consumers, which is enshrined in the second subparagraph of Article 40(3) of the EEC Treaty and which includes the prohibition of discrimination on grounds of nationality laid down in the first paragraph of Article 7 of the EEC Treaty, comparable situations must not be treated differently and different situations must not be treated in the same way unless such treatment is objectively justified. It follows that the conditions of production or consumption may not be differentiated except by reference to objective criteria which ensure a proportionate division of the advantages and disadvantages for those concerned without distinction between the territories of the Member States ...

27 The contested provision provides that the term 'cremant' in combination with the name of the specified region shall be reserved for quality sparkling wines psr made in France or Luxembourg which satisfy the conditions provided for in the second paragraph of Article 6(4) of Regulation No 3309/85 and which were produced in accordance with the special rules laid down for their manufacture by those two Member States.

28 It thus appears that the term 'cremant' refers primarily not to the origin but the method of manufacture of the quality sparkling wine psr, in particular that provided for in Article 6(4) of Regulation No 3309/85. Since the quality sparkling wines psr sold under the Spanish graphic trade mark 'Gran Cremant de Codornfu' satisfy the conditions provided for by the contested provision, it follows that provision treats comparable situations differently.

29 It is therefore necessary to ascertain whether such treatment was objectively justified.

30 In that respect the reason given for the reservation of the term 'cremant' was concern to protect a description traditionally used in France and Luxembourg for products of specific origin.

31 It is common ground that the first national measures providing in France and Luxembourg for the use of the term 'cremant' as a 'traditional description' were adopted in 1975. Codornfu, however, has been traditionally using its graphic trade mark containing the words 'Gran Cremant' to designate a quality sparkling wine psr since at least 1924.

32 In those circumstances the reservation of the term 'cremant' for quality sparkling wines psr manufactured in France and Luxembourg cannot validly be justified on the basis of traditional use, since it disregards the traditional use of that mark by Codornfu.

33 The Commission observes, however, that it follows from the wording of the contested provision, according to which the term 'cremant' must be followed by specification of the region of production, that the term 'cremant' refers not so much to the method of manufacture of a quality sparkling wine psr as to its origin.

34 In that respect it must be observed that according to the contested provision the term 'cremant' is in essence attributed on the basis of the method of manufacture of the product, since the specification of the region of production serves only to indicate the origin of the quality sparkling wine psr. The origin thus has nothing to do with the attribution of the term 'cremant', which is not associated with a geographical connection.

35 The different treatment has therefore not been objectively justified and the contested provision must be declared void. 36 In view of the foregoing it does not appear necessary to consider the other pleas in law put forward by Codornfu."

3 Challenging the Validity of Community Regulations

As we poured a few drops of olive oil on our salad we called to mind *P Union de Pequeños Agricultores v Council of the European Union*[8] where the Court was once more concerned with the standing of the claimant to challenge the validity of a Community regulation. In this context the Court considered the impact of the standing rules on the right to effective legal protection and also considered the principle of sincere cooperation. The court said this:

"32 As a preliminary point, it should be noted that the appellant has not challenged the finding of the Court of First Instance, in paragraph 44 of the contested order, to the effect that the contested regulation is of general application. Nor has it challenged the finding, in paragraph 56 of that order,

---

[8]   Case C-50/00 [1-06677].

that the specific interests of the appellant were not affected by the contested regulation or the finding, in paragraph 50 of that order, that its members are not affected by the contested regulation by reason of certain attributes which are peculiar to them or by reason of factual circumstances in which they are differentiated from all other persons.

33 In those circumstances, it is necessary to examine whether the appellant, as representative of the interests of its members, can none the less have standing, in conformity with the fourth paragraph of Article 173 of the Treaty, to bring an action for annulment of the contested regulation on the sole ground that, in the alleged absence of any legal remedy before the national courts, the right to effective judicial protection requires it.

34 It should be recalled that, according to the second and third paragraphs of Article 173 of the Treaty, the Court is to have jurisdiction in actions brought by a Member State, the Councilor the Commission on grounds of lack of competence, infringement of an essential procedural requirement, infringement of the Treaty or of any rule of law relating to its application, or misuse of powers or, when it is for the purpose of protecting their prerogatives, by the European Parliament, by the Court of Auditors and by the European Central Bank. Under the fourth paragraph of Article 173, '[a]ny natural or legal person may, under the same conditions, institute proceedings against a decision addressed to that person or against a decision which, although in the form of a regulation or a decision addressed to another person, is of direct and individual concern to the former.'

35 Thus, under Article 173 of the Treaty, a regulation, as a measure of general application, cannot be challenged by natural or legal persons other than the institutions, the European Central Bank and the Member States ...

36 However, a measure of general application such as a regulation can, in certain circumstances, be of individual concern to certain natural or legal persons and is thus in the nature of a decision in their regard ... That is so where the measure in question affects specific natural or legal persons by reason of certain attributes peculiar to them, or by reason of a factual situation which differentiates them from all other persons and distinguishes them individually in the same way as the addressee ...

37 If that condition is not fulfilled, a natural or legal person does not, under any circumstances, have standing to bring an action for annulment of a regulation ...

38 The European Community is, however, a community based on the rule of law in which its institutions are subject to judicial review of the compatibility of their acts with the Treaty and with the general principles of law which include fundamental rights.

39 Individuals are therefore entitled to effective judicial protection of the rights they derive from the Community legal order, and the right to such protection is one of the general principles of law stemming from the constitutional traditions common to the Member States. That right has also been enshrined in Articles 6 and 13 of the European Convention for the Protection of Human Rights and Fundamental Freedoms ...

40 By Article 173 and Article 184 ..., on the one hand, and by Article 177, on the other, the Treaty has established a complete system of legal remedies and procedures designed to ensure judicial review of the legality of acts of the institutions, and has entrusted such review to the Community Courts ... Under that system, where natural or legal persons cannot, by reason of the conditions for admissibility laid down in the fourth paragraph of Article 173 of the Treaty, directly challenge Community measures of general application, they are able, depending on the case, either indirectly to plead the invalidity of such acts before the Community Courts under Article 184 of the Treaty or to do so before the national courts and ask them, since they have no jurisdiction themselves to declare those measures invalid ... to make a reference to the Court of Justice for a preliminary ruling on validity.

41 Thus it is for the Member States to establish a system of legal remedies and procedures which ensure respect for the right to effective judicial protection.

42 In that context, in accordance with the principle of sincere cooperation laid down in Article 5 of the Treaty, national courts are required, so far as possible, to interpret and apply national procedural rules governing the exercise of rights of action in a way that enables natural and legal persons to challenge before the courts the legality of any decision or other national measure relative to the application to them of a Community act of general application, by pleading the invalidity of such an act.

43 ... it is not acceptable to adopt an interpretation of the system of remedies, such as that favoured by the appellant, to the effect that a direct action for annulment before the Community Court will be available where it can be shown, following an examination by that Court of the particular national procedural rules, that those rules do not allow the individual to bring proceedings to contest the validity of the Community measure at issue. Such an interpretation would require the Community Court, in each individual case, to examine and interpret national procedural law. That would go beyond its jurisdiction when reviewing the legality of Community measures.

44 Finally, it should be added that, according to the system for judicial review of legality established by the Treaty, a natural or legal person can bring an action challenging a regulation only if it is concerned both directly and individually. Although this last condition must be interpreted in the light of the principle of effective judicial protection by taking account of the

various circumstances that may distinguish an applicant individually ... , such an interpretation cannot have the effect of setting aside the condition in question, expressly laid down in the Treaty, without going beyond the jurisdiction conferred by the Treaty on the Community Courts ....

46 In the light of the foregoing, the Court finds that the Court of First Instance did not err in law when it declared the appellant's application inadmissible without examining whether, in the particular case, there was a remedy before a national court enabling the validity of the contested regulation to be examined."

4 Protected Designations of Origin Revisited: The Parma Ham Case

It was now time for some strengthening food and we turned to consider the Parma ham which was beautifully packed and which awaited our attention. We recalled that in relation to the protection granted by designations of origin the Court in *Consorzio del Prosciutto di Parma and Salumificio S. Rita SpA v Asda Stores Ltd and Hygrade Foods Ltd.*[9] had said this:

"62. It should be noted that, in accordance with Article 30 EC, Article 29 EC does not preclude prohibitions or restrictions on exports which are justified inter alia on grounds of the protection of industrial and. commercial property.

63. Community legislation displays a general tendency to enhance the quality of products within the framework of the common agricultural policy, in order to promote the reputation of those products through inter alia the use of designations of origin which enjoy special protection ... That tendency took the form in the quality wines sector of the adoption of Council Regulation (EEC) No 823/87 of 16 March 1987 laying down special provisions relating to quality wines produced in specified regions ... repealed and replaced by Council Regulation (EC) No 1493/1999 of 17 May 1999 on the common organisation of the market in wine ... It was also manifested, in relation to other agricultural products, in the adoption of Regulation No 2081192, which, according to its preamble, is intended inter alia to meet consumers' expectations as regards products of quality and an identifiable geographical origin and to enable producers, in conditions of fair competition, to secure higher incomes in return for a genuine effort to improve quality.

64. Designations of origin fall within the scope of industrial and commercial property rights. The applicable rules protect those entitled to use them against improper use of those designations by third parties seeking to profit from the reputation which they have acquired. They are intended to guarantee that the product bearing them comes from a specified geographical area and displays certain particular characteristics. They may enjoy a high reputation amongst consumers and constitute for producers who fulfil the condi-

[9] Case C-108/01 [2003] ECR 1-05121.

tions for using them an essential means of attracting custom. The reputation of designations of origin depends on their image in the minds of consumers. That image in turn depends essentially on particular characteristics and more generally on the quality of the product. It is on the latter, ultimately, that the product's reputation is based ... For consumers, the link between the reputation of the producers and the quality of the products also depends on his being assured that products sold under the designation of origin are authentic.

65. The specification of the PDQ 'Prosciutto di Parma', by requiring the slicing and packaging to be carried out in the region of production, is intended to allow the persons entitled to use the PDQ to keep under their control one of the ways in which the product appears on the market. The condition it lays down aims better to safeguard the quality and authenticity of the product, and consequently the reputation of the PDQ, for which those who are entitled to use it assume full and collective responsibility.

66. Against that background, a condition such as at issue must be regarded as compatible with Community law despite its restrictive effects on trade if it is shown that it is necessary and proportionate and capable of upholding the reputation of the PDQ 'Prosciutto di Parma' ...

78. Consequently, the condition of slicing and packaging in the region of production, whose aim is to preserve the reputation of Parma ham by strengthening control over its particular characteristics and its quality, may be regarded as justified as a measure protecting the PDQ which may be used by all the operators concerned and is of decisive importance to them ...

79. The resulting restriction may be regarded as necessary for attaining the objective pursued, in that there are no alternative less restrictive measures capable of attaining it."

5 Precedence of EU Law, State Liability and Other Delicacies

Inspired by *Amministrazione delle Finanze dello Stato v Simmenthal SpA*,[10] decided in the context of veterinary regulations governing the import of Veal and Beef into Italy, we started talking about the principles laid down there which have been followed ever since. This led to a long discussion of the interrelation of Union law with national law, the obligation of national judges to apply Union law notwithstanding a conflict with national law. The discussion became involved and at this point John produced a bottle labelled Tocai friulano from Italy (now a little past its best it must be said) and another labelled Tocaj from Hungary. We tried the Italian one first with the remains of our salad and kept the Hungarian one for later. We called to mind

---

[10] Case 106177 [1978] ECR 00629.

Regione autonoma FriuZi-Venezia Giulia and Agenzia regionaZe per Zo sviluppo ruraZe (ERSA) v Ministero delle PoZitiche AgricoZe e Forestali[11] and I remembered that the Court had there ruled on homonymity – a word which, after the Tocai friuliana seemed difficult to pronounce with my accustomed clarity – and had ruled that a Commission decision preventing the Italians from continuing to use the word tocai as from a date in 2007 was lawful.

But John's rucksack was not yet exhausted and he fished out some bananas which we could eat with the Royal Tokaji Aszu 6 Puttonyos. Bananas, he pointed out, qualified as part of this meal under several heads. For a start, there was the leading competition *United Brands Company v Commission*,[12] an early case in the bananas litigation which continues to reverberate down the Union's legal corridors.[13]

At this point my head started swimming with cases all concerned with food or drink in some of which John or I had been concerned at one stage or another -Dassonville[14] and Cassis de Dijon[15] which started a whole line of case law in relation to measures having an equivalent effect to quantitative restrictions, *Commission v France*[16] and *Commission v UK*[17] on differential taxation as between spirits, wine and beer, Joined Cases *Brasserie du Pecheur* and *Factortame*[18] which laid down the ground rules for the civil liability of a Member State for breach of Union rules, *Courage v Crehan*[19] which was concerned with the rights of a party to a tied-house agreement unlawful under Community law to sue the other contracting party and *Marks & Spencer Ltd v Commissioners of Excise*[20] dealing with the principles of effectiveness and legitimate expectation.

I woke up with the happy thought that, should John after his retirement decide to organise a picnic course on European Union law from his delightful house in Burgundy, I might be invited – to eat and drink while listening to expositions by the next generation of Union lawyers.

---

[11] Case C-347/03 [2005] ECR 1-03785.
[12] Case 27176 [1978] ECR 00207.
[13] See joined Cases C-120/06 p and C-121106 P FlAMM [2008] ECR 1-06513.
[14] Case 8174 [1974] ECR 00837.
[15] Case 120178 [1979] ECR 00649.
[16] Case 168178 [1980] ECR 00347.
[17] Case 170178 [1983] ECR 02265.
[18] Cases C-46/93 and 48/93 [1996] ECR 1-01029.
[19] Case C-453/99 [2001] ECR 1-06297.
[20] Case C-62/00 [2002] ECR 1-06325.